ESSAYS
ON SOME OF THE FIRST PRINCIPLES
OF METAPHYSICKS, ETHICKS, AND THEOLOGY

HISTORY OF PSYCHOLOGY SERIES

GENERAL INTRODUCTION

The historically interesting works reprinted in this series helped to prepare the way for the science of psychology. Most of these books are long forgotten, but their relevance to the field is unmistakable. Many of the writings on mental and moral philosophy, published before the dawn of scientific procedures, have much to commend them to present-day scholars. These books serve as groundwork for a fuller account of the background from which the field emerged, and they should be attractive to students who seek in the past for hints of the future direction that certain types of research can take. Each work will have an Introduction stating the provenance and significance of the book and will add appropriate biographical information.

ROBERT I. WATSON
General Editor
University of New Hampshire

ESSAYS
ON SOME OF THE FIRST PRINCIPLES
OF METAPHYSICKS, ETHICKS, AND THEOLOGY

ESSAYS
ON SOME OF
THE FIRST PRINCIPLES
OF METAPHYSICKS, ETHICKS,
AND THEOLOGY
(1824)

BY ASA BURTON

A FACSIMILE REPRODUCTION
WITH AN INTRODUCTION
BY JAMES G. BLIGHT

SCHOLARS' FACSIMILES & REPRINTS
DELMAR, NEW YORK
1973

PUBLISHED BY SCHOLARS' FACSIMILES & REPRINTS, INC.

P. O. BOX 344, DELMAR, NEW YORK 12054

© 1973 SCHOLARS' FACSIMILES & REPRINTS, INC.

REPRODUCED FROM A COPY IN

AND WITH THE PERMISSION OF

THE UNIVERSITY OF MICHIGAN LIBRARY

PRINTED IN THE UNITED STATES OF AMERICA

Library of Congress Cataloging in Publication Data

Burton, Asa, 1752-1836.
Essays on some of the first principles of metaphysicks,
ethicks, and theology.

(History of psychology series)
Reprint of the 1824 ed., printed by A. Shirley,
Portland, Me.
Includes bibliographical references.
1. Psychology—Addresses, essays, lectures.
2. Ethics—Addresses, essays, lectures.   3. Theology
—Addresses, essays, lectures.   I. Title.
B908.B7316   1973   150   73-4839
ISBN 0-8201-1114-7

INTRODUCTION

WILLIAM JAMES' two-volume *Principles of Psychology* had its long-awaited debut in 1890 before an appreciative and admiring readership of psychologists and philosophers. Those volumes, it has been contended, launched psychology in America and reduced to obsolescence all pre-Jamesian American psychology. A psychological revolution was initiated which decisively altered the character of American psychology. Thereafter, according to this view, the field became almost completely divorced from theology and discussions of faculties, and re-wed to the experimental method.

As in the case with many successful revolutions, the vanquished have been treated harshly. American philosophy in the century before James has been referred to as the "Glacial Age".[1] American psychology in this period, on the other hand, has become so obscure that it has not been "dignified" with a derogatory epithet. To most scholars, it seems, pre-Jamesian American psychology is a myth. Only Jay Wharton Fay has undertaken an extensive attempt to rouse historians of American psychology from their apathy concerning the earlier period. Unfortunately, his monograph, *American Psychology Before William James*[2], contains minimal interpretation and narrative to accompany his admirable compilation of quotations. No integrative history of pre-experimental American psychology has ever been written.

Psychological thinkers prior to 1890 have fared far better in the hands of historians of philosophy and theology. Unencumbered by doctrinaire adherence to experimentalism or any other prevailing trend in contemporary psychology, they have discovered psychological revolutions that were profound and exciting, just as that which followed the appearance of James' textbook. One such event occurred in 1824 with the publication of the *Essays* of Asa Burton (1752-1836).

The son of a Congregational minister, Burton received his divinity degree from Dartmouth in 1777 and was ordained two years later at Thetford, Vermont, where he remained for life. He was not primarily a writer or scholar, having published only about twenty sermons in addition to the *Essays*. Most of his energy seems to have been directed toward building his own congregation and promoting educational institutions in Vermont. He helped organize two academies, was a founder

v

of the University of Vermont, and served as trustee of Middlebury College. Despite his lack of scholarly productivity, Burton has been described by Herbert Schneider as the initiator of the era of psychological textbooks in America[3] and by Joseph Haroutunian as the author of "the first full-blown, systematic treatise on . . . the 'faculty psychology'."[4] The implication is that Burton's volume has much in common with those of James: each was a novel formulation which prefigured a dawning era. Each was a pivotal work.

It is obvious, however, that while James is still regarded as pertinent to modern psychology, Asa Burton and his contemporaries are cloaked in anonymity. Their lengthy discussions of numerous faculties, appetites, and powers appear "medieval" in their outlook and quite irrelevant to the current scene. Their psychology is out of vogue and psychological historians' ignorance of its basic issues and assumptions is profound. Until the issues, controversies, and key figures in American pre-experimental psychology are understood far more clearly than is presently the case, no legitimate estimate can be made concerning the historical significance of the early period. In order to appreciate the historical pivot accomplished by Burton's *Essays*, it is necessary to understand a few essential aspects of his intellectual milieu. To that end the following discussion and schematic outline is provided (see Fig. 1).

Faculty Psychology in America

Burton was a New England Congregational minister and, as such, he was heir to the Calvinist heritage of American Puritanism. The psychological system of the first American intellectuals viewed the mind as a myriad of faculties (e.g., reason, will, fancy, the affections, imagination) which transmitted perception into action via a very complex mechanical process.[5] Seventeenth-century thinkers like Thomas Shepard, Thomas Hooker, and Samuel Willard conceptualized the cognitive process as a sort of synchronized gear-shifting operation. The truth or falsity of a percept would be judged by reason, it would then have certain affections or emotions attached to it, and after passing under the jurisdiction of numerous other faculties the information would make its way to the will for execution of appropriate action. The will was generally held to be bound by the judgment and dictates of reason, "the queen of the faculties".

The chief function of this psychology was to provide an explanation of that all-important event in the life of a Puritan, the conversion experience. The perception of God's holy word, both written and spoken, was said to traverse the mental faculties in much the same manner as any other perception. Most Puritan thinkers hypothesized that the spiritual light present in the conversion experience operated most directly upon the faculty of reason. Consequently, most Puritan sermons employed a rigorously logical method of discourse known as the "plain style". Man, they believed, is above all a rational creature who will respond to reasonable argument.

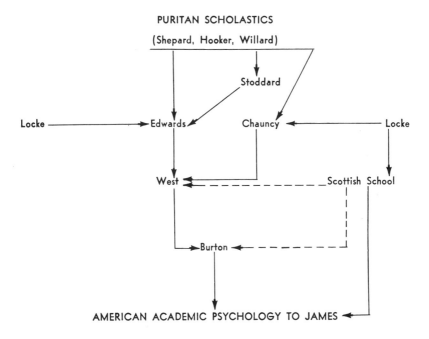

Fig. 1. FACULTY PSYCHOLOGY IN AMERICA. Lines of influence are designated by arrows. Dotted lines indicate that the Scottish influence seems likely but cannot be proven. Locke appears twice because Edwards used the empiricist, faculty system to help found one tradition, while Chauncy emphasized Lockean rationalism, and helped found the tradition which culminated in Unitarianism.

Yet it could not be denied that many conversion experiences were anything but rational. They were affairs of the heart, which was the theoretical repository of the affections. It is not surprising, therefore, that concurrent with the emphasis upon the rational faculty, there existed an equally strong tradition known as "the preparation of the heart". The dual emphasis in Puritanism on the rational intellect and affectionate piety was held necessary to explain the pervasive re-alignment of mental gears that constituted the Puritan notion of conversion.

For a number of years, the contradictory emphasis upon piety and the intellect, upon man as both a rational and as an irrational creature, survived intact. The first serious challenge to the dualistic doctrine to come from within orthodox American Puritanism was provided by Solomon Stoddard (1643-1729), a minister at Northampton. His revivalist preaching, theological and psychological systems, and his relatively lax ecclesiastical policies were indicative of his appeal to the affections.[6]

The revivalist heart-psychology initiated by Stoddard was incorporated by his grandson and successor in the Northampton pulpit, Jonathan Edwards (1703-1758), into the most influential psychological system to be developed in America before James. Combining traditional Calvinist determinism, Stoddard's emphasis upon the heart, and Lockean empiricist psychology, Edwards fashioned a view of psychology which would influence American thought on the topic for a hundred years. With Locke, Edwards reduced the ponderous list of faculties to two: the understanding and the will. Furthermore, Edwards did not use the term "faculty" in the traditional sense. He implied that the understanding and the will, with its associated affections, were merely fictions or constructs which proved useful in explaining cognition. These two "faculties" were said to be aspects of a unified cognitive process which he often referred to as "a sense of the heart."[7] To illustrate that cognition is a unified process combining elements of both the rational and the irrational Edwards often used examples such as the following:

> There is a distinction to be made between a mere notional understanding, wherein the mind only beholds things in the exercise of a speculative faculty; and the sense of the heart, wherein the mind does not only speculate and behold, but relishes and feels . . . The one is mere speculative knowledge, the other sensible knowledge, in which more than the mere intellect is concerned; the heart is the proper subject of it, or the soul, as a being that not only

beholds, but has inclination and is pleased or displeased. And yet there is the nature of instruction in it; as he that has perceived the sweet taste of honey, knows much more about it, then he who has only looked upon, and felt of it.[8]

A related aspect of Edwards' thought was the elucidation, in psychological terms, of a rigorous Calvinist determinism. If a man is restricted by what Edwards called "natural necessity", he is not free. A man is not "free" to leap over a tall tree because certain natural restrictions prohibit it. But what of the situation in which nature does not seem to prohibit the execution of an act; cannot one choose between alternatives? Edwards replied that, indeed, choices are made, but those choices are themselves determined by "moral necessity".[9] Though a man may consciously choose to act in a given manner, that choice is a function of man's universal adherence to an underlying hedonistic principle. Men are constructed such that they must choose that which they perceive to be the most pleasureable or least painful. That perception, in turn, is the end result of the rational-affectionate process of cognition. What appears to consciousness to be willful volition is what modern psychologists might call a pre-determined response to a perceived stimulus. The infusion of grace in the conversion experience thus becomes a re-orientation of the cognitive apparatus so that human perception coincides with God's perception.

So logical and forceful were the arguments of Edwards that, given his psychological assumptions concerning "a sense of the heart", his conclusions seemed inevitable to many of his contemporaries. The only apparent way to successfully counter Edwards was to reject these assumptions. This approach was taken by numerous individuals who were outraged by Edwards' assertion that man is, to a large extent, an irrational creature who has no free will.[10] One of the first to adopt this strategy was Charles Chauncy (1705-1787) of Boston. He resorted repeatedly to the older scholastic faculty psychology in order to buttress his attempt to re-assert that man is reasonable being, and to establish the belief in an independent and sovereign will.[11] Somewhat later, Samuel West (1730-1807) proposed a tripartite division of the faculties into perception, propension, and volition.[12] Perception and propension (the affections) were both said to be externally determined, while volition was held to be free. For evidence, West appealed to consciousness. We are, he stated, "Conscious, that many things take place in consequence of our acting . . . ."[13] West rejected any underlying hedonistic principle to which choices might be attributed. Thus by approximately 1800, man was held by certain "liberals" like Chauncy and West to be both rational and free. The conclusions were made possible by the apparently unconscious dismantling of Edwards' unified cognitive process into a number of segmented faculties. It was far easier to defend the freedom of the will when it could be assumed, using data from consciousness, that an independent will did indeed exist.

Any doctrine of free will, irrespective of its psychological assumptions, was bound to be objectionable to an orthodox Calvinist. In fact, West's doctrine of free will appears to have had little direct influence on American psychology, which was being written at this time primarily by Calvinists. Though in some respects West was far ahead of his time, he was laboring under the handicap of trying to establish freedom of the will in an era in which, due to the pervasive influence of Edwards, the very existence of an independent will was doubted. The alleged superficiality of West's appeal to consciousness was soon enthusiastically exposed by exponents of orthodoxy who upheld God's sovereignty and man's absolute dependence upon Him.[14]

Burton's System: Common Sense Determinism

A number of psychological issues remained in doubt, however, after absolute omnipotence was again attributed to the Calvinists' God. Asa Burton appears to have been the first thoroughly deterministic Calvinist to quarrel with Edwards' arrangement of the faculties. Especially troublesome to Burton was Edwards' reduction of the number of faculties to two. Burton, like Chauncy and West, does not seem to have understood Edwards' unique use of the term "faculty". He may have found independent support for his concern in the writings of the early members of the Scottish School, especially Reid.[15] The Scots with their hardheaded appeals to common-sense and consciousness would have found an appreciative audience in Burton, whose "common sense" repeatedly told him that the understanding and the will, as he understood Edwards' use of those terms, were not the only faculties.

Burton replaced the Edwardean scheme with the first formal alternative to Edwards' that proved acceptable to even the most deterministic Calvinists. The extent of the Scottish influence on Burton is difficult to assess, since he provides no references and he states in his introduction that the *Essays* are more a function of "his own powers" than of "the English, Scotch, French, and German authors" (p. 3). This claim must, however, be contrasted with his naive realism, appeals to common-sense, and his frequent use of the data of consciousness to prove that his particular tripartite division of the faculties was the correct one. By the time Burton wrote his *Essays*, Reid had already developed these three characteristics into cornerstones of the emerging Scottish School. Whatever the extent of the Scottish influence, there is little doubt that despite their differences, Burton's principal debt is to Edwards. With Edwards he maintains the distinction between natural and moral necessity that had made Edwards so unpopular among those who were dedicated to demonstrating the existence of a free will. "Were it not for moral necessity," he contended, "liberty would rest on an uncertain foundation. For sometimes we might will as we wish, and sometimes we might not" (p. 126). The implication is that the strongest motive is that which is perceived as providing the greatest pleasure or least pain. There is not freedom of willing, for Burton, in the sense that there are acts which are not motivated by one's subjective estimate of the potential pleasure or pain that can be derived from them.

Adherence to such a deterministic doctrine did not lead Burton to the fatalistic position that human choices are inconsequential. On the contrary, like most Calvinists, he felt compelled to show that man is a "moral agent", i.e., capable of actions which might be considered right or wrong in an absolute sense. In this way man could be held responsible for his acts and justifiably rewarded with everlasting grace or punished with everlasting damnation. In his psychological explanation of moral agency, Burton makes his most significant departure from Edwards and his most original contribution to the development of psychology in America. Edwards' representation of the faculties was held to be inadequate because it failed to recognize the singular attachment which exists between feeling and action. Edwards had said that cognition and perception are continuous; there is an intellectual and an affectionate component to every perception, hence to every resulting action. Burton countered by formulating a system of three independently functioning faculties: understanding, taste, and will. Based upon the introspective evidence of consciousness he proposed that the understanding perceives, the taste feels, and the will acts. Taste, a term which Burton originated and which he used interchangeably with "heart" and "affections," was designated as the seat of moral agency. In an important passage he held that

> Feeling is the spring of action. If a moral agent were deprived of the faculty of taste, and were as incapable of pleasure and pain as material bodies are, he would be as inert as they (p. 58).

It is obvious that Burton did not mean to re-establish man's rationality or free will. Man is essentially moved by his taste. In addition, "the will is only an executive faculty. It is no more than a servant to the heart, to execute its pleasure" (p. 91). Burton retained his Calvinistic determinism and Edwardean emphasis upon the affections. His system of independent faculties, unlike that of Chauncy or West, was strictly a function of his dependence upon the data of consciousness.

There is, however, an aspect of Burton's notion of taste which is wholly contrary to the psychology of Edwards. Though Edwards spoke of the "faculties" of the understanding and the will, he was implying a completely unified, indivisible, perceptual-cognitive-motivational process. Burton, on the other hand, no longer speaks of a unified mind. In his system there are three independent faculties, each with its own province within which it is sovereign. Burton's faculty of will was, therefore, not free in the "liberal" sense, but it had been isolated and given well specified functions. Burton's relationship to the question of the will in pre-Jamesian American psychology is represented in Fig. 2.

The significance of Burton's elaboration of an acceptably deterministic tripartite arrangement of the faculties may be illustrated via an analogy with Descartes' separation of mind and body. Descartes' well known dualism held that mind and body are utterly different but interactive entities. LaMettrie, however, then applied Descartes' persuasive description of automata to man, and was left with the first modern vision of man as a thoroughly mechanistic organism. Burton also emphasized the interactive nature of two constructs: will and taste. Soon after the appearance of his *Essays*, however, psychological thinkers influenced by him and by the like-minded Scottish School cut the Edwardean knot of "moral necessity" which was said to bind will and feeling. They held that the will of man is free. Without the will-taste dichotomy provided by a deterministic Calvinist like Burton, it is unlikely that there would have been a knot to cut, just as LaMettrie's mechanism would have been inconceivable without the earlier believeable dualism of Descartes.

EARLY AMERICAN PURITANISM

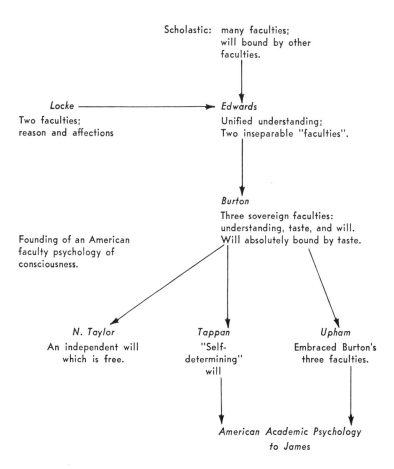

Scholastic: many faculties; will bound by other faculties.

Locke ⟶ Edwards
Two faculties; reason and affections
Unified understanding; Two inseparable "faculties".

Burton
Three sovereign faculties: understanding, taste, and will. Will absolutely bound by taste.

Founding of an American faculty psychology of consciousness.

N. Taylor
An independent will which is free.

Tappan
"Self-determining" will

Upham
Embraced Burton's three faculties.

American Academic Psychology to James

Fig. 2. THE PROBLEM OF THE WILL IN PRE-JAMESIAN AMERICAN PSYCHOLOGY.

Burton and American Psychology, 1824-1890

Burton's attempt to integrate Edwardean psychology with the data provided by his own consciousness appears to have had two important consequences. First, after the will had been extricated from the "understanding" of Edwards, it was a relatively small step for other Calvinists to dissolve the link of moral necessity which was said to render the will merely an executive faculty. This was accomplished principally by Nathaniel Taylor (1786-1858) in whom the doctrine of the freedom of the will triumphed.[16] A second result of Burton's efforts was what Schneider has called "the founding of a faculty psychology of consciousness".[17] Soon after the publication of Burton's *Essays* a number of textbooks appeared which expounded the new three faculty psychology. The most influential of these volumes, T. C. Upham's *A Philosophical and Practical Treatise on the Will*[18] and H. P. Tappan's *A Review of Edwards's "Inquiry into the Freedom of the Will"*[19] reveal the considerable influence of Burton.

It is clear that Burton was a transitional figure in pre-Jamesian American psychology. One foot was rooted deeply in the past; psychology for Burton was still of little intrinsic interest. Rather he considered it useful primarily because "he who knows himself correctly may have just conceptions of God" (p. 7). By this criterion Burton must have considered his psychology to be quite useful, for he concludes, not surprisingly, that

> the attributes of God are all comprised in three; benevolence, knowledge, and power, answering to the faculties in men called the heart, the understanding, and will . . . (p. 307).

Despite the undeniable theological overtones of the *Essays*, Burton was also breaking new ground. His persistent appeals to common sense and to the data of consciousness was to be reinforced by the Scottish position which was to dominate in America throughout much of the nineteenth century. His tripartite arrangement of the faculties seemed more reasonable to Calvinists of his era than did the earlier arrangement of Edwards. Though the publication of the theological psychology contained in the *Essays* coincided with the movement among American psychological thinkers to divorce themselves from theological concerns, his system of faculties was nevertheless adopted and his "will" was declared to be free.[20] Asa Burton helped open the door, perhaps to a greater extent than he wished, for the development of a vastly different view of man's psyche than that which preceded him.

JAMES G. BLIGHT

University of New Hampshire
January 1973

NOTES

1. I. Woodbridge Riley, *American Philosophy, the Early Schools* (New York: Dodd, Mead, 1907).
2. New Brunswick, N.J.: Rutgers University Press, 1939. Fay does, however, provide the most extensive treatment of Burton's system that is currently available.
3. *A History of American Philosophy*, 2d Ed. (New York: Columbia University Press, 1963), p. 203.
4. *Piety Versus Moralism: The Passing of the New England Theology* (New York: Harper & Row, 1970), p. 250.
5. For a thorough treatment of this period of American psychology see Perry Miller, *The New England Mind: The Seventeenth Century* (Boston: Beacon Press, 1962).
6. See especially his *Safety of Appearing* (Boston, 1689). It should be noted that this is not the conventional view of Stoddard. A more extensive treatment of Stoddard in this context is presented in James G. Blight, "Solomon Stoddard and the Dissolution of the Puritan Faculty Psychology," *Journal of the History of the Behavioral Sciences* (in press).
7. The brief outline of Edwards' position which is presented here is derived, in part, from an interpretation first offered by Perry Miller in his *Jonathan Edwards* (New York: Sloane, 1949).
8. Jonathan Edwards, *A Treatise Concerning the Religious Affections*, ed. John E. Smith (New Haven: Yale University Press, 1959), p. 272.
9. Jonathan Edwards, *Freedom of the Will*, ed. Paul Ramsey (New Haven: Yale University Press, 1957).
10. Excellent treatments of the early controversy over Edwards' notion of "the will" may be found in Edwin S. Gaustad, *The Great Awakening in New England* (New York: Harper, 1957), and Miller, *Jonathan Edwards*.
11. *Seasonable Thoughts on the State of Religion in New England* (Boston, 1743).
12. *Essays on Liberty and Necessity* (Boston, 1793).
13. Ibid. p. 26.
14. Chief among this group were Jonathan Edwards, Jr. (1745-1801) and Nathanel Emmons (1745-1840). Contrasting interpretations of their positions and importance may be found in Frank H. Foster, *A Genetic History of the New England Theology* (Chicago: University of Chicago Press, 1907), and Haroutunian, *Piety Versus Moralism*. Foster characterizes Edwards, Jr., and Emmons as villains responsible for the demise of the will in American thought, while Haroutunian's account emphasizes the continuity between their views and those of Edwards. On the whole, Haroutunian offers a much more balanced account.

15. Burton's *Essays*, though not published until 1824, appears to have been written much earlier, in the period 1800-1804. Reid's *Intellectual Powers* (1785) and *Active Powers* (1788) were known in America by 1800, thus they could have had some impact on Burton. See the following for related information concerning Burton and the *Essays: Dictionary of American Biography*, 3:340-41; Thomas Adams, "Memoir of Asa Burton, D.D.," *American Quarterly Register*, 1838; William B. Sprague, *Annals of the American Pulpit*, (Vol. 2), 1857.

16. *Lectures on the Moral Government of God*, 2 vols. (New York: 1859).

17. Schneider, *History*, p. 207.

18. Portland, Me.: Hyde, 1834.

19. New York: Wiley & Putnam, 1838.

20. The separation between theology and psychology was not complete until William James. James McCosh, for instance, wrote an influential theological, common sense psychology as late as 1887. Cf. *Psychology: The Cognitive Powers* (New York: Scribners, 1886) and *Psychology: The Motive Powers* (New York: Scribners, 1887).

ESSAYS

ON SOME OF THE FIRST PRINCIPLES

OF

METAPHYSICKS, ETHICKS, AND THEOLOGY.

****

By ASA BURTON, D. D.

PASTOR OF THE CHURCH OF CHRIST IN THETFORD, VERMONT

PORTLAND:

PRINTED BY ARTHUR SHIRLEY.

1824.

INTRODUCTION :

Containing preliminary Observations.

THE AUTHOR of the following essays, when he first entered on the study of theology, felt the importance of forming a just and true theory of the human mind. This feeling prompted him to read with attention all the most noted and distinguished authors, he could find, on the subject of pneumatology.—He expected, by studying them, to digest a true system. This course he pursued for several years. When he had carefully attended to English, Scotch, French and German authors, instead of finding increased light, his mind was more darkened and perplexed with respect to several parts of this very important subject. Failing of success in this way, he determined to lay aside reading authors, except occasionally, and make an attempt by an exertion of his own powers, to arrange his thoughts systematically on the principles and operations of the human mind. In this way, he has succeeded, in some good measure, to his own satisfaction.— That theory of the mind, which was the result of much study, and which he had taught students in divinity under his care ; which was generally approved by them, and which they frequently urged him to publish, it is the object of these essays to illustrate and explain. In doing this, he determined not to adopt the plan or theory of any author he had ever read, for this reason ; he does not agree, except in part, with the system or plan of any preceding author. He, however, approves many things they have advanced, and views them as having reflected much light on this science. He feels himself much indebted to them, for a number of important suggestions, which have afforded him much assistance in the work before him.

As it is not his design to follow others by adopting their theories ; so he does not write in opposition to them, any further than is necessary to support his own opinions. His object is to illustrate, as far as he proceeds, the true theory of the human mind ; and avoid all disputation, as far as can be done consistently. In the essays on the mind, he means to take *facts, experience,* and *common sense* for his guides. He does not design to form a system on any other principles, than those which are self-evident,'or capable of demonstration. Whatever opinions respecting the mind he may advance, which do not agree with *experience,* with *facts,* and the *word* of God, are to be rejected. For principles, which contradict daily experience, cannot be true. Principles, which do not agree with the lives, and conduct of mankind, are not to be received. And if they do not accord with what the word of God teaches us concerning the characters of sinners and saints, they are false. All the external, visible actions of mankind, whether virtuous or vicious, may be traced back to first principles in the mind. By these principles we can account for the conduct of all men, or for the events which take place in the moral world, as well as we can explain the phenomena of nature, by the first principles in natural philosophy. Hence no hypothesis is to be admitted as true, which does not agree with experience, with facts respecting our visible conduct, and with the word of Jehovah.

Again. As every science is founded on what may be justly termed *first principles,* so this is especially true with respect to the science of theology. And no person can be considered as understanding systematically any science, if he is unacquainted with its first principles. And whosoever will examine the subject carefully, and candidly, will find, that *intelligent existence* contains the first principles of divinity. It is generally granted, that if a person does not understand the subjects of *moral agency,* and *liberty,* there are many other subjects connected with these, of which he cannot have a consistent view, and which he cannot satisfactorily explain. Of course he is not a systematic, or good divine. But a knowledge of moral agency and liberty involves a knowledge of the principles and operations of the mind. Hence these principles and operations are the *foundation* of divinity. Without a knowledge of these, a person is not acquainted with the foundation on which divinity, considered as a superstructure, rests. This shows the importance of a thorough acquaintance with the first principles, and the operations of the mind.

These essays therefore, are designed as an *introduction* to divinity. The author's great object, in explaining what appears to him to be the true theory of the mind, is, to assist the student in acquiring a systematic and consistent knowledge of divinity. He does not purpose to attend to any questions, or disquisitions relative to the mind, which are not necessary to answer this end. Whatsoever will not, in his view, serve to reflect light on subjects in theology, does not come within the compass and design of his plan.

It has been found by experience, that the *classing of objects* assists the memory, and renders the acquisition of knowledge more easy, and rapid. This is the plan the author designs to adopt with respect to operations of the mind. If certain qualities are found to belong to a number of individual existences, they are classed together, and denominated by some general name. For instance : We find many individuals are endued with *life* and *motion ;* they are formed into a class, and called *animals.* Though these properties are common to them all, yet some of these individuals possess properties, which others do not ; for this reason a general class is divided into a number, called *species.* Man is one species of animals ; beast, bird, and so on, are other species. Hence, among individual existences, according to the various qualities with which they are endued, there is a generic and a specific difference. In like manner, the operations of the mind are not all of one kind, but they differ from each other ; for which reason they ought to be formed into distinct, general classes ; and these general classes may be divided, according to their specific differences. This method will give a systematic arrangement to the several divisions of mental operations. It will greatly assist the memory ; and help the student in acquiring a clear, and distinct knowledge of the principles and operations of spiritual substances.

Authors have pursued different plans in the study of the human mind. Some have not only attended to its faculties and operations, but have in connexion with them attended to all the objects with which the mind is ever conversant. This leads them into a very extensive field, in which a student is in danger of being lost. In these essays, the author has pursued a different course. He has attended, as far as possible consistent with perspicuity, to the faculties of the mind, and their operations, without describing the numerous objects of perception and choice.

Others have not only attended to all the materials of knowledge with which the mind is furnished ; but have considered particularly the connexion, relation, similitude, and association of objects or ideas, and shown how one suggests and leads to another in a regular train or series. And on the principle of suggestion, resemblance, or association, have formed their system of classification. This view of objects has not been attempted in the following essays.

Again. In forming distinct classes in the views taken of the mind, different methods may be adopted. For instance, we may classify the operations of our faculties, and also the objects of the mind. This is a double classification, which serves to confuse, instead of elucidating the subject of the mind. It is also needless. For the objects with which we are acquainted are already formed into distinct classes, including both the genus and species. Hence, to give a systematic view of the mind nothing more is requisite, than to form its operations under each faculty into distinct classes. The plan adopted in these essays, of confining the attention to the faculties and operations of the mind itself, excluding a consideration of the objects of perception, feeling, and volition, as far as could be done with perspicuity, presents the mind with all its operations to view in a much narrower compass. And the more concisely any subject is discussed, if it is done perspicuously, the more easily, and distinctly will it be understood by the reader.

If it be admitted, that the animal, vegetable, and inanimate creation are three general classes, which include all the individuals of the material creation with which we are acquainted ; the addition of another general class would be needless, and serve to confuse and lead the mind away from the truth. When these are divided into species, the work is done, and all material existences are clearly and systematically arranged. In doing this, there is no need of considering the faculties or operations of the mind.

So in relation to the mind, when the number of faculties with which it is endued, and the operations of each faculty with the real difference between them are known, the way is then prepared to form them into general and specific classes. And in doing this, there is no need of attending to the several classes into which the material world is divided.—And if *perceptions, sensations* and *affections,* and *volitions,* include all the operations of the mind ; these three general classes are sufficient. Form these three general classes into their *specific* divisions ; then the work of classifying is finished, and a systematic view of the mind is formed. And this seems to be the only rational plan for accomplishing that end.

The existence of an eternal, independent, absolutely perfect being, is the first principle in divinity, and the foundation on which the whole superstructure rests. Every doctrine, then, in theology, must be explained in consistency with his character. But how can this be done, by any person, unless he has just, clear, and distinct views of the character of God? Hence, generally, all, who teach divinity, begin with proving the existence of God, and giving a description of his character. If any err concerning the character of Jehovah, errors will prevail through their whole system of sentiments, in a greater or less degree. And all we know of God is by the revelations, or displays he has made of himself in his *works* and *word ;* or by *actions* and *declarations.* These are the *signs* by which he is made known. All existences produced by him are either *material,* or *immaterial,* or what we call spiritual. The material creation contains but a comparatively faint display of his character. Here we see no communications of his nature, or moral attributes. We behold goodness displayed, but see no *inherent principle* of goodness in any material being. We discern no inherent principles of action ; nothing, which constitutes intelligent *agency.* Hence material existences, however great, are not viewed as rational *agents,* or as rewardable for any of their operations.

But God is an *agent* worthy of love, service, and praise, on account of the various operations of his agency. And no where do we find, through the vast extent of his works, a real resemblance of himself, but in immaterial, spiritual beings. Such beings are rational *agents.* And the mind or soul of man is the most perfect agent in kind or nature, to be found in this world. Man sustains the highest rank among all creatures on earth, which have *life* in themselves, from the lowest, smallest insect, through every rising grade. In him, then, we may expect to find the most perfect, and entire resemblance, in kind, of Jehovah. It must, therefore, be evident to every reflecting mind, that we cannot have just, and correct views of God, as the first, eternal, and infinite agent, any farther than we form just, and correct ideas of man, as an agent. Hence the study of *man* is the most important, and interesting, and useful study. He, who knows himself correctly, may have just conceptions of God.

Man is an agent. He is endued with such powers, and is capable of such operations, as to be considered a *moral* agent ; a being, who is a proper subject of praise and blame, and of future and endless rewards. Hence arises the interesting, and important inquiry, what powers, qualities, or faculties, are necessary to render a moral agent worthy of praise or blame, and of final rewards ?—This inquiry will lead to the discussion of many very interesting subjects; such as the following : In what does agency properly consist ? Is it some inherent, abiding, primary principle of action ; or no more than a simple exercise ? Can all our actions be traced back to some primary active principle in us, from which they all proceed ? What is the difference between the natural and moral powers of the mind ? What powers, or faculties are necessary to constitute a complete moral agent ? And when these are ascertained, then the question arises, *why* are they requisite to make such an agent ? This is a question which I have, as yet, never found answered, in any systematic, or satisfactory manner, by any author, who has published on this subject. Yet it is one of the most important subjects to be clearly understood in the whole range of subjects, which relate to moral agency ; and one which reflects by far the most light on this inquiry. In what does that liberty consist, which is considered necessary in a moral agent ; and why, for what reasons, is it requisite ?

When questions of this complexion are answered correctly, then a person knows what things are needful to constitute a perfect, moral agent ; and he also clearly discerns the *reasons* why they are necessary. A person may then, and not before, be said to understand the subject of moral agency ; and the ground on which praise and blame may be predicated of man ; and why final rewards suited to his character are perfectly just and proper. This knowledge will enable him to form just views of the being and character of Jehovah. He can then explain and unfold to view the divine character ; and describe in a consistent, and systematic manner all the doctrines and precepts of the Bible. But, until he is acquainted more or less distinctly with the subject of moral agency in the light above exhibited, his mind must be full of darkness, confusion and uncertainty respecting the leading, and fundamental doctrines of the gospel.

These observations are sufficient to show, and impress on every mind, the importance of commencing the study of theology with a discussion of leading ideas, which relate to the subject of moral agency. This is the first subject with which the student's mind ought to be occupied ; and his attention to it should be continued, until he clearly understands it. He is then prepared, and not before, to understand systematically the doctrines of divinity ; and he cannot well fail of forming consistent views of the doctrines of the gospel from the beginning to the end ; in case his powers of mind are sufficient to qualify him for a teacher.

It will be granted that every sentiment, when explained, which does not agree with moral agency and liberty, ought not to be admitted as a doctrine of the gospel ; for every doctrine actually taught in the bible is consistent with moral agency and liberty. But how is it possible for any divine to know the doctrines he believes do agree with the true theory of moral agency and liberty, unless he is previously acquainted with that theory ? Does not this clearly show, that correct views of moral agency lay the foundation for a consistent explanation of gospel doctrines ? Of course, in digesting a system of divinity, he ought to begin with the study of this subject.

Again. It is well known that the systems of divinity embraced by Calvinists and Arminians differ widely. This difference arises in part from different views of the subject of moral agency and liberty. The latter say, that necessity destroys the liberty essential to a moral agent. Hence they reject, as far as they can consistent with themselves, every doctrine, which implies necessity. But Calvinists admit that one kind of necessity not only agrees with liberty, but is necessary to its existence. Hence they can believe in those doctrines, plainly taught in the Bible, which imply this necessity. This shows that divines do in fact differ in their sentiments, according to their ideas of that liberty, which is consistent with moral agency, or praise and blame. They must then begin with the study of moral agency and liberty, and fix their principles on this subject, before they are prepared to explain the word of God, and adopt, or reject the doctrines it inculcates. These and many other considerations show, that we ought to begin the study of divinity with forming consistent views of the subject of moral agency. But to have consistent views of this subject, we must attend to the faculties and operations of the mind. When every thing is considered, which might and ought to be, it is ve-

B

ry evident, that we ought to begin the study of divinity with the study of the human mind. If we agree here, and are consistent, we shall agree in all the leading doctrines of the bible.

The author is aware that many, at this day, are greatly prejudiced against all kinds of metaphysical reasoning and investigation ; and are disinclined to read discussions of that character. It is not expected that persons of this class will attend to the following essays Yet some subjects are so abstruse, and the truth so difficult to be explained, that a close metaphysical investigation is necessary, and in no other way can light be reflected on them. And this is especially the case with all subjects, which respect the mind, moral agency, liberty, necessity, and worthiness of praise and blame. Must we remain ignorant of all these subjects, which are in fact the foundation on which a whole system of divinity rests, because what is called a metaphysical investigation is necessary to understand them ? If we proceed on this ground, and attend to no subject which requires patient, and accurate reasoning ; the course of mankind will soon be retrograde. Instead of making new discoveries and advances in the field of science, each succeeding generation will be less informed ; mental imbecility will ensue ; and the most important and practical truths will be involved in darkness.

Metaphysical reasoning strengthens the rational powers of the mind ; and begets a habit of close attention, and patient investigation. But those, who content themselves with superficial views, and are willing to remain ignorant of every thing, which requires mental exertion to understand, will soon find their powers weakened, and mere declamation will constitute all their excellence and worth. But the author hopes we have many in our nation yet, who are willing to give every subject, and especially the human mind, that laborious and thorough investigation, which is requisite to the attainment of a competent knowledge. And he flatters himself, that these essays will afford them some light and assistance in their study of the mind ; and serve as a clue to further inquiries ; and thus enable them to explain and defend those doctrines of our holy religion, which at this day are attacked with great zeal, by men who have not neglected mental discipline. If these essays should be useful to any in these respects, he will feel himself repaid for all his trouble and labor.

The author has nothing to say in defence of his stile. He confesses he has always attended more to ideas and matter, than to the ornaments of speech ; and is willing to acknowledge he has been too negligent in this particular. He has made it his aim to avoid all vulgar expressions ; and to use words, which shall not offend, if they do not please. The main character of stile at which he has carefully aimed is *perspicuity*. If he has failed in this, he will lament it ; though he trusts there will not be much complaint arising from this source. A desire to be well understood, is the only excuse he has to make for repeating so frequently the same word in a sentence, and the same idea in different words. On abstruse subjects, perhaps any person would find it difficult to use what is called an eloquent style. An argumentative style must differ in its character from others.

Some of the essays too were written in too much haste, owing to numerous avocations & interruptions, incident to the care of a large church & society. He begs the candor and patience of the reader, hoping his attention will be so occupied with the sentiments advanced, as to make every allowance for imperfections of style, as far as the most liberal candor will admit. Nothing but diffidence, and a backwardness to appear in print on subjects so often discussed by learned men, has kept these sheets from the public eye for several years. But he has finally yielded to the judgment & importunity of particular friends. He expects various opinions will be embraced concerning what is here written, and different feelings excited. But he hopes no one will form a hasty opinion, or condemn any sentiment advanced, unless he can detect the fallacy of the reasoning by which it is supported. The author is advanced in age, and has no expectation of living to hear what may be said for or against the system he espouses. He believes however, there are those, who, if they agree in opinion with the author, will be able to defend him, and repel the attacks which may be made. He has, therefore, nothing more to say, but to leave the work with God, to bless and give it success, as far as what is published may be agreeable to his mind and will. What is written was with a view of affording assistance to candidates for the ministry of the gospel, and to defend in general that system of doctrines called the reformed, or Calvinistic creed. The author earnestly prays it may not in any respect prove injurious to gospel orthodoxy ; but rather a means of increasing the true light, and of diffusing it through the world.

ESSAY I.

On the Faculties of the Mind.

All existence, as far as human knowledge extends, is either material, or immaterial; corporeal, or spiritual. And though it is generally granted, that certain properties, aside from their operations, are essential to matter, yet this is not acknowledged to be true, by some, with respect to the mind. It becomes, therefore, necessary to inquire whether the mind has properties, or faculties, antecedent to the operations of *thinking, feeling*, and *willing*, and distinct from them. However, what is meant by a faculty of the mind ought to be, in the first place, explained. There was a time, when the word faculty was first used. It was then used to express some idea which the speaker then had. What was it? If the original meaning of the word is retained in our language, it was at first used to signify a *preparedness* in the mind for certain operations. It communicates no more than a *simple idea*. Hence it does not admit of a logical definition.

The way many have taken to evade truth, and silence an antagonist, has been to request a definition of words; and if they cannot be defined, they are said to be used without any meaning. Many do not consider, that some words are incapable of any definition, and yet may be well understood. This is true of every word which conveys only one simple idea. Would it not be impertinent for any person to ask another, to define the terms *pain* and *pleasure*? The reason is, they are terms, which convey simple ideas. All such terms are incapable of any logical definition. There is but one way to explain them, which is to use some other terms, of the same meaning, which are better understood, if there are any of this class. The word faculty is a term, which conveys a simple idea, and can no more be defined, than we can define the word *pain*. Yet it no more follows from this, that no such property, which is called a faculty, exists, than it follows, that there is no such thing as pain, because it cannot be defined. And there is no propriety in asking for a definition of simple terms. If all persons would keep in view the difference between simple and complex terms, they would never ask for a definition of the former, nor deny the reality of a thing merely because it cannot be explained by a definition. There is reason to think, that some reject certain truths because the words, which convey truth, cannot be defined. This appears to be one reason, why some disbelieve the existence of faculties, as antecedent to exercises, because the word is undefinable. Some do not believe in the existence of faculties, because they have not, what they call, a *consciousness* of their existence. They are conscious of their fruits, or operations, and this is sufficient. Will any person affirm that pain has no cause, has nothing which occasions it, when he has no consciousness or knowledge of that cause, or antecedent? No ; he infers, from the pain he feels, the existence of something which produced it. And he may as safely infer the existence of faculties, from their operations or exercises. Hence, candor will admit the existence of faculties or properties of the mind, though they cannot be defined, and though we have no consciousness of them except by their operations.

By a faculty, then, I mean a preparedness, a fitness, a capacity, or an adaptedness of the mind for those various operations, of which we are daily conscious. And I would here give notice, that I shall use the term operations in these essays, to denote all the thoughts, feelings or affections, and volitions of the mind. Every thought is an operation ; every affection, and every volition, is an operation of the human mind. I shall generally use the word in this extensive sense. And now the inquiry is, whether there is in the mind a faculty or preparedness for thinking, a preparedness for feeling, and a preparedness for willing ; or whether there is not ; and whether these faculties are antecedent to every operation of the mind, and objects of distinct consideration. Some believe that faculties and operations are as distinct objects, as motion and the body moving ; and that the former are antecedent to the latter. Others, in philosophical discussions, deny this distinction. Some arguments will now be adduced to show, that such a distinction ought to be admitted.

1. This distinction is so obvious to common sense, that it has been admitted by all nations, in every age of the world. This is evident from the general construction of languages. In ev-

ery language, verbs are used, which always have a nominative case, expressed or implied. A nominative case denotes an agent, or something capable of action. And a verb expresses the act of the agent. Accordingly we say, the understanding thinks, the heart feels, the will chooses and refuses. This mode of expression is common to all languages, and is founded on this distinction, that the faculties of the mind are objects as distinct from their acts or operations, as matter is from motion. If we deny this distinction, and say the mind is nothing more than a composition of thoughts or ideas, feelings and volitions, or as some have said, a bundle or union of exercises, then, to be understood, we must alter our mode of conversation and writing. Instead of saying the understanding thinks, the heart feels, the will chooses, we must say, thoughts think ; feelings feel love, and hate ; volitions choose and refuse. And this destroys all distinction between verbs and their nominatives ; an action is the nominative and the verb at the same time.

Some to avoid this difficulty say, the proper mode of expression is this ; the mind thinks, feels, chooses. Actions ought to be predicated of the mind, instead of faculties. This supposes the mind and its exercises are not synonimous ideas ; that the mind is one thing and its exercises another: This solution of the difficulty implies the same distinction between the mind and its actions, as has been made between faculties and their respective operations. Here it may be asked, what is the mind ? Is it a number of faculties or properties, united ? This will not be granted by those who deny the existence of faculties. Is the mind nothing but various exercises united ? Then to say, the mind thinks and acts, is only saying, that exercises think, and act, or that exercises exercise, and acts act ; and thus the objector involves the very difficulty he is attempting to avoid. It may be still asked, what is the mind ? Will it be said it is an essence ? Then it is an essence that thinks and acts. Is it agreeable to common sense, and the common use of words, to predicate actions, exercises, or operations of an essence ? An essence is often supposed to be the substratum or supporter of properties ; but to predicate actions of it, is a new thought, and an improper use of words. But has any one a clear and distinct idea of the meaning of the word essence ? Can he tell what it is ? Has he a consciousness of any such thing ? If not, how does he know, that things which exist have an essence ? Does he infer it in this way, that properties must have an essence, or something to support them? Then he believes some things, of which he has no knowledge by consciousness. Hence it does not become such a person to deny the existence of faculties, for the want of a knowledge of any such properties of the mind by consciousness. We may as consistently infer the existence of faculties, from those operations of which we are conscious, as we can infer an essence from the existence of properties.

Again ; it may be said, it is not the mind, or any particular faculties which operate ; but it is the person, who acts.—Here it may be asked, what is a *person?* Is he a being? Is his being a union of properties, or of exercises? If the former be admitted, then the thing contended for is granted. If the latter be affirmed, then all the absurdities, which attend the theory that exercises act, return upon us. Objections of this kind, when fairly examined, have no weight. Hence, notwithstanding the evasions which have been noticed, the argument retains its full force, which is this, that we must admit the *difference*, on which the distinction is founded, between faculties and their respective operations ; or believes an opinon, which has prevailed in all ages without any particular bias in its favor, is false ; and also alter the general construction of all languages. This opinion, which has so generally prevailed in all nations, of a difference between faculties and their operations, has been proved from the construction of every language among men. And mankind have not been led to embrace this opinion by any particular bias or prejudice ; for, it is presumed, no such general bias can be named.

2. From our actions and operations we may safely infer the existence of faculties.

That we think, feel, love, hate, choose and refuse, is certain. What is it, which thinks, which loves, which chooses ; something or nothing? It must be one or the other. Will any one boldly say nothing acts? Nothing operates? If this is too absurd to be admitted, it must be granted that where there are operations, there is something which operates. By what particular name shall it be called? If it be said it is the mind, or the person, which acts ; it has been made evident these evasions, instead of invalidating the argument under consideration, involve absurdities too gross to gain belief. That property of the mind which is employed in thinking, has been generally called the understanding. And it is by the will the mind chooses and refuses. As it is absurd to predict actions of nothing :

and equally absurd to predicate actions of themselves, or of actions; and as they must be predicated of something, from them we infer the existence of faculties. From our thoughts, we infer the faculty called the understanding, which thinks, or perceives objects ; and from our feelings or affections, we infer a feeling faculty ; and from our volitions, we infer the faculty termed the will, which chooses and rejects. And there is no way to avoid this inference, unless we say there may be operations without an operator ; which is as inconsistent, as to assert there may be design without a designer.

3. If we have no faculties, mankind are not agents. Agents act, or operate. But agency exists, antecedent to actions. Now if men have no faculties, what constitutes that agency which is employed in thinking and choosing, and which by its operations becomes visible ? Is it actions, operations, or exercises ? Is perception, or volition the agent which perceives, or wills ? Then agency and action are the same thing ; and we return to the former absurdity, that actions act. If it be granted that men are agents in thinking, in choosing, in all their operations, then something exists antecedent to all our exercises. If we say it is the mind, still what is the mind ? We have seen where interrogations of this kind lead us.

If we say men are not agents in thinking or willing, and are to be considered only as the *subjects* of such operations, how can this afford any strength to an objector ? If we are not agents, who act, and nothing more than subjects acted upon, what in this sense constitutes us subjects ? Whatever it be, it must exist before it can be acted upon. It must be a substance of some kind or other, wholly distinct from the operations of some other agent upon it. Indeed, let us view this subject in whatever light we may, a being must exist before he can think, feel, or will. The operations of thinking, loving, hating, and choosing are *objects*, as distinct from the *being* of whom they are predicated, as any two objects in existence. This is so evident, that no person can deny it, who has given a proper attention to the subject. This is certain, that neither actions, nor exercises, nor operations, constitute this being. What then is this being ? Nothing but a mere *essence*, or substrátum ? This will not be pretended, if what was said respecting it under the first argument receive proper attention. What are called the understanding, heart, and will, constitute the human mind. Whether these properties have an essence, or substratum, for their support ; and whether this substratum is the divine agency, or something else, are questions, which do not in the least affect the subjects considered in these essays. I therefore leave them to the decision of others. That to our *being* do belong such faculties as have been mentioned, the arguments which have been used, fully evince. However, if any persons wish for further proof, I refer them,

4. To the word of God. This corresponds with the reasons which have been offered. God is the author of our being. He is perfectly acquainted with the nature and properties of our minds. He can give us a just description of men. According to his word, men possess three distinct properties or faculties. An understanding, which is the seat of knowledge ; the heart, which is the fountain of depravity ; and the will, as the cause of all the visible effects wrought by us.

The last time Christ appeared to his disciples after the resurrection,it is said," then opened he their *understanding*,that they might understand the scriptures." Here the understanding is that faculty, by which his disciples were to obtain a knowledge of the great doctrines of the gospel. By this they would perceive the truth ; and become acquainted with the gospel scheme of salvation, and be able to teach it to others. Also Eph. 1. 18. " The eyes of your *understanding* being enlightened, that ye may *know* what is the hope of his calling, and what the riches of the glory of his inheritence in the saints." The *eyes* of the understanding were *enlightened*, for this purpose, that saints might *know*, or clearly and distinctly *perceive* the objects of their hope and desire. Many passages might be cited of the same import, which teach us, that the understanding is that faculty of the mind, by which we *perceive* or obtain a knowledge of divine truth.

And the scriptures teach us that the heart is another distinct faculty of the mind, and the source of all moral good and evil. Christ says, " A good man, out of the good treasure of his heart, bringeth forth that which is good ; and an evil man, out of the evil treasure of his heart, bringeth forth that which is evil ; for of the abundance of the heart his mouth speaketh." Here the heart is represented as either a good, or evil treasure, fountain or source, from which good and evil, as streams, proceed.   And there is a plain distinction made between the *heart*, and the *good or evil* which proceeds from it. In another place Christ says, " For out of the heart proceed evil thoughts, murders, adulteries, fornications, thefts, falsewitness, blasphemies." Our Lord taught, if a man look on a woman, and lust after her, he hath committed adultery with her in his heart already ; by the sins mentioned in this passage, not only *external acts*, but the *internal motions* or *desires* of the heart are included. Here an evident distinction is made between the *heart*, and the evil affections, or *desires* which proceed from it. They are as distinct, as a fountain, and the streams which flow from it ; and are so represented by our Lord. These passages, and many others which might be adduced, do not represent the heart as the seat of *knowledge*, but as the *source* of moral good and evil. Hence they make a plain distinction between the *understanding* and *heart*, and between *them* and their *operations*. *Perceptions* of truth are the operations of the understanding ; and the *affections* are the operations of the heart. These things are clearly taught by the passages to which we have given attention.

And the *will* is represented in scripture as another distinct faculty of the mind. " Which were born, not of blood, nor of the will of the flesh, nor of the *will* of man, but of God." Regeneration is a great change, wrought in man. This effect is produced in the heart, but the will of man is not the cause of it. The will of man produces many effects ; some it cannot produce. And this change in the heart is one of the latter. Here the will is mentioned as a *cause* in man, which produces effects ; and is clearly distinguished from the heart, in which regeneration is wrought. Again we read, " For prophecy came not in old time by the *will* of man ; but holy men spake as they were moved by the Holy Ghost." Whether men shall sit or walk, keep silence, or speak, and many other actions, depend upon the will. But foretelling the events of future ages does not depend on their will. Here, according to the representation of the Spirit, the will is a *cause* of many *effects ;* and the will and its operations are no more one and the same, than a cause and its effect are the same thing. The will by its volitions or exertions produces effects. This is its office.

Hence the scriptures teach us that the mind is created with three distinct faculties, whose operations are very different from each other. *Perceptions* of objects are the operations of the understanding. The *affections* are the operations of the heart. And *volitions* are the operations of the will. These distinctions are founded on a real difference, and are taught and supported by the holy scriptures. To view the human mind as possessed, or, if any prefer it, composed of three distinct faculties, which are to be considered as existing *antecedent* to their operations, and to which very different operations are severally ascribed, are truths supported both by reason and scripture.

****

ESSAY II.

Of the Understanding.

Matter is a general name given to all *corporeal* beings, or to all kinds of existence which are inert ; which never act, except when acted upon. Mind, or spirit, is the general name, by which all intelligent, active beings are distinguished. What the essence of matter is, we know not. We are acquainted with its properties, and their operations and effects. This comprises all our knowledge of matter. And we know not what the essence of mind, or spirit is. It is endued with certain properties. This we are obliged to believe, or renounce our claim to common sense. We are also acquainted with the operations of the mind, and the effects they produce ; and this comprises all our knowledge, at present, of spiritual existence.

The faculties of the mind are its essential properties. By these the mind acts, and produces effects. Its operations are generically different. For this reason they cannot all be considered as operations of the same faculty. Hence, philosophers have been led to consider the mind possessed of two faculties or properties, called the *understanding* and *will.* Whether it is endued with any other faculties or not, will be determined in subsequent essays. At present, I shall confine myself to the understanding. This faculty is undefinable ; for two reasons. 1. It is an individual property. 2. It is simple in its nature. And of individual, simple existences, no one can give a logical definition. If a person does not know what is meant by the terms solidity, extension, perception, pain, and volition, it is not possible to give him a knowledge of them by any definition whatsoever. An attempt to define such words, has occasioned darkness and confusion, instead of clearer knowledge. Where such words are not understood, all that can be done is to explain them by other words, with the meaning of which persons are better acquainted. By the understanding, then, I mean a preparedness, or an adaptedness, or a fitness in the mind, if these words are better understood, for a certain class of operations. Many are apt to conclude, if they cannot define a word, it has no meaning. Hence they infer, there is no such faculty as the understanding, because it cannot be defined. And they might as well conclude there is no such thing as pain, because it cannot be defined. Hence, though the understanding cannot be defined, yet this is no objection against its being considered a faculty, nor any evidence against a belief of its existence.

Perceptions are the operations of this faculty. By a *perception*, a *thought*, an *idea*, I mean the same thing, the same operation of the mind. A perception must have an object ; and the same is true with respect to thoughts and ideas. When we perceive, there is something perceived ; when we think, we think of something ; and when we have an idea, we have an idea of something. Whether, when material objects are perceived, we see the objects themselves, or only their images, as some suppose, is a question which it is not the design of these essays to determine. In whatever way it be determined, the design which lies before me will not be materially affected. I would, however, give notice that, by the objects of perception, I mean the objects themselves, and not any image or representation of them. I shall take it for granted, that a material world really exists ; that when I see a tree, it is the tree itself, and not its image, which I perceive.

Different theories have been adopted and supported concerning our perceptions, thoughts,or conceptions. Some of the ancient philosophers believed, that men do not see the objects created, but their *forms*, which they called *phantasms*, or *images*. And modern philosophers have advanced various other theories on this subject. Of late there has been much dispute concerning the sense in which Locke used the term *idea*. Whether he meant the real object existing, or some image of it in the eye. Some have denied the existence of a material world ; and such various opinions have given rise to skepticism, which has been carried to a great length. It is not my object to attend to any of these various theories, either to state, explain, defend, or confute them. But as I have observed, it will be taken for granted through these essays, that a material world does exist, distinct from the mind ; and that all objects, of which we obtain a knowledge through the medium of our bodily senses, are real existences. It is objects as they exist, which we see, whether properties or modes ; and not images, or representations of them.

It may now be observed, that in all the operations of the understanding three things are to be noticed ; an agent, an operation, and an object. These are the things meant in the construction of all languages, by nouns when in the nominative case ; by verbs ; and nouns in the accusative or objective case. I perceive a man. *I* is the agent, in the nominative case ; *perceive* denotes its action or operation ; and *man* is the object in the objective case. There cannot be a perception without an agent, and an object. And the mind is so formed by its Creator, it can *perceive* objects ; it can be pleased, or disgusted with them ; it can make exertions to produce external, visible effects. This *preparedness* in its formation to *perceive*, is the understanding. Can the same simple faculty be the subject of operations so different, as *perceiving, feeling*, and *willing* are ? This is so unphilosophical, that but few have ever admitted it. Writers have, therefore, generally adopted the division of the mind into the faculties of the understanding and will. And according to this division, all the operations of the understanding are perceptions. Hence any operation, which is not a perception, does not belong to this faculty. But feeling is not a perception ; and volition is not a perception ; they are not, therefore, operations of the understanding. Every perception has an object. But a mere feeling of pleasure or pain has a *cause*, but not an object. And a volition is not a perception, but the *cause* of some effect. All these operations of the mind differ from each other, and ought to be distinguished. By confounding them, our views of the mind are darkened to such a degree, we know not what to affirm or deny consistently with truth. One perception does not differ from another in any respect whatsoever, unless in such particulars as these, that one is more distinct and clear, and another more confused and obscure. But whether clear or confused, they are perceptions. The objects of perception may widely differ from each other ;

yet this difference is in the objects seen, and not in the perceptions. And as all those operations of the mind called perceptions, thoughts, or ideas, are in their simple nature alike, they form *one distinct class.* Hence by perceptions, I mean one distinct class of operations, as by animals, is meant a distinct class of beings. These operations belong to the understanding, and to no other faculty. Every one will see there is no propriety in classing them with volitions, or sensations of pleasure and pain. Whatever operations, therefore, may be properly called perceptions, belong to the understanding. They cannot, without confounding things which widely differ from each other, be classed with any other operations, such as sensations and volitions ; nor be referred to any other faculty. I trust it is now made evident, as far as I have proceeded, that perceptions are the only operations of the understanding : that it is the office of this faculty to think and perceive : and that we can no more account for perceptions without a faculty to perceive, than we can account for actions without an agent.

****

ESSAY III.

Of the Objects of Perception.

The individual objects of perception are almost innumerable. However, most, if not all of them, may be arranged under the following heads.

1. *Simple existence.* When we see an object, we perceive a thing which is a real being or existence. For if there were no existences around us, there would be no objects of perception. We must have a conception of existences, before we can analyse or combine them. We may and do perceive objects as real existences, without taking into consideration their properties, relations, or connexions with other things. And viewing an object as having nothing more or less belonging to it, than barely its being, is what I mean by a perception of existence. Some may say we have a perception of some ob-

jects which have no real existence, and are nothing but creatures of the imagination ; as a horse, for instance, with wings. But we have an idea of a horse and of wings, things which really exist, before we place wings on a horse. So that this creature of the imagination is a combination of things which have a real existence, in such a manner as they are no where found to exist. The things, horse and wings, have an existence, but not united in the manner they are in this particular instance. All combinations of objects are formed of things which have a real existence. Those objects of perception, which are only mere existences, are very numerous.

2. *The properties* of which all existences are possessed, are objects of perception. All primary, & what some call secondary, and others occult, qualities, whether of matter or spirit, are objects of perception. These, also, are very numerous.

4. *Relations* are objects of perception. The relations of cause and effect, of things with respect to time and place, and all other relations, come under this head. A relation is an object of perception. We see the relation one thing bears to another. And there is no other way by which we can obtain a knowledge of relations, but by perception.

Relations, such as cause and effect, time and place, resemblance, contrast, contiguity, or any other which can be named ; these relations, as well as the things, are objects of perception. This is all, which is necessary to my purpose ; for it is not designed to discuss these several relations ; or show how one suggests another in a train of thoughts, or to attend to the laws of association or suggestion. This would lead into a wide field, far beyond the limits proposed. All which is requisite, to answer the end herein aimed at, is, for the reader to notice, that however numerous and various the objects of perception are, yet the perceptions of them are alike. Whether we see a being, or its properties, or relations, our perceptions are as similar in their nature, as numerous drops of water are similar. Hence perceptions of the relations of objects form one generic class of operations of the understanding.

4. *Truth and falsehood* are objects of perception. We perceive the agreement or disagreement between the subject and predicate of a proposition. When it is affirmed that snow is white, we clearly perceive this quality belongs to snow. This is a perception of truth. But if it be affirmed, that snow is black, as we perceive no such quality belonging to snow, we

see the affirmation is a falsehood.—Every affirmation, and every denial, is true or false. For whatever is affirmed of any subject, is true or false. Whether it be true or false, we learn by perception. Hence truth or falsehood are objects of perception.

5. *The right and wrong of actions* are objects of perception. The right and wrong of actions imply some prescribed rule of duty. Those actions of moral agents, whether internal or external, which agree with the rule of duty, are right ; and those, which do not agree with it, are wrong. When actions are compared with the rule of duty, we perceive they agree or disagree with it ; and this is a perception of right and wrong. The rule of duty, the action, and their agreement or contrariety, are each of them objects of perception.

6. *Good and evil*, both natural and moral, are objects of perception. Our ideas of good and evil are relative. Whatever, in the natural and moral world, tends to happiness ultimately, is good.—Now all things, which can be viewed in relation to happiness or misery ultimately, tend to one or the other ; and may therefore, with propriety, be termed good or evil. When we say a thing is good or evil, the meaning is, it tends to happiness, or misery. Hence a perception of the tendencies of things, is a perception of good and evil.

I am not certain, that all the objects of perception are included under these general divisions. But I think of no others at present. Some, perhaps, will say, the objects mentioned under one head, are included in another ; there was, therefore, no need of so many divisions. This may be true. Yet, perhaps, on more mature consideration, these divisions will not be thought too numerous.

Whether our knowledge of all objects is obtained by *sensation* and *reflection*, or not, is not my design to determine. Because it is not necessary to elucidate the subjects principally aimed at in these essays.—Mankind frequently say, they have a knowledge of such and such objects. Now what is intended by the knowledge of an object ? Any thing more than a perception of it ? Feeling or sensation is not knowledge. By sensation we may acquire a knowledge of many objects. Yet sensation is one thing, and knowledge another. And no one willpretend that acts of the will constitute any part of our knowledge. Acts of the will may be objects of knowledge, but not knowledge itself.—Of course a perception of objects comprises

D

all our knowledge. Whatever, then, is known, is perceived ; and whatever is an object of knowledge, is an object of perception. We have a knowledge of existence, of the properties of beings, of their relations, of truth and falsehood, of right and wrong, of good and evil. And are there any other objects of knowledge, which are not included under one or the other of these divisions ? If not, then these contain all the objects of perception. But if there be other things, which are not included under either of these general heads, yet if they are known, they are only objects of perception.

This essay may now be concluded with a brief recapitulation of a few ideas. Perceptions, we have seen, form one general class of the operations of the mind. These belong to the understanding, & to no other faculty. The understanding acts, or operates. Perceptions are its operations. And the objects on which they terminate, or which are perceived, have been briefly arranged under several heads. When I say the understanding *acts*, I do not mean, it produces its own exercises. But I speak in this manner, to conform to the common use of words.

It is hoped the reader will carefully observe, that it is not designed in this work to show how external objects affect the bodily senses of seeing, hearing, smelling, tasting, and feeling ; or in what way by these senses the mind is impressed or affected ; or in what manner *sensations* are produced in the mind, by the operation of objects on the bodily organs. That sensations are produced, we know is a fact by experience. But the manner in which objects affect the mind, is an inquiry foreign from my present design.

****

ESSAY IV.

Of the Memory.

Some consider memory as a distinct faculty. Whether it is or not, depends on the nature of its operations. No one will suppose, that sensations, or affections, or volitions, are acts or operations of the memory. But the latter are perceptions ; & on that account may be called operations of the understanding. They either have only a specific difference from other operations of the understanding, and so belong to that faculty ; or they have a generic difference, and ought to form a distinct class of operations. Whether they differ generically, or only specifically, from the operations of the understanding, is the inquiry to which I shall give immediate attention.

A few days since, as I passed along, I saw a house of a certain form, dimensions, colour and situation. No one will suppose the eye can see. It is only an organ, or medium, through which the mind sees external objects. It was, therefore, my mind, which perceived the house at that time. What other name, beside seeing, or perceiving, shall we give to this act of the mind ? Whether we call it seeing, perceiving, conceiving, or by any other name, yet the act or operation is the same. Names do not alter things. This operation of the mind, I have hitherto called a perception. I give it this name, because I know of no other word, by which it can be more properly designated. At this moment I remember that I saw the above house. I recollect its form, dimensions, colour, and situation.

It will be granted, that remembering is an operation of the mind. What is the difference between this operation of the mind, and the one I had, when I first saw, and had a direct view of the house ? The object is the same. The house was the object, when I saw it ; it is the object now, when I remember it. Then I saw it ; and now, when I remember it, I see it. Remembering, then, when considered as an act of the mind, is seeing or perceiving. Here are two operations of the mind ; one respects a present, the other, a past object. Wherein do they differ ? It is believed it is not in the power of any man, to show any difference between these two operations, unless it be this ; one is more clear, the other more indistinct. Each is a perception of a house. And this is true respecting all the operations of the memory. There is a difference with respect to the objects. The object I now perceive before me, is *present.* When remembered, it is *past.* An interval of time has passed, between the first and the second perception of the same object. And when an object is recollected, it may be attended with a full persuasion, that it is the same object I once saw ; that I am the same person now I was then ; and that a period of time has intervened. Yet that operation, called remembering, is the same in kind with the one I had, when the object was present to the mind. Both are perceptions of the same object. But with relation to the object, and the two perceptions of it, there is the difference of past and present. Though an interval of time, a day, a month, a year, has passed, between my first seeing an object and remembering it, yet the object is the same, and each perception of it is the same in kind. Also there may be this difference, that when the object is present, the perception of it is more clear and distinct, than when it is remembered. But a perception is the same operation in kind, whether it be clear and distinct, or obscure and indistinct. This, however, may be true of perceptions of present objects, as well as those which are past. Again, I now see a house. A year hence I travell the same way and see it again. Would any suppose there is any difference between the first and second perception I have of that house, because an interval of a year has intervened ? Surely not. Yet there is no more difference between my seeing a house yesterday, and recollecting it to day, than between seeing it a year since when I passed it, and again to day, when I pass it again. For in both cases a portion of duration has succeeded, between the first and second perception of the same house. Indeed, the more this subject may be examined, the more obvious it will appear, that remembering, considered as an operation of the mind, is a perception of an object. And this perception differs no more from any other perception, than any two perceptions differ from each other. They are individual operations of the same kind, and may be numbered first, second, and third, as they succeed each other. Two or more individual things may be similar, and for this reason be called by the same name, as is the case with the same sort of rays of light.

Though all the operations of the mind are perceptions of objects, and being alike ought to be classed together ; yet on account of a difference attending the objects, they are subdivided into several distinct *species* of operations. And to each division a name is given, by which it may be ever after designated and known.—Present and past constitutes a difference between objects now seen, and those remembered. This is one difference. An object, which is now seen, is present to the mind. I look, not back, nor forward, but directly at it. When I recollect, I look back ; the object is not present before me. An object remembered is attended with a belief of personal identity ; a present object is not. On account of these differences between the objects remembered and those which are not, all these perceptions of past objects are formed into a distinct class, and to this class or division the name *memory* is given.

Hence it is as unphilosophical to say remembering is not perceiving objects, as to assert that a horse is not an animal. And we may as consistently say, that horse is not the name of one class of animals, as say that memory is not the name of one class of the operations of the understanding. And hence it is not philosophical to consider memory a distinct faculty. For there is no ground to believe there are any more faculties belonging to the mind, than there are classes of operations of different *kinds*. It is agreed, that loving, hating, choosing, refusing, are operations of different kinds—so different, that the faculty, which perceives, cannot love and hate. This is the reason, which has induced philosophers to admit the existence of two, if no more, distinct faculties, which they call understanding & will. But is it not as easy for the same faculty to perceive past, as present objects? If it is, what necessity is there of supposing two faculties, understanding and memory, to account for a perception of present and past objects? Even such a supposition will not account for it. It is a fact, that we perceive the objects which are before us, and those which are past. But *how* we perceive either, no person can tell. We may, then, conclude, there is no sufficient reason, nor any necessity, for considering memory to be a distinct faculty. We ought to view memory only as a name given to one class of the operations of the understanding. If any, however, choose to consider the memory as a *power* of the understanding, I have no objection to it. For by it nothing more can be meant, as far as I can conceive, than the ability of the understanding to perceive, or recal past objects. That it has a power, or ability, or can recal or remember them, is granted. For it is a fact, it does recollect them; and what it in fact does, it can or has power to do.

It may be inquired, if remembering is perceiving, what is the object? I answer, the object recollected is the same object perceived, when first presented to the mind. If it be asked, where is the object, when remembered? Answer, where it was, when we first obtained a knowledge of it. If any ask, how we remember or recal past objects? Answer, I know not. I know it is a fact, but cannot describe the manner of it. I cannot tell *how* we perceive present objects. These are inquiries beyond my reach.

Having made it evident, that the operations of memory are only perceptions, and the difference between them and other perceptions are such circumstances as present & past, and not the perceptions themselves except the relation of time ; having shown the dissimilarity of the circumstances attending the objects, as the reason why they form a distinct class to which the name memory is given ; & that this class of operations are operations of the understanding, and of course there is no reason or necessity for considering and calling the memory a distinct faculty, the principal objects of this essay are answered. Many other things which might be observed respecting the memory, as they do not come within the design of these essays, receive here no particular attention.

It is granted, that several relations between objects afford great aid to the memory. One object suggests another ; and a present object, by a relation of resemblance, or place, or some other relation, suggests a past object, or revives in the mind a perception of an object, which had been previously received. Hence it is granted, that the various relations of objects are of great use in recollecting, or reviving past objects, or objects which had been previously seen. But when we consider the perception of a present, and the perception of the same object at another time, those perceptions or operations of the mind are similar ; and for this reason are operations of the same faculty.

****

ESSAY V.

Of Judgment and Reason.

Judgment and reason are distinguished by some writers, and considered as different operations of the mind. It is apprehended that the difference, if any, is very small. Judgment is agreed to be an act of the mind. It is that act by which one thing is affirmed or denied of another ; or it is an assent to the truth of a proposition. And this assent to the truth or falsehood of a proposition is an act of the mind.

But what act or operation of the mind is it ? Is it a sensation, or a volition ? This is never pretended. It must then
be a perception. For we experience no other operations than
perceptions, sensations, and volitions. All our operations
may be included in one or the other of these general classes.

That the act of the mind, which is called judgment, is only
a perception, will be evident from a further attention to the subject. *Man is a rational being.* This is a proposition. For
it has a subject, copula, and predicate. Man, which is the subject, is an object of perception. And rationality, which is the
predicate, is an object of perception. I perceive that the affirmation is true ; which is only perceiving the agreement between
the subject & predicate of this proposition. If we were to attend to a hundred propositions, we should find an assent to their
truth or falsehood is only a perception of the agreement or disagreement between their subjects and predicates. Hence,
judgment is nothing more or less, than the *perception* of the
truth or falsehood of a proposition.

In the next place, what is reason ? It is a power of the understanding to infer one proposition from another. This process of inferring one thing from another is called reasoning.
There is no necessity of adducing proof of this, because it is
granted. The only question is, what acts of the mind are employed in reasoning ? *I think.* From this I infer another
proposition, which is, *I exist.* For I clearly see non-entity
cannot think or operate. But as I do in fact think, it is certain, the being intended by the pronoun *I* in the proposition has
existence. The operations of the mind are limited. From
this I infer, that mankind do not know or comprehend all
things. For if men knew all things, as God does, their minds
would not be limited. This inferring one proposition from
another, is reasoning. In this process of the mind none of
its operations are employed, but perceptions. As perceiving
the agreement or disagreement of the predicate of a proposition
with its subject, is termed judgment ; so perceiving the agreement or disagreement of one proposition with another is reasoning. When I perceive the truth of this proposition, *I think,*
or the mind of man is limited, I clearly perceive other propositions must be true ; that I do exist, and that mankind do not
know all things. Of course, reasoning is perceiving the agreement or disagreement of one proposition with another.

With a self evident proposition another is connected. All

propositions, which are true, are connected as links in a chain. And when we attend to a self evident proposition, we perceive the connexion between it and another, and between this last and another ; and so on in a regular progression. The mind acts by perceiving the connexion between one proposition and another, is all that can be meant by inferring or deducing one truth from another. And it must be evident to any attentive mind, that in this process, which is called reasoning, there is only a perception of the agreement, relation, or connexion of one truth with another. Perceiving these agreements, relations, or connexions, is reasoning. By perceiving these agreements, the mind is advancing in knowledge, and there is room for it to proceed in discovering truth in an endless progression. For the field of science is unlimited. And from this view of the subject it is obvious, if there were no self evident propositions, there would be an end to all reasoning. The mind would have no where to begin. If it could not directly, and intuitively perceive the truth of one proposition, it could never perceive any to be true, and must forever remain in a state of doubt and uncertainty. All conclusive reasoning is founded on self evident propositions, of the truth of which we are convinced by intuition or direct perception.

The way is now prepared for us to attend to those things, which constitute an agreement and a difference between judgment and reason. For in some respects they agree, and in others they differ. They agree with respect to their object. Truth and falsehood are their objects. When one thing is affirmed of another, the affirmation is true or false. Perceiving the truth or falsehood of the affirmation, is that act of the mind called judgment. For, judging a proposition to be true, is perceiving the agreement of the predicate with the subject, or the truth of the proposition. And judging a proposition to be false, is nothing but a perception of its falsehood.

Judgment respects particular propositious, and the agreement of a predicate with its subject, or its disagreement. But in reasoning, two propositions are taken into view. By compairing them we perceive, that if this proposition be true, *I think*, the other must be true, that *I exist*. Perceiving the agreement between one and another proposition, is reasoning. This is inferring one truth from another. In this process there are two acts of the judgment. We perceive the truth of the first and of the second proposition. Hence in reasoning, two, three, or more judgments are united. The difference between judgment and reason is this. Judgment is an individual act of the mind ; it respects the truth of one proposition only. But in reasoning, several acts of the mind are connected. One judgment or perception of the truth of a proposition, is a necessary help to discern the truth of another. In reasoning,there is a succession of perceptions. The mind, from viewing one,passes to the contemplation of another proposition ; and in its progress perceives the truth of the several propositions, and their connexion and agreement with each other. Yet in judging and reasoning, no acts of the mind are employed, but those perceptions, or those operations which belong to the understanding.

It is true, other operations are connected with our perceptions. For instance, the will confines the attention to a subject ; and when truth is perceived, and new discoveries made, the heart is *pleased*, and emotions are excited. Yet every person must know, that those volitions and the pleasure we experience, are not perceptions of truth or falsehood. A pleasant or painful sensation is not a perception ; and volitions are not perceptions. This is evident to every person, who has given attention to the operations of his own mind. Though affections and volitions may accompany perceptions, yet it is by the latter we obtain a knowledge of truth and falsehood.

Whether or not all truths are contingent or necessary, according to the division made by some, is not my object to determine. It is the great object of these essays to describe the difference between the operations of the human mind, and class them according to their differences, and present them in a systematic order to the reader's view. In order to this, it is not necessary to attend to the objects of perception,any further than to show the ground and reason of the several classes into which the operations of the mind ought to be divided. And though there may be a difference between contingent and necessary truths, yet each of them is an object of perception. In a proposition, where there is no necessary connexion between its subject and predicate, still the latter may agree with the former ; and when this is perceived, we judge the affirmation to be true. And when I affirm that two and two are equal to four, though this is necessarily true, yet it is the understanding which perceives it. Hence contingent as well as necessary truths, are objects of perception only.

E

Now objects of perception differ in certain respects from each other. This difference is the reason of forming them into distinct, specific classes. Accordingly, those operations of the understanding which have for their object the truth or falsehood of particular propositions, ought to be classed together ; and this class ought to have a name, which is commonly known by the term *judgment*. And those operations of the understanding, which are employed in deducing one truth from another, form another class, which is called *reason*. So the terms judgment and reason ought to be used, as the names by which those perceptions are designated, which have the truth and falsehood of propositions for their object.

Hence judgment and reason are not faculties of the mind. They ought not to be considered as faculties, unless their operations *generically* differ from perceptions. But we have seen there is no such difference. For judging is only perceiving the truth of a proposition ; and reasoning is only inferring one proposition from another. In this process, when the truth of one proposition is perceived, the truth of another immediately connected with it, is perceived. Each act of the mind in judging and reasoning is a perception. And between one perception and another, there is no difference. As life, or motion, is the same, though it be predicated of a thousand individuals called animals ; so perceptions, however numerous, belong to the understanding. For this is the only faculty which perceives. Yet, as the objects of perception differ in particular respects, they are divided into several classes, to designate, and remind us of this difference. When the word remembering is used, I know the objects recollected have been seen, but now are past. And the words, judgment and reason, remind me, that the truth and falsehood of propositions are contemplated. Hence the reason, why different names are given to the same operations of the understanding, is not because they differ in their kind or nature ; but because the objects of those operations differ from each other.

Having said sufficient to make this subject plain, we may now proceed to another class of operations, which belong to the understanding.

ESSAY VI.

On Conscience.

Various are the opinions respecting conscience. Some metaphysicians term it a *moral faculty*, a *moral sense* ; while others consider it synonymous with the dictates of reason, or the judgment we form of our moral conduct. Amidst such a conflict of opinions, it becomes us to examine this subject with candor and impartiality.

And 1. It is not the immediate and direct office of conscience to teach us truth, or falsehood. Truth and falsehood are not the objects of conscience, any farther than is necessary to ascertain their moral qualities. Conscience is not employed in determining what propositions are true, or false ; this belongs to the province of reason.

But 2. Conscience judges of the moral qualities of actions. Our actions are either right or wrong, good or bad. And it is the office of conscience to distinguish these qualities. But to determine the qualities of our actions, we are to compare them with some general rule or principle. Self evident propositions of the moral kind, are general principles by which we determine moral qualities. Some actions ought, and others ought not, to be performed. When we do what ought to be done, our conduct is right ; but when we do what ought not to be done, our conduct is evil. It is a self evident proposition, that I ought to do by another, as he ought to do by me, in similar circumstances. From this I infer, that if my neighbor ought to love me, I ought to love him. Although, from self evident principles, we may draw many just conclusions, yet in many things we are liable to err. Through the strength of corrupt inclinations, the influence of prejudice, and the want of light, we may judge amiss, respecting what we ought, or ought not to perform. We, therefore, need some infallible rule for our guide. The moral law supplies an infallible rule. This is prescribed by our Maker, who cannot err. The moral law makes nothing right or wrong ; but is founded on eternal principles of right. Our hearts and actions are either right or wrong, antecedent to the consideration of the written law of God. God knows, without the possibility of error, how we ought to feel in all cases, and how we ought to live in all the relations we sustain. And whatever we ought to do, *that* God requires of us ; and whatever we ought not to do, *that* God prohibits. The moral law, considered as a rule of conduct, contains nothing but requirements and prohibitions. As these are given us by our Maker, who cannot err, the moral law is an infallible rule, or guide, conformably to which we ought always to feel and live. This is our teacher. This is the rule, with which we ought to compare our hearts and our lives. If our hearts and our actions agree with this rule, they are right; but if they disagree, they are wrong. If any thing is wanting in the heart, which ought to be there, as love to God, there is a *defect*, which is a transgression of the law. And if any thing be found in the heart, which ought not to exist there, as hatred to God, there is an *excess*, which the law prohibits. Then the moral law is an infallible rule, by which we are to judge of our conduct.

3. Conscience compares our hearts and actions with this rule, and judges of them according to their agreement or disagreement with it. This comparing implies two things; first a perception of the rule; 2. A perception of the things to be compared with it. Or in other words, it implies a knowledge of each. We must have a knowledge of those things severally, which we compare together. A knowledge of the law as a rule of duty, is neither more nor less than a clear and distinct perception of its requirements and prohibitions. The law then, as a rule of duty, is an object of perception. The heart and its actions are to be compared with this rule. And a knowledge of these, is a perception of them. So far as we have a distinct perception of the heart and its exercises, or affections, we have a knowledge of them.

Now, when we clearly see what the law requires and forbids, and distinctly perceive the objects to be compared with the law, then we can compare the latter with the former. When the comparison is made, we cannot avoid perceiving an agreement or disagreement. For our hearts and their operations do agree or disagree with the rule of duty. And this agreement or disagreement can be known by perception only. And it is the office of conscience to judge, whether our hearts and actions are right or wrong, good or evil. In this case conscience judges. But what is intended by the judgment of conscience? This judgment is certainly an act of the mind, and it is that act by which we affirm or deny. By which we say, our characters and conduct do, or do not, agree with the rule of duty, and thus pronounce them right or wrong. But this act of conscience, which is styled its judgment, is nothing but a distinct perception of the agreement, or disagreement of our hearts and lives with the rule of duty. Supreme love to God is a right, a holy affection; and supreme love to the world is idolatry, a sinful affection. This is the judgment of conscience. But this judgment of conscience is no more, than a clear perception, that supreme love to God is a holy affection, and supreme love to the world is a sinful affection. If any person will attend carefully to this judging of right and wrong, he will find he can make nothing more of it, than perceiving right and wrong. The terms right and wrong, good and evil, holy and sinful, are adjectives, which denote the qualities of our hearts and actions. Two or three propositions may convince us, that conscience is nothing, but the judgment we pass upon our conduct ; and this judgment is nothing, but a perception of the agreement, or disagreement of a predicate with its subject.

Solomon was wise. I perceive the affirmation agrees with the subject. This is judging the proposition to be true. *Solmon was benevolent. God is good.* Nothing is affirmed of these subjects, but what I perceive to be true. This perception is judging the proposition to be a truth. But when we perceive, or judge, that Solomon was benevolent, and that God is good, we only see or judge, that their characters are right or holy. The qualities affirmed of them are right and holy, consequently they are worthy of approbation. *Satan hates God.* Here I perceive what is affirmed of Satan to be true. This is judging him to be a sinful being. Then *perceiving* the wickedness of any being, and *judging* him to be wicked, is one and the same thing. And perceiving the righteousness of any being, is the same thing with judging him to be a good, a holy being. There has ever been a distinction maintained between natural and moral attributes. *God is powerful.* In this proposition, power, a natural attribute, is ascribed to Deity. *God is benevolent.* Here a moral attribute is ascribed to him. Then we may distinguish propositions into two kinds, *natural* and *moral.* In propositions, where nothing but a natural attribute is ascribed to the subject, all we have to do is to judge, whether the affirmative be true, or false. But this determines nothing respecting the moral character of the subject. When I say, *God is powerful,* and perceive what is affirmed to be true, yet this does not determine his moral character. A powerful being may be either sinful or holy. But when I say *God is benevolent,* a perception of the truth of this proposition, determines his moral character. Natural propositions are true

or false ; but determine nothing respecting the moral character of the subject.   Moral propositions are true or false.
They also determine the moral character, whether it be right
or wrong, holy or sinful.   In each of these two kinds of propositions, it is the business of the mind to judge, whether they
are true or false.   Judging, we have already seen, is nothing
but a perception of the agreement or disagreement of the predicate with its subject.   Then those acts, which are called our
judgments, and those acts, which are termed conscience, are
the same kind of acts.   For they are nothing more, nor less,
than perceptions of the truth or falsehood of propositions.
Wherein then, does conscience differ from judgment, or reason ?   When we consider the operations of conscience, judgment, and reason, as *acts* of the mind, they do not differ.   But
the objects perceived differ.   Truth and falsehood are the objects of reason.   Right and wrong are the objects of conscience.   They also differ with respect to the sensations they
produce in the heart.   A perception of truth affords pleasure.
A perception of right conduct gives greater pleasure.   From
the consideration, that a perception of right and wrong is attended with a more strong and lively sensation of heart, than a
perception of truth and falsehood, many, probably, have been
led to believe that conscience is a sense ; and that its operations,
considered as acts of the mind, are different in their kind from
the operations of reason.   It is generally agreed, that the office of conscience is to teach us what is right, and what is
wrong ; what we ought to do, and what we ought not to do.
By what acts of the mind, beside those called perceptions, can
we determine what is right, or what is wrong in our characters
and conduct ?   Can we determine by our feelings or affections ?   A pleasant or painful sensation is a feeling.   If a person's conduct pleases me, is it certainly right ?   If we make
our feelings the standard by which to judge of the characters
and conduct of moral agents, we shall find the same character
and conduct, at the same time, both right and wrong.   For it
is not unfrequent, the same character and conduct please one
person, and disgust another.   The divine character affords
pleasure to saints, but pain to sinners.   If *feelings* be the cri-
teria, saints will say, the character of God is holy and good.
But sinners will say, it is evil, and hateful.   Both cannot be
true.   Our feelings, then, are no correct standard by which
we can determine what is right, and what is wrong.   Can we

ascertain what is right, and what is wrong, by our affections ? Love and hatred are affections.

Is it certain, because I love a character, that that character is worthy, holy and good ?   Or because I hate a character, does that determine the character to be evil, sinful, and hateful ? Good characters are often hated, and evil characters are often loved.   We, therefore, can determine nothing concerning the goodness, or wickedness of characters or conduct, by our affections.   And no one will pretend, that by willing or choosing, we can ascertain what is right, or what is wrong.   Surely our refusing any thing does not determine that thing to be evil ; nor does our choosing a thing determine it to be good. For bad characters are often preferred to good.   Sinners prefer wicked characters to that of Christ.   Perceptions, feelings, affections and volitions, are operations of the mind, of which we are conscious.   We know we have them.   And those include all the operations of which we have any consciousness. But neither feelings, affections, nor volitions constitute what we term conscience.   We do not, by these, judge one thing to be right, and another wrong, as we have already seen.   It then follows, that perceptions constitute conscience.   Indeed, a view of right and wrong, good and evil, is antecedent to any feeling, affection, or volition, excited by a conviction of right or wrong.   Good qualities can neither please, or disgust ; be loved or hated ; chosen or rejected, until they are perceived, or we have a knowledge of them.   When we learn by the dictates of conscience, that the character and conduct of a moral agent are very evil, then we may feel a disgust and hate them. And when we are informed by conscience that a character is holy and good, then we may be pleased, and love it.   Then every person must see, that conscience performs its office, and informs us what is right, and what is wrong in characters, *before* they give us any pleasure, or pain, or excite any love, or hatred, or preference.   Then perceptions must constitute conscience.   Because its operations are antecedent, in the order of nature, if not of time, to all our feelings, affections and volitions ; and must be distinct from them.

Here it is well to observe, that conscience respects *our* conduct, and not the conduct or characters of others.   When we say we cannot in conscience do certain things, we do not mean, that others cannot in conscience do them.   For the dictate of *their* conscience may greatly differ from *ours*, respecting the same thing. When we see wickedness in others and condemn them, it is not common to say *our conscience* condemns them ; but our reason. Though in approving or condemning others, the same operations of the mind are implied, as in approving or condemning ourselves ; yet with relation to the former we say, our reason condemns them ; but with respect to the latter it is common to say, our conscience condemns us.   This shows that conscience and reason contain the same operations of the mind.   But to these operations we do not give the name of conscience, only when *our* conduct is approved or condemned. Hence the operations of the mind, or of the understanding, when *our* conduct is to be judged, approved or condemned, are called our conscience ; but when the conduct of *others* is approved, or disapproved they are stiled *reason*.   Hence conscience in judging of moral conduct is restricted to *our* actions, and does not extend to the actions of others.

But it may be said, that conscience is a *moral sense*.   If it be a sense, what are its operations ?   Do we by this sense perceive the qualities, which are denominated right and wrong, good and evil ?   Then its operations are perfectly similar to those of the understanding.   Why then is it not precisely the same, to say and believe that the understanding perceives moral qualities, as to say, a moral sense perceives them ?   If the operations of the understanding, and of this moral sense, are the same ; are nothing but perceptions of moral qualities ; then the understanding and this moral sense do not differ, but are perfectly similar.   If by a moral sense, some persons would imply a faculty different in its nature from the understanding, they use the term without any meaning.   If the operations of this moral sense are perceptions, then the moral sense and the understanding are the same faculty.   The question then returns, what are the operations of this moral sense ?   Are they feelings of pleasure and pain ?   Are they affections or volitions ? We have already seen, that by operations of this kind, we can never ascertain the nature of moral qualities.   If these are the operations of a moral sense, this *sense* is wholly inadequate to the purposes, for which its inventors designed it.   But as all the operations of the mind, of which we have any knowledge, are included either in the class of perceptions, or in the class of feelings and affections, or in the class of volitions ; and as the two latter classes do not contain the operations of this moral sense ; it follows, that perceptions must be the operations of this moral sense. Then this moral sense and the understanding are the same faculty ; or the word has no meaning in our language.

The word *sense* denotes *feeling*. To have a sense of right and wrong, and a feeling of them, are the same, considered as operations of the mind. A feeling is either a pleasant or painful sensation. Surely where there is no pleasure or pain, there is no feeling. So that feeling is a pleasant or painful sensation. If a moral sense is a feeling, it is either a pleasant or painful sensation. And if such feelings judge what is right and wrong, then we shall pronounce our conduct to be right, if it is agreeable ; and wrong, if disagreeable to us. In this way we shall often reverse the decisions of the divine law. This is one reason why men so often err in judging their moral conduct ; they are influenced by their feelings to approve what is agreeable to them, and to disapprove what is unpleasant. If, then, by a moral sense is meant a feeling, it is the most unsafe, erroneous standard of moral conduct, which can be invented. For this plain reason, that nothing is more commonly wrong in man, than his *feelings*.

If a moral sense is not a feeling, which very few will pretend on a close examination, what do the advocates for it mean by the terms ? Do they mean by it an *intuitive perception* of right and wrong in moral conduct ? So that without comparing our conduct with any rule, we perceive *intuitively* the moral quality of every action, as we suppose is the case with God in judging of moral conduct ? We suppose he sees intuitively what is right and wrong. Now suppose he has given to men the same faculty, which some call conscience ; some call it a moral sense, and many say it is his vicegerent in men, teaching them intuitively the moral qualities of their acts. Concerning this, I remark, 1. If it be true, mankind would never err, or differ in their judgment of moral conduct. But this is not the fact. The same person has judged differently, concerning the *same conduct* in himself at different times. Numerous facts might be mentioned to verify this. How often has the same person one day judged certain amusements to be innocent, right and lawful ; and the next day utterly condemned them. And mankind often, in fact, differ in their judgment of the same conduct, one pronouncing it right, and the other wrong. These are facts. And they prove that men often err, in their judgment of moral conduct in themselves and others. This is

F

sufficient to prove, that mankind have no faculty by which they can, in all cases, judge intuitively what is right and wrong. There is no such vicegerent implanted in them. 2. Judging intuitively always respects self evident propositions ; and no other. I am not against granting, that some moral actions are self-evidently sinful,and others holy. All who admit there is a God, who ought to be the supreme ruler of the universe, must see rebellion against him is wrong,& obedience right,as soon as they hear the terms pronounced. No process of reasoning is neces-sary, to produce conviction of such moral truths. And with respect to a great part of our moral conduct, the moral pro-perties of our actions are so nearly self evident,that a very short process of reasoning is sufficient to convince. With respect to some parts of moral conduct a regular process of reasoning is necessary. Seeing that, in some cases, a very brief process is sufficient, many persons have embraced the notion of a moral sense, or power of judging in all cases instantly and intuitively. 3. Whether we judge intuitively or not concerning moral con-duct, we ought to inquire what operations of the mind are con-cerned or employed in judging. If any proposition, whether natural or moral, is self evident, we know it by *perception*. We immediately perceive the truth or falsehood of the natural, or the right or wrong of the moral proposition. In this case we do not judge by our *feelings*, but by *perceiving* the fact. If any moral propositions are not self evident, but a shorter or longer process of reasoning is necessary to come to a final judgment ; through the whole process of reasoning *perceptions* only are concerned. We perceive the *action* to be judged ; the intermediate propositions by which we at last perceive its agreement or disagreement with the rule of duty. The oper-ations of the mind employed in the train or series are percep-tions ; perceptions of the rule of duty, of the actions to be judged, and their agreement or disagreement with the rule. Hence, when this moral sense is examined, we see, in this last sense of the terms, they contain no other operations of the mind, but the *perceptions* of the understanding.

We have now considered this moral sense as a *feeling* ; also as a faculty by which it is said we perceive intuitively what is wrong or right. We have seen in the first sense of the terms, it cannot be true ; and in the last sense, they imply no opera-tions but perceptions. And I cannot invent any third sense, in which the terms, *moral sense*,can be used. And as the terms, in the sense in which they are perhaps generally used, contain no operations of the mind but perceptions; it follows that a moral sense has the same meaning with the term conscience. It is another name denoting the same operations with conscience, or signifying the same thing. Hence a moral sense, if it mean any thing, is synonimous with conscience as I use it.

We will now return and give some further attention to the operations of conscience. When a person has a clear perception of the excellency of God's character, he distinctly sees why he ought to love him supremely. He clearly perceives that supreme affection is due from him to his Maker. A perception of what is due from him to God, is the same thing with a dictate of conscience. Conscience dictates such love, which is perceiving such love is due to God. He, also, at the same time, clearly perceives, that hating God is a sinful affection. Perceiving this, and remonstrating against it, is the same thing.

When a person hates God, perceiving this hatred is condemning, censuring, and blaming himself. And perceiving that he loves God, is justifying, approving and assenting to his worthiness of love. Then condemning, censuring, remonstrating, considered as acts of the mind, are only perceptions of wrong affections and conduct in a moral agent.

Again, the law saith, thou shalt not commit adultery; and Christ saith, if a man lust after a woman in his heart, he hath in his heart committed adultery with her already. Now when I compare the lust or desire with the law, I clearly perceive lust is prohibited, and that our Lord's assertion is true. If a person commits adultery, and perceives his sin, he condemns, censures and blames himself. Thus conscience operates. But blaming, condemning, censuring, and the like, are acts of the mind. And when considered as acts of the mind they are only perceptions of a wrong heart and conduct in the moral agent, who has committed the sin.

It must now appear abundantly evident, that the operations of conscience are perceptions, and do not differ in their nature from other perceptions, which are operations of the understanding. But the objects perceived, are different. Right and wrong, good and evil, or moral qualities, are the objects of those perceptions called conscience. Now these perceptions, which have moral qualities for their object, are classed together. And this class of operations of the understanding are called *conscience.*

As terms are used to express the views of the mind in relation to moral actions, of a different meaning from those in common use with respect to truth or falsehood, it may reflect further light on the subject to notice them. Because different terms are used, many judge they express different operations of the mind, and in this way deceive themselves.

With respect to conscience, we say it *approves* and *disapproves, accuses* and *condemns.* Reason we say *perceives, judges, determines,* and *pronounces* one proposition to be true and another false. As such different terms are used, we conceive they express very different operations of the mind. Let us now examine the meaning of the terms.

When reason judges and pronounces one proposition true and another false, it is generally agreed, that this means no more, than *perceiving* the agreement or disagreement of one proposition with another, or of the predicate with its subject. And this perception is an operation of the understanding. In judging what is true or false, we compare the subject predicate of propositions, and one proposition with another. And perceiving their agreement or disagreement is judging them to be true or false.

But moral actions are compared with the law, the rule of right and wrong. *Perceiving* the agreement of our actions with the rule, is *approving* them ; they are judged to be good, or right. *Perceiving* the disagreement of our actions with the rule, is *disapproving,* and *condemning* them, or judging them to be wrong. It is believed a person cannot affix any other meaning to the terms approving, acquitting, or disapproving, accusing and condemning. These terms then, mean no more than a *perception* of the agreement or disagreement of our actions with the rule of duty. I know there are other operations connected with this perception, to which attention will be soon given.

We also read of a *pure* conscience. The conscience is pure, when it does not accuse and condemn, but acquit and justify us. A pure conscience then, implies no more than a clear perception that our conduct is right. And a defiled conscience is a clear perception of actions as wrong.—A conscience void of offence is the same ; it does not condemn ; it perceives nothing wrong. A *good* and *evil* conscience is nothing more than a perception of good or evil in our conduct. And other expressions of a similar meaning in relation to conscience ought to have the same meaning affixed to them. Of this every one may be convinced by giving proper attention to two things.—1. That all the operations of the mind, which we ever experience, are included in three general classes—as *perceptions* of objects, *feelings* or *affections*, and *volitions*. Every operation belongs to one or the other of these classes. As there are three distinct clases of operations, it is evident the mind is composed of three distinct properties, or *faculties.* The understanding perceives, or sees ; the heart or taste *feels,* or has *affections* ; the will chooses, or has volitions.—And certainly there is no occasion for more faculties, than there are distinct classes of operations,operations different in their nature. Hence, 2. Conscience is not a faculty. If we consider it a faculty, we must predicate of it operations different from others in *their nature.* But we must say it *perceives.* For we cannot have a knowledge of right and wrong, but by comparing our conduct with the known rule of duty. This comparing certainly implies a *perception* of the rule, and a *perception* of *actions* ; and when actions are compared with the rule, then there is a *perception* of their agreement or disagreement with it. Thus far the operations of conscience are the same with those of the understanding. Then if we say, that conscience also *feels* ; has affections, which are sinful or holy ; we attribute to it operations different in their nature from perceptions. In this way we make the same faculty capable of operations distinct, and different in their *nature.* But we know a faculty is a *simple property,* so cannot be defined. Now can a simple property have operations so different in their nature as *perceptions,* and *feelings* or *affections* ? Can the same simple property *see* and *feel* ? To suppose this is irrational, and unphilosophical. For if its simple nature is to perceive, it cannot feel ; and if its simple nature is to feel, it cannot perceive. For a simple property cannot be the foundation of operations different in their *nature.*

Now we see, that conscience does *perceive ;* it therefore does not feel. As it perceives, if we call it a *faculty,* it is the same with the understanding. But of what use is it to have two perceiving faculties ? So if we say, it is the nature of conscience to *feel,* to love and hate ; then it cannot perceive. And if its nature is to *feel,* it is, if a *faculty,* the same with the heart or taste. And of what use is it to attribute to the mind two *feeling* faculties ? These observations, I hope, are sufficient to satisfy every one, that there is no propriety in viewing conscience as a distinct faculty. As it is not a distinct faculty ; then the terms approve,disapprove,pure,defiled,& those of a similar import, mean no more than a clear perception of the agreement or disagreement of our actions with the rule of duty. When we perceive that our actions agree with the rule, we say conscience is pure, undefiled, without offence ; it approves, instead of accusing and condemning us as polluted, guilty creatures. This approving is also *peace* of conscience. When conscience accuses and condemns, there is no peace.

Having shown what conscience is, we shall now attend, 4. To the feelings it excites in the heart. This is necessary, in order to show, that the operations of conscience and the feelings they excite are operations of a different kind, and ought never to be blended. We may now give attention to a class of feelings, which always attend on the operations of conscience. —These are feelings, which are either *pleasant*, or *painful*.

When a person has committed *theft*, and reflects on his conduct, he clearly *perceives* he has transgressed the laws of God, and of men. He then *sees* he is exposed to disgrace, shame, and punishment ; that he may in this world be detected, and punished ; and will certainly have his guilt exposed to the view of an assembled universe at the judgment day, and receive the punishment his crime deserves. His conscience condemns him as a transgressor ; the crime, the disgrace, the danger of punishment, all combine to wound him deeply, and excite strong wishes that he had never done the deed.

Such pains and desires are the operations of the heart or taste. And these feelings are expressed by different terms ; such as *remorse, regret, compunction*, and *stings of conscience.* If he is so hardened, that his conduct does not give him much pain, his conscience is said to be deceived, blinded, stupified, seared, or dead. Such expressions are *figurative ;* they ascribe to conscience the feelings of the heart ; or the feelings conscience produces in the heart are predicated of conscience itself. As when we say, reason *loves* the truth, and *hates* deception and error ; we do not mean, that love and hatred are operations of reason ; but they are connected with it, and produced by it in the heart. When reason discovers truth, the heart loves it ; and hates error, when detected by reason. The feelings connected with reason, though they belong to the taste, are figuratively ascribed to reason.—So the painful feelings excited in the heart on account of sin, are ever connected with a perception of wrong conduct in ourselves. And because they are connected with the operations of conscience, they are figuratively attributed to conscience.

Hence, when a person's conduct agrees with the law of God and he perceives it, pleasant feelings are excited in the heart. Thus he has peace of conscience ; it not only approves of his conduct, but his conscience is said to *rejoice*, to have joy in the holy Ghost.

Hence, to understand the operations of the mind distinctly, we must attend to them carefully, and refer each operation to its proper faculty. And though operations follow each other, and are connected in a train ; yet we ought not to view all those thus connected as operations of the same faculty. But we ought to distinguish them according to their natures, and refer them to the classes and faculties to which they belong ; and not suffer ourselves to be imposed upon by figures of speech. When we say reason delights in demonstrating truth, and loves the truth, and hates deception ; here we ought to distinguish between the operations of reason, and the *feelings* connected with it. Reason itself is nothing but a train of perceptions, which have for their object the truth or falsehood of propositions. But those perceptions are attended with pleasant feelings, which do not belong to reason, but the heart.

So the proper operations of conscience are only perceptions, which have for their object a *rule* of duty, *actions*, and their agreement or *disagreement* with the rule. These perceptions are always followed by *pleasant* or *painful feelings* in the heart, with their attendant desires. And these feelings, sometimes the strongest we ever experience, belong properly to the heart, though we often ascribe them figuratively to the conscience. In strict propriety of speech, therefore, we should say conscience includes operations both of the understanding and the heart. It cannot, however, be considered a distinct faculty.

Benevolence is a most amiable quality. When we perceive, or have a knowledge of this quality in another, if our hearts are right, they are pleased. They delight in such a character, approve it, and commend it. Such feelings are excited, whenever we perceive amiable and virtuous qualities in any moral agent. But those feelings constitute no part of conscience ; for a perception of those qualities is antecedent to those feelings, and is the cause which produces them. And

those feelings are as different in their nature from the perceptions of moral qualities, as any other operations whatever ;
yet they attend all the operations of conscience. But this is
no evidence that they constitute any part of conscience. For
operations, totally different in their nature, may accompany
each other, and be closely connected in point of time.

Vices are hateful qualities. When a person has committed
murder, and we obtain a perception or knowledge of his criminality, displeasure and indignation are immediately excited.

These feelings, which accompany our knowledge of crimes
committed by others, have their seat in the heart. There is
no similarity between them and perceptions of moral qualities ;
consequently they are not operations of conscience, but strong
feelings, produced by a perception of criminal conduct in others. Thus distinguishing, as we ought, between the operations of conscience, and the strong and lively feelings or affections they produce, whether pleasant or painful, sinful or holy,
is of great importance to a correct notion of conscience.

That we may have accurate views of conscience, we proceed to consider three things, the *objects* of conscience ; its
operations, considered as acts of the mind ; and the *effects*
they produce. Right and wrong, good and evil, are predicated of our hearts and conduct. The heart is an object ; its
affections are objects ; and our actions are objects. When
these objects are viewed as subjects, right and wrong, good
and evil, are predicated of them.

These words, good and evil, denote the nature or qualities
of these objects. And these qualities too are objects. For
the predicate, as well as the subject of a proposition, is an object of perception. Then our *hearts* with their *operations*,
and all our *actions*, with their *qualities*, are the *objects* which
conscience regards. These objects constitute what we term
duty. The word *ought* implies the idea of duty. We say,
we ought to have a right heart, right affections, and right actions. And so far as our hearts, affections and actions are right,
duty is performed. And our hearts and conduct ought not to
be wrong, evil or sinful. But if they are wrong, duty is not
performed, we are transgressors. As it is the office of conscience to inform us of our duty, it must inform us what is right
and what is wrong. And it is evident, we cannot ascertain
what is duty, when it is not self evident, but by comparing our
hearts and conduct with self evident truths, or some infallible

rule of right and wrong. By comparing our affections and actions with a self evident duty, or with the moral law, we ascertain what is duty. Then duty, or our hearts and conduct with their qualities, are the *objects* which conscience takes into view. This will clearly show, that the operations of conscience are *perceptions*. For there are no other operations of the mind, by which objects can be seen, or known. We do not learn the nature of hearts and conduct by feelings, or affections, or volitions. It is solely by our perceptions. A perception of an object & its moral quality, is a knowledge of what ought,or ought not, to be. Then perceptions are the operations of conscience. These perceptions produce pleasure or pain. These sensations are the effects of conscience on the heart ; and they are as different from perceptions, as effects are from their causes. For we have already shown, that sensations are not the operations, but the effects, of conscience. And they ought to be viewed wholly different in their nature, and to be carefully distinguished from them.

Then our conclusion is this : that those perceptions of the understanding, which have the right or wrong of our hearts and conduct, or in a word our duty, for their object, are classed together, and called *conscience.* Or conscience may be thus defined : it is the understanding itself, when it takes cognizance of our own motives and actions, compares them with the standard of duty, and then acquits or condemns.

****

ESSAY VII.

Recapitulation.

The object of this essay is to recapitulate the principal ideas contained in the preceding essays, in a brief manner, that the reader may see them in a narrow compass. And

1. The understanding is a faculty of the mind. This faculty is a property of the mind. *Understanding, heart, will,* are words, which express different properties of the mind.

G

2. A faculty is a preparedness, a fitness, an adaptedness of the mind, to be the subject of definite operations. The same property does not prepare the mind to see, feel, and choose. There is no way to account for operations so different in their nature, but by supposing the mind to be possessed of different properties, or faculties.—Hence the different operations of the mind have led philosophers to consider it as having distinct faculties, or properties.

3. A faculty is as distinct from its operations, as a body is distinct from its motions. Hence a faculty is antecedent to its operations, and the foundation of them.

4. The construction of all languages is a direct proof of the existence of faculties. All languages have verbs; and every verb has a nominative case. The nominative case is the agent; and the verb expresses the action of the agent. *I perceive.* It is certain the mind does not perceive objects by the same faculty, by which it feels; nor by that, by which it prefers one thing to another. It is by the understanding only that the mind perceives. Accordingly we say, the understanding is a perceiving faculty. That mankind have, from time immemorial, considered the mind possessed of this faculty, is evident from the construction of all languages. Indeed it is a truth so evident, the words we use in talking and writing prove we have ideas of faculties, and believe in the real existence of such properties. It is a self-evident truth. If any deny it, they must be left to themselves. For it is vain to reason with persons, to convince them of the truth of self-evident propositions.

5. The word *perception* is used to signify all the operations of the understanding. I use this word in this sense, because I know of no other, which will more aptly express the operations of this faculty. Perception is an act of the understanding. The acts of the understanding may be, and often are, called ideas, thoughts, notions, and the like; but perception appears to me to be as proper a name of every act or operation of this faculty, as any that can be used. And perception is the name I give to every operation of the understanding.

6. Perceptions, which are operations of the understanding, are very numerous. Simple apprehension as an act of the mind, or the perception of an object. Conception is an act of the understanding. Memory, reason, judgment, and conscience, as we have shown, are operations of this faculty. This is true with respect to imagination; which is a perception of

objects combined in such a manner as to answer the design of the agent. Apprehension, conception, judgment, reason, memory, conscience, imagination, fancy, which are words abundantly used by philosophers who treat upon the intellectual powers of the mind, are names by which the acts or operations of the understanding are designated. For the understanding is the only intellectual faculty belonging to the mind. And when we attend to the meaning of these words, as applied to acts of the mind, it is obvious they cannot designate any other operations,th n those which I call perceptions. If persons will take the trouble of attending to the meaning of the above words, he will find they differ very much from the words feelings, sensations, affections, or volitions. They are, then,nothing more or less, than those acts called perceptions, thoughts, or ideas. An act of the mind is a simple operation. It cannot be defined. Seeing, thinking, apprehending, conceiving, remembering, reasoning, judging and the like, express acts of the understanding. These acts are not affections, desires, or volitions. These acts are perceptions. Seeing an object, conceiving of an object, remembering an object, and so on, is perceiving it. When perceptions are considered as acts of the mind, though called by different names, yet they are alike. It is not possible to point out any difference between one perception and another, considered as acts or operations of the mind. Being similar, of the same kind, they constitute one *general class of operations.* As all creatures, who have life, are classed together and called animals, so all those individual operations of the same kind are classed together, and called perceptions. But

7. This general class is subdivided into several distinct classes, to each of which a name is given. Though all the operations of the understanding are of the same kind, for which reason they constitute but one class ; yet their objects differ. Where there is a perception, there is something perceived. This something, whether it be a substance, a property, a quality, a mode, or relation, is the object of perception. And the individual objects are as numerous as the perceptions. The objects are not of the same kind ; they differ from each other in a variety of respects and circumstances. These differences among the objects, is the ground and reason of dividing our perceptions into several classes. Some objects have been seen, and are past ; when seen again, they are recollected. These

perceptions constitute a class by themselves ; and this class of perceptions is called *memory.*

Truth and falsehood constitute another class of objects. These are objects of perception. For we know what truth is, when we perceive it. Those perceptions, therefore, which have truth and falsehood for their object, constitute another class, which is known by the name of *reason*, and *judgment.*

Right and wrong, good and evil, form another class of objects. And those perceptions, which have the right and wrong of our own conduct for their object, constitute another class, which is called *conscience.*

All the operations of the understanding form one general class called perceptions. This general class of operations is divided into several specific classes. And each specific class has some name given it, by which it is known ; as simple perception, memory, judgment, reason and conscience. And the difference among the *objects* of perception, is the reason why our perceptions are formed into distinct classes. As those divisions are necessary in order to have a clear, distinct, and systematic view of the mind, so to facilitate the communication of our knowledge of the mind to others, it is necessary to give those several classes distinct names.

This mode of attending to the operations of the mind, appears to me far preferable to that generally adopted by metaphysicians. They generally begin by dividing the mind into two faculties, understanding and will ; and say, those are the only faculties belonging to it. Then they proceed to talk about the memory, judgment, reason, and conscience ; and frequently call each of these a faculty. Then the reader is confused ; he asks himself, does the writer mean, as he first said, that the mind has but two faculties ; or that it has six or seven ? For he calls judgment, reason, memory, conscience, imagination, and the like, faculties also. What does he mean ? Then when they write concerning the operations of these faculties, are these only one kind, or very different kinds of operations ? This he cannot determine from their manner of writing. Of course, he is left in the dark respecting the nature of the operations of these several faculties, as they are pleased to call them.

And after he has gone through a long treatise of philosophy on the human mind, though he has acquired many useful ideas, yet he has obtained no systematic knowledge of the mind. The ideas he has acquired have no proper arrangement ; neither does he see their connexion with first principles. Hence the reader has acquired only an indistinct and confused notion of the mind, and its operations. One great object here is, to give the reader a clear, and systematic view of the mind. Whether I have done it, as far as I have proceeded, he must judge.

I would observe one thing more, and close this essay. If any one should prefer considering memory, reason and conscience different *powers* of the understanding, I will not contend with him. If he says the understanding has a power of perceiving, or recollecting past objects ; and a power of perceiving truth, and inferring one truth from another ; and a power of perceiving the right and wrong of actions ; still all the operations of these powers are perceptions. And of course, these several powers only designate the several classes into which the operations of the understanding are divided. One power denotes one class, and another power another class of operations. Hence, whether we consider memory, for instance, as a power of the understanding, or as the name given to one class of perceptions ; still it is either the perception of past objects, or the power of perceiving them. So we consider all the operations of the understanding as similar in their nature ; and divisible into as many classes, if no more, as are above enumerated and specified.

****

ESSAY VIII.

Of Taste.

Taste is another faculty of the mind, distinct from the understanding, and also from the will. There are several considerations, to which our attention must be directed for the elucidation of this subject. The reader who wishes to examine it impartially, is requested to suspend his judgment, till he has weighed the considerations here presented, and seen the relation and connexion of the several parts with each other.

1. Taste, like the understanding, is undefinable, being a simple property. It can be explained only by using other terms of nearly the same import. It is that preparedness, adaptedness, or disposition of the mind, by which the mind is affected agreeably or disagreeably when objects are presented to it. We know it is a fact, that some objects please,and others disgust us. It is a fact, that we are conscious of sensations or emotions, which are sometimes agreeable, sometimes painful. These emotions belong to the mind. They must have a cause. Those things which produce pleasure or pain, whether they are material or immaterial, are the *objects* that affect us. These objects operate, and thus occasion sensations or emotions. Their operation necessarily implies a *subject*. Taste is the subject operated upon, when objects afford us either pleasure or pain. The understanding is not the subject on which they operate : for that has perceptions, but not emotions ; it is a perceiving, but not a feeling faculty.—To say the mind is the subject, is not satisfactory. What is the mind ? Is it a simple existence without properties ? An existence simple in its nature cannot be the subject of operations so different in their kind, as perceptions, pleasant and painful sensations, and volitions.

How the same simple nature can see, *feel* and *produce effects,* is to us unaccountable. Philosophers have, therefore, been led to view the mind, like all other substances, as possessed of different, distinct properties, or faculties. Operations of different kinds, which we experience, have led them generally to make two faculties, called understanding and will. The same reason which induces them to admit two faculties, will require them to acknowledge three ; which we design to make evident in its proper place. It will appear further on, that we have as much reason to view the taste as a faculty, as we have either the understanding or the will. And taste is that faculty by which the mind is pleased or disgusted by the objects which affect it. This faculty is the subject on which they operate, when we experience agreeable or painful sensations or emotions. These sensations do not belong to the understanding, nor to the will ; as I shall show hereafter. Taste is the faculty to which all operations of this kind belong. If we had not the bodily sense, which is called taste, food would neither please or disgust us.

By a mental taste, the mind is pleased or displeased with

all objects with which it is conversant. There is a great similarity between that bodily sense, called taste, and this mental
faculty, by means of which all objects affect us in an agreeable or disagreeable manner. On account of this similarity,
this mental faculty is called the taste. I know of no other
word, which will, according to its common acception, more
fully express the nature of this faculty. And for this reason I
use it. The word of God calls this faculty, the *heart*. And
whenever I may use the word heart to signify a faculty of the
mind, I mean the same thing by it, I do by the word taste.
Can the mind perceive ? Then its nature and construction
are such, that it is prepared for this kind of operations. Can it
feel, or be the subject of painful and pleasant sensations ?
Then its nature is such, that it is prepared to be the subject of
this *kind* of operations. Do we infer, from our perceptions,
the faculty which is called the understanding ? Then, from
our feelings, we as safely infer the faculty we call taste,
or the heart. And to suppose there may be perceptions and
sensations, without any subject to which they belong, is absurd. And to suppose a subject, which has not different properties, but is simple in its nature, can perceive objects, and also
be pleased or disgusted with them, is equally absurd. The
different faculties, which belong to the mind, prepare it for
operations of different kinds. This is as evident, as it is that
the different construction of material bodies prepares them for
different operations.

2. The taste, or the heart, is a *feeling* faculty. Although
this has been noticed already, yet it deserves a further and
distinct consideration. Both pleasant and painful sensations
are *feelings*. Every one knows what pain is, and what pleasure is, by experience. Pain is a sensation, and pleasure is a
sensation ; pain is also a feeling, and pleasure is a feeling.
Pain and pleasure are simple operations, which cannot be defined. Yet all persons are acquainted by experience with the
meaning of these terms. The terms pleasure and pain, sensation and feeling, when applied to acts of the mind, are applied
to the same class of operations. When I am pleased or disgusted, I feel ; I have a sensation or emotion excited. And the
taste is the only feeling faculty, which belongs to the mind.
And material objects, when perceived through the medium of
our senses ; and all the operations of the mind, when they are
objects of perception or reflection, either please or disgust us.
The heart is never in a perfect state of indifference. Objects,

when seen, always affect it, more or less. Yet the feelings of pleasure and pain excited by objects are often so faint, so feeble, that we do not observe them. In this state we say we are indifferent. It is true that we may be very nigh to a state of indifference ; yet, at the same time, we have some feeling. This faculty is in the highest degree *sensible*. Its nature is so tender, so lively, so susceptible, that every object we perceive must affect it. And our being in such a state, that we do not know we have any feeling, is no certain evidence we do not feel. It is pleasant to behold the light. But ask a person, whether the light of the sun excites in him an agreeable sensation ; and he will often be at a loss for an answer. Yet reason informs him, if his senses are not disordered, that it is always a source of more or less pleasure. We seldom reflect on the pleasure we receive from those objects which are the most constantly in view ; and for this reason are apt to say, we are indifferent towards them. We are apt to think we are indifferent towards all objects, which do not excite so lively sensations of pleasure or pain, as to gain our particular attention. Yet there are sufficient reasons to conclude, that mankind are never in a state of perfect indifference, or totally without any feeling. If not, then all objects affect us more or less.

Again ; all our sensations of pleasure and pain, however different the objects are which excite them, are operations of the same faculty. Many seem to suppose, that the mind has as many feeling faculties or powers, as there are differences in the kinds of objects which affect us. But there is no ground for such an hypothesis. The reason why objects of different kinds may and do affect the same faculty, will be attended to in the next essay. Here I shall attempt to show we have but one faculty which is capable of feeling. It will be agreed by all, that our bodily senses neither perceive, or feel any thing. The eye does not see the light ; the ear does not hear sounds ; but the understanding, through the medium of the senses, perceives light, sound, and every other object of sense. It is true, we often ascribe to our senses, those operations which belong only to the mind. We say the eye sees, the ear hears, the palate tastes. But these are figurative expressions. Seeing, hearing, smelling, and the like, are operations of the mind, not of the senses. The bodily senses are mediums through which the understanding becomes acquainted with external objects. They are necessary mediums, in the present state, to the perception of material, external objects. Hence the deaf have no perception of sounds ; and the blind have no perception of light, or of colours. Does it follow,because different senses are necessary to a knowledge of external objects, that we must have as many perceiving mental faculties as there are bodily senses ? Is it by one faculty of the mind that we perceive light and colours, by another sound, by another odours ? This is not pretended by any philosophic writer, with whom I am acquainted. Seeing, hearing, and the like, are operations of the same faculty. Through the eye, the understanding perceives light and colours ; through the ear, sounds ; and through the other senses, all the other objects of the senses.

In like manner, neither the eye, or ear, or any other bodily sense, is the subject of pleasant, or painful sensations. It is the faculty of taste, which is pleased with light, with colours, with sounds, and other objects of sense ; or which is disgusted with them. The senses are only mediums, through which external objects excite agreeable and disagreeable sensations. And to suppose we have as many feeling faculties, as there are different kinds of objects which affect us,is an hypothesis without evidence to support it, or end to be answered by it. Most philosophers treat of a power of the mind, they call taste ; the objects of which are beauty, novelty, and grandeur. These objects produce agreeable sensations. So, also, light and colours, melodious sounds, honey, and a thousand other objects, produce agreeable sensations. And what is the difference between one agreeable sensation and another, or one painful sensation and another, when we view them as acts or operations of the mind ? There is evidently no difference in their nature. One may be more lively, strong, or greater in degree, than another. Still, each operation of this kind is a sensation. Though the objects may be of various and different kinds, yet the pleasure or disgust they give us, considered as operations of the mind, are nothing but sensations. An excellent character pleases us ; a bad character may disgust us. Natural beauty, and moral beauty, may each afford us much pleasure. And every operation of the mind, when it is an object of perception, or reflection as some call it, will please or offend us. But as every emotion excited is either a pleasing or painful sensation, they are all operations of a similar nature.

And when nothing is taken into view but the sensations themselves, we can discern no difference in their natures. In de-

H

gree they may differ. One is a more pleasing, or more painful sensation, than another.—When we attend to the objects, which please or offend us, we see a great difference among them. Yet we know it is a fact, that objects, however different, have the same effect on the mind ; they either please or disgust us, in a greater or less degree.

Also, by attending to the objects which affect us, we learn, that some of our sensations will have a good, and others a bad tendency. And when we attend to our feelings with a view to ascertain their moral quality, we are not contemplating the feelings themselves, but their *tendency*. The feelings, and their tendency, are distinct objects of consideration. When the feelings of pleasure or pain are the only objects considered, we can view them in no other light, than merely as operations of the same kind. Every drop of liquid is in its essence a liquid. There is no difference between the essence of one drop and another, when considered merely as a liquid. Yet liquids produce very different effects. And from the effects they produce we learn how differently they operate. Yet liquids have the same construction. And sensations, however different the objects which excite them, or however different their tendencies, are nothing more nor less than sensations, when viewed only as acts of the mind. To account, then, for those numerous feelings of pleasure and pain which we all experience, it is not necessary to suppose we have a number of distinct, individual feeling faculties. For that faculty, which can be pleased or disgusted with one object. can be affected in the same manner by millions. Enough has been said, I trust, to make it evident, that all our pleasures and pains are operations of the same faculty, which is called the taste, or heart. The *manner* in which objects affect this faculty, is beyond my ability to describe. I profess not to be acquainted with the *modus operandi* of any thing. I shall, therefore, say nothing respecting it ; but

3. Show that taste is the spring of action in all moral agents. —Feeling is the spring of action. If a moral agent were deprived of the faculty of taste, and were as incapable of pleasure and of pain as material bodies are, he would be as inert as they. Of this every candid person must be convinced. It is a truth so obvious, but little can be said to make it plainer. In case persons could perceive objects as clearly and distinctly as they now do, yet were not in the least degree either pleas-

ingly or disgustfully affected by them, they would remain in a state of rest, or inaction. For, in this case, they have no incitement to action ; no motive to influence them in the least degree. There is no object, which pleases them, to be sought ; nor any, which disgusts them, to be avoided. For they are totally destitute of any feelings ; nothing affects them, they are in a state of perfect indifference. If they could perceive the good and evil qualities of objects, as they now do, yet they would have no idea that they could profit or harm them, in any possible way. If they are crushed under the weight of mountains, they suffer no harm, because they feel no pain. As it is evident, if we were as incapable of pleasure and pain as stones are, that we should be inactive beings ; it follows, that feelings give rise to all the actions of moral agents. It follows, that the taste is the *primary principle* of action in them. For this is the only feeling faculty they possess. Pleasure stimulates to action, to obtain the agreeable object ; and pain excites actions, to avoid disgustful objects. And it is impossible for moral agents to experience daily pleasure and pain, and continue in a state of inactivity. Where there is feeling, there will be action. When there is no feeling in bodies, they are inert ; they never move, only when acted upon by some foreign agent. The feelings of pleasure and pain constitute the only active principle, of which we have any knowledge, in any beings in the universe. Hence the faculty of taste is not an inactive, dormant principle. It is the most operative, energetic, active principle in the universe, that has ever come within our knowledge. This is the primary principle of action in God, and all intelligent creatures. His feelings gave rise to the grand fabric of the universe ; they give rise to all the works of providence. For we are expressly informed, that all things were created for his *pleasure ;* that is to gratify the feelings of his heart.—Hence, then, in this faculty we find the primary spring of action. This principle is always operating ; hence the reason why moral agents are always acting.

4. Taste is a *moral* faculty. Here is the fountain of all vice and virtue. Every moral agent is sinful, or holy, according to his character ; and his character is good or bad according to the nature and temper of his heart. If the heart be good, the fruit will be good ; but if the heart be evil, the fruit will be of the same nature. This truth is taught by our Saviour. " The good man, out of the good treasure of the

heart, bringeth forth good things ; and the evil man, out of the evil treasure of his heart, bringeth forth evil things." It is generally agreed that action is necessary to vice and virtue ; that any existence, destitute of active principles, is not an agent, of course vice and virtue cannot be attributed to him. Neither is he a proper subject of praise and blame. But if an active principle is necessary to constitute a being a proper agent, and a proper subject of praise and blame, then this principle is either vicious or virtuous. All the moral good and evil, belonging to a moral agent, must consist in the active principles which govern him. Otherwise, the power of action is not essential to vice and virtue. A ball, when in motion, is operating or acting. For in its course it produces many effects ; and among others, puts an end to a man's life. Yet we do not consider it a proper agent, or guilty of murder, or deserving of blame. And why ? One reason is, it has no inherent principle of action, and did not put itself in motion. Hence we attribute the evil it produced, to the agent who put it in motion. This makes it evident, that in order for any being to be vicious or virtuous, he must be an agent ; and to be an agent, he must possess an active principle ; and from this principle all the good or evil he ever does proceeds. This active principle, then, is either a good or evil fountain, which contains in itself all the streams, whether sinful or holy, which flow from it. This principle, therefore, comprises all vice and virtue. But we have shown, that the heart, or faculty of taste, is the primary principle of action in moral agents ; and is, therefore, either vicious or virtuous ; or, in one word, a moral faculty. But this is a particular, to which it is not my design to give much attention in this place ; as it will come under consideration, when I treat of moral good and evil.—The particulars to which we have attended in this essay show us clearly, that there is a wide difference between this faculty and the understanding. The understanding is a *perceiving* faculty, but is never the subject of sensations. It never *feels* any thing. The faculty of taste is a *feeling* faculty. It never perceives any object. Perception does not belong to it ; but it is very susceptible of feeling. It is the subject of all our pleasures and pains. The understanding is not a moral faculty ; because it is not the spring or principle of action. But the heart is a moral faculty. It is active in its nature, and the primary principle of action in moral agents. It comprises in itself all vice and virtue. These are evident and essential differences between the understanding and the taste ; and show us that they are totally distinct faculties, from which operations of a different nature proceed.

****

ESSAY IX.

Of Appetites.

The appetites constitute a subject as difficult to understand and explain as any one, perhaps, that appertains to the human mind. A patient, and careful attention is necessary in the reader, while examining this intricate and important subject. With it is connected several interesting truths. And an understanding of it is requisite to a knowledge of human nature. For the appetites comprise every principle of action, and constitute the faculty of taste of which we have taken only a general view.

When we attend to the numerous objects, which either please, or disgust us, we find great differences among them. Light, and colours, food, and drink, sounds of every tone, odours of every species, solidity, extension, and all the objects of the senses, are very dissimilar. Though they may have a similitude to each other in some respects, yet in many others they widely differ. Truth and falsehood, good and evil, beauty and deformity, amiable and odious characters, are objects, which differ from each other, and from the objects of sense. Yet such varieties of objects please or displease us. How can we account for this ?

We know the blind never experience any sensations from light and colours, nor the deaf from sounds. By the eye we cannot distinguish sounds, nor by the ear light. From this, if from no other source, we may safely infer, that the senses are differently constructed, and suited to the nature of the objects from which the mind derives different sensations. All the senses are necessary to the existence of those internal feelings.

which we experience. ، By one sense only we become acquainted with but few objects. All the five senses are necessary to
the knowledge we now have of external things, and the sensations they produce in our hearts. Something similar to our
bodily senses must belong to the heart, or we can never account for the numerous sensations we experience from objects
dissimilar in their kind and nature. Will the same internal
sense, which is pleased with light, and colours, delight also
in sounds, both grave, acute, lively, and solemn? Will the
same internal sense be pleased with both vice and virtue? If
all mankind have but one internal, feeling sense, how comes it
to pass, that objects, which please one, disgust another? How
can this phenomenon in the moral world be accounted for?
It is a known fact, that objects which are agreeable to one person, displease another. This is not owing to the bodily senses. For these senses are not the subjects of either pleasure or
pain. The heart is the only subject of agreeable and painful
sensations. The bodily senses are only mediums, through
which the heart is affected.

God has so constructed the heart, or the faculty of taste,
there is a preparedness or adaptedness in it to be pleased with
objects of one kind, and a preparedness to be pleased with objects of a different kind. That objects very different from
each other do please us, is a fact. From this fact we may
safely infer, the heart is adapted in its nature to be pleased with
objects of different kinds, as different as vice and virtue, sounds
and colours. A preparedness to be pleased with a *definite class*
of objects, is what I mean by an appetite. One person is
prepared to be pleased with virtue. This is an appetite for
virtue. Another has not this adaptedness in his heart, he has
not, therefore, an appetite for virtue. This is the reason,
one person is delighted with virtue, and another is not. This
particular preparedness of the heart to be pleased with a definite class of objects, is the sense in which I shall use the word
appetite. Using it in this sense, I give it a more extensive
meaning, I grant, than writers commonly do. For this reason
it is conceived necessary to be somewhat particular, in explaining the meaning I affix to the term. Attention to the operations of the heart leads us necessarily to view it as endued with
such distinct fitnesses to be pleased with objects of different
kinds. To this particular fitness I give the name appetite,
because I know of no other word in the English language by

which it can with greater propriety be called. If any would prefer the word sense, or relish, if they use them to mean the same thing, I have no objection. I may sometimes use them to avoid a frequent repetition of the same word. But when I do, I shall mean by them the same thing the word appetite signifies.

When I have attended to an enumeration and illustration of some of our appetites, I will then attempt to show the difference, between them and the faculty of taste. Our appetites are either natural, or acquired. Some of those with which we are born are the following.

1. An appetite for food. When born, we are prepared to take more or less satisfaction in the different kinds of food, which are suited to nourish the body. An appetite for food is called hunger, and an appetite for water is termed thirst. When we analyze hunger, we find an uneasy sensation, with a desire for food, that it may be removed, ever attends it. This sensation and desire are the *operations* of this appetite. The appetite, and its operations, are distinct objects of consideration. Care ought to be taken never to confound them. Between all our appetites and their *operations*, this distinction ought to be made. If the taste was not prepared to be pleased with food, we might use it, yet we should never experience the sensation of pleasure in eating, nor a desire to enjoy it. An appetite is antecedent to all its operations, and is the subject of them. It has a being, when its operations are not experienced. The heart, therefore, is always prepared to be the subject of those operations, which belong to the appetite of hunger. For this preparedness is the appetite itself.

This appetite is attended with an uneasy *sensation*, what some would call a hankering, and a *desire* for something to remove it. Food is the object, which will remove the uneasy sensation. As soon as we have learned this fact, then food is the particular object of desire. When we eat, food not only removes the uneasiness, but affords us pleasure. This appetite, then, is attended with three distinct operations ; uneasiness, desire, and pleasure.

This uneasy sensation is a feeling of the appetite. When this exists, it feels, it hankers, it desires food, it longs for it. Its desires are strong or weak, in proportion to the degree of the uneasy sensation. This feeling will produce all the actions necessary to obtain food. It is, therefore, an *active principle*.

an original spring to those actions necessary to get food, which is the only object that can afford gratification. In like manner, each individual appetite belonging to the heart is a principle of action. They are the primary, self-moving, exciting causes to all the actions requisite to the attainment of those objects, which will gratify them. When an appetite is gratified, it ceases to operate, until uneasiness begins again to arise.

The great design of God, in implanting in the heart this appetite of hunger, is very obvious. The design of it is the preservation of life. Food is necessary to the life of the body. And this appetite is the only active principle, which will move us to get and eat the food necessary to the preservation of life. In this view it is an important principle, and answers a most valuable purpose.

What has been said respecting hunger, is true in relation to thirst. These are distinct appetites. For we may be hungry, without thirst; and be thirsty, without hunger. Hence an appetite for food will not prompt us to seek for water. Though they are distinct, yet the same operations belong to each of them, and each of them is a principle of action. I need, therefore, give no further attention to the appetite of thirst.

2. *The natural affections* constitute a distinct appetite. These include the parental, filial, and fraternal affections. The propensity to exercise them may be called a *particular* and *distinct appetite.*

It is a fact, that all parents have a feeling for *their* offspring, which they never experience towards the children of other parents. Their own children afford them pleasant sensations. From this feeling arise desires and exertions to preserve their lives, their health, and to provide for them, and promote their prosperity and happiness. These are facts.—And those we consider and call our offspring, include that *class* of objects, with which this appetite is pleased. This, like the other, is a *feeling* appetite ; it is an internal, *active* principle ; and another law of our nature by which we are daily governed. And those possess it, who are not as yet parents ; and it will operate as soon as they have any offspring.

And the design of God in giving to men this appetite is obvious. It is the principle, which will stimulate them to take a watchful care of their children in *infancy,* and to do all they can to render them useful, and respectable in this world.

Hence it is a necessary, and very useful, active principle, as long as our race is to inhabit the earth.—The same general remarks will apply to the other natural affections.

3. The prospensity of the different sexes for social intercourse is another appetite ; an active principle, a law of our nature, implanted in man for the propagation and continuance of the human race, until time shall be no more. What has been said concerning the other appetites, is applicable to this law of our nature.

4. Another appetite implanted in the heart is generally called *pity*. We find it is a fact, which all experience more or less, that when we see any of our fellow mortals in a state of pain and distress, and unable to help themselves, an uneasy sensation is excited. Their distress, misery, and helpless condition, excite in us a *painful sensation*. We find the ready way to remove the pain we feel, is to afford them help and relief. Desires arise at once to afford them assistance, and exertions are made for this purpose. And as soon as they are relieved, and freed from the miseries they suffered, the pain we felt is removed. Then we have no more feeling for them, than for others, who need not our help.

The object of this appetite is the distress and misery of mankind. Experience teaches, that it is a very *active* principle, and a law of our nature, like other appetites. And the design of God in giving it, is evident ; to stimulate us to afford help to the helpless. Were it not for this, many would die in extreme misery, who now are preserved alive.

5. An appetite to be pleased with *novelty* is implanted in us. Mankind are much pleased with *new* things ; with new discoveries and improvements in the arts and sciences. This disposition to be pleased with objects which are *new* to us, is an active principle in us, exciting us to every exertion of mind and body necessary to make new discoveries. This is the principle, which stimulates mankind to exertion to improve the mind, to acquire knowledge, and make advances in the fields of art and science. Deprive men of this stimulus, they would sink down into a state of ignorance, and mental darkness, and remain contented in it. So far as a mind improves, *new objects* are discovered. These new discoveries are one source of our entertainment and happiness in this world.

6. Another appetite with which Adam was created is termed

I

benevolent. The character of God, the happiness of intelligent beings, divine truths and doctrines, holiness, the law and
service of God, are the class of objects with which this appetite
is pleased. This is lost by our apostacy from God. Hence
the reason why men in a natural state are not pleased with this
class of objects.

If all men had this appetite, perfect both in *kind and degree*,
so as to be always under its influence ; then all the other appetites mentioned would be innocent, and would require indulgence only in agreement with the divine commands. But it
was the pleasure of our Maker that the others should remain,
even after this was lost ; for the preservation of our race, and
for our sustenance and comfort. In all those persons who are
born again, to whom the love of holiness is restored, the other
appetites are again brought into subjection ; though they have
a warfare while they remain on earth. In heaven, the use of
their animal appetites having ceased, the appetites themselves
will cease also. Their benevolence will be perfect, and will
forever be their only *active principle*, as it is in Jehovah. God is
love ; and all his ransomed will become like him.

Whether these are all the appetites implanted in us by our
Maker, or not, I will not affirm. These appear to be the *principal*, if not the whole.—There are some appetites which are
acquired, commonly called *habits* ; as the love of labour, intemperance, and the like ; but as those are not natural, I shall give
no further attention to them.

All the appetites, which have been enumerated, may by use
and cultivation, be increased ; they may also in certain ways
be diminished. For instance the appetite for novelty, by use
and cultivation, may be increased, and become more vigorous ;
and it may be almost eradicated by certain indulgences ; and
it may prompt men more to one kind of discoveries, than another. And here we might go into a discussion of numerous
things, which would in many ways reflect more light on this
subject. Still, however strong a propensity may be felt to
explore a field so widely extended, it must be restrained and
denied. Because the design of these essays is only to give a
general view of the faculties and operations of the mind, without following any one main branch in its various ramifications
to their extremities. The general view proposed will occupy
sufficient time ; and present a clearer description of human

powers and exertions, than would be obtained by attending to almost innumerable particulars.

II. I shall now adduce *proof* of the theory advanced.

1. It is a fact, that appetites may be lost and restored, without affecting, in the least, those which remain. This proves that the appetites are distinct from each other, like the bodily senses. For instance : Adam was created with a benevolent appetite or relish. This prepared him to delight in that class of objects called holy and divine. The character of God, of Christ, of saints and angels ; the holy law of God, his service, the doctrines of the gospel ; these objects form one class, which afford delight and satisfaction to a benevolent relish. They are not a source of pleasure to any other appetite of the heart. Adam lost this appetite at the fall ; and his posterity are born without it. This is the reason why this class of objects are not relished or loved by men.

Still, the loss of it did not affect, impair, or destroy the other appetites with which Adam was created, and with which his posterity are born. In regeneration, this is again restored ; yet this does not alter the nature of the other appetites ; any more than giving eyes to the blind alters the nature of the other bodily senses.

Again ; our offspring affords pleasure and gratification, to the appetite known by the name of parental affection. This may be lost. The word of God informs us, there are some parents without natural affection ; and there are some, who in fact appear to be wholly destitute of it. Yet when this is lost, all the appetites and their operations remain the same.

As persons may be, and in fact have been, deprived of one and another appetite, without affecting or altering the nature and operations of those which remain ; we have sufficient evidence that they are as distinct from each other, as our bodily senses are. Were not this the fact, the loss of one would destroy the others.

2. It is evident that different and distinct appetites belong to the heart, from this consideration : that if this were not a fact, the loss of an appetite would be the destruction or annihilation of the faculty of taste.

To illustrate this truth, it may be observed : Solidity is an essential property of matter ; and so connected with other properties, that deprive matter of this property, extension, form, and impenetrability are destroyed ; in a word matter is annihilated. Also *feeling* is essential to every bodily sense. And if the senses were not so distinct and different, that the loss of one sense would not affect the others ; depriving a person of one sense would destroy all bodily *feeling ;* the body would have no more feeling, than lifeless matter has.

To apply these remarks ; we are to remember the heart is a *feeling* faculty, the subject of pleasant and painful sensations. And if the appetites were not so different and distinct, that the loss of one would not impair another, the loss of one would annihilate all feeling in us ; we should not be the subjects of pleasure and pain, any more than dead matter is.

Observe further ; animal is a generic term ; it includes all beings which have life and a principle of action, or loco-motion. Life and motion are common to all the individuals belonging to each species. Now, if the several species were not so different and distinct, that destroying one species would not be destroying another ; the annihilation of one species would annihilate every other, or destroy the genus. But the fact is, by the loss of an appetite we sustain no injury, only this ; that the class of objects, which had been a source of pleasure, no longer delight us. As when a person loses his sight, light and colours are no more objects of pleasure ; but his hearing and other senses remain the same.

One appetite *prepares* us to be pleased with one particular class of objects ; as benevolence, for instance, prepares us to be delighted with that class of objects called *divine* ; hunger is an appetite which prepares us to be pleased with *food ;* parental affection is an appetite, which prepares us to be gratified with *our offspring ;* an appetite for novelty prepares us to be delighted with new discoveries ; and so with respect to each of our appetites. Accordingly, divide all the objects, which have ever pleased or disgusted mankind, into distinct classes ; we shall then find that mankind have implanted in them distinct appetites, which prepare them to be affected pleasantly or painfully with all objects, which ever come within the range of their perceptions or knowledge. And these appetites, conjointly viewed, constitute the faculty termed taste or the heart.

3. As further proof of this theory it may be observed, it is the only theory which agrees with the word of God.

God is perfectly acquainted with the human mind, with its faculties and operations. For he is the Creator of the soul. And though it is not his design in his word to give us a theoretic description of it; yet he has not revealed any thing, which does not perfectly agree with its real and true theory. Hence, when any sentiment is advanced concerning the mind, which does not agree with what the bible teaches, it ought to be rejected as false.—This is the case with the greater part of all the theories, which have been hitherto published. They contain sentiments, which can never be reconciled with bible doctrines; and especially the sentiments advanced concerning the heart, or will, or active powers, as they are commonly called, are most at variance generally with the word of God, and for this reason should be rejected.

According to what God teaches in his word, it must be admitted as a fact, that appetites may be lost, and restored, without any infringement of moral agency. If the loss of *any* appetite would destroy our agency and accountability, it would be the loss of a benevolent appetite. For the loss of this affects us more than the loss of any other could do. Yet God informs us that Adam lost it; all his posterity are born destitute of it; and when any person is born again, this appetite is created in him. Still, under these changes we are the same moral accountable agents, and are so treated by our Maker.— The theory, then, advanced in these sheets agrees with the word of God. And it is the only theory, it is believed, which can be made to agree with it.

According to the theory, man at the fall did not sustain the loss of any *faculty ;* and when born again, no *new faculty* is created. Nothing, but an appetite, is lost and restored.—But according to the theories generally advanced, the mind has but two faculties, the understanding and the will ; and the latter is simple in its nature, without any appetite belonging to it. It is considered as simple as volition itself. Hence those who say the will and its operations are distinct, to be consistent, must say that Adam at the fall lost the faculty called the will ; and that when a man is born again, that faculty is again created. For that which is *simple* in its nature, if any part of it is destroyed, is wholly destroyed. And if the will is nothing but a succession of volitions, as some say ; then if holiness is lost, and total depravity ensue, Adam after the fall had a will entirely different in *its nature* from the will he had in a state of innocence. But not to dwell on this here, the view which has been given of the faculty of taste agrees with the word of God, with facts, and with the daily experience of mankind.—

For they find they have such appetites as have been described. All know they have hunger, and thirst, natural affection, a relish for novelty, and all the other appetites named.

The understanding *perceives*, but never *feels ;* the heart *feels,* but never *perceives* any thing. Seeing objects, and the feelings of pleasure and pain, are very different operations. These appetites are *active* principles, and the laws of our nature by which all men are governed. Go through the world, and you will find every person actively employed, in pursuit of the objects which are most agreeable to his appetites ; and there is no way to produce a change in the conduct of mankind, but by effecting an alteration in those active principles. Hence, though the motives to live a holy life far outweigh the motives to idolize the world ; yet no person will lead a holy life until a new and benevolent appetite is created in him. And though mankind can never alter the nature of their appetites ; yet they may be improved and corrected, by education and proper cultivation. The more the taste for beauty, novelty and grandeur, is improved in *correctness* and *delicacy*, so much the more all the appetites are refined from those vulgar, immoral, and degrading acts, and keep men within the limits of decency and propriety. Here, did it comport with my design, much might be said on the subject of cultivating, restraining, and improving the taste and its appetites ; in order to adorn a character as far as it can be without the ornaments of grace. But this pertains rather to rhetoric than metaphysics.

It is much more important to form correct views of this faculty, than of any other belonging to the mind. Because this governs, in many respects, the understanding and will, and puts all the wheels of active life in motion ; it is the primary cause of all the happiness and misery, of which men are the authors ; and when viewed in the deity, it is the first, efficient cause, which has given being to *every thing* which exists through the universe. It is also the fountain of all moral good and evil ; and the endless felicity or misery of intelligent creatures depends on its nature. Hence too much attention cannot be given to it. Thus far we have only attended to the taste as a faculty of the mind, to give a general view of its nature ; as the only faculty capable of pleasant and painful sensations ; the only active and moral principle in man, with a general description of its appetites or propensities. I have said nothing concerning its operations. This will be the subject of the next essay.

****

ESSAY X.

Of the Operations of Taste.

Having given a general description of the taste as a faculty, with the several appetites which belong to it ; its *operations* now claim our attention. The method proposed is to explain and give a distinct view of them ; and then divide them into their several classes.

I. Explain the operations of this faculty.

The *affections* and *passions* comprise all the operations of this faculty. The affections and passions do not differ in their nature. The real difference is circumstantial. When any emotion is *suddenly* excited, and is *strong* and *vivid*, and is *soon* moderated, it is called a *passion*. And those sensations, which *gradually* increase, which *continue* and *abide*, are termed *affections*. For example ; *anger* is commonly called a passion. This is *suddenly* excited, operates with greater or less *violence*, and *soon subsides*. If it continues a long time, it is then generally designated by another name.

Love is generally viewed as an affection. This emotion begins, and increases gradually. It seldom becomes very violent or strong ; and is commonly lasting. But if it is ever suddenly excited, and is very *strong* and violent in its operation, it is then considered a passion ; and is very apt, after a short time, to subside, or cool down into a moderate flame. A similar difference between other emotions would be evident on a particular examination. A *sudden* excitement; *strength* or *violence* of operation ; and *short* continuance ; and *sudden* abatement of an emotion, are the particular circumstances attending a passion. And this difference between some emotions of taste and others, is distinguished by the words, affection and passion. As the *nature* of each is the same, it is not very important to spend much time on these particular differences. We may now proceed to an analysis of the affections.

Love is an affection. It implies two distinct operations. The first is a pleasant *sensation*, and then a *desire* for the enjoyment of the object, or for its prosperity and happiness, if capable of it. This every person knows by experience. Select any object you love, and then attend to your own feelings; and you will say, there is something in it pleasing and agreeable, and you feel a desire to possess and enjoy it. This desire will be fervent, or faint, in proportion to the degree of pleasure it affords.

Hatred, the opposite of love, is an affection. Here the sensation excited is *painful*. The object is unpleasant and disagreeable. The feeling is often expressed, by saying of the object it is deformed, and odious. Then arises a *desire* to shun the object, to have it removed from your sight. The only difference, therefore, between love and hatred as operations of taste is, the sensation implied in the former is pleasant, in the latter it is painful ; in the former the desire is to enjoy the object ; in the latter to avoid it. These definitions include all our affections and passions. The operations they imply are either *pleasant sensations*, with a *desire* to enjoy the object, and other desires friendly to it ; or *painful uneasy sensations*, with a desire to shun the object, that the pain it occasions may be removed. So sensation and desire belong to every affection. On particular examination, every one will find that anger, envy, revenge, joy, delight, sorrow, grief, or any other affection, contains nothing more or less than pleasant or painful sensations, with correspondent desires. It is, then, an object of inquiry, why all the operations called affections are not designated by the same name. Why are not all the affections, in which the sensations are pleasant, termed love ; and those where the sensations are painful, hatred ? If sensations and desires are the ingredients in every affection and passion, why do we call them by so many different names ; as hatred, anger, envy, love, joy and delight ?

The reasons are two. One is, to distinguish the difference in the *objects* of the affections. The other is, to mark the different *circumstances* attending them. This will be best explained by examples.

Envy and revenge, whether called affections or passions, are uneasy, painful sensations with their attendent desires. The object of envy is *superiority* in a rival. The object of revenge is recompense for some *injury* received. Their operation is different. The design of one is to *retaliate*, and of the other to *deprive* a person of his superior merit. To mark such differences, one is called revenge, and the other envy. Then if we understand their meaning, we see the difference between them.

Take anger and revenge for another example. Anger is a painful sensation, with a desire to injure its object. And revenge is the same. The painful sensations of each are excited by some injury ; and the desire of each is to retaliate, or repay the injury. The difference between them is this ; anger is an emotion suddenly excited, operates openly and violently, and is soon spent and subsides. Revenge *continues*, perhaps for months and years, operates more *slowly* and *privately*, and cannot be satisfied, until the injury is repaid. When sudden anger becomes rooted, abiding, and inveterate, it is then called malice or revenge. As there are these differences between them, they are designated by different names.

So when we hear a person is very angry, we expect he will soon become cool and calm. When we are informed a person is full of revenge towards another, we expect it will continue until retaliation is effected. Anger is like a violent storm, which is soon over ; revenge like a slow, but sure poison, which sooner or later destroys life.

Love and hatred are sensations, with their attendant desires. In one the sensation is pleasant ; in the other, painful. The desire of one is the good of the object ; the aim of the other is to injure it. In such respects they differ ; and to mark the difference, one is called love, the other hatred. Yet, viewed as operations of the heart, love is a sensation and desire ; and hatred is the same.

Pride is a pleasant sensation. Elevation or distinction is the object, which excites it. Desire attends it, which is to rise to the pleasant, exalted station. Humility is a pleasant sensation. The object which excites it, is self-abasement. Its desire is, to take a low place. But no person knows by experience what humility is, unless he is born again. To the unrenewed this definition will appear strange ; because their abasement ever excites painful sensations. In them it is merely the mortification of pride.

Grief, sorrow, repentance, are painful sensations, attended

J

with desires for the removal of their causes. Sin, now hated, is the cause of these sensations in real christians ; and they are commonly attended with other sensations, which are agreeable. Joy is a pleasant emotion, united with a desire for its increase and continuance.

But enough has been said, to give every one a clear and distinct view of the operations of taste. And all know by experience, that some affections operate with more strength or vivacity, than others ; and that the same affection is more lively at one time than another. Here, also, it is proper to observe, that the affections are not under the control of the will. My meaning is, it does not depend on a person's will, whether objects shall please or disgust him ; whether the taste of honey shall be sweet, or bitter. The sensations which objects will excite, depend on the nature of our appetites, and of the objects which surround us. Though the first emotions produced are not under the control of the will ; yet both reason and the will may enable us to regulate, restrain, and govern them. But as it is not the design of these essays to attend to the restraint and government of the affections, we may observe, that they differ much in their *strength* and *vivacity*. Sometimes the affections are very cool and calm ; and sometimes towards objects of great importance mankind seem to be almost indifferent. At other times, they operate with great force and activity. This variation is produced by different circumstances, as they occur from time to time, which will be passed by without investigation.

It may here be observed, that mankind are always governed by their feelings, or affections. The appetites are the only principles of action implanted in our nature ; and by these active principles our conduct must and will be governed. Hence the affections, which are the operations of the taste, will regulate the conduct of men. It is as impossible for mankind to act in opposition to their strongest feelings at the time, as for matter to move in opposition to the laws of attraction and gravitation.

Again, all the affections *tend* to either *good* or *evil*. Active principles always have a *tendency* to some end ; and this tendency must be, either to promote or destroy happiness ; and is therefore, to either good or evil.—These observations give a general view of the affections, which are the operations of the faculty called taste.—The next object, which claims attention, is a division of the affections into their distinct classes.

It will be remembered, that the affections contain two parts; *sensations,* either pleasant or painful in different degrees, and *desires* for the enjoyment of the agreeable, or avoidance of the disagreeable objects. As all the affections are composed of the same operations, sensations and desires, they form one *general class.* Being entirely distinct in their *nature* from *perceptions,* they cannot be operations of the same faculty. The general class called perceptions, are the operations of the understanding. But the affections are so different in their nature, they must belong to some other faculty or property of the mind, which is called taste. Hence there is as much reason to believe the mind is endued with this faculty, as the one termed the understanding.—In order to see clearly the ground of dividing this general class, the affections, into several distinct, specific classes, it is necessary to observe,

1. The operations of the heart in infancy.

If we proceed on the belief that to the taste belong the several appetites, which have been illustrated, we are led to notice in the first place the one called hunger. An infant is born with this appetite. We might, then, expect to find the infant *pleased* with food, and manifest a *desire* after it. And this we find is the *fact.* The infant is evidently pleased with food, and especially such as is best suited to its nature. Its desire for it is evident from its crying for it, and being immediately pacified on receiving it. These operations of hunger are some of the first visible in an infant ; and thus far verify the theory which has been advanced.

The appetite also, called filial affection, operates, and manifests itself in an infant ; and becomes more evident as it increases in years. A child is more pleased with its parents, than with other persons ; and manifests a strong desire after them, when they are absent. Such feelings are some of the first, visible in children. They become more evident through infancy and childhood, for several years ; but commonly decrease, when they arrive to the age in which they become parents themselves.

The appetite for novelty operates in infants. Those objects which are new to them gain their attention, and excite strong desires to obtain them. As new objects are sources of pleasure to them, they are fond of hearing and reading stories, novels, and plays. As such pursuits are generally hurtful, it is desirable that their attention be early turned to the study of the arts and sciences, where new objects will be daily unfolding to their view. This study strengthens the mind, stores it with useful knowledge, and good habits are formed, instead of bad. And whenever the young and tender mind is highly pleased with new discoveries, and manifests so strong desires after them, as to occupy its powers in a close investigation of snbjects, we may expect such persons will make great advances in the field of knowledge, and become eminent, respectable, and useful.

The operations of the appetite of pity will not be visible so early in life ; because more or less knowledge and experience are necessary to give opportunity for its exercise. But young children will suffer pain, when they see others in distress ; if they do not so early in life exert themselves to relieve them. They do not yet know by experience, that this is the ready way to remove the pain, which the distress of others excited.—And according to the theory advanced, we shall not discover any of the operations of a benevolent appetite in infants, or children, or any others, until born again ; because they are born without this appetite. Hence they never manifest any pleasure in religion, or divine objects, or in any acts of spiritual devotion ; or any sincere desires after communion with their Maker. On the contrary, they show an aversion to religious exercises ; the reason of which will appear in its proper place.

Enough has now been said to show, that the *first* operations of taste in infants and children, are those of the appetites above mentioned.—And to understand this part of the subject more clearly, it is needful to remark, that the several classes of the objects, which are presented to the appetites, afford *pleasure* on their own account. To illustrate this observe, that food is *in itself agreeable*. No reason can be given, why it gives us pleasure. To say, it is because food suits us, is no reason. For the words agreeable and suitable, have the same meaning. So we may say an object is agreeable, because it suits our nature ; and it suits our nature, because it is agreeable. We find it is a fact, that some objects are so suited in their nature to our nature, that they please us ; and we can assign no other reason, why they do please. Hence we say of all such objects, that they are in themselves, on their own account or nature, sources of pleasure to us. And in the same sense some objects are in their nature disagreeable, sources of pain. And we can give no reason why it is thus, but that God has so ordained it. And were it not thus, we could never arrive at any first principles, and could never attain any real knowledge. If there were no self-evident truths, there would be no point at which to begin to reason ; it would be no matter where we began, or whether we traced things backward or forward ; we should never arrive at a *first cause*, or *final end*. So if there were nothing in itself good or evil, we could never arrive at any first source of good or evil ; or at any final end or state of enjoyment or suffering. But God has so formed us, and objects around us, that some of them are in their very nature agreeable, and others disagreeable. We here learn by experience, as well as the word of God, how we must conduct to obtain happiness and avoid misery.

And the first sensations, experienced by persons in their early infancy, are produced by objects in themselves agreeable, or disagreeable. Hence mankind soon learn what will render them comfortable in this life, and what will make them unhappy. This we could never know, were not some objects in their nature agreeable, and others disagreeable. This being the case, we seek the one, and avoid the other. These sensations, and the desires we have to enjoy the objects which produce them, are the *first operations* of taste mankind experience. These operations, to distinguish them from others, form a class, which are properly styled *primary affections* ; because they are the first affections mankind have after they are born. If you now have a distinct view of this class of affections, you see they are affections produced in us by objects in their nature agreeable or disagreeable. And the objects, which produce this class of affections, are not so numerous, as those which belong to the next class to be considered.

Even young children learn, that they can purchase such articles as they love, with *money*. Then money is an object, which gives them pleasure ; but not for its own sake, or as an object in itself agreeable. They can give a good reason why they love it ; because they can buy with it food and other pleasant things. This shows more clearly what is meant by objects in themselves agreeable, and those which are not. With respect to the former, no reason can be given why they please ; in relation to the latter, we can always give good reasons why they please us.

In like manner, as persons advance in life, they find that with lands, and flocks, and labour, they can raise and procure food, and other objects in themselves agreeable. Then those objects become sources of pleasure, and objects of desire. They are pleased with them and desire them, because they can with them obtain other objects in themselves agreeable. Here is another class of affections. Those affections we have for objects which are not in themselves agreeable, but which are valued as means of obtaining those in their nature pleasant, may be called our *secondary affections*. They are a second class of affections, which mankind have, after the first class.—The objects, which produce this class of affections, are *very numerous*. They include all the objects, which are properly the *means* by which we purchase or obtain things in themselves agreeable.—To these there is scarcely any end.—If we had not the first, we should never have the second class of affections just named. We should never love money or land, if we could not obtain with it some object in itself agreeable. Hence they are really a *secondary class* of *affections*. There is only one other class, which claims attention.

We often see children, as well as men, manifest anger, hatred, revenge, envy and malice.—If a child has any thing in its possession, with which it is much pleased, whether in itself agreeable or not ; if another child should take it away, and refuse to return it, anger rises in the breast of the injured child. In this case, one child *opposes* the other in the gratification of his primary or secondary affections, no matter which. For opposition to any of our primary or secondary affections, will produce the affections or passions called anger, hatred, revenge, &c.—These passions ought to be formed into a distinct class, which may be called malignant. These passions are *malignant* in their nature, the sources of some of the greatest crimes ever committed by man. This class may then be said to comprise the *malignant affections*, or *passions*. I will now show, that these passions are always produced by opposition made to our primary or secondary affections.

Whatever objects are sources of pleasure to a man while in a natural state, if we supply him with them, he will not experience any dislike to us. Our conduct towards him harmonises with all the feelings of his heart ; we act precisely as he would have us. He has no ground of uneasiness with us ; and cannot be offended, while we thus treat him. He views us as friends to his feelings & happiness. And he will feel the same kind of affection for us he does for food, or money, or any other objects of his primary or secondary affections.

But if we alter our conduct, take from him objects which he loves, or oppose him in his plans to obtain them ; and are daily crossing, disappointing, and opposing his feelings and pursuits ; he will then view us as his enemies, and anger, and other malignant passions will begin to operate. All this is verified by innumerable facts from day to day. And these facts fully prove, that malignant passions are excited by opposition in some way made to our primary or secondary affections.— Hence the reason why mankind live together in peace, so long as they treat each other in a friendly manner, and their interests do not clash together. But when they thwart, cross, and oppose each other in their feelings and pursuits, anger, feuds, quarrels, and wars ensue.

While God gives men fruitful seasons, and his providences are gratifying to their feelings, they speak well of their Maker, and extol him for his goodness and mercy. But when his providences are crossing and afflictive, they begin to murmur, and view him as a hard master. Hence the reason why the Jews sang praises to God in such sublime and animated strains at the red sea, and in a few days after murmured, and complained, and rebelled against his authority. Hence the reason why sinners, in a state of security, do not feel any opposition rise in their hearts against God ; but under convictions of truth, often have their enmity strongly excited. In security, they seldom reflect enough on his character, or law, or government, to realise that they are all arrayed against them as sinners. Of course no opposition arises in their hearts. But under real convictions of truth, they clearly see his character, law, and government are such, that they must reform or perish. They often feel as a stubborn criminal does, when the law condemns him for his crimes. He is angry with the law, with his judges, and with all who take the side of order and justice. He is angry, because they are so opposed to him ; because he is not suffered to live, perpetrating crimes with impunity, as he wishes.

This is a sentiment, to which Christ's ministers ought to give a careful attention. Some from the sacred desk will teach the unrenewed, that their hearts are full of hatred and opposition to God ; and this they apply to all sinners, both the stupid, secure, and unawakened, as well as those, who are under strong conviction. The careless, secure sinner says, this preaching is not true. I do not hate and oppose, and fight against God. He knows this, because he has never felt or experienced any such hatred and opposition.

The truth is this. Sinners are born wholly destitute of love to God ; and of this they may be convinced. But they may not, for many years, have any positive hatred and opposition to him. They have the seeds from which hatred, murmuring, and opposition will spring up, whenever events favor their growth. Till such events take place as excite opposition, they pursue the objects which suit their appetites, and treat God with indifference and neglect. They seldom reflect on his character or government, and have very erroneous ideas of his real character. God is not in all their thoughts. And they are willing He should do his pleasure, if he will permit them to do as they please with impunity, and grant them the prosperity they desire. Thus they live without feeling any opposition in their hearts to God. So far are they from this, that if they prosper in worldly blessings, & meet with no crossing events, they experience what is called natural gratitude ; and will speak of God as a very good and kind being, worthy of love, and thankfulness and service. Indeed they will talk in a way which, as far as professions go, manifests much love and gratitude, as though they were his real friends. And from this flow of feelings and affections within, which are excited entirely by their prosperity, they often make themselves believe they do love God, and are real christians.

At the same time, if providential events cross and oppose their desires, and hedge up their way, then a complaining, murmuring and rebellious disposition is excited. Also if their consciences are enlightened, and they have so much conviction of truth as to see that the holy character of God, his law and government, are directly against them as sinners, and that, if they do not repent, and turn to God, they must be forever miserable ; then all their inward desires are opposed, and crossed. For their desire is, to live as they wish with impunity. And when they see this cannot be, that if they live in sin they must suffer eternal death ; then their opposition will rise against God. And when by conviction they further see they are wholly dependant on God for that new heart, which is necessary to life ; and of course their eternal state is suspended on his holy, and sovereign pleasure ; they then have views, which are in all respects against them and opposed to every desire of their hearts. With this light their hearts rise, often, to a fearful height of opposition. They look on God as a hard master, a cruel tyrant ; and they would in their rage dethrone Him, if they had power. And abundant experience teaches, that there is nothing which will excite so great enmity and opposition to God, as his absolute sovereignty. When this is held up to view in the doctrines of decrees and election ; and when seen and realized by a sinner, his heart swells with enmity and rage. The reason is, there is nothing so perfectly opposed to a sinner's heart, as his entire dependance on the pleasure of God, to be lost as a transgressor, or be saved by grace.

Hence there are but two conditions, in which real hatred and opposition of heart to God will arise. One is, when providential events cross and oppose their *primary* or *secondary desires.* The other is, when sinners are under a real conviction of truth. But so long as all providential events harmonize with a sinner's desires ; and so long as they do not see, or realize the opposition of the divine character and government to their selfish and perverse inclinations ; so long they are free from the operations of positive hatred to God ; although the seeds of enmity are latent in their hearts, and only wait for occasions of being elicited, and manifested to themselves and their fellow men, as they are now manifest to the eye of God.

Our primary affections form one class of the operations of our taste ; secondary affections, a second ; and our malignant passions, a third. These three classes include all the operations of this faculty. It is presumed no one can name any affection or passion, which is not clearly contained in one or another of the classes I have named.

These are the active principles, the laws of our nature, which put every wheel in motion ; and from which have proceeded all the evils, and crimes, which have been committed in this world. In scripture they are called lusts. So when the question is asked, from whence come wars and fightings ; the answer is, from the lusts which war in our members.

These principles are sufficient to explain the conduct of men. By them it is easy to account for all the actions of moral agents, and assign the reasons of their conduct in every condition of life. If a person makes the accumulation of property, or high stations of honor, or scenes of pleasure, his

K

great and principal object; if he defrauds, commits theft, or murder; or if he is moral, kind, liberal, and performs acts of charity and benevolence; it is easy to show, that such and all his other actions proceed from these principles or affections. The principles here advanced agree with facts, and with the observation and experience of all men. Is not every one sure and certain, that he perceives objects, not only their existence, but their properties, modes, and relations? Is he not sure, that he perceives truth and falsehood, good and evil, right and wrong? Can he doubt whether he is a feeling being, a subject of pleasure and pain; or whether he has desires to obtain some objects, and to shun others; or that he has affections and passions? Can he doubt whether his feelings excite him to action? And if he were to make it an object of inquiry, what principles and motives governed him in any of his particular pursuits in life, could he not ascertain them? And he would always find that his actions proceeded from these inward, active principles, which he knows operate within him. Upon these principles, we may reason as correctly and safely concerning phenomena in morals, as we can on the first principles in natural philosophy concerning the phenomena in the material world. We should find some facts more difficult to account for, than others; and some, perhaps, inexplicable. This is to be expected in every science. With respect to men, I see no great difficulty in accounting, on the principles advanced, for their actions and conduct in the several grades and stations of life. And the profession of a minister is such, it is one part of his study to account for the conduct of mankind. In this way he explains their characters, shows them what they are, and opens to their view the inward springs of action, and the external effects they will produce, so clearly, that persons often think that some one has informed him of their feelings and conduct. To me it appears impossible for a minister to explain the character and conduct of man in the most convincing manner, unless he is acquainted with those internal, active principles, which govern all men. Before I had any clear, distinct view of them, many things appeared dark, and mysterious, which now are as obvious as day light. On the application of those principles, in explaining and accounting for the actions and conduct of mankind, I will detain you no longer at this time. For their truth and application will appear more clear and evident, as we pass on to other subjects, and especially to explain the operations of the will, and the nature of liberty, and the motives by which all are influenced. For the sake of assisting the memory, I shall conclude this essay by a brief repetition of the leading ideas, and those most important to be remembered, which have been explained concerning taste.

The taste or heart is a distinct property or faculty of the mind, which prepares it for those operations called the affections and passions. To this faculty belong several distinct appetites, such as hunger, pity, natural propensities or affections, and love of novelty, implanted in us by God for our preservation, comfort, improvement, and well being, while in the present state of existence. This is a *feeling* faculty, the subject of all our pleasant and painful sensations ; the *primary* spring, or principle of action. It constitutes *agency* ; is the seat of all vice and virtue ; and is of course a moral faculty.— Without it, mankind would be inactive beings, like all existences incapable of feeling.

Each affection and passion contains two operations ; a *sensation* either pleasant or painful ; and a *desire* to obtain the object, if agreeable, or to avoid it, if disagreeable. These two operations, *sensation* & *desire*, combine to form every affection and passion. Hence all the affections, in their nature simply, are similar ; though they differ much in vivacity and strength. Sensations and desires are the only operations of this faculty ; & being perfectly similar, they form another moral class of operations of the mind, termed the affections and passions. And as this class is totally different in its nature from the class called perceptions, there is no way to account for them but on this ground, that the mind is endued with the property denominated taste.

The general class of operations called the affections is divided into three distinct classes. The first operations experienced by a human being in infancy and childhood, are for objects in their nature agreeable or disagreeable. These being the first experienced, are classed together, and called our *primary affections*. When affections are excited by objects which are indifferent in themselves, but which are regarded as necessary *means* of gratifying other desires, they form another class, denominated *secondary affections*. They are the second operations which we feel, and arise from the preceding or primary class. And when men have their primary or secondary affections crossed and disappointed, either by God or man, the sensations of hatred, anger, malice, envy, or revenge, are excited. These form a third class, called the *malignant passions.*

The appetites, from which these classes of operations arise, are distinct laws of our nature by which all men are invariably governed. And by a proper application of them, all the actions and branches of conduct in men, in their various pursuits, may be accounted for and explained. When these are understood aright, then we have a knowledge of human nature, and not till then ; I mean a knowledge of the principles, which govern men.

****

ESSAY XII.

Of the Will, and its Operations.

Scarcely any writer, that I now recollect, has considered the heart and will to be distinct faculties. They have generally been treated as one and the same. Yet I hope to make it appear that they are distinct faculties, and ought not to be blended with the understanding.—The want of this distinction has occasioned much confusion in the discussions of this subject.

The will and its acts are as different as the subject and predicate of a proposition. Accordingly the will is considered as a subject, and volitions are the operations predicated of it. We therefore say, the will chooses and refuses. And voluntary exertions are the only operations, which properly belong to the will. There is certainly a preparedness or adaptedness in the mind, for operations of this particular kind. If there were not, it never could choose or refuse. For the mind cannot have those operations, to which it has no adaptedness. A square body is not adapted to that kind of motion called rolling. There is no adaptedness in matter for the operations of thinking, and feeling. And if the mind were not prepared to be the subject of those operations termed perceptions, feelings, and volitions, it could no more perceive, feel, and choose, than matter itself can. But the mind does think, feel, and choose.

These are facts, which prove undeniably, that it is prepared for these several operations. And a particular preparedness, fitness, or adaptedness for that kind of operations called volitions, is what I mean and understand by the term *will*, considered as a faculty of the mind. Some will say, this is no definition. I grant it is not. It is impossible to define simple ideas. Can any one define pain, or pleasure ? If I were to say, the will is a power to choose and refuse, or a capacity for voluntary exertions, as many do ; yet I might be requested to define power, and capacity. For these as really need defining, as the term will itself. The truth is, no one can give a logical definition of any simple thought, or existence. They can be illustrated by other words, which are better understood, if such words can be found. The will, then, is a preparedness of the mind for voluntary exertions.

We may now take into consideration the operations of this faculty. Those I call *volitions*. Every volition has an object. When we choose, there is something chosen. And the thing chosen, is what I mean by the object of volition. The immediate object of volition, is generally the motion of the whole body, or some one of its members. When I make a voluntary exertion to move my hand, the motion of the hand is the immediate object of this exertion. I move my hand to take my pen. I keep it in motion, that my pen may continue to move in making letters, and words. This is done to answer further purposes and ends. I may move my hand to take a sword, to put it in motion for my defence, or to produce some other effect. If an end is to be obtained, and a number of effects are necessary to obtain it, these are produced by volitions, or voluntary exertions. The first effect produced is some bodily motion. This is necessary, in order to produce the next effect in the arrangement ; and this in order to the next in succession, until the desired end is attained. The motion of the body, or some of its members, is the *first* effect produced by the exertions of the will. Then the other effects, necessary to the end, follow each other in a regular succession. This motion of the body, or first effect produced, is what I mean by the *immediate object* of volition. Other effects produced, intervene between the first and the last, which puts us in possession of the object or end sought. The last effect is the *ultimate object* of volition. And those effects, which intervene between the first and the last, are its *intermediate objects*.

Whenever the will makes exertions to produce bodily motion, the motion follows, unless prevented by superior force. And all the effects willed follow, unless superior strength, or resistance of some kind, prevent them. And all these effects which God has connected with our voluntary exertions, are in our power ; and no others. If God had established the same connexion between voluntary exertions and flying, as he has between them and walking, we could move from one place to another by flying, as easily as we now can by walking. And ten thousand effects, such as stopping the earth in its orbit, or overturning the Chinese empire, are effects, which we could as easily produce by one single exertion, if God had connected them with it, as we can now walk or speak. When the connexion between the will and the motion of the hand, is destroyed by a paralytic stroke, we can no more move the hand, than create a world. Hence those effects, and those only, which are connected with our volitions, are in our power. Whatever is connected with the will, we can do ; and whatever is not, is beyond our reach. The body and its members are, in general, under the controul of the will ; and every other thing, as far as is necessary to answer all the purposes of moral agency.

Not only the body, but the understanding, is more or less in the power of the will. We find by experience we can turn our thoughts from one object or subject to another. We can confine our attention to any particular subject ; and, if it wander, call it back again. Our thoughts are evidently under the control of the will. The will can turn them in any direction ; recal them, when they wander ; and confine them to the investigation of subjects, whenever necessary. If our thoughts were not in our power, we should make very slow, if any advances, in scientific knowledge. We should also be, in a great measure, incapable of acting, and attaining the objects of our desire. At best, we should be very imperfect agents. But this will be more particularly considered in another place. This we know is true by experience, that the direction of our thoughts, and the motions of the body, as far as is necessary, are connected with the will ; each of them is subjected to its power. Yet it must be acknowledged, that human power is very limited. There are many things to which we are utterly incompetent. God has, however, given us as much power as is necessary for us, in the grade of existence which we occupy. We have sufficient power, if the heart were rightly inclined, to avoid every thing which is prohibited, and do every thing required of us, by our Lord and master. We have sufficient power to be good and faithful servants unto the death. And more power than this we do not need.

I shall now proceed to show the difference between the operations of the *heart*, and those of the *will*. Here let it be remembered, that pleasant and painful sensations, and the desires which accompany them, are the operations of the heart. And volitions are the exertions of the will, to produce the effects necessary to gratify the feelings of the heart. Hence,

1. It must be evident to any reflecting, candid mind, that neither a pleasant or painful sensation is a volition. Is the exertion a person makes to move his hand to take an orange, the same thing with the pleasure it gives him? Is the pain a person has, when his teeth ache, the same operation in kind with the exertion he makes to extract them? Every person's experience teaches him, that sensations, and exertions to move the body, are operations generically different. He must know, if unbiassed, that volitions, which have the motion of some part of the body for their object, are neither agreeable or painful sensations. He must know it to be a fact, that pleasure and pain produce no visible, external effects. A person may contemplate distant objects with great pleasure, for days and weeks, without one motion towards them. But if he makes exertions to attain such agreeable objects, bodily motion, and other effects immediately follow. He cannot make an exertion to move his hand, and at the same time keep it at rest. But objects may please, and displease him, yet he remain at rest. This is a fact. Hence bodily motions and other effects, which are connected with the will, have no immediate connexion with our sensations, either pleasant or painful. If sensations and volitions were operations of the same kind ; if a sensation were a volition, the former would produce the same effects the latter produces. But this we know is not a fact. We know, that an exertion to move the hand is followed by its motion. But an object may please me, and no motion or effort to attain it, follow. Experience then teaches, that sensations and volitions are totally different operations.

2. Volitions and desires are not operations of the same faculty. I have already observed, that the immediate object of volition is bodily motion, some action, to produce some effect. Now, though desire has an object, yet its object is not an ac-

tion, or an effect. Therefore the objects of volition and desire are not the same. I desire meat, or drink. But meat and drink are not actions. To obtain those objects many effects may be necessary. These, if connected with the will, are the objects of volition. Now if desire and volition were the same, their objects would be the same. But we know it is a fact that they are different. I may desire meat or drink, and yet not one effect follow necessary to obtain them. But when I will these effects, they follow, they are produced.

We may desire what we do not will. A man, who is thirsty, desires drink ; yet, for certain reasons, may not make one exertion to obtain it. The drink may, at the same time, be before him, and within his reach. If he makes an exertion to take it, the motion necessary follows, and the drink is brought to his mouth. If desire and volition were the same thing, if a desire is a volition, his desire for the drink would bring it to his mouth. We might proceed to notice this difference in a hundred other particular instances. But it is not necessary. For every person, who is intimately acquainted with the operations of his own mind, must know, that many objects may be desired, yet no exertions may be made to obtain them. Hence a desire is not a volition. If it were, the effects necessary to obtain the objects of desire would follow, as soon as it existed. For the moment we make exertions to move the hand or foot, and produce other effects, these motions and effects follow. This is a decisive proof that a desire is not a volition. And every person's experience daily decides this dispute. Do not all persons know they frequently have desires to visit friends and neighbors, yet make no exertions to accomplish the object ? Yet if a desire is a volition, the moment they have such a desire the exertion is made, and the visit would soon be accomplished. It appears then that those persons, who consider desires to be volitions, have never given much attention to the operations of their own minds.

3. Whether objects shall please or disgust us, does not depend on any thing in us, except our nature ; but whether they shall be chosen or not, depends on our pleasure. Our nature, and the nature of objects, are such, they will please or displease us. Does it depend on our pleasure to say, whether beautiful colors, and melodious sounds shall give us pleasure ? Or whether discordant sounds, and fetid scents shall offend us, or not? Pleasure and pain are not produced by choice ; neither can

choice prevent them. Whether we will or not, some objects will please us, and others will disgust us. But whether they are chosen or rejected, depends on our pleasure. Many objects, which are agreeable, are rejected; and many, which are disgustful, are chosen. For instance, sometimes food, which is agreeable to the taste, is refused, and disgustful medicines are chosen and received. Though these things, and many others, will be agreeable or disgustful to our taste, and it is not possible for us to prevent it ; yet we can choose, or reject them. This shows, that our voluntary exertions depend on our pleasure ; but our pleasures, pains, and desires do not depend on the will. Or in other words, the operations of the will are under the government of the heart, but the operations of the heart are not under the government of the will. But if our feelings of pleasure and pain, and desires, (which are the operations of the heart, or taste,) are volitions, then our volitions are governed by our volitions ; which is absurd.

The will is influenced and governed by the heart. Our desires give rise to volitions. When I come to a right and left hand path, for certain reasons I may desire to take one, and for other reasons desire to travel the other ; & the strongest desire will finally prevail. My choice, which moves my body in either path, is determined by my strongest desire. And as the will never determines itself, & is influenced by the strongest desire, desire is not an operation of the will. For that, which determines the will, is not an act of the will. And as our feelings & desires govern and determine the will, they are not acts of the will, but antecedent to them. But this argument will be set in a more clear and forcible light, when we attend to the influence of motives, and consider what it is that determines the will. The evidence of its truth will appear with increasing strength from several subjects, which will be discussed in their proper place. I shall now

4. Observe, that vice and virtue have their seat in the heart, not in the will. This constitutes an essential difference between these two faculties.

When the divine character is clearly exhibited to the view of an attentive mind, and a person has a consistent knowledge of it, and is filled with joy, is not this a holy joy ? What is holy joy, but a true delight in the character of God ? When he contemplates the government of God, and rejoices that the Lord reigns, is not this a holy rejoicing ? This joy is attended with ardent desire for the increasing displays of the glory

L

of God. He may have an ardent desire, that sinners might submit to the will and government of God. Are not these holy desires ? But this joy is only an emotion of pleasure, excited by the character and government of Jehovah. These holy desires are those which attend such agreeable sensations. And this delight in God, and this desire for the glory of his name, are the ingredients of that affection called love to him, and his government.

When a person of this character has a knowledge of himself, and sees that he has sinned against a holy God, his heart is broken and contrite for sin. He has what the scriptures call repentance, and godly sorrow. These feelings of his heart are attended with earnest desires to overcome all remaining wickedness, to be delivered from the dominion and pollution of sin, and be holy as God is holy. Is not this sorrow for sin a holy sorrow, and these desires holy desires ?

Another person, when he has a clear view of God's character and government, is filled with pain. He has strong desires to dethrone God, or rise above him, that he may sin with impunity. Are not these operations sinful affections ? Who can deny it ? Have not these two persons hearts totally different in their nature ? Are not their feelings as different as sin and holiness ? But their feelings are nothing but *affections* ; which are, as I have shown, the operations of the taste or heart. These affections exist, antecedently to those voluntary exertions, which they make in order to gratify their desires. Hence holy and sinful affections exist antecedently to volitions, which are the only operations of the will. For persons may have all these affections, without making one exertion to move the body or to produce any other effects. Such exertions, by which I mean volitions, are not necessary to the existence of these affections. And if voluntary exertions were made to produce such affections, it would avail nothing ; for the heart is not under the power of the will. A person by willing can no mo e produce love to God in his heart, than he can produce a world by willing it. If any reader is not convinced of this truth, he may convince himself by making the trial.

A person injures his neighbor. The injury the latter has received excites revenge in his heart. It gives him pain, which is attended with a desire to be revenged, the first opportunity, by taking his neighbor's life. I ask, does not this feeling, called revenge, constitute the crime termed murder? Our Lord says, if a man look on a woman, and lust after her, he hath committed adultery with her in his heart already. What is this lust, but a desire for the commission of the sinful act? This our Lord calls adultery. Indeed, the more any person attends to this subject, the more he will be convinced, that no operations of the mind are sinful or holy, but those which are termed the affections and passions. And these, it has been shown, are the operations of the heart. They have a full and complete existence, antecedent to those operations which I call volitions.

Of course our volitions cannot be considered as vicious or virtuous, any more than the operations of the understanding can be viewed in this light.

There are two reasons, why vice and virtue are seated in the heart or affections, and not in volitions. 1. The heart or taste with its affections are the primary principle of action. All the actions may be traced back to the heart, as the primary fountain from which they proceed; and they cannot be traced back any further, or to any antecedent principle of action in a moral agent. From the heart all good and evil proceed. The moral character of man, then, is just what his heart is. 2. The will is only an *executive* faculty. It is no more than a servant to the heart, to execute its pleasure. The will is no *primary* principle of action; its office is to obey the commands of the heart. Accordingly, for all the good or evil produced by the will, the heart only is praise or blame worthy; or every moral agent is to be blamed or praised, on account of the good or evil heart in him.

Hence no one need be surprised at the sentiment advanced. For the more he reflects upon it, the more he will be convinced it is correct, and accords with the word of God.

This will appear more evident to any candid person, if he duly considers the end to be answered by our voluntary exertions. These exertions are made to gratify the feelings, or affections of the heart. The man, who has revenge or murder in his heart, makes exertions, and employs his bodily powers, to put an end to the life of his victim. What is the design of all those motions and effects, produced by the will, but to gratify his revenge? This is the great design of all our volitions, to produce those external effects necessary to gratify our affections and passions.

Now is there not a generic difference, between those operations which are sinful or holy, and those which are neither vicious or virtuous ? There can be no operations of the mind, between which there is a more essential difference in their very nature or kind. And it is perfectly unphilosophical, and serves only to confuse us in our investigations, to class those operations together, which have a generic difference. Our volitions then are operations, which cannot be classed with the affections, nor be considered as operations of the heart. They, therefore, form a third general class of operations. They are not operations of the understanding ; for there is no likeness between them and perceptions. And for the same reason, they cannot be considered as the operations of the taste or heart. They must, therefore, be referred to the will. Volitions are the operations of this faculty, and of no other. This general class does not admit of any subdivisions into specific classes. For every volition is designed to answer the same purpose ; which is, the production of those effects, which are necessary to obtain the objects of the affections. The will is a servant to the heart. It is given to execute its wishes, and put it in possession of those objects, which gratify and satiate its feelings. As every voluntary exertion answers the same purpose, one volition does not specifically differ from another. Of course this general class of operations is not divisible into any specific classes.

Some have attempted to account for the manifest difference, which exists between our affections and volitions, by making a distinction between *immanent and imperate* acts of the will. By immanent acts they mean, if I understand them, what I call the affections and passions. And by imperate acts, those operations which I call volitions. They therefore consider those immanent and imperate acts to be operations of the same faculty, called the will. But from what has been said, it is evident, this is classing those operations together, which generically differ from each other.

Why do not philosophers consider all the operations of the understanding, and the affections, as constituting but one general class of operations, and as belonging to one faculty ? The reason is, they see no similarity between intellectual perceptions and affections. A perception is not a feeling either of pleasure or pain, nor a desire. And pleasure and pain, and desires, they clearly see, are not perceptions. Hence classing them together would be improper, and create confusion. It would be confounding things which differ, and destroying all those distinctions which are necessary to the acquirement of scientific knowledge. For a person has no more than a confused notion of things, who does not make distinctions, where there are differences; or point out the difference between one thing and another. As perceptions and affections generically differ, philosophers have distinguished them, and formed them into distinct classes; and so they have admitted the existence of two faculties. And for the same reason they admit two, they ought to grant there are three faculties. For when we attend to the affections and to volitions, it is evident there is a generic difference between them. It is evident that pain, pleasure, and desires, are not volitions; and have no similarity to those voluntary exertions, which produce effects on the body, and in other things around us. For these affections do not immediately produce any external effects; they are effects themselves produced by the heart, and are either virtuous or vicious. For it has been shown, that vice and virtue belong to the heart only, and its operations, or affections. There is, therefore, no more propriety in classing the affections and volitions together, than in making but one class of the affections & perceptions. The affections & volitions so widely differ, that they naturally divide themselves into two distinct, general classes. Of course, they cannot belong to the same faculty; and the distinction concerning immanent and imperate acts, is inconsistent and useless. Those who make this distinction, divide the affections and volitions into two general classes; for the difference between them is so great, they cannot avoid admitting it. But to grant it, and then refer both classes to the same faculty, is unphilosophical, and creates confusion of ideas.

But the importance of admitting that the mind has three faculties, will appear more clearly and fully in some of the subsequent essays. I have now finished what I intended to say on the faculties of the mind, and their respective operations. The numerous operations of the understanding I have called by one general name, *perceptions*. I think I have made it evident, that every operation of this faculty is a perception. Those perceptions are divided into distinct, specific classes, termed reason, memory, conscience, judgment, imagination. And the numerous operations of the taste or heart, are known by the name of *affections*. This general class is divided into several specific classes, termed primary, secondary, and malignant affections. And the numerous operations of the will are known by the term *volitions*. This class does not admit of any divisions. These three general classes, *perceptions, affections,* and *volitions,* include all the operations of the mind. It is presumed no person can name an operation,which is not included in one or the other of these classes. As these several classes generically differ, for the same reasons that two faculties have been admitted to belong to the human mind, it is necessary to admit a third.

****

ESSAY XIII.

General Observations on Moral Agency.

Very different opinions concerning moral agency and liberty, have prevailed among the learned. This has occasioned very warm disputes, and numerous treatises. Of the different theories which have been advanced, very few, if any, agree wholly with facts and experience. The different opinions which have been embraced are included, I believe, either in the Arminian scheme, or the Calvinistic. Each of these schemes has been warmly defended by the ablest pens. Though the parties have widely differed, yet on some points they have been agreed. In this essay it is my design to show how far they are agreed, and in what particulars they differ ; which will prepare the way for a more distinct discussion of the subject in the next essay.—The great dispute has been, and is still, what is necessary to constitute a being a real agent, and proper object of praise and blame, and a proper subject of rewards. To constitute such a being it is agreed,

1. That he must be *an agent.* It is agreed on both sides, that a being, who is not an agent, is not a proper object of praise or blame. But what is agency ? Respecting this, different opinions have prevailed. And here is the proper place to discuss this subject. The words *cause, agency, effi-*

ciency, action, are used in so many different senses, and their meaning is so ambiguous, that it is very difficult to explain their meaning. This, however, I shall attempt, so far as is necessary to understand the subject under consideration.

Whatever begins to exist is an effect, and must have a cause. And in things, which do exist, many changes and alterations take place. All such changes are effects, which must have a cause. And the causes must be adequate to the production of such effects, or they could not have an existence. These are first principles, which no candid person will deny. To the production of an effect a cause must *operate,* must *act.* For it does not appear to be possible for an inoperative, inactive cause, if it may be called a cause, to produce any effect. A proper cause then is something, which is in its nature operative and active. The operation of a cause is what we mean by *action,* and by *activity, energy* and *efficiency.* This implies a distinction between the *thing,* which is a cause, and its *action,* or *operation.* If the nature of a thing is such, that it will operate and act, and produce effects, whenever there is an opportunity for it, it is a proper cause; it is an active, efficient cause.

If any being has a principle in him of this nature, a principle which is active and operative, he is an *agent.* This active principle constitutes agency. In this active principle his agency consists. All things which exist either *act,* or are acted upon ; they are either *active* agents, or *passive* subjects. And perhaps there is nothing in existence, of which both action and passion may not be predicated. A ball, when put in motion by some impulse, is acted upon. It is passive, or suffers the force of the impulse. But when we view it in motion, and in relation to some effect it produces, it acts and is the cause of effects. Motion is the action of the ball. And the effect it produces is greater or less, in proportion to its weight, magnitude, and velocity. In receiving an impulse, it is passive ; in moving and producing effects, it is active. These observations are true with respect to all inanimate existences. But though such kinds of existence, viewed in one relation, may be considered as acting, and as causes of effects ; yet they are not *agents,* according to the sense in which this word ought to be used, when we treat on the subject of moral agency. Because their motion does not proceed from any *operative principle* inherent in them.

Some say a cause is only an *antecedent,* and an effect the con-

sequence of this antecedent; and that this is all we know concerning what we call causes and effects. They seem to exclude all idea of energy, activity, or efficiency, as belonging
to the nature of a cause. If they would admit, that energy,
activity, or something of this nature, is inherent in some
causes, there would be no ground of objection to their view of
causes and effects. But if all energy or efficiency is denied,
as existing in any cause, it is difficult to see how we can account for the existence of any effect, or what they call a consequence. And if it is granted, that God is an efficient cause ;
that in him is energy, activity, which constitutes Him an active agent ; why may not man be endued with the same principle, so as to make him an active agent ? His being dependent, and his powers limited, are no objection of any weight
against viewing him an active agent. If God can create a dependent, limited being, why can he not endue him with an *active*, dependent, limited, principle of action ? I see no objection
of weight against this, and of course prefer viewing a moral
agent as really having in his heart the same active, energetic
principle, as we suppose God possesses. It is granted this active principle in man, which renders him an agent, is dependent and limited. So is his being ; yet he is a real being, distinct from God.

Mankind possess an internal principle of action. They
have one property, which is active in its nature. This property or quality we call the heart, or the faculty of taste. Its
nature is such that all objects will please or disgust it, in a
greater or less degree. It is true, the pleasure and pain are
often so feeble as to be wholly unnoticed, and we are prone
to say, that we feel nothing. We pay no attention to feelings, which are very feeble and faint. When they are strong
and lively, they gain our attention. Yet there is no reason to
believe we are perfectly indifferent, or without any feeling in
the view of objects, at any time. But we are not apt to consider any feeling a real pleasure, or pain, unless so lively and
strong as to gain our attention. Feelings, which pass unnoticed, we are apt to say are no feelings ; and of course are
indifferent towards objects, which make such slight impressions. But we have reason to conclude from the nature of the
heart, that every object makes some impression, though perhaps
feeble. It must be obvious to any person of reflection, that an
existence, which has no feeling quality, or is incapable of

pleasure and pain, has no internal principle of action. And this is one essential difference between active, and inactive beings. The former are endued with feeling, the latter are not. This constitutes one essential difference between material and spiritual substances. It is presumed that if matter, which is now inert, were endued with feeling, it would immediately discover appearances of activity. If it were the subject of pleasure and pain, it could not remain in a state of rest. Such feelings would put it in motion. Mankind, when their feelings of pleasure or pain are very faint, find no difficulty in continuing in a state of almost total rest, and inactivity. But when their feelings are very acute and strong, they find it is impossible to remain inactive. How animated and active a person is when filled with joy. How active and spirited, when he is angry. With what zeal and life the avaricious, the proud, the ambitious, the voluptuous, pursue their respective objects. But whence arises all this activity ? From the pleasure they feel, in view of the objects of their pursuit, or expect to derive from them, when attained. With what speed persons flee from danger, when they apprehend it ; and with what zeal they use means, when in distress, to gain relief. What is the cause which excites them to action in such cases ? It is pain. Hence pleasure and pain are the springs of action in moral agents. Deprive mankind of this feeling principle ; let them become as incapable of pleasure and pain, as rocks are, and they would be as inactive. Motives would have no influence upon them. There would be no spring to action in them ; nothing to excite them to seek one thing, or avoid another. We might multiply facts to prove, that a quality, or faculty, susceptible of pleasure and pain, is the only active principle in the universe. It is the primary, original cause of all existences, and of all the changes which they undergo. And the more any person attends to this subject, the more he will be convinced of its truth.

Hence the heart, or the faculty of taste, being the only property of the mind which is susceptible of pleasure and pain, is the principle of action in moral agents. We have once distinguished between a cause, and its operations or actions. The heart is a cause ; its operations, such as pleasure and pain, and their attendant desires, are its *actions*. The heart, when it is pleased or displeased, and has desires to avoid disgustful objects, or to enjoy those which are pleasing, is operating, and

M

produces the effects designed. The first and immediate effects it produces are *volitions ;* and by means of these and bodily motions, it produces all the effects necessary to reach the ends desired. This, then, is in man the primary and original cause of all his actions, and motions, the source from which they all proceed. The heart constitutes human agency, and efficiency. This is the only primary, active, operative cause belonging to his nature, The will, it is granted, operates and acts. But it is not a primary principle of action. Its operations and acts are effects produced by the heart. This brings more clearly into view, what I aimed to prove in the preceding essay, a generic difference between the heart and the will. The actions of the will do not proceed from any activity in itself. They are the effects of a prior cause, which is the heart. The heart, then, is an active principle ; the will is not, any more than a ball, when in motion. Like the ball, it is put in motion, or derives its activity from the heart, the preceding cause. This is true, if a being incapable of feeling would be inactive. For if men did not feel, the will would never act. Hence feelings are antecedent to volitions, and the cause of them. This shows, that the heart and will are distinct faculties ; so different, that one is an active principle, and the other is not.

And beings, who are endued with an active principle, are agents ; but those destitute of any such principle, are not, in the proper sense of the word, agents ; they are only the instruments, which agents use in the accomplishment of their wishes.

Objects impress, or act on the heart. And while objects are impressing it, the heart is constantly operating, and producing effects. If objects could not, and did not, impress the heart, motives would have no influence. For their influence consists wholly in the impressions they make. When they please or displease, they impress us. If they did not have this effect, we should be neither pleased nor offended ; and of course, should never act at all. But objects, or motives, are not agents ; they are only a *means* of action. They are not endued with any principle of action. They are not the subjects of pleasure or pain. But they are necessary means, or occasions of action, or of the operation of what we call active causes.

In the sense explained it appears, that the Deity is acted upðn. The ultimate end of all his operations, is something in itself agreeable to his benevolent heart. This end gives him pleasure. By pleasing him it acts upon his heart, or impresses it, and by thus impressing it influences him to pursue the plan necessary to attain his ultimate end. But the end, which influences him, is not an agent ; is not the cause, which gave existence to this world, and the events of providence. His heart is the primary, original cause of the existence of all things.

As I observed in the beginning of this essay, it is agreed on all sides, that man must be an agent to be a proper object of praise and blame ; yet they differ with respect to the thing in which agency consists. Some say it consists in a self-determining power. Different persons have entertained different notions concerning that kind of agency, which is requisite to praise and blame-worthiness. I grant that if man is not an agent, he is not a proper object of praise and blame. Because nothing could be imputed to him as his act. For no actions are properly his, but those which proceed from an active principle inherent in him. What this active principle is, which constitutes the agency, and efficiency of man, as well as of God, I have laboured to prove and illustrate under this first particular head. I now hope it is evident to every unbiassed mind, that the heart, which is the only feeling faculty, is the primary original cause in man of all his actions. This constitutes him an agent ; an active being. It also appears, that he has the same kind of agency, that his Maker possesses. The difference between the divine and human agency is this ; one is derived, the other is not ; one is dependent, the other is independent ; one is finite, the other is infinite. Yet men are complete agents ; for they are endued with a principle of action. And many of those, who say the will is the only active principle in man, grant, that if men had not a capacity for pleasure and pain, they could not be moral agents ; because having nothing to influence them to act, they would not act at all. If they had not this capacity, no object would ever please or displease them. We should, therefore, be forever in a state of indifference, in which state it would be impossible to act. This is the manner in which many Calvinistic divines reason, who at the same time say, that the will constitutes human agency.

But when they say this capacity is necessary to action, is it not the same as to allow it is the primary original principle of action, and that principle which constitutes agency ? If they do not mean this, their words, in my view, have no meaning. For saying, without this capacity men would never act, or be moral agents, is the same as to assert, that this capacity is the primary spring of action, and constitutes human agency. Their capacity, therefore, for pleasure and pain, is, as far as I can see any meaning in the thing, the very same thing with what I call the heart, or faculty of taste. Hence persons of this sentiment have no ground to object against the scheme advanced in these essays, if they will be consistent with themselves.

Again. If by a self-determining power Arminians mean some cause in man which determines the will, or produces volitions, they have no ground to object against what has been advanced in this essay. And furthermore, if they will be consistent with themselves, they must embrace the scheme hitherto illustrated. For I have endeavoured to prove, that there is a cause in man, which determines the will, and gives rise to every voluntary exertion. Though motives have influence, yet they are not the causes, or agents, which produce volition. So that when we say motives determine the will, we do not mean they are agents ; or have any active principle ; or do any thing more, than merely as means influence us to act, or give an opportunity for the active principle in man to operate. The real, active cause, which determines the will, or gives rise to volition, is in man, and a property of his nature. In this sense a person may be truly said to determine his own will. His heart has power over the will, and does determine all its acts. If this, then, is all that is meant by a self-determining power, mankind truly possess it. Of course in this particular Arminians and Calvinists may be agreed.

We may now inquire, why that agency, which is granted to be necessary to praise and blame, is called *moral*. It may be observed here, that many other beings, as well as men, are represented as *acting*. Hence we say, the sun sets and rises ; the moon changes ; the water runs ; the wind blows ; and of almost every thing which exists, action is predicated. They are represented, in the construction of all languages, as possessing principles of action. What original notions gave rise to such modes of expression, is foreign to my design to inquire. Such expressions are common in all languages. Yet we know, inanimate existences have no inherent principles of action.

Hence, when they are called, or represented as agents, it is in a figurative sense only. Beings, which are not agents, in the literal and proper sense of the word, we know are not objects of either praise or blame. Hence the modes of expression in all languages direct us to two different kinds of agents. One kind is worthy of praise, and blame ; the other kind is not. To distinguish one from the other, we call one a *moral*, the other a *natural* agent. When those words are used to qualify the term agent, they mean, that the *moral* agent is a proper object of praise or blame ; the *natural* agent is not. They therefore are used to denote what beings are, and what beings are not, deserving of praise or blame. To communicate my idea readily to another, that man is worthy of praise or blame, I only say, he is a *moral* agent ; and for the same purpose I say of another being, it is a natural agent, neither deserving of praise nor of blame. I grant, when I call any thing, which has no principle of action, an agent, the word is used in a figurative sense.

Having now shown, what agency in man is, and why he is called a *moral* agent, I proceed to add,

2. That it is agreed on all sides, that a moral agent is a proper object of praise and blame.

Few, if any, deny that men are agents. The dispute is not, whether men are agents ; but as it respects this point, in what does their agency consist ? To this we have already attended.

It is, also, generally granted, that men are proper objects of praise and blame ; deserving of approbation, or disapprobation, according to their good or bad condcct. Still it is a matter of some debate, what is necessary to render man a proper object of praise and blame ? What kind of agency is necessary ? Whether an understanding and knowledge are requisite ? Then, if they agree that certain properties are necessary to constitute a proper moral agent, it is disputed, why they are necessary. Some assign one reason, and some another.

3. It is in general agreed, that a moral agent is a proper subject of rewards. This but few deny. But the inquiry is, what is necessary to constitute a being a proper subject of rewards ? Some assert one thing, and some another. Respecting this question they dispute with great warmth.

4. Also, it is agreed generally, that liberty is necessary to render man a complete moral agent. But what is liberty ? Is it consistent with necessity, and why is it requisite ? These several subjects have not been settled to universal satisfaction.

It is a matter of some importance to learn, with respect to a subject which has caused almost endless disputes, how far the parties are agreed, and in what views they disagree. One great object of this essay has been to show how far parties are agreed.

It appears on examination, that they generally admit, that man is an *agent*, a proper *object* of praise and blame, and a proper *subject* of rewards. And it also appears, that the following points are yet subjects of debate—what is agency? Why is it necessary, and what other properties are requisite, and why, to constitute a person a fit object of praise and blame and a fit subject of rewards? Ascertaining the points of agreement and disagreement, prepares the way for terminating such uncomfortable disputes. In the next essay, I shall prosecute the inquiry, with a hope of contributing to such a result.

****

ESSAY XIV.

Particular reasons given, why certain properties are necessary, to constitute a being a proper, and complete moral agent.

It is agreed, 1. That agency is necessary to constitute a *moral* agent. 2. That a moral agent is a proper object of praise and blame. 3. That he is a proper subject of rewards. The great inquiry is, what is requisite to constitute such a being? And when we see, why the different properties in succession are necessary, we can answer the general question ; can determine what is needful to render a being a complete and entire moral agent. For a being, who has every quality requisite to action, and to make him a fit object of praise and blame, and a proper subject of rewards, is a complete moral agent. I shall, therefore,

I. Show why the faculty called the understanding is necessary, to constitute a being of the above description. When we see *why*, then we shall see *it is* necessary.

1. The understanding is necessary to *agency*. The understanding is not an active principle, yet it is necessary *to action*. Some things are necessary to the operation of active powers or principles, so that without them they cannot act.

The heart is an active principle, and the understanding is necessary to its operation generally, if not universally.—Pleasure, pain, and desires, are the operations of the heart. By these every effect is produced, which is attributable to the agency of man. But in order for objects to please or offend us, they must be perceived or known. Objects of which we have no knowledge, do not affect us. And so long as we remain ignorant of them, they are not objects of our desire or pursuit. The only way objects, considered as motives, influence us to act, is by pleasing or disgusting us. But they cannot in this manner influence us to act, unless they are seen. Objects, which might have a powerful influence, can have none, so long as we have no knowledge of them. We hence see, that a perception, or knowledge of objects, is necessary to excite desires in us ; and this is requisite to action. For we shall never act, only when there is something influencing us. And the only way by which they influence us to act, is by pleasing or offending us ; and as they do not give us either pleasure or pain unless they are seen or known, it is evident knowledge is necessary to the operation of the heart.

Knowledge of every kind belongs to the understanding. Hence, without this faculty, man would not be a complete agent ; because his active principles would have no opportunity to operate. This, then, is one reason why the understanding is necessary to an entire agent. For to this end, man must not only be an agent ; but there must be opportunity for the operation of his active powers.

2. Without the faculty of understanding mankind could not, generally, obtain the objects which please them, or avoid those which disgust them.

To the attainment of ends, plans of operation are requisite. The means necessary to any particular end must be discovered, arranged, and connected. When this is done, a plan of operation is formed. The way is then prepared, for the heart to obtain the object of its desire.

But what faculty of the mind devises means and ways to accomplish our ends, and forms plans of operation ? None, certainly, but a perceiving faculty. It is the office of the understanding to show the heart, how it can attain the ends it wishes. It is the eye of the mind to guide the heart in the way, which will lead it to the end or object it wishes to enjoy, and from the object it wishes to avoid. Suppose a man had a heart, but no understanding. He could feel, if an object were presented ; but he could see nothing. Suppose it possible that an object could affect him ; he could see no way to attain what he loved, or to avoid what he hated. He could not act by aim or design ; for he would see nothing to aim at. He could not devise means for accomplishing any purpose ; he would grope in uncertainty and darkness.

If a man can perceive objects, and in this way be affected and influenced by them to act ; if he can perceive and devise the means requisite, to direct his actions to the end desired ; he is thus far a perfect and complete agent. For this purpose, the faculty of understanding is necessary. If man could act without an understanding, yet he would be a very imperfect agent. These reasons show, why the understanding is necessary to constitute man a complete and proper agent.

3. The understanding is necessary to render man an object worthy of praise and blame, and a proper subject of reward.

If we had not this faculty, we should have no knowledge of vice, or virtue ; nor any conception of the meaning of the words, censure, blame, approbation, praise, and rewards. If blamed or praised, we should not know why, or for what cause. If we were rewarded with good, or with evil, we could not know why we were thus treated ; nor have any idea of the righteousness of our judge, from whose hand we receive rewards. For, if we had not an intellectual faculty, we should have no conception or knowledge of any thing whatever. But is a being a proper object of censure, or approbation, for any of his actions, who has no idea of vice and virtue ; and who consequently cannot know what is intended by censure and praise ? Is a being a fit subject of rewards, who has no conception of good and ill desert, or of the justice and propriety of his conduct who distributes rewards ? Earthquakes, tempests, pestilential disorders, are great evils in the natural world. But we never think of blaming and punishing them. The sun, rain, and fruitful seasons, are great blessings in the natural world. But we have no thought of praising and rewarding them. One reason why we do not is, we know they can have no understanding of the things implied in censuring, praising, and rewarding them. Hence no end would be answered by treating them in such a manner.

It is then very evident, that beings which have no intellect, and are incapable of acquiring knowledge, are not proper objects of either praise or blame ; or fit subjects to be rewarded with good or evil. Beings, which have not the faculty of understanding, are incapable of knowledge ; and therefore they are not suitable objects to be censured or praised, or fit subjects to be rewarded. Hence they are not proper and complete moral agents. Accordingly, this faculty is necessary, for the reasons given, to constitute any being such an agent as is intended by the terms moral agent.

I now proceed to show,

II. Why the faculty of taste, or the heart, is necessaay to form a complete moral agent.

1. It is necessary to constitute an intelligent being an *agent*. Agency, and the primary spring of action, are the same thing. It will be generally, if not universally, agreed, that our intellectual faculty is never the subject of either pleasure or pain ; or it is not a feeling faculty. But as we are in fact the subjects of pleasure and pain, it follows, that the heart is the only feeling faculty belonging to the human mind. Suppose a person had an intellectual faculty, but had no heart, or faculty of feeling ; would he ever act ? Those, who have ever given much attention to this question, are ready to answer, he would remain inactive, unless moved by some external force. And any one may be convinced of this truth, by a little attention. For though this person might perceive objects, yet they would not affect him ; he would be and continue in a state of perfect indifference. And the impossibility of acting in such a state, has been so clearly, and demonstratively shown by several authors, it is needless for me to spend time in proving it. On the other hand, it is impossible for a being, who is pleased or displeas'd with objects, to remain in a state of rest, or inaction. When his pleasures and pains are faint and feeble, he will not act with much force. Yet the nature of man is such, he cannot continue long in a state of feeble effort. For inaction begets uneasiness ; and action becomes necessary for the removal of the pain, occasioned by inaction. Also, if he did not act, his appetites must remain ungratified. In this state, their cravings and hankerings would increase, and render his condition very painful. By creating this uneasiness, they ever incite man to

N

action to obtain the objects, which, by satisfying their cravings, remove their uneasiness. Even when the body is at rest, the heart of man will keep his mind employed, and devising means to gratify his desires. And the activity of the heart is as really displayed, in turning the attention of the mind from one object to another, and in confining it to the investigation of subjects, as in moving the body, and producing external, visible effects. When all these things are duly considered, it is evident the heart is always acting, either on the mind, or the body ; and producing effects of some kind or other. The heart, then, is the primary principle of action in moral agents. In this the agency of man consists. It is an inherent principle of action in man ; a property and law of his nature. Hence all the actions of men are *their* actions ; the operations of a principle of action, which is a property of their nature, and constituent part of their being. So that the actions of men cannot be attributed to any being, but themselves.

As this faculty constitutes agency, if man were destitute of it, he would not be an agent.

2. This faculty is necessary to constitute man *worthy of praise and blame*. It is granted, that vice and virtue are not predicable of the understanding. It will also be granted, that a being, who is neither virtuous nor vicious, is not deserving of censure or praise. He is not a proper object of approbation or disapprobation. It has also been shown, in the essays on taste and its operations, that vice and virtue are not predicable of any faculty of the mind, but the heart. And the reason is, no other faculty is a principle of action. It is not, therefore, necessary here to prove, that vice and virtue have their seat in the heart, this having already been done. It therefore follows, that as vice and virtue belong to the heart, and are essentially necessay to render a being worthy of praise and blame, if men did not possess this faculty, they would not be proper objects of either censure, or approbation. This faculty then is essentially requisite, for the reason now assigned, to constitute a moral agent.

3. This faculty is necessary to render men *rewardable*.—Future misery is the reward of the wicked, and happiness the reward of the righteous. Wickedness of heart prepares the former for eternal death ; holiness fits the latter for eternal life. Beings, therefore, incapable of pleasure and pain, cannot be rewarded. They cannot be made either miserable or happy.

We never think of rewarding or punishing inanimate things, however useful, or hurtful. We know they are incapable of rewards, because they are incapable of pleasure and pain. And as the heart is the only feeling faculty belonging to man, deprive him of this, he is then incapable of receiving rewards. With this faculty, he can be rewarded with good or evil, according to the defect of his character. But without it, he is no more rewardable, than any part of the inanimate creation. But a being incapable of rewards, is not a complete moral agent.

This faculty, then, is necessary to constitute a man a proper moral agent. For the first reason assigned, it is requisite to make him an *agent*. For the second reason given, it is necessary to render him a fit *object of praise and blame*. And for the third reason, it is needful to render him *capable of future rewards*. It is, therefore, absolutely requisite to constitute him a proper moral agent. This is the most essential, and important faculty belonging to the subject of moral agency ; and the most difficult of any to be understood clearly and distinctly.

III. *The will* is a necessary faculty in moral agency. If a wheel is wanting in a clock, it is imperfect. It is not prepared to answer the end for which it was made. It was the design of God in the formation of man, to make him capable of accomplishing his wishes, of manifesting his real character, and serving his Maker. That he might be qualified for these ends, that faculty termed the will was necessary. The will is, therefore, necessary,

1. To render us *capable of gratifying our appetites, and desires*. Here let it be remembered, that volitions are the operations of the will ; and by volitions, I mean, those voluntary exertions with which bodily motions, and the direction of the understanding are *immediately connected ;* and by which those other external, and visible effects are produced, which are necessary to obtain or avoid the objects at which we aim. These are necessary, to gratify our wishes and appetites. When the heart desires the enjoyment of an object, and the understanding has formed a plan for its attainment ; unless the plan is carried into execution, the heart cannot be gratified, or accomplish its wishes.

For instance, a person wishes to visit a friend at a distance. To effect this, measures must be concerted and pursued. To concert a scheme agreeable to the desires of the heart, is the office of the understanding. When the plan is formed, the understanding has done its duty ; for it is only a servant to the heart. To execute the plan, many things must be put in motion, and a train of effects must be produced. It is the office of the will to produce them. And by exertions, which are called volitions, they are produced. The plan is executed ; the heart obta'ns its end, and is gratified. When the plan is executed, the will has performed its duty; for it is only a servant to the heart. Thus the will is an executive power. By this power, the heart gratifies its appetites and desires, obtains whatever it esteems good, and avoids whatever it esteems evil, as far as God sees it best to prosper our exertions. Is man a complete agent, is he such an agent as he would wish to be, unless he is able to reach his desired ends ? If he had not this faculty, he would be incapable of performing any external actions. However strong his desires might be, he must remain in a state of rest, and never obtain the ends desired. To constitute a perfect agent, two things are necessary. First, a principle of action ; a primary, operative cause, inherent in his nature. Secondly, this active principle must be able to produce all the effects, necessary to obtain its desired ends, and the ends for which it is created. Such a principle constitutes complete agency. And in order for this agent to be thus efficient, two other things are necessary. First, an understanding, to form plans of operation ; and secondly, a will to execute them. And each of these faculties must be under the command, control, and direction of the heart. If they are, then the heart, which is an active principle, is *able*, its agency is *sufficient*, to accomplish all its desires and ends, as far as God sees best, on whom all created beings are dependent. Hence we see, that unless man had a will, and unless his will had been subjected to the command of the heart, he would not have been a perfect agent. He would not have been able to carry any plan into execution, or to gratify any of his appetites and desires. And, unless he had been able to do this, his agency would not have been complete. So the will is necessary to a perfect agent. Some may here ask, why God, in forming men, did not immediately connect bodily motions, and other external actions and effects, with the desires of the heart ? Why was it necessary, that this power, called the will, should interfere, between the heart and external visible actions ? Answer, why men were not made differently, does not belong to us to determine. God knew what was necessary, to constitute such a being as man perfect in his kind. Such a being he has made him. To say he might have been made differently, and answer the end of his being as well, is dictating to our Maker, and exalting ourselves above him. Our only business in our investigations is, to get a clear knowledge of man, as he is made ; and the perfect adaptedness of his being to the end for which he was created. It does not belong to a child to dictate to a clock maker. But when the machine is finished, he may examine it, and learn its perfect adaptedness to the end for which it was designed. And we find the will is a necessary faculty, in beings formed as we are.

2. The will is necessary, to a full *performance of all the duties* enjoined us by our Maker.

We are servants of God. And if we have every thing necessary to perform faithfully the services required of us, in case the heart is right, we are qualified for the station we fill. The divine commands, in general, respect two things ; the temper of the heart we ought to have, and the actions we ought to perform. The temper of the heart they require is that, which is implied in love to God and our neighbour. These two commands comprise all the divine requirements and prohibitions, as far as they respect the heart. But external actions, as well as a right internal temper, are required of us. For instance, we are required to remember the sabbath, to keep it holy. All the external actions implied in this command, we are bound to perform. We are also required to clothe the naked, and feed the hungry. And all the external actions, necessary to the performance of this duty, are implied in the command. So that commands, generally speaking, respect the heart and our outward actions. So far as outward actions are required, the will is necessary to the performance of them. For it is by the will only, that these actions are performed. Hence, without this faculty, we could not obey the commands of God so far as they respect our outward conduct. We might have the temper of heart required ; but could not, without the help of the will, perform the external part enjoined. The will, therefore, is a necessary qualification to the performance in full of the duties required. Without this, we should labour under a natural inability. And without an understanding to learn and know the will of God, we should be under a natural inability to obey his commands. But an understanding sufficient to know his pleasure,

and a will to perform every external duty required, constitute
a natural ability to serve the Lord.

3. The will is necessary *to manifest the nature and character of
the heart.* A person, who has a holy character, ought to be
praised by his fellows, and treated well by his Maker. If his
character be bad, he deserves the censure of his fellow men,
and the disapprobation of his Judge. Now the heart of man constitutes his moral character. Every person's heart is virtuous
or vicious; and therefore, in a moral sense, is good or evil, deserving of approbation or censure. But men cannot be acquainted with each other's hearts, or characters, only by external signs or actions. These are the indices of the heart, the
signs and interpreters of its nature. As by the fruit a tree
bears, we learn its nature ; so by these external fruits, we obtain a knowledge of each other's characters. Without this
knowledge, we could not make proper distinctions in our treatment of men. But it is the will, which produces those external fruits from which we learn the characters of men. Hence,
without this faculty we could have no knowledge of men's characters, and could not see the righteousness of God in the final
distribution of rewards. For a knowledge of every person's desert is necessary, to see his righteousness in rewarding.

These are the faculties requisite to constitute a moral agent.
I have also assigned the reasons, why they are necessary; and
have made it evident, I trust, that if either of them were wanting, man would be an imperfect agent. But these properties
render him a complete agent. He has all the agency and efficiency needful, to all the purposes of a finite, dependent being. They render him also a proper object of praise and
blame, and a rightful subject of rewards. For a being of the
description I have given, will forever appear to us to deserve
praise or blame, and a good or evil reward, according to the
nature of his character.

An infant, when born, has the faculty called the understanding, which qualifies him for an endless improvement in knowledge. He has, also, the faculty termed the taste, or heart,
which prepares him to be the subject of agreeable and painful
sensations, and all those desires which attend them. He is endued with a principle of action, which will never cease to act
through interminable ages. He has, moreover, the faculty called the will, which prepares him to perform any actions, and
produce any effects, necessary to gratify his appetites and de-

sires, as far as infinite wisdom may see best. He has the faculty necessary to devise means and form plans for the accomplishment of his desires. He has the faculty requisite to carry them into execution. He has the faculty or principle of action, which puts every thing in motion. It can turn the understanding from object to object; and confine its attention, when and where it will. It can employ the will in executing its wishes and purposes. Such an infant, then, is thus far an entire and perfect moral agent. It is prepared for action and improvement.

But one thing more is wanting to render man a finished, complete and perfect agent; that is liberty. What that liberty is, which is considered as essential to moral agency, and why it is necessary, and other inquiries connected with these, will be the subject of the next essay.

****

ESSAY XV.

Of Liberty ; and the reasons why it is necessary to form a complete, perfect, moral agent.

This essay will comprise a discussion of two questions: What is liberty?—and, Why is it necessary to a perfect moral agency? To prepare the way, I shall inquire, Whether any *power* or *operation* of the mind is liberty?

1. It will be granted, that our *intellectual* faculty does not constitute liberty. Liberty is never, unless figuratively, predicated of the understanding, or of any of its operations. No author, that I recollect, considers perception, or reason, or memory, or judgment, or conscience, as constituting liberty. It will be granted, that liberty does not belong to the understanding, or any of its operations.

2. Is the *pleasure* or the *pain*, which in a greater or less degree we derive from objects, liberty? Is liberty the same thing as being pleased, or disgusted? Is any person at liberty to say, whether objects shall please or disgust him? If so,

then we have power to create our own happiness and misery. And if men have this power, why do they groan under exquisite pains for days, for months and for years? Is any person at liberty to determine, whether a bodily disease shall give him pain or not ; or whether natural objects, or divine objects, shall please, or disgust him? When we consider how averse all mankind are to pain, and how ardently they seek happiness, if it depended on their determinations whether they should be happy or miserable, we have reason to conclude that all misery would immediately be banished from this world. But mankind know that happiness and misery do not depend on their determinations. Or it does not depend on their determinations, whether objects shall please or displease them. It is true, they can by prudent conduct avoid many causes of pain, and render their circumstances more comfortable. Still, whether the object they have shunned, or the one they have attained, shall give them pleasure or pain, does not depend on their determinations. When I have purchased an orange, it does not depend on me to say, whether I shall relish or disrelish it. Our pleasures and pains depend on our nature, and the nature of objects with which we are conversant. All we can do is to avoid those, which we know are disgustful, and get possession of those, which we learn by experience are agreeable, as far as our power extends. Therefore, a pleasant feeling is not liberty, neither is a painful sensation liberty ; nor are we, in any sense, free to determine whether objects shall please or offend us.

3. Do our *desires* constitute liberty? If a desire to obtain or shun an object, is liberty; then, so far as we have desires, we have liberty. But it no more depends on us to say, whether we shall desire to obtain, or avoid objects, than to say, whether they shall please or disgust us. If an object disgust us, a desire will arise to avoid it ; and if it please us, and is attainable, we shall desire the enjoyment of it. Desires will attend our sensations. We cannot prevent it.

Again, if a desire of the heart is liberty, then, when persons have desires, they are free. But when a person is bound with chains, he may desire to walk. But is he at liberty to walk, when his feet are bound with fetters? It will be granted that, in this situation, he has not liberty to walk. Yet he may, and persons often have, in such a condition, desires to walk. And if desires are liberty, then persons have liberty to walk, when their feet are bound with cords ; or they have liberty, and at the same time, have none. This is a direct contradiction; and makes it evident, that a desire is not liberty. Whatever liberty is, it is something totally distinct from sensations and desires. And hence liberty does not consist in any of the operations of the heart, or taste.

4. Does liberty consist in *volitions?* Are volition and liberty synonimous terms? If so, then a person is free, as far as he has voluntary exertions. But in the case just mentioned, where a person has his feet bound with fetters, he has at that time no liberty to walk? Yet he may make, and persons in such a condition often do make, powerful and voluntary exertions to walk. If such exertions constitute liberty, persons have it, and exercise it. But I believe it will be granted, that in this condition they have no liberty to walk. Hence volitions are not liberty, unless contradictions may be true.

It may be said, though volition is not liberty, yet persons may have liberty to will, or make voluntary exertions. They may be free to make such exertions, even when bound. This is readily granted ; but it does not determine what freedom is. It is not volition, nor any antecedent sensation or desire. What then is meant by this liberty to will, to choose, or refuse ?

Though very few, if any, expressly say that volitions are liberty ; yet many assert, that liberty is as essential to volition as fluidity is to water. What is the meaning of such an expression ? We say, water is a fluid. Do they mean, then, that a volition is liberty ? We have seen this idea implies a contradiction, as soon as we view it in relation to some given effect. By the fluidity of water, may be meant its adaptedness to run or move towards the centre. Do they mean, then, when they say volitions are free, there is an adaptedness in them to some effect ? Is an adaptedness in volition to move the hands or feet, the thing intended by liberty ? I believe few will assert this. Do they mean by the expression, that volitions are free, as we say, water is fluid ? What are they free to do ? When a person is bound, are his volitions free to produce walking? No. For this would imply a contradiction. Do they mean, persons are free to choose, to will ? This makes liberty consist in something antecedent to volition, and fairly gives up the idea, that volitions are free. For to say, volitions are free, and to say we are free to choose, are very different things.

When I am bound with fetters of iron, am I at liberty to make voluntary exertions to break my fetters ? I am. No man

O

can deprive me of this liberty. No man can prevent my willing, or choosing. Men cannot bind the will. But are my voluntary exertions at liberty to loosen the chains on my feet? They certainly are not. I do not enjoy the liberty necesssary to produce the effect aimed at. It is agreed, that in this condition I am not at liberty to walk. Hence it may be said, I am at liberty to make *exertions* to walk ; but I am not at liberty to walk, or to *produce* this effect. All that is contained in the last sentence, the distinction it presents to view, it is presumed, will be readily granted. And according to this distinction, I am free, antecedent to willing. I am at liberty to choose ; to make voluntary exertions. I am in this state of liberty antecedent to choosing. Were this not true, it would be as impossible for me to make these exertions, as it is to arise, and walk. I cannot walk ; because I do not enjoy the liberty necessary to this event. And, if I did not enjoy liberty to choose, I could not make one exertion with a view to walking.

Now every one may see, liberty and walking are not the same thing. For a liberty to walk is antecedent to the event. And volition and liberty are not convertible terms. For a liberty to make *exertions* to walk is antecedent to making them. Hence it is obvious, that liberty and volition are not the same thing.

5. Is liberty *some power*, which the mind possesses? Some say, liberty is a power to act or not to act. This notion of liberty many have labored to support.

In this definition of liberty it is important to know what is meant by *action*. Choice is an action, or exercise. It is an act of the will. And bodily motions are called actions. All those visible, external effects, which moral agents produce, are stiled their actions. While they are talking, travelling, laboring, they are acting. Every volition, and all the effects which volitions produce, are the actions of moral agents. The action they intend, is to be understood in one or both of these senses. Hence, when they say liberty is a power to act or not to act, they mean it is a power to will or not to will ; or a power to perform, or not perform external actions. They, therefore, make the same distinction between *power* and *action*, as is commonly made between a *cause* and *effect*. Their power is a cause, and action is the effect it produces. Having explained what appears to be their meaning of the phrase, " liberty is a power to act or not to act," let us examine it with respect to external actions.

External, visible actions are effects, and must have a cause. But what is the cause of these external actions? Volitions certainly. Willing to walk, produces walking. In like manner, willing, or voluntary exertion, produces every other external effect, which can be attributed to us as agents. Their power, then, to perform or not perform these external actions, is volition. For volition is the power, that produces those effects or actions. Hence, as liberty is a power to act, or produce such external effects, and it is our volitions which produce them, then volition is liberty. For we see, this power is volition ; and they say, this power is liberty. Of course, liberty and volition are the same thing. That this is not a just notion of liberty, we have already shown.

We may now examine their power in relation to the acts of the will. Here we are to view volitions as effects, and the power of which they speak is the cause of them. Here the difficulty is, to learn what they mean by power. We will grant there is such a power as they contend for ; and our object now is, to ascertain what it is. A power, and its operations, are objects of distinct consideration. For a power, if it do not operate, if it remain in a dormant state, will never produce any effect. It is by operating that it produces effects. Now the question is, what will put this power in operation ? Some antecedent power ? What will put that in operation ? Some other antecedent power ? We see this is only running back *ad infinitum*, without ever arriving at a first power. To ascertain what they must mean by this power, if they mean any thing, the following self-evident propositions demand attention.

1. If mankind were as incapable of the feelings of pleasure and pain, as rocks are, they would be as inactive. And if they have a capacity for pleasure and pain, yet—2. If there were no objects in existence, they would still remain inactive. And, 3. If objects did exist, yet if they were never in the least degree to give them any pleasure, or pain, they would still remain inactive. Three things, then, are absolutely necessary to action. 1. A capacity for pleasure and pain. 2. Objects to please and disgust us. 3. Real pleasure, or pain, excited by those objects. Each of these is so essential to action, if either is wanting, no action will exist ; the universe would never have had any existence. And these propositions appear to me to be self-evident. The first is certainly a self-evident truth. And

if any should say the other two are not, they must admit, they are necessary inferences from the first proposition. If men had no capacity for pleasure and pain, they would be as inactive as rocks. For they would be as destitute of any active principle as inanimate matter. There is no excitement to action, in a being which has no feeling. For feeling is the only internal excitement. Hence if no objects to affect him existed, he would not feel, or be the subject of pleasure and pain. And if objects do exist, yet do not impress him, as those do not which are not seen, or come in contact with our bodily senses, or be presented in some other way to the mind, still he has no feeling. And where there is no feeling, there is no excitement to action ; and where there is no excitement, actions can never have existence. Whether these remarks render the three first propositions above stated any more evident, is a doubt in my mind. If they have been made more evident, it is because I have stated them in different words ; and not because the illustrations are clearer than the propositions themselves.

This conclusion now follows ; that if a power to act or not to act means any thing, a capacity for pleasure and pain must be the thing intended by it. Because, without such a capacity existing some where, there would be no such thing as action in the universe. For powers incapable of pleasure and pain will never act. They have no excitement in their nature to action. They are incapable of being put in operation, by any quality inherent in them.

Hence, according to the definition of liberty we are now examining, it is a capacity for pleasure and pain. But is this the true idea of liberty ? Is any man at liberty to say, whether objects shall please or disgust him or not ? This notion of liberty has been already refuted.

From the whole that has been said in this essay, it appears, that liberty does not consist in any power, or operation of the mind. Neither a capacity for pleasure and pain, nor sensations of pleasure and pain, nor desires, nor volitions, constitute liberty. Hence liberty is not a quality of the mind, or of a moral agent ; unless we consider a privilege a quality. We may now proceed to show what liberty is.

The unlearned define liberty in different words ; yet their definitions amount to the same thing. And their definition is the result of their feelings and experience ; and of course is as just as any given by the learned. They commonly say, *to act as they please is liberty.* So far and so long as they can act as they please, or as they have a mind to act, they enjoy all the liberty they can conceive of, and all they desire. Perhaps a better definition than this cannot be given of liberty. Let us now attend to the things implied in it.

1. What do they mean by action ? By this they undoubtedly mean two things ; *willing*, and the *effects* which are connected with the will. They, therefore, would distinguish between *liberty of will*, and *liberty of action*. For they might enjoy the one, and not the other.

2. What do they mean by pleasure ? They say they are free, when they can act according to their *pleasure*. They mean their wishes, or desires. If objects please them, it is their wish to obtain them ; if they disgust them, they wish to avoid them. It is their pleasure to obtain whatever pleases, and shun whatever offends them ; which is no more than saying, it is their desire to enjoy the former, and avoid the pain the latter gives them. These are the only ideas of importance to be attended to, in their definition of liberty. Accordingly, when they have desires to get possession of an object, which pleases them, they wish to have every act exist necessary to their end. The first act is volition. Their desire prompts them to a voluntary exertion, which is the first thing necessary to their end. If any thing should *restrain*, or prevent their putting forth the voluntary exertion to which their desires prompt them, they would say they are not free, their liberty of choosing according to their pleasure is abridged. And if any thing should *constrain*, or oblige them, to choose or will any thing contrary to their desire, they would view their liberty of choice detroyed. If two objects were before a person, one of which was very pleasing, and the other very disgustful to him ; if he was effectually *restrained* from choosing the agreeable, & was *constrained* to choose the disagreeable object, I ask, would he not feel and say, that his liberty of will was abridged, and destroyed ? In this case a person is restrained from choosing agreeably to his desire, and constrained to will in opposition to it. If this were a law of our nature, obliging us to will in direct opposition to our feelings and desires, would not mankind be in a most unhappy condition ? Let any one reflect, how he must feel in such a state, to have his will always crossing and opposing his desires ; he must at once be convinced, such a condition would be most unhappy and afflictive.

On the other hand, if he never finds any thing preventing or hindering his choosing objects according to his wish, does he not enjoy all the liberty of will he can desire ? With respect to liberty of will, what more can a person desire, than to will according to his wishes ? Or, than to have the acts of his will subject to his pleasure ? This is the highest liberty of will, of which it is possible to form any conception. The will operates, or acts, free from the influence of any *restraint*, or *constraint*. There is no power, which does or can restrain men from willing as they desire, or constrain them to will contrary to it, except the divine power. Between the strongest desire of the heart, and choosing the object of that desire, God has established an infallible connexion. He certainly will not exert his power in opposition to his own appointment. Hence he will never oblige men to exert their wills in opposition to their desires. And no other power in the universe can destroy a connexion, which he has established. Accordingly the liberty of the will never will, and never can, be abridged. Hence mankind do, and ever will, enjoy the privilege of willing agreeably to their desires, or pleasure. This *privilege* is liberty. And this privilege is made sure and certain to men, by the unalterable determination of Jehovah.

When I say, we are at liberty to will according to our desires, my meaning is, according to the strongest desire, at the time we make our choice. Mankind often have desires, each of which cannot be gratified at the same time. When desires contend, the strongest will prevail, and determine the will. We have now explained what is intended by liberty of will. Our state and condition is such, that we enjoy uninterruptedly the privilege of choosing according to our strongest desires. No power, which operates as a restraint or constraint, can deprive us of this privilege.

Liberty of action is a privilege of acting, externally, agreeably to our voluntary exertions. When a person's feet are bound with cords, he is not at liberty to walk. If he exerts himself for this purpose, a superior force operates against him, and deprives him of the privilege of acting agreeably to his exertions. This force is a restraint ; it prevents the existence of the action willed. And when a person is carried by a superior force to prison, contrary to his will, his liberty is destroyed. This constraining force produces effects contrary to what he wills, and deprives him of the privilege of acting according to his choice

Thus liberty of action may be, and sometimes is, abridged. God has established a general, but not a universal connexion between voluntary exertion, and the action, or effect, willed. Accordingly mankind generally, though they do not always, act according to their choice. This liberty may be destroyed by *restraining* and *constraining* forces. And when we are made to act contrary to our wills, the actions are not ours ; as agents, we do not produce them, and of course are not answerable for them.

Can any person desire any other or greater liberty, than to act as he wills ? When those actions follow, which his will is exerted to produce, what more can he desire ? But this privilege God has granted to mankind, and made the enjoyment of it, generally, sure to them by his unalterable determination. Hence he has given to man all the liberty, which it is best for him to enjoy.

That I have given a just idea of liberty, may appear more evident by attending to first principles in relation to action.

1. If we were as incapable of pleasure and pain as inanimate matter is, we should never be the subjects of desires. In this unfeeling state, we should not have any idea of good or evil. No person can, at first, get an idea of pleasure and pain, without knowing them by experience. And till he knows what pleasure and pain are, he cannot have a notion of relative good and evil. If men could perceive, as they now do, and at the same time had no more feeling than lifeless matter, they would not know what ideas the terms pleasure and pain, good and evil, convey. As well might a man born blind know what is meant by light and colors ; or a deaf man, what is meant by sounds. This is too evident to be denied. But if mankind had no feelings, and no idea of good and evil, desires could not possibly have an existence. For good and evil are the only objects of desire. Whatever is agreeable, we desire to attain ; and whatever is disgustful, we wish to avoid. But are objects ever desired by us, however good or evil in reality, if they are unknown to us ? When we have once felt pleasure and pain, whatever we apprehend will give us pleasure is desired ; and whatever in our view will give us pain, we feel an aversion to it. Hence if we had no feelings, we should have no idea of good and evil, and no desire for one object or aversion to another. Accordingly, that the feelings of pleasure and pain are necessary to the operations of desire, is a first principle, which all ought to admit.

2. If mankind had no feelings and desires, they would never act ; or, in other words, they would never seek one thing, or avoid another. For they would exist in a state of perfect indifference. If no objects are desired, none will be sought. This is a truth so evident, nothing can make it plainer.

3. In a state in which mankind have nothing to seek, volitions and external actions are needless. For in every volition and external action, the attainment or avoidance of some object is aimed at. But in a state of perfect indifference, we should never aim at any thing. Of course, there would be no occasion or use for voluntary exertions, and external actions.

4. Liberty, therefore, would be a useless privilege. Is it a privilege to be at liberty to act according to our pleasure, when actions are needless, and when we have no pleasure to gratify? Is a freedom to act as our pleasures, desires, or inclinations, would dictate, of any worth, where such operations have no existence ?

Keeping these things in view, we may easily see what liberty is, and how the idea of it is first acquired. Children are very fond of play things. A top affords them much pleasure. They have strong desires to amuse themselves with it. Whilst playing with it, without the least hindrance or opposition from any quarter, they enjoy liberty. They follow their inclinations, will and act as their desires prompt them, without any opposition. But if a restraint could be laid on their minds, so as to prevent those voluntary exertions which are necessary to put their bodies in motion, they would then experience an opposition to willing. This would give them uneasiness, and excite complaints. Because they cannot will as they wish. There are hindrances and obstacles in the way. If, also, they should will to run, and some person were to hold them and prevent the actions willed, then they experience opposition. This would give them uneasiness, and excite complaints.

Now they have experienced two very different conditions. The first in which they acted agreeably to their wishes, without opposition or hindrance ; the other, in which they experience such opposition as wholly prevents their acting as their inclinations prompt them. These two conditions they will compare together, and discern a great difference in them. The ideas they have of this difference they cannot communicate without words. That condition in which they act without any hindrance, is called a state of freedom or liberty ; a state in which they act freely. In this state they enjoy what is called liberty or freedom. And what is this, but the privilege of willing and acting according to their wishes and inclinations ; or pursuing the objects of their desire without any hindrance ? They might call the other condition, in which opposition prevents their acting as they wish, a state of bondage ; a state in which they do not follow their own inclinations, but are obliged to act contrary to their desires, and as other agents dictate. Hence liberty implies a state or condition, in which moral agents act as they please : a state in which they experience no hindrance, no opposition, and meet no obstacle to prevent their going the way their hearts lead them.

This teaches, that all our sensations of pleasure and pain, and our desires, are antecedent to the need or use of liberty. For if we did not experience these operations, there would be nothing to prompt us to will, or act, in any sense. There would be no end for us to answer by any exertion, because there is nothing which we have the least inclination to seek. But when we experience these desires, then we wish to act without any hindrance. The privilege of gratifying the feelings of the heart, without any hindrance, without meeting any opposition to prevent the actions which are necessary, is an object earnestly desired. This privilege, or liberty of acting, is highly valued by every moral agent. So that liberty is a precious privilege, rather than a quality or property, or any operation of the mind. Liberty does not consist in any action or operation of the mind ; but is a privilege of acting without any obstacle to prevent. It is an absurdity, to say that liberty and voluntary action are the same thing. If voluntary exertion is an action, and this action is liberty, then liberty is action of action. Liberty of action is a very common phrase. And if liberty and voluntary exertion are the same thing, and voluntary exertion is also an action, then liberty and action are convertible terms. Use the word action instead of liberty, then the liberty of action is nothing but *the action of action*. Those who assert that liberty is nothing but voluntary exertion, have no way to avoid this absurdity. But if liberty is the privilege of acting according to our wishes and inclinations, without any thing to restrain us, this absurdity is avoided. When mankind will and act agreeably to their wishes and desires, without experiencing any restraint or constraint, do they not

P

act freely ? Do they not enjoy perfect liberty ? Can they conceive of any greater liberty than this ? Is there any other *kind*, which they would prefer to it ?

I know many in answer to these interrogations would say, they wish for liberty to fly, to create, to gratify all their desires by a single act of the will. This, they might say, is a higher and more desirable kind of liberty, than any which mankind now enjoy. This statement, I would observe in reply, contains a fallacy. The thing, which they call liberty, is power. And by giving the thing a wrong name, they deceive themselves. By liberty to fly, to create, and the like, a power is the thing intended. If by power is meant volition, then a liberty to fly, for instance, is only willing this event. This is making an act of the will and liberty the same thing ; which we have already seen cannot be true. And if by power is intended a *connexion* between an act of the will and the thing willed, so that the latter shall follow the former, then by a liberty to fly they mean no more than this connexion. Whether power is an act of the will, or a connexion between willing and the thing willed, still liberty and power are not the same thing. This has already been proved. But to illustrate this fallacy more fully, let it be observed,

1. A moral agent aims at some end in every action. When he is sick, health is an object or end desired.

2. To the attainment of ends, means are necessary. Means must be used to recover health ; for this is the appointment of Jehovah. God works by means in the attainment of his ends. And according to his ordination men cannot obtain their ends, only by using the means adapted to them. If God had seen fit, ends might have been connected immediately with the will. Then nothing would have been necessary to obtain health, when we are sick, but to will it. But the determination of God is such, we cannot attain our ends, except by the intervention and use of means.

Now a person, when sick, is at liberty to use means to recover his health. He is at liberty to will, and to act, He enjoys this liberty, this privilege, and is using it. He has not power to recover health by a single act of his will, nor to give efficacy to the means he uses. Hence mankind enjoy liberty, and use it in pursuit of their ends ; when at the same time they have not power to attain them. Does a person's inability to recover his health abridge his liberty ? Surely not ; he may act with perfect freedom, as long as he has life. Do not mankind act freely, as their inclinations lead them, when laboring in the field, and attending to other pursuits of life? Yet it is not in their power, in innumerable instances, to obtain their ends. This shows there is a plain and obvious distinction between liberty and power. Men may act freely in pursuit of their ends, yet not have power to obtain them. If liberty and power were the same thing, and if men have not power to arrive at the ends they seek, they have no liberty. This notion of liberty contradicts facts. Because we know by experience it is a fact, that we are acting freely in numerous instances, where we have not power to attain what we seek, and so finally fail of it. Hence to say, a power to attain our ends is liberty, is to assert we are not free, while acting freely; which is a manifest absurdity.

To bring these remarks to a point, attention to the following things is necessary. I have a strong desire to visit a friend, who lives west from this place. A volition, which would move my body westerly, would accord with my desire. If some power should constrain me to will an opposite motion of the body, the will would act contrary to my desire. In this case I do not enjoy liberty of will. For liberty of will is a privilege of willing as my desires dictate. And if I will to have my body move to the west, yet some force carries it to the east, then liberty of action, in this instance, is destroyed. For actions directly contrary to those willed take place. But so long as the will obeys the heart, and actions are obedient to the will, I am free. I will and act agreeably to my desire. I enjoy the liberty of willing as I wish, and of acting as I wish, and in the exercise of this liberty I visit my friend. At the same time I have not power to visit him by flying over the distance he is from me. Hence our object, when we wish for liberty to fly, is power, not liberty.

We may wish to have liberty *extended*; to have a thousand events connected with the will, which are not. To have this wish gratified, our power must be *enlarged*. If God had connected flying, or the creation of a world, with an act of the will, as he has the motion of our hands, we could as easily fly, and create, as we now can move our hands. This enlargement of our power is an object ardently desired by many. By an increase or enlargement of our power in this way, our liberty would be extended beyond its present limits. But if our liberty was extended by an increase of power, it is still the same kind of liberty—a liberty to will and to act as we please. Our liberty is not greater, unless its extension is the thing meant.

If it be extended, this does not alter its nature. And it is by us-ing the words power and liberty as synonimous, that men de-ceive themselves, when they plead for a different *kind* of liberty. And this fallacy is now detected by distinguishing, as we ever ought, between liberty and power.

Liberty of action is extended, as far as external actions or events are connected with the will. A greater number of events might have been connected with the will, than now are, if God had seen fit. But connecting other events with the will, is not altering the nature of the liberty of action; it is only extending it further, or rendering it less limited. We may therefore say, that mankind cannot conceive of any kind of liberty, preferable to that which they enjoy; nor can they have any greater liber-ty, unless the extension of it is greater liberty. But they may desire more power; and no degree of power short of omnipo-tence will satisfy the unrenewed heart.

6. We may now inquire, whether liberty is consistent with ne-cessity. It is the opinion of many, that every kind of necessity is inconsistent with liberty. For a clear elucidation of this part of the present subject. the word *necessity* must be defined. It is not my design, however, to explain all the senses in which the words *necessary, necessity, impossible, unable,* and the other like terms, are used. I shall define the word necessity, so far as is requisite to a conclusion, whether any *kind* of necessity is inconsistent with liberty.

A certain and infallible *connexion* between causes and their effects is one thing meant by necessity. If a cause might oper-ate, and its effect might be prevented at one time, and be pro-duced at another, the effect is not necessary. And in this case, there is no certain connexion between the cause and the effect. For the connexion is not infallible, it may be destroyed. But where the connexion between causes and effects is certain, there the effect is necessary. Water will run towards the centre. Between this motion of water towards the centre, and the cause which produces this motion, there is an infallible connexion. This motion of water is a necessary effect. When force is used to destroy this connexion, ineffectually, we say it is *impossible* to overcome it. The meaning is, no force applied, in this in-stance, is equal to the force of the cause. In this sense the word *unable,* and many others of the same import, are used. In such instances, causes operate without producing the intended effect. We may, therefore, to prevent a needless circumlocution in conveying our ideas, divide necessity into *natural* and *moral*. This distinction is not founded on any difference there is in the connexion between causes and effects, where the connexion is certain and infallible ; but on the difference there is in the terms related, or connected. Hence the certain connexion between moral causes and their effects, is what I mean by a *moral necessity*. And the infallible connexion there is between natural causes and effects, is what I mean by a *natural* necessity. These are the only kinds of necessity which come into consideration, when it is to be determined, whether necessity is inconsistent with liberty. We may inquire,

1. Whether *natural* necessity is inconsistent with liberty.— Nothing, as I have already observed, can destroy liberty of will ; as will appear clearly, when we attend to moral necessity. I shall therefore, under this particular, consider natural necessity in relation to liberty of action. Here it is granted, that natural necessity is inconsistent with liberty of action. For instance, if a person wills the motion of his hands or feet, and the motion does not follow, liberty of action is destroyed at this time. Some cause in this particular instance operates, which is more powerful than the exertion of the will ; and produces *rest*, an effect opposite to the one intended. Here the connexion between the will and the effect willed, is destroyed ; and the effect, which the opposing cause produces, is necessary. Here it may be said, that the person was *unable* to move his hands or feet. It was *impossible* for him to do it. The operating cause, whatever it be, which renders the act of the will ineffectual, *restrains* him. And all restrints, which prevent the existence of the effect willed, destroy liberty of action. Restraints do not destroy liberty of action, unless they prevent the effects willed.

Again. If a person's will is exerted to move his body westward, and it is moved eastward, here the connexion between the act of the will and the effect willed is destroyed. In this particular instance, some cause or other operates with more force than the will, and renders its exertion ineffectual. Here the person experiences what is called a *constraint*. An effect contrary to the one willed takes place. When a constraning cause is sufficient to produce an effect opposite to the one willed, liberty of action, at that particular time, is destroyed.

When effects, different or opposite to those willed, take place, liberty of action is destroyed. The causes, which operate in such cases, are more powerful than the will, and overcome it.

And such causes are the things intended by *restraints*, and *con-straints*. All restraints and constraints, which are sufficient to produce effects opposite to those willed, destroy liberty of action. This, however, is but seldom the case. Generally, the effects willed take place. But when those effects exist, which are opposite to those willed and intended, we are not accountable for them. They are not *our actions*, but the effects of the cause which produced them. And we do not act according to our pleasure, unless the effects follow which are necessary to gratify our desires.

2. Inquire, whether *moral* necessity destroys liberty.

Mankind are the causes of many effects. Thousands of events are attributed to them as the cause. They are agents. They act, and produce effects. Yet it may be well to observe, they are not the *independent, efficient cause* of one effect. They are dependent on God, and cannot produce any effect without the concurrence of his agency, or contrary to his determination. Having observed this to prevent mistakes, I may now say, that the *feelings* and desires of the heart are the cause of every volition. The taste, which is the only feeling faculty of the mind, constitutes agency. It is the primary cause in man of all his actions. Those which do not proceed from this cause, are not *our* actions, but the actions of some other agent. This internal cause, by its operations, produces *every volition*. It puts the will in motion. And volitions are the first and immediate effects it produces. Between this cause and volition, God has established an infallible connexion. No power but his own, is sufficient to destroy this connexion ; and he will not destroy, what he has determined shall exist. Hence the reason, why liberty of will can never be abridged. When there is nothing to prevent our willing according to our desires or inclinations, we enjoy liberty of will. Nothing can prevent this, because God has established a certain connexion between the strongest desire of the heart, and volition. This connexion is *moral* necessity. And this necessity renders liberty of will absolutely sure and certain.

Were it not for this moral necessity, liberty of will would rest on an uncertain foundation. For sometimes we might will as we wish, and sometimes we might not. It would be altogether uncertain, whether such volitions would follow as we might wish. The will might act in opposition to our inclinations. If it did, we could never carry our desires into effect. Not only so, but the will might produce effects in opposition to our desires. But now it must be obedient to the heart. It must will the effects we wish to have exist.

Would any man feel contented to be in a state, in which he could neither will nor act according to his wishes, nor gratify any of his desires? But if there were no connexion between the heart and the will, no person would be able to will events, which it was his desire to have exist. He would not be able to act according to his inclinations and wishes. His condition would be very unhappy. And if there were a connexion, but not certain, then it would be a matter of uncertainty when he should and when he should not act as his inclinations dictated. This would be a very undesirable condition for such an agent as man.

But the connexion between the heart and the will is certain and infallible. It cannot be destroyed. It, therefore, infallibly secures liberty of will to every moral agent. This necessity or connexion, let it be remembered, is not liberty. Liberty is the privilege of willing as we wish. And this necessity secures this privilege to us. Our liberty of will, therefore, is certain, as this necessity is infallible. Hence moral necessity is so far from destroying liberty, that it is the foundation on which it rests. Take away the foundation, and our liberty is effectually destroyed.

In the next place, are liberty of action and moral necessity *consistent with each other?*

The immediate design of volition is, to put the body or some particular member of it, in motion; and by this means to produce other external effects, which are necessary to obtain the objects desired. If I have a desire to eat an apple lying on the table before me, by an exertion of the will my hand is moved directly to it, and from thence to my mouth. It it be growing on a tree, and I wish to enjoy it, the body must move to it, and by a stroke of my staff the stem must be broken, that it may fall to the ground. Here not only bodily motions, but the motion of other things, as the staff, for instance, are produced. These are the effects of volition. And as it is by the instrumentality of the body, that we produce alterations and effects in other things around us, the immediate operation of the will is on the body And by means of the body every other effect is produced, requisite to the attainment of the objects of our desire. And it is often the case, that a series of external effects are necessary to reach our desired ends. Accordingly, all the effects contained in such a series are the objects of volition, and are produced by it ; and the last effect in the series is the ultimate object of the will.

It is therefore easy to see, when there is nothing to prevent the existence of the effects willed, that we enjoy liberty of action without any interruption. If I make exertions to walk directly east, and nothing prevents my moving in this course, I certainly enjoy all the liberty of walking in this direction which can be conceived of, or desired. But if by the operation of some cause I am *restrained*, or prevented from walking in this direction ; and at the same time am *constrained* by some superior power to move in a western course, my liberty of walking easterly is destroyed. Causes, which prevent my acting as I chose, are restraints ; and those, which make me act, as I would not, are constraints. Of course, both restraints and constraints, so far as they operate, abridge liberty of action. And those effects which are produced by extrinsic causes or agents, whether restraining or constraining, are not *our actions*. Because they are not the effects of our will, but of some foreign cause or agent, external to us, which we have not power to resist ; and we are not accountable for them. But if restraining or constraining causes operate in opposition to the will, yet the will overcomes them, and produces the actions intended ; then the actions are our own, and we are responsible for them. Because they are such as were intended, and are produced by the operations of the will. And so far as constraints and restraints oppose the will, liberty of action is impeded, but not destroyed, if the will at last overcomes. We always act freely, when we do the thing intended. And when the thing intended is done without any impediment, we enjoy the most perfect liberty of action. But so far as the will is opposed, liberty is abridged ; or we do not act so easily and freely. It is now evident, that when we act as we choose, we enjoy liberty of action. We are now to inquire, whether necessity destroys liberty of action.

Such a *connexion* between causes and effects, as renders the existence of the latter *absolutely certain*, is *necessity*. Such effects are always necessary. Accordingly a certain, and infallible connexion between volition, and the effect or action willed, is necessity. If we act freely, they certainly follow the exertions of the will. Does this necessity destroy liberty of action ? So far from it, that without it we should be wholly deprived of liberty. If such an infallible connexion, between the will and the action willed, were not established, the will might exert itself, but no effect would follow. But does a person enjoy liberty of action, if the effects intended and willed cannot be produced ? But if the actions chosen certainly follow, he enjoys liberty in the highest perfection. So far then as the connexion between volition and the action willed is certain, liberty is secured. Accordingly, if any external cause by its operation destroys this connexion, it takes our liberty of acting as we wish entirely from us. God has not established an absolute infallible connexion, between every volition and its intended effect. Had he seen fit to do this, liberty of action could never be destroyed, in any one instance, any more than liberty of will. As this connexion is not universal, does not extend at all times to every volition, this is the reason why liberty of action may be, and sometimes is, destroyed. For sometimes external causes, and other agents, by their operations prevent the existence of the actions which we will. Or, in other words, by the influence of constraints or restraints this connexion is destroyed, and the actions chosen do not follow. When this is the case, in every such particular instance we are deprived of our liberty. Accordingly this infallible connexion between the thing willed and the will, or what is here called necessity, is essential to the enjoyment of liberty. So far as this prevails, our liberty is secured; and as often as it is destroyed, we are deprived of liberty. Every one must therefore see, if he attends candidly to the subject, that this necessity is so far from destroying our liberty, that it is essential to the preservation and enjoyment of it.

Let us suppose a person to have strong desires to visit a friend. Volitions are necessary, we know, to accomplish his wishes ; and also external actions. By the operation of his desires, volitions are produced; and by the operation of volitions, external actions are effected. If there was no connexion between the desires of the heart and volitions, desires would operate in vain. For no volitions would follow. And if there were no connexion between the will and external actions, the operations of the will would be ineffectual. Of course the person could never visit his friend. But if a connexion is established, between his desires and volitions, and between his volitions and external actions, then he can act as he pleases, and gratify his heart in visiting his friend.

If the matter was left wholly to man, which would he prefer,

Q

that condition in which no such connexions are established, or that in which they are? He would certainly choose the latter. And if the latter, then the necessity by which he acts, corresponds with his own feelings. And it is obvious, from what has been said, if no such connexion had been established by our Maker, his creatures never would have enjoyed any liberty of will, or liberty of action. So that the necessity of choosing as we feel, or according to our pleasure, and acting as we choose, is essential to the existence and enjoyment of liberty. And our Maker has granted and secured this privilege to us, by establishing an infallible or necessary connexion between our desires and volitions, and between our volitions and actions. There is, therefore, no ground to object against this kind of necessity, as being inconsistent with liberty.

One great reason, why so many consider necessity as inconsistent with liberty, arises from their using words without any definite meaning. Another reason is, they indulge themselves in a careless, indefinite mode of reasoning. Because necessity sometimes destroys liberty of action, they infer it is always, and in every sense, inconsistent with liberty. This, all will see, is false reasoning. If all would affix a definite meaning to their terms, and reason correctly, they would not so often reject the truth, and embrace errors, as they now do. But this requires so much attention, mental exertion, and labor, they are not willing to submit to it. And to justify themselves in the indulgence of this mental indolence, they are always declaiming against metaphysicks as a fruitful source of error. Yet it is believed, that if all men should neglect that correct mode of *thinking* and *reasoning*, which at this day is called metaphysicks, it would not be many ages before truth on moral subjects would be generally banished from the world, and errors universally prevail. When a person asserts, that necessity destroys liberty, would he wish to have it made certain that he should choose and act according to his pleasure, or not? If all men desire the privilege of choosing and acting according to their pleasure, and to have this made infallibly certain, why do they declaim against necessity?

Furthermore, if our pleasure is what Arminians mean by a self determining power, we surely have it. For our pleasure is, to act according to the desires of the heart. And all our volitions and actions proceed from the heart. If objects please us, desires arise to enjoy them ; and those desires give rise to all the volitions and actions necessary to have possession of them ; and in obtaining them we act according to our pleasure ; and when we enjoy them, our pleasure is done. If acting in this sense according to our pleasure is what they mean by a self determining power, (viz.) that our pleasure produces our volitions ; it is granted that we have this power. But this power destroys *indifference*, and is consistent with *necessity*. To say we have a power to produce, and govern our pleasure, is false ; but to say we are governed by our pleasure is true, and corresponds with our wishes. If then they admit our pleasure, in the sense explained, is a self determining power, to be consistent they must also admit our ideas of liberty. If they would do this, the dispute between them and us would be ended.

****

ESSAY XVI.

Whether liberty is necessary to vice and virtue; and, if not, for what purposes is it requisite, in moral agents ?

It is, I believe, a general opinion, that liberty is necessary to the *existence* of vice and virtue. But the truth of this sentiment may be questioned. And if, when examined, it should not appear to be well founded, the inquiry will be, why is liberty requisite in a moral agent ? For all will grant, that without it mankind would be very imperfect moral agents. I shall, therefore, inquire,

1. Whether liberty is necessary to the existence of vice and virtue. According to the description given of liberty in the preceding essay, any person will clearly perceive, it is not essential either to vice, or virtue. For vice and virtue must exist antecedent to the need, or use of liberty. For an illustration of the truth in relation to this subject, let the following suppositions be carefully examined.

Suppose a person to have an inveterate hatred against his

neighbor, which will lead him to take his life on the first favorable opportunity; I ask, is he not a murderer? Does not this hatred, or as the law defines it, this malice prepense, constitute the sin, or crime, denominated murder? From the time this hatred exists in his heart, is he not a murderer in the sight of God? He says, in his word, he that hateth his brother is a murderer. And if we had a knowledge of his heart, should not we view him in the same light? If vice and virtue belong to the heart, it is certain that this person is guilty of the crime called murder. For taking the life of a neighbor, is only the fruit or effect of a murderous disposition. Let us suppose further, that this person is born with this hatred, not only to his neighbor but to all mankind, which will prompt him to take the lives of his fellow men, as often as he judges he can do it with impunity. Is he not born with a murderous heart? If mankind knew he had this disposition, would they not have the same view of his heart, they have of the heart of one who has committed a murderous deed? Would they not stand in fear of him? Would they not watch him, and guard themselves against his assaults? I may now ask, is liberty necessary to the existence of this murderous disposition? The person, according to the supposition, is born with it. Is his birth an effect of his choice? Is this disposition a voluntary action, or the fruit and effect of his will? Is it an effect, which was produced by the operation of this person's agency? Surely not. And if not, the liberty of this person was not necessary to the existence of this murderous disposition.

Again. Suppose a person is born with a benevolent disposition of heart. And such a supposition is not impossible; for many believe, that some persons are sanctified from the womb. Is not this benevolent innate disposition a moral virtue? Does it not lay a foundation in him to be pleased with the divine character and government? Will it not, as an internal active principle, influence him to serve God with fidelity and delight? But was the liberty of this person, in any sense, necessary to the existence of this benevolent disposition? We may as well suppose the exercise of liberty in an agent is necessary to his *very existence.*

Furthermore. Calvinistic divines believe, that all mankind are born with depraved, corrupt hearts. And it is presumed, they will not assert, that the depravity of heart with which they are born is produced by their *own voluntary exertions.* And if they say, this depravity consists in voluntary exertions, yet they will not believe, that the agent produced them. For this would represent him as acting *voluntarily*, before he had any volition. It implies the same absurdity, which is implied in saying that a person creates himself. It is obvious, that, with respect to those appetites or dispositions with which we are born, they are not produced by our agency. We are no more the cause of them, than we are of our own existence. It is as inconsistent to suppose, that we produce our own faculties, as our own existence. And if it be said, we have no faculties, and the mind is nothing but our various mental operations united, still our *first* operations are not produced by us. For if operations constitute the mind, till they exist, there is no mind in being to operate. Accordingly the *first operations*, which constitute the mind, the mind could not produce ; unless it can act before it exists. To suppose the mind is nothing but operations united, does not relieve any difficulty. For then the *first operations*, which according to this scheme must be called the heart, constitute that depravity with which we are born. It therefore clearly follows, that all, who believe we are born with depraved hearts, must admit, that this depravity is no more our production, than our own existence is. Of course liberty is no more necessary to the existence of original depravity than it is to our having a being in this world. Neither is it necessary to original holiness of heart.

Adam was created in the image of God. And Calvinists believe he was created in the moral, as well as in the natural, image of his Maker. Accordingly he was created with a benevolent heart. And this benevolence of heart was no more the effect of his agency, than his own existence. Was his liberty necessary to his own existence? Could no tsuch an agent, as Adam was, be created, unless he exercised liberty in his creation ? If not, it was impossible for such an agent to be produced. For he could not exercise liberty, before he existed. And the exercise of liberty was not necessary to the existence of a benevolent heart. For this was a quality given him in his creation. And he could not act *freely* in its production. For agents cannot act at all, much less freely, before they have existence. His liberty, therefore, considered as an agent, was not necessary to the existence of a benevolent heart.

These observations will apply with equal force to prove, that men do not act freely in that change wrought in them, termed regeneration. If in this change something is created, as Calvinists believe there is, it is not produced by the agency of man. For it is granted, he has not power to *create* any thing. As the virtuous disposition, or exercise, or whatever it may be called, is not produced by man as the agent, but by the power of God, the sinner exercises no liberty in the production of it.

Liberty is the privilege of a moral agent ; a privilege of acting according to his pleasure, or as his feelings dictate. Such an agent must exist, antecedently to the need, or use of liberty. And if he is a complete moral agent, he has moral as well at natural faculties. And his moral faculty must be vicious or virtuous, the moment it has existence, as has been made evident in a previous essay. If this cannot be denied, it is certain that liberty is not necessary to the existence of either vice or virtue in the heart of moral agents. This is not only evident from the description given of liberty in the fourteenth Essay ; but it is true, if we adopt the opinion generally received respecting it. Orthodox divines have commonly said, that liberty is a *power* of willing. If the will, or a power of willing, be a just definition of liberty, then the terms will and liberty mean the same thing. According to the definition, it is asked, whether the will is vicious, or virtuous, or neither ? If it be answered, that the will is either virtuous, or vicious, then nothing is predicated of the will, but what may be affirmed of liberty, if liberty and will are the same thing. It therefore follows, that the liberty of moral agents is either virtuous or vicious. But the will did not produce itself. It was not created by man, but by his Creator. And as man, considered as an agent, did not exercise any liberty in the production of his will, because he did not create it, yet the moment it exists, it is either vicious or virtuous; it is therefore evident, that liberty is not necessary to the existence of vice and virtue in a moral agent. For no agent can exercise liberty, before it exists. It is said by many, that the faculty, or power of willing, is liberty. And it is created with the quality of vice, or virtue. But the will, with either of these qualities, is not produced by man, but by his Creator. And the will, the moment it exists, with the quality of vice or virtue, constitutes the depravity with which we are born. And as men do not exercise any liberty in the production of this depraved will, their liberty is not necessary to its existence ; and of course it is not essential to the existence of vice and virtue.

Some however say, that liberty consists in spontaneous, voluntary exertion. They also assert, that all vice and virtue consist in voluntary exertions, or exercises. This makes liberty, volition, vice and virtue, the same thing. According to this representation, the first volition of a moral agent constitutes his orignal depravity. But who is the agent that produces this first, depraved, vicious volition ? Is man the agent ? If not, then there is no liberty exercised by him in the existence of that, which constitutes his original depravity. But if it be said, that man is the agent, in this case, because voluntary exercises constitutes agency, this involves on absurdity. For it makes agency, and the effect it produces, the same thing. Because it is said, that volition is agency ; and volition, at the same time, is the effect it produces. This cannot be true with respect to the first original volition in man, whatever it may be in relation to those which are subsequent to it. Therefore, according to this definition of liberty, it is not necessary to the existence of that original depravity with which men are born. For with respect to this first volition, which constitutes their original depravity, and from which all subsequent vicious exercises proceed, they were not at liberty to have it, or not to have it.

Furthermore; what is meant by the phrase, liberty is necessary to the existence of vice and virtue ? Does it mean, that the original fountain of either vice or virtue in man, is produced by himself, and he is at liberty to produce it, or not ? Whether the original depravity of man consists in taste, or will, or the first voluntary operation of the will, will any say, we create or produce them ? We might with as much propriety say, we create ourselves. For no man can create a taste, or a will, or the first exercise of his will, any more than he can create himself. If not, he certainly is not at liberty to be either vicious, or virtuous, any more than he is at liberty to exist, or not exist. Indeed, in whatever light we may view the subject, it is apparent, that liberty is not necessary to the existence of either vice or virtue. For whether we shall be created with either a vicious or virtuous character, does not depend on our pleasure, any more than our being.

Some are often objecting to this representation, saying, if a sinful inclination does not depend on our exertions, we are not blameable. This will be attended to, under the subject of praise and blameworthiness. Here it may be observed, that all who believe the doctrine of total depravity, grant we are born with

corrupt hearts. These will admit, that liberty is not necessary
to the existence of vice or virtue.

Whether the dealings of God with Adam, as especially his establishing a connexion between his moral character and that of
his posterity, was inconsistent with wisdom and justice, is a
subject distinct from the present. We know it is a fact, that
Adam's posterity derive a depraved heart from him. And all,
who believe God is holy, wise, and just, will admit that the connexion he did establish between our first parents and their posterity was consistent with his attributes, whether they can clearly see the consistency or not. The author has written on this
subject, and advanced a theory which was new to him, never
having seen any part of it in print ; but whether he will ever
publish it is uncertain. It is in his view a theory that avoids the
difficulties, which have hitherto attended it, and which agrees
with reason and facts.

But though liberty is not necessary to the existence of vice
or virtue, yet is it essential to render us worthy of praise and
blame ? It would appear, on examination, that it is no more
necessary to praise and blame, than it is to the existence of vice
or virtue. But as the subject of praise and blame is discussed
in a subsequent essay, to prevent repetitions, the reader is referred to that for satisfaction on this point. We may now consider,

II. For what ends, or purposes, liberty is necessary in a moral agent. Though it is not essential to one thing, yet it may
be for another. And it is requisite for the following purposes.

1. If we did not enjoy the privilege of choosing as we wish,
and acting as we choose, we should not be complete agents. A
complete agent is capable of choosing and acting agreeably to
the desires of the heart. So that, if he has desires for objects,
yet is not at liberty to put forth those volitions, and produce
those external actions necessary to obtain the objects of his desire, and avoid the objects of his aversion, he is not a complete
agent. For a complete agent is able to attain, generally, whatever he loves, and shun whatever he hates. If God had not established a connexion between our desires and volitions, and
external actions, we might have desires, but they would never
produce any effects, nor be able to reach the objects which
would gratify them. In this case the agency of man would be
very imperfect, and incomplete. Accordingly a liberty to choose

agreeably to his wishes, and to act as he chooses, is essentially necessary to complete agency.

2. It is necessary for us, in order that we may act out the internal inclinations of the heart. The desires of the heart would
never appear in any external acts, if we had not the liberty of
choosing and acting. Of course moral agents could never have
any knowledge of each other's characters. As we have no intuitive view of each other's hearts, and become acquainted with
each other's characters only by external, visible signs, or actions, if the heart was incapable of manifesting itself in this
way, we must forever remain ignorant of each other's deserts. But it is necessary, to answer many purposes in the
moral government of the world, for creatures to have a knowledge of each other's characters. And in order to this, liberty
of choosing and acting is requisite.

3. It is necessary to social intercourse. We might have
strong desires, yet if we could not express them, we could not
have any social intercourse with each other, nor with our Maker.
For if he did not enjoy the same liberty, the desires of his heart
would not be manifested. And without a knowledge of his
character, we could never enjoy him. As true happiness consists in the enjoyment of God, and the social intercourse of holy
creatures with each other, liberty is essentially necessary to our
present and future felicity.

4. It is necessary, in order for us to render unto God *all* that
service, which he requires of us. Generally, to do the things
required of us, external actions are necessary, as in teaching,
reproving, exhorting, and many other duties. But if we had
not the liberty of choosing and acting, the most benevolent heart
could not perform all those duties, which are enjoined.

I now ask, is a person a complete agent, who is not at liberty to attain the objects he desires, or to manifest the internal feelings of the heart, or to have social intercourse with men, or perform the duties required of him? If not, then liberty is necessary to answer ends unspeakably interesting and important.

If we did not enjoy the liberty of choosing and acting agreeably to our inclinations and desires, we should be very imperfect, and incomplete agents. But our Maker has established a
connexion between our original appetites, or primary principles
of action, and all our subsequent actions ; which are necessary
to the accomplishment of our pleasure, and the gratification of our
desires. This established connexion secures to us the privilege

R

called liberty, and enables us to act as we please, and renders as complete agents, as far as this connexion extends.

＊＊◆＊◆◆◆◆＊◆＊

ESSAY XVII.

On Motives, with their influence in determining the will.

By a motive, I mean any thing which moves, excites, or induces an agent to act ; to choose one thing, and refuse another. Motives are causes of action. I do not mean, that they are efficient, independent causes ; but they are, what are commonly called secondary causes. They are as really the causes of our voluntary actions, as rain, heat, and the earth, are causes of vegetation. They are the ground and reason of our acting, at all times, as we do act. Motives may, therefore, be divided into two general classes, *internal* and *external.*

1. By internal motives, I mean, every thing in the heart or taste, which stimulates to action. The appetite of hunger impels, or excites, to action. The same is true with respect to all the appetites with which we are born.

Our affections and passions excite to action. They operate as causes, which put the will in motion. They produce, or give rise to voluntary exertions. This agrees with the experience of all men ; for all experience the operation of these internal principles, and find they are stimulated by them to every action they perform.

Every language also is constructed on a belief, that we are governed by our internal appetites, and our desires to obtain that which is agreeable, and avoid whatever is painful. Hence arise the phrases, in every language, of being impelled by hunger, thirst, and the passions. Indeed deprive moral agents of those internal principles of action, their agency would be destroyed, and all action would cease.

These internal principles are antecedent to all our voluntary exertions. They move us to act. They are the internal causes, which produce volitions. These internal motives govern, and determine the will. Hence it is wholly improper to say, that these internal principles are governed by motives. They are the *primary* principles of action in moral agents, and of course are not governed by antecedent principles within us ; for there are none, which are antecedent to them. Being *primary*, they are not governed by any principles we possess ; but they govern, direct and determine the will. This faculty is entirely under the influence of the heart ; but the heart is never directly under the influence of the will. Having explained what I mean by internal motives, I shall attend,

2. To the influence of external motives. External motives include all objects, which either please or disgust us. Every individual object which pleases, excites us to those actions, which are necessary to obtain the agreeable object. And all those objects, which displease, excite us to those actions, which are necessary to avoid them, that we may shun the pain they might occasion. All objects, therefore, of every kind, whether agreeable or disagreeable, when in view of the mind, are motives to action. I say, in view of the mind ; because objects, which are not perceived, or of which we are wholly ignorant, can never please or disgust. Of course, till they are perceived, they have no influence. This will lead us to consider the influence of motives.

How do external objects operate on the mind, and influence it to action ? It is wholly by *affecting* it. And they never affect it any farther, than they excite painful, or pleasant sensations. Agreeable and painful sensations are feelings ; and the only feelings we ever experience. It is by exciting such sensations, that external objects affect us. If we could perceive external objects without experiencing either pleasure or pain, they would not affect us. In relation to all such objects, the mind would be in a state of perfect indifference. For to be in a state of indifference in relation to any object, is to be unaffected by it. But we are unaffected, if the object is neither agreeable, nor disagreeable. But when objects either please or disgust us, we are then no longer in a state of indifference ; we are affected either for or against them. Objects, so far as they please or displease, impress us ; and when they do neither, they make no impression. Hence they act upon the mind by exciting pleasant or painful sensations. And the whole influence of external motives consists in the impression they make on the mind. So far as they affect or impress the mind, they influence us to action; and 'no farther. Here it is well to observe, that as the heart, or taste, is the only feeling faculty of the mind, or the only faculty which is the subject of pleasure and pain, it is the only faculty, which is affected and impressed by external objects. And when objects are perceived by the understanding, they always affect the heart agreeably or disagreeably, in a greater or less degree; though they often affect us so slightly, that we take no notice of it. But the heart is never in a state of indifference in relation to any object, when in view of the mind. When external objects impress the heart, they excite it to action; and it is in this way only, that motives have influence. This may be more clearly explained by observing, that three things are always necessary to action. These are, as observed in a former essay, *a faculty* which can be the subject of pleasure and pain; *objects* to make an impression upon it; and an *impression* actually made, through the medium of the understanding.

This shows in what sense motives, both internal and external, are necessary to give rise to volitions; or, in other words, to determine the will. Every volition is an effect, which must have a cause. And our internal principles of action, together with external objects, are the secondary causes, which produce volitions. And unless these causes operate conjointly, the will would never be determined. External objects, by pleasing or displeasing, excite internal principles to action, and by their actions or operations, volitions are produced; the will is put in motion, and exerts itself to give existence to every subsequent act, requisite to attain the objects at which an agent aims.

Having explained in what sense I use the word motive, as including both the internal and external cause of volitions, and the manner in which external objects have influence in determining the will; we may proceed to consider the *strength* of motives.

These appetites or propensities of the heart, with which we are born, are the primary principles of action in moral agents. Our pleasures, pains, and desires are the affections, or operations of our appetites. They are the cause of our voluntary exercises. And our desires are weak or strong, in proportion to the strength or weakness of our appetites. The keener our appetite of hunger is, the stronger is our desire for food. And this is true with respect to all our appetites and desires. The strength of an appetite is not always the same; it may be one hour strong, and the next weak and faint. Hence the reason why our desires for the same object are one day warm, and the next cool and languid. And the strongest appetite, while it remains the strongest, has the governing influence. They are often operating also in opposition to each other. The drunkard, for instance, has a desire to gratify his appetite with spirituous liquor, and a desire to keep the money he must part with to purchase it. Both these desires cannot be gratified, at the same time. There is a struggle, a warfare between them. In this warfare the strongest will prevail, and the weaker will be denied. Within a short period, the weakest may become the strongest; aud when this is the case it will prevail, and the other must be denied. Thus the desires of the heart are constantly opposing each other, with less or greater strength ; and by the strongest desire we are always governed. Between the strongest desire, and a choice of the object desired, there is an infallible connexion. Hence the strongest desire determines the will, and the will determines our external conduct. Accordingly the strongest desire is what I mean by the strongest *internal motive*. And the strongest desire is always strong, in proportion to the strength of its appetite. It is therefore of no consequence, whether we say the strongest appetite, or the strongest desire, determines the will ; because both assertions are true.

This shews the reason, why the conduct of mankind in this world is so changeable. It is because our appetites and desires are daily gaining the ascendancy of each other. And when an appetite becomes stronger, than the one which had previously governed, there will be an immediate change in the agent's conduct. If the same appetites and desires governed us uniformly, our conduct would not be variable. This is one reason why there is no change in the divine conduct. God is forever influenced by the same benevolent desire. He is therefore ever pursuing the same measures, and seeking the same end. And as saints and angels in heaven, are always governed by benevolent desires, their conduct will be uniformly and eternally consistent.

But it is time to show what *external motive* is the strongest. By external motives I mean all those objects, which, by affecting the heart, influence the will.

It has been shown, that external objects determine the will, by affecting the heart. When several objects are in the mind's view, the object which is the most agreeable, and from which the most pleasure is expected, is the *strongest motive*. For the object, which is the most agreeable, will excite the strongest desire in the heart, with which the determination of the will is connected. Because we always have the warmest desire for that object, which is, all things considered, the most agreeable. Hence the most agreeable object is the strongest motive ; and will have the most influence, so long as it affords the most satisfaction. This is the object, which makes the deepest impression on the heart, and excites the strongest desires. Of course this object will be chosen, or preferred to others which are less pleasing, at the time the will is determined.

Furthermore, objects which are disgustful, the will rejects. It chooses to avoid them. Hence that object, among many, which is the most disagreeable, has the greatest strength or most influence in determining the will. It must be obvious to any one, that when two objects are disgustful, if both cannot be rejected, the one most disagreeable will be avoided by voluntary exertions. On the whole, those external objects are the strongest motives, and have the most influence, which are the most agreeable, or the most disgustful ; the former to determine our choice in favor of the object, and the latter against it.

From the above illustrations it is evident, that internal and external motives perfectly harmonize in determining the will. For between the strongest desire and choice, there is an infallible connexion ; so, also, between the most agreeable object, all things considered, and choice. To see, therefore, their united and harmonious influence, let it be carefully observed, that the most agreeable object excites a stronger desire, than an object less agreeable ; and the strongest desire always determines the will ; and the most agreeable object is uniformly chosen. If, then, we consider motives as secondary causes of volition ; these internal and external motives or causes, of which an explanation has been given, jointly operate in producing the same effect, or determining the will for or against the same object.

It is foreign from my object at this time, to inquire what things, or how many, are taken into consideration, to render one object more agreeable than another. For whatever they may be, still it remains true, that the most eligible or agreeable object determines the will. And to ascertain what determines the will, is the great object of this Essay. I may not use words according to their more common sense, when I call an internal principle of action a motive ; yet these internal principles do as really have influence in determining the will, as external objects. And I have wished to bring into view every thing, which in fact has

143

influence in the determinations of the will. If I have succeeded in this respect, my end is answered. From what has been offered on this subject it follows—

1. That the heart is a faculty antecedent to, and the foundation of a particular class of exercises or operations. The design of external objects, considered in the light of motives, is, to excite action. They can have no influence in answering this end, but by exciting painful, and pleasant sensations. This is the first effect they produce ; and unless this effect is produced, no exercises will follow. When these sensations are produced, desires, and other exercises follow. If motives excite pleasure and pain, they *act ;* not as agents, but as means, or secondary causes. And there must be a *subject* for them to operate upon. For to suppose operations without a subject, implies the greatest absurdity. It implies, that they operate on nothing. But that subject is not the understanding ; for that is incapable of either pleasure or pain. Their first and immediate operation is not on the will. For the pleasure and pain they produce are not volitions, but the cause of volition. There must be, therefore, another faculty, which is the subject on which they operate. And this faculty we call the *taste,* or heart. Thus by considering external objects as motives, which excite us to act, such a faculty as the heart is proved to to exist, which is antecedent to, and the foundation of all its exercises.

2. It follows, if there be no such faculty as the heart, distinct from the will, motives have no influence in determining the will. When we have clear, just and distinct views of objects, if they afford neither pleasure nor pain, we are in relation to them in a state of absolute indifference. In this state, we have no feeling, no inclination, no desires, for or against the objects we perceive. It is self-evident, that a being in this state can never act. He is totally without any inducement to action. It is impossible for him to prefer one object to another ; or to choose or refuse. Volitions, or acts of the will, never can have existence. This has been demonstrated by writers, more than once or twice. They accordingly insist, there must be a bias, preponderancy, or inclination, for or against an object, before it is possible for it to be chosen. The moment an object pleases, or appears agreeable, there is a bias, or inclination in its favor ; and when an object appears disgustful, there is a bias against it. Then the mind is no longer in a state of indifference. Hence the pleasure

we feel in view of an object, is a bias in favor of it ; and the pain we feel is a bias against it. If such a bias, or inclination towards or against an object be necessary ; or, in other words, if we must feel either pleasure or pain, in view of objects, *before* choice can exist, then it clearly follows, first, that pleasure and pain are not volitions, because these sensations must exist antecedent to choice ; and secondly, that this bias, or pleasure and pain, are not operations of the will, but of some other faculty. But it is agreed on all hands, they are not operations of the *understanding ;* because this is a *perceiving*, not a *feeling* faculty. If it be said, they are operations of the *conscience, or a moral sense ;* then it must be granted, that conscience, or a moral sense is a *feeling* faculty ; and if a feeling faculty, it is *the heart*, or what I mean by taste ; for this is a feeling faculty. If it be said, these operations belong to a *capacity* of pleasure and pain, which is essential to moral agency ; then it is obvious this is a feeling capacity, and of course the very thing I mean by the faculty of taste. It is therefore certain, that the faculty which I call the heart or taste, though by others it may be termed the conscience or a moral sense, or a capacity of pleasure and pain, is the subject of that bias, that pleasure or pain, which is necessarily antecedent to the existence or possibility of choice, or the operations of the will. And there is no way to account for the existence of volitions, only on the ground of the existence of a *feeling* faculty, distinct from the will. Those, therefore, who will not admit the existence of a faculty susceptible of pleasure and pain, distinct from the will, can never account for the existence of voluntary exercises. And those who deny the existence of faculties, antecedent to the exercises, are in the same predicament. And to be consistent with themselves, they must deny the influence of motives wholly ; or agree with Arminians, that we can act in a state of perfect indifference ; or say, that volitions are produced by the *immediate agency* of Deity, without the influence of motives. Then the warnings, admonitions, threatnings, and promises, presented to view in the word of God, are wholly useless, and never can have the least influence.

Every candid mind must be convinced by its own reflections, that motives have no influence, any further than they affect, or are agreeable or disagreeable to the agent. We may judge many things to be good, useful and excellent, which are not agreeable to the heart. Of course they are not chosen, however strongly judgment may determine in their favor. Our judgment informs us that the character of God is infinitely excellent ; but it is not agreeable to the natural heart ; and therefore, in opposition to judgment, the will rejects him. The will never follows the dictates of the understanding, any farther than they are agreeable to the heart. This is evident from daily facts. Hence objects must be agreeable to the heart, to attract the will. And agents never choose objects, unless they are agreeable ; nor reject them, unless they are disagreeable. Their agreeableness is the reason why they are chosen ; and their disagreeableness the reason why they are rejected. But the reason of choice is always antecedent to choice. After volition exists, no reason, no motive can alter it. The influence of motives is antecedent to choice. So far as objects please, they incline us to choose them ; and so far as they disgust, they incline us to reject them. This is the manner in which they influence and govern us. Hence there must be something in an agent, to be pleased or disgusted, previous to choice ; or motives have not, neither can have, the least degree of influence. And if motives do not influence in this way, what reason can be given, why any object is chosen ; or why one thing is preferred to another ? Those therefore who deny the existence of such a faculty as the heart, distinct from the will, to be consistent, must admit the Arminian doctrine of indifference ; and assert, that we choose and refuse objects in a state of perfect indifference. For if they admit, that the influence of motives is previous to choice, and is the reason of course of our choosing them, they grant the very thing for which we contend. And if we choose and refuse in a state of indifference, then motives have no influence ; we are never governed by them. And we act very inconsistently to present objects to the view of an agent, with a design to induce him to act. And if we admit the influence of motives, we must grant the existence of that feeling faculty, which I call the heart. But grant that a moral agent is possessed of the faculties of understanding, taste, and will, and the influence of motives is easily discerned. For then, when external objects are in view of the mind, the agent's heart is affected by them ; it is pleased or disgusted, and desires are excited. Those desires, thus excited, govern and determine the will. And this shows what we all find to be true, that the heart is never controlled by the will ; but the will is always under the government and influence of the heart. Objects will please or disgust us, and it is not in the power of the will to prevent it. It is not in

S

the power of the will to cause us to love and hate ; or to prevent it. But the will is always obedient to the command of the heart. It is always exerted to produce those effects, which are necessary to gratify the cravings and desires of the heart. And as by motive is intended every thing which is a secondary cause, or a means of volition ; motives are properly divided into two classes, internal and external.

Whether we say the will is determined by the greatest apparent good, or greatest uneasiness, or any other motive, what is contained in this Essay does not disagree with such opinions. For if objects of choice are painful, there is uneasiness ; if agreeable, there will be uneasiness until the objects are obtained. And to choose according to the greatest apparent good, is in fact to be governed by sensations excited, which are the most agreeable, or painful. For it is ever most agreeable to reject and shun objects which are painful, if this can be done. We are then always governed by motives, according to what is written in this Essay.

****

ESSAY XVIII.
On the Nature of Good and Evil.

The division of good and evil into *natural* and *moral* is proper. Under these two divisions, every kind of good and evil is included. And the difference there is among things called good and evil, is the ground of this distinction. To ascertain this difference, and thereby show the propriety of this division, is the object of this Essay. It is necessary first, to get clear and distinct ideas of the nature of good and evil in general ; and then proceed to investigate the ground on which they are distinguished into natural and moral. Hence my present design is, to obtain clear conceptions of the nature of good and evil, both natural and moral.

Good and evil may be divided into *absolute* and *relative*. Whatever is good in itself, or in its own nature, is an absolute good. An absolute good is self-evident. No reason can be given, why we esteem it a good.

Happiness is an absolute good. Every one knows what happiness is ; what an agreeable feeling or sensation is. This all know by experience. And every moral agent who has experienced agreeable sensations, is *certain* that happiness is a good thing. It is impossible to convince any one to the contrary. Neither can any moral agent give *any reason*, why he accounts it a good thing. He is not convinced of this fact, by reasoning ; but by feeling, or possession. No proposition is more self evident than this, that happiness is a good feeling. We say, it is self-evident, that whatever is, is ; and that a whole is greater than a part. It is equally self-evident, that whatever is good, is good ; or that good is good. But to say, that happiness is a good thing, is only saying, that this good, called happiness, is a good. For a pleasant or good feeling, is happiness ; and happiness is a pleasant or good feeling.

Some make a distinction between *pleasure* and *happiness.* Can we mean by pleasure any thing less or more, than pleasant sensations ; and do not the same sensations constitute happiness? It is granted the pleasures of mankind, derived from worldly objects, are vain and unsatisfying ; and that there is no happiness or pleasures, but in God, which are durable and perfectly satisfying. There is no other happiness worthy of the pursuit of rational beings. And I can see no ground for any distinction between them, but the one here admitted.

Not only is happiness an *absolute good ;* but the greatest sum of happiness is the *highest possible good.* For it is evident, by attending to the ideas the terms express, that an absolute good, increased to the greatest possible measure, is the highest possible good. Greater good than this cannot have existence. For it is absurd to say, there can be greater good than the greatest.

And as every moral agent esteems happiness a good thing ; increase it to as high a degree as his capacity will admit, he then will possess as great a sum of happiness as his nature will contain. Or, in other words, he possesses all the good his capacities will admit ; the greatest good to which an individual can arrive, unless his capacities are enlarged. Hence the highest happiness of which an agent is capable, is his highest good.

And that, which is the highest good of an individual, is the highest good of society. Societies are composed of individuals ; and the collective good of all the individuals, constitutes the absolute good of the society. Accordingly, the sum of all the happiness the individuals possess, is the sum of happiness existing in that society. And if the individuals possess as much happiness, as their natures will admit ; the happiness of all added together, constitutes the highest good that society can have, unless the capacities of the individuals are enlarged. Hence the greatest happiness a society *can* possess, is its highest good. The greatest possible sum of happiness, therefore, is the highest good of the universe. For a greater good than the greatest, cannot exist.

I may now say, that the greatest possible sum of happiness, is not only the highest good of the universe, but the *only absolute good* in it.

Some have supposed, and professed to believe, that *holiness* is an absolute good ; and of course, the highest good of the universe. If it be an absolute good, it is the highest good. And as this position is believed by many, it is necessary to say something to evince that it is an error

I will suppose a society of beings, each of whom is perfectly holy ; yet happiness is a feeling they have never experienced, and never will. Is their holiness any benefit to them ? If they were devested of holiness, in case pain were not to be the consequence, would their condition be rendered worse ? No ; for their condition is precisely the same. For whether they are holy, or not holy, they have existence without feeling either pleasure or pain. Some may say, this is not a supposable case ; because, if beings are holy, they will be happy. If this were granted, still it is a supposable case ; because holiness and happiness are distinct things. As they are not the same, but objects of separate, distinct consideration, we may suppose one to exist without the other. Furthermore, holiness and happiness are not inseparably connected. Perfectly holy beings may suffer pain ; as was in fact the case with our Savior, who was perfectly holy. The above supposition is, therefore, admissible ; and clearly shows, that holiness in the universe without happiness, would never be esteemed as a valuable property or benefit. And this makes it evident, that holiness is not an absolute good.

Again ; suppose a moral agent to continue in existence without experiencing any pleasure or pain, yet capable of improvements in many branches of science ; I ask, could he ever have any idea of good and evil ? Could you communicate to him an idea of pain, or pleasure ? No ; if he were born blind, you could as easily give him an idea of light and colours. For we do not obtain a knowledge of pleasure and pain, by reasoning ; any more than we do of light and colours. To have an idea of pleasure and pain, a person must be the subject of them. And without an idea of pleasure and pain, the words good and evil would be perfectly unintelligible to him. You might tell him, that holiness is a good, and sin an evil ; but he would not apprehend the meaning of the terms good and evil. This I think every one must grant. This proves, that holiness is not an *absolute*, but a *relative* good. Indeed, without happiness, why not as well to be without holiness, as to have it ; to be stones, as men ? Of what value is a universe, however holy, if there be no happiness ? But I need not spend time in showing, that holiness is not an absolute good. This is so evident, that every one must be convinced of it, who is not under an undue bias in favor of some beloved system.

From what has been said it is evident, that happiness is an absolute good, and the *only* absolute good ; and that the highest possible sum of happiness, is the greatest good of the universe. I now add,

2. That *pain* is an *absolute evil*. This is self evident. Every person knows by experience, that pain is an evil. It is thus viewed, and dreaded, by every one. Yet no one can give a reason, why he views it to be an evil, or why he dreads it. If pain, or misery, is an evil in itself ; then the greatest sum of misery, is the greatest evil which can exist. That being, who is perfectly miserable, suffers the greatest possible evil. Now every one will grant, that pain is an absolute evil. And, as it is the direct opposite of happiness, to be consistent, every one must grant also, that happiness is an absolute good.

3. Every thing, except happiness and misery, is good or evil in a *relative sense* only. When a reason can be given, why one thing is good, and another evil, they are relatively good and evil. We consider them good or evil, on account of their *relation* to absolute good and evil. When we view things in this relation, if their *tendency* is to happiness, we pronounce them good ; but if their tendency is to destroy happiness, or produce misery, we pronounce them evil. But to prevent mistakes, it is necessary to observe,

1. That to judge aright respecting the nature and tendency of things, we must take into consideration their *ultimate tendency*.

For many things afford *present* aud *immediate* pleasure, which tend ultimately to destroy happiness. This is true with respect to many sinful courses and practices. They often afford those who follow them much present satisfaction and pleasure ; yet they tend ultimately to misery. In like manner, a godly life, such as the apostles and primitive christians lived, exposed them to persecution, and brought upon them in this life many extreme sufferings and tortures. Yet the ultimate tendency of holiness is to happiness However much present pain holiness may occasion ; yet, as its ultimate tendency is to happiness, it is a good thing. And however much present pleasure sin may afford ; yet, as its ultimate tendency is to misery, it is an evil.

We cannot, therefore, judge correctly concerning the good or evil nature of things, by the *immediate* effects they produce. To judge aright, we must take into view their *ultimate* effects ; and pronounce them good or evil according to their ultimate tendency.

2, It is necessary, also, to explain, in what sense the word *tendency* is here used. We say, the tendency of all bodies on the surface of our earth is towards its centre ; yet we know many things may be made to move in a direction from the centre.

We say, however, their tendency is not to ascend, but to descend towards the centre of the earth. By tendency, therefore, in this instance, we mean, that according to established laws in the natural world, bodies meeting with no obstruction will move directly towards the centre, and will never rest till they reach that point. This direct course of water for instance, in its motion to the centre, is what we mean by its tendency to the centre.

We say, the tendency of poison, arsenic for instance, is to destroy life. Yet it may be used in such a manner, as to remove disorders, and restore health. According to the laws which prevail and govern, arsenic in its direct course will produce one effect after another, till its operation finally puts an end to life. Its direct course, in its operation, is to the extinction of human life. This direct course is what we mean by its *tendency.* Things in this world are, by their Maker, connected one with another, intermediately, and with some ultimate end. According to this establishment, things produce effects one after another, in a regular train, till they reach their final term or end. According to the connexions God has established, their direct course, in their operation, is towards their ultimate end ; and in such end they will terminate, unless, by some means or other, this established connexion is broken, or interrupted. This direct course of things to some ultimate end or point, according to established connexions, is their tendency. Now, according to established connexions in the moral world, the direct tendency of holiness, in all its operations, is ultimately to happiness. This is what I mean by its tendency. And the direct course of sin is, in all its operations, to the destruction of happiness ultimately. And this is what I mean by its tendency. And there is no way, of which we have any knowledge, by which a sinner can avoid being ultimately miserable, except by becoming holy. And a holy character, continuing holy, cannot be finally miserable ; unless a different order of things should be established in the moral world.

Also, though arsenic may be a means of restoring health to the sick ; yet, in order to this, its direct course or operation must be destroyed, or interrupted. Hence, though it may, by interrupting its course, or compounding it with certain other things, be a means of health ; yet, we do not view this to be its natural tendency. So, although sin may occasion good to the universe, yet its direct course or operation is to make the sinner finally miserable. So all will say, its tendency is to evil, and not to good, ultimately. Having explained what I mean by the tendency of things ultimately, whatever their present immediate effects are ; it may be said, that the reason why we call some things good is, because they tend to absolute good ultimately ; and the reason why we term some things evil is, because they tend to the destruction of absolute good ultimately, or to absolute evil. Or, we call some things good, because their ultimate tendency is to happiness ; and we call things evil, because they tend ultimately to misery. Here I would just observe, that whatever tends to misery, tends to destroy happiness ; and whatever tends to happiness, tends to prevent misery. Hence to say, that a thing tends to destroy happiness, is the same as saying it tends to misery ; and to say, it tends to destroy misery, is the same thing with saying it tends to happiness. The preceding illustrations lead to the following important conclusions.

1. We judge all relative good, whether natural or moral, to be a good, for one and the same reason.

Why do we consider the sun, the rain of heaven, a good constitution, and health, to be blessings ? Because they conduce to happiness. For the same reason we view every thing in the natural world to be be a good thing, or a blessing.

Why do we consider holiness, with all its operations and exercises, to be good ? Because they promote happiness. This is their motive and tendency. If the question were asked respecting every individual thing, whether natural or moral, why we consider it to be a good thing, or a blessing ; in answer, we must assign one and the same reason. We should say, because it tended ultimately to the promotion and increase of happiness. It is presumed no other reason but this can be given, why we judge things to be good, whether natural or moral.

If we should say, we consider one thing good on account of of its utility ; another on account of its excellency ; another for its beauty, or on any other account ; still this is only saying, in other words, that we esteem things good, because they tend to happiness ultimately. For can any thing with propriety of speech be called useful, excellent, amiable, beneficial, or profitable, which does not tend to happiness ? It must be granted, that every thing has a tendency, either to happiness or misery. Accordingly, things which do not tend to happiness, tend to misery. Can we with any propriety apply to such things the terms useful, or excellent, or amiable, or any other epithet of similar import ? If not, then they are designated by such qualifying epithets, because they tend to the happiness of the universe ; I mean, to the greatest sum of happiness. Indeed it must be obvious to every person, who reflects candidly on the subject, that things are called good on account of their tendency. And if on account of their tendency, it must be for their tendency to happiness. For no one will call any thing good, which tends to misery, unless he views it in some other, very different relation. The same thing, it is granted, may be viewed in different relations ; and be called good or evil, according to the relation in which it is viewed ; still it will be termed good or evil according to its tendency, in that relation, in which it is viewed. That is a good, which does good ; and that does good, which promotes happiness, or absolute good. And nothing else can be termed good, without an abuse of words.

As every thing is called good for the same reason, on account of its tendency to happiness ; natural and moral good are not distinguished by the terms natural and moral because they have different tendencies. If however all things are viewed good for the same reason, it may be asked, why are they divided into two classes, and marked with the words natural and moral? There must be a difference, which is the ground and reason of this distinction. To this I purpose to attend in the next Essay; but now proceed to add,

2. That for the same reason one thing is termed evil, every thing is so called, whether it be a natural or moral evil. Why are earthquakes, wars, famines, pestilences, and all bodily diseases, viewed as evils? Because they destroy happiness. This is their tendency. If these evils were to prevail *constantly, universally*, and *eternally*, could created beings be happy? Could a holy being, if always tortured with an acute disease, be considered a happy being? Natural evils, if they were to prevail universally, would destroy happiness as certainly as moral. So far as they do prevail, happiness is destroyed. Why is sin considered an evil? For the same reason; because it destroys happiness. This is its invariable tendency. And so far as it prevails in this world, misery abounds. In hell, where sin reigns uncontrolled, the inhabitants are perfectly miserable. It is then true, that natural and moral evils, are evils for the same reason; because they tend to misery, or absolute evil. Accordingly, the reason, why evils are distinguished by the epithets natural and moral, is not on account of their different tendencies; for their tendency is precisely the same.

Some may object and say, according to the above reasoning, the same thing may be both good and evil. For instance, moral evil tends to misery, and for this reason is an evil; it is also an occasion of happiness, and for this reason it may be termed good. Hence the above reasoning proves too much; and therefore proves nothing.

Answer. 1. We say, poison tends to destroy life; and is, therefore, an evil thing; yet it is sometimes the means or occasion of preserving life; and when viewed in this relation, it is a good thing. Still, is it the tendency of poison to preserve life? Does it not naturally destroy life? Whenever it is the occasion of preserving life, its tendency is counteracted, by being connected with other ingredients. Let a person feed upon it constantly, and it will soon put an end to his life. We say, the tendency of sin is to the misery of the sinner; yet we say it is the *occasion* of good to the universe. But is it not true, that its *tendency* is to misery; and is it not for this reason called an evil? But,

2. The words occasion and tendency have different mean-

T

ings. When we say sin is the *occasion* of good, what do we mean? We mean; that it is not the *cause* of good; it is not its *nature* to produce good; it is *not owing to sin*, but to the wisdom of God, that it is ever the *means* of good. God makes use of it to promote an end, which it tends to destroy. Hence its tendency is counteracted. A man in anger makes use of his hand, or some other instrument, to put an end to a person's life. Here the instrument is not the cause, but the *occasion* of death. The person, who used it, is the *cause* of the death. When therefore we say, sin or any other evil is the occasion of good; we mean, some agent has made it a *means* of good, *contrary* to its nature and tendency, Hence, though evil may be made the occasion of much good; yet its proper tendency and nature is to evil. And we do not judge of the nature or tendency of any thing, by the good or evil it may *occasion*; but by the good or evil it will *produce* in its operation, if not counteracted.—Religion has been, not the cause, but the occasion of many sore persecutions; and sin is, not the cause, but occasion of much good; yet the tendency of religion is to happiness, and the tendency of sin to misery. And we judge things to be good or evil according to their tendency, but not by the good or evil which they may occasion. Hence the objection has no force, to invalidate what has been said to show, that we denominate all things good or evil for precisely the same reason.

3. It follows, that all kinds of good and evil, natural and moral, have the same *nature*; which is either good or evil. Natural and moral good have the same nature; natural and moral evil have the same nature. We learn the nature and tendency of things by the effects they produce. If misery is the awful effect all created beings would suffer, in case nothing but natural evil universally prevailed, then its nature and tendency is to produce misery. But if every created being was to be constantly afflicted with the excruciating pains of an acute disease, then it is the nature of that disease to produce nothing but misery. The same will hold true with respect to every other natural evil.

The nature of sin is to produce misery. If every being in the universe was to live forever under the entire dominion of sin, universal misery would prevail; this is the effect it would produce. Hence it is the nature and tendency of both natural and moral evil to produce misery, or absolute evil. Their natures then are precisely the same.

In like manner, if nothing but natural good universally prevailed, universal happiness would be the result : and if every being were perfectly holy, universal happiness would be the result. So that natural and moral good, if they universally prevailed to the exclusion of all evil, would produce the same effect. Of course, their nature is the same. It cannot be denied, therefore, that natural and moral evil have the same nature ; also, that natural and moral good have the same nature. Whether the nature of moral evil is not more destructive, than that of natural evil ; and whether moral good is not more conducive to happiness than natural, are questions which do not in the least affect the above reasoning. For two things may have the same nature, although one may be more destructive, or salutary in its operation, than the other.

I have been more particular on this head, than I otherwise should have been, with a view to detect an error which many have embraced ; which is, that evils and goods are distinguished by the terms *natural* and *moral*, because their natures and tendencies are totally different. But, I apprehend it has been fully proved, that their natures and tendencies are the same ; and that natural and moral evils, are evils for the same reason ; and that natura' an l moral goods, are good also, for the same reason. We must, therefore, search for other differences, as the ground of the division of good and evil into natural and moral. This will be the subject of the next Essay.

****

ESSAY XIX.

Of the Reasons, why good and evil are distinguished by the terms natural and moral.

Where there is no difference, there is no ground for a distinction. The distinction therefore, which is under consideration, and has long prevailed, implies a difference.

The person, who first made this distinction, had in his own

view, sufficient ground for it. And mankind, for many ages, have considered the distinction well founded. It has been shown, in the preceding essay, that the difference in the *nature* of moral and natural good and evil is not the reason of the distinction.

With a view to elucidate this subject, I will divide all things which exist, into natural and moral agents. Some may say, there are no natural agents. For all things which exist, except moral agents, are no more than *means* and *instruments;* & it is improper to denominate them agents. Though this will be granted, yet for the sake of elucidation, the distinction may, for the present, be admitted. According to this distinction, many will say, that things are called good and evil according to the nature of the agents to which they belong. Good and evil qualities, belonging to a natural agent, are denominated natural ; and similar qualities, belonging to a moral agent, are called moral. And this account of the matter may satisfy many. But inquisitive minds will ask, what is the difference between a natural and moral agent ? It is as necessary to know the ground of this distinction, as of that under consideration ? In answer to this inquiry, it is well to observe, that the difference between a natural and moral agent is very obvious. A natural agent is destitute of all the properties, which are necessary to constitute a moral agent. Moral agents are beings, who have the properties, or faculties of understanding, heart, and will. But all other agents are totally devoid of these properties. All beings possessed of these properties are proper objects of praise and blame. But there is no propriety in praising or blaming those existences, which are destitute of these properties. Every quality, therefore, whether good or evil, is denominated *natural*, which belongs to a being that is not a proper object of praise and blame ; and qualities, whether good or evil, are called *moral*, if they belong to beings who *are* proper objects of praise and blame. In other words, by natural good and natural evil is meant, that which belongs to a being, which has not the properties necessary to render it a fit object of praise and blame; and by moral good and moral evil, is intended that which belongs to a being, who has the properties necessary to constitute such an object. Accordingly, when we say, the light of the sun is a *natural* good ; we mean, however great a blessing the sun is, it deserves no praise. But why not? Because it has not the properties, which are requisite to render it a fit object of praise or blame.

For it has no intelligence, no voluntary exertions, no feeling, or principle of action. In like manner, when we say all affections or desires are morally good or evil, we mean, they belong to beings who *are* proper objects of praise and blame. But why are they proper objects of praise and blame? because they have all the properties necessary for that purpose. But what are those properties? Understanding, Taste and Will. This shows that there is a wide difference between natural and moral agents. And the distinction of good and evil into natural and moral, is designed to teach us this difference, without using circumlocution. Now, when we say the light of the sun is a natural good, we know the idea intended to be communicated is, that the sun, by its light, promotes happiness, but deserves no praise. But by moral good is meant, that the subject of it is an object, which deserves praise. So that by this distinction, we do, in a short and easy way, give each other to understand that one being is, and another is not, a proper object of praise and blame. Hence, when we say diseases, earthquakes and tempests, are natural evils, the meaning is obvious; these are not proper objects to be blamed. And when we say, that wars, thefts, murders, frauds, and the like, are moral evils, we know the meaning is, that the authors of these evils are deserving of blame and censure. The same holds true with respect to moral and natural good.

This distinction and division being once made and understood, our meaning is obvious, when we use the terms natural and moral. These terms include a train of ideas, which all understand, who understand the ground of the distinction. All those evil qualities and events, which do not imply a desert of praise or blame in the agents, are classed together and called natural evils; and those evils, which imply a desert of blame, are classed together and called moral. So all things, which are good, are divided into classes, called natural and moral. This classification renders the communication of our ideas short and easy. And if this distinction were not made, and its appropriate terms were not adopted, we should be compelled to use many more words than we now do, on almost every topic. It is necessary, however, to observe, that every thing belonging to a moral agent, which may be termed either good or evil, is not of a moral nature. The understanding is not considered a moral faculty, nor its operations moral exercises; because mere intellect is not a principle of action. If mankind were endued with no other faculty than the understanding, they might reason correctly, and increase in a knowledge of truth ; but they would never do any thing, which is either good or e- vil ; they would be totally inactive beings. Nothing but an active principle will ever prove useful, or hurtful. And as mere intellect is not in its nature active, and for this reason will never promote or destroy happiness, it is not a moral faculty, nor its operations of a moral nature.

The understanding may err, and errors may be the *occasion*, but not the *cause* of evil. If errors are considered as evil, be- cause they are the occasion of evil, they come under the class of natural evils. So also, if correct reasonings and acts of judgment are termed good, because they may be the occasion of good; they are merely a natural good. The understanding is under the command of the heart. It is employed, as the heart is pleased to direct, in devising means and ways to do good or hurt. It is employed in concerting wise and benevo- lent, or wicked and pernicious schemes, according to the pleas- ure and direction of the heart. The heart of Paul employed his intellectual powers, before his conversion, in devising means and ways to eradicate the christian religion from the earth ; but when he became a good man, his heart employed his un- derstanding in concerting plans to spread it through the world. According to this example, all mankind make use of their un- derstandings to do good or hurt, as their hearts please to direct. So the understanding is as really under the power and influence of the heart, as our hands or feet. And the operations of the former are no more of a moral nature, than the motions of the latter.

The same is true with respect to the will. This faculty is under the entire influence of the heart. Mankind never choose or refuse, contrary to the pleasure of the heart ; but all their voluntary exercises are according to its highest pleasure. It has been shown, that the pleasure of the heart is antecedent to all voluntary exercises ; and mankind always act freely, be- cause they always act according to their pleasure. But if the will was not under the influence of the heart, men could not act according to their pleasure ; and of course could not be free agents. Previous to his being renewed, Paul's heart employed his will to carry into execution the schemes, which his under- standing had formed, to destroy christianity. But after his conversion, his heart employed his will in executing plans, to extend the knowledge of the Saviour through the world. In like manner, the will of every man is under the direction and influence of the heart. Now as the will is under the influence of the heart, its exercises are not of a moral nature. The operations of the will produce every external effect, and always prove useful or hurtful. For this reason they are termed good, or evil. But they are not in a moral sense good or evil, for the same reason that the operations of the understanding are not. All our voluntary exercises therefore, belong to the class of natural good or evil.

The motions of the hands, and other members, sometimes do good, and sometimes mischief ; and for this reason such actions are termed good and evil. But no one supposes the actions of the hands and other members are, in a moral sense, either good or evil, And why not ? Because the good and evil they produce do not proceed from them as the cause ; but from the heart, which uses them to do good or hurt, according to its pleasure. Such external actions are viewed as good or evil, in a natural sense only. And for the same reason, we must consider all operations of the understanding and will in the same light.

From these remarks it follows, that all the operations of the understanding and will, and all our bodily actions, so far as good and evil may be predicated of them, belong to the class of natural goods and evils, It also follows, that nothing but the heart and its operations is of a moral nature, belonging to the class of moral good and evil. And one reason why the heart only is to be denominated morally good or evil is, this is the only *primary principle* of action in moral agents.

As we can trace streams back to their original fountain ; so we can trace all the actions of men back to their original fountain ; and this is the heart. And we can go back no farther. We find nothing in man antecedent to the heart, which is active, or the cause of any actions. The heart then is the *primary* and *original cause* of all the moral good and evil, which can be predicated of men as agents. This is the cause, source, or fountain of all moral good and evil in man.

The affections and passions are the operations of the heart. They flow as directly from it as streams from a fountain. They are the operations of the heart, as perceptions are of the understanding, or volitions of the will. And as streams are of the same nature with the fountain from which they proceed ; so the affections and passions are of the same nature with the heart. The heart is a moral faculty; and its operations are of a moral nature. These only belong to the class of moral good and evil. The understanding and will are not moral faculties, because they are not *primary, active* principles. Of course the operations of these faculties are not moral. So far as it is proper to call them good and evil, they are to be referred to the class of natural good and evil.

It may by some be said, that as the operations of the will are *connected* with the heart, they ought to be viewed as moral exercises. But this does not follow. Things of different natures are connected. There is a connexion between the understanding and the heart; yet it does not follow that the operations of the understanding proceed from the heart, or are of the same moral nature with the operations of the heart. There is as real a difference between volitions and affections, as between affections and perceptions. This has been made evident in those essays, which treat on the faculties of the mind. Hence, though the will is connected with the heart, yet its operations are not the operations of the heart, any more than perceptions are; and of course, are not of a moral nature.

To bring this essay to a close, let the following things be considered. A tree has fallen, and killed a man. Does it deserve blame? No; because it is not a proper object of blame. Why is it not? Because it has not the faculties necessary to render it a *designing agent*.

One man kills another. Does he deserve blame? We will answer, yes: But why? Because he has all the faculties, which are necessary to constitute him a *designing agent*, or a complete moral agent. But does blame belong to the understanding, which devised the means by which life was taken away? No. To his will, which executed the scheme devised? No. To the hand and dagger by which the victim was stabbed? No. But why are not these deserving of blame? Because they were not active principles; they were only the instruments or means, by which the murderous purpose was effected. What then renders the murderer deserving of censure and condemnation? His heart. But why? Because it is an active principle and the primary cause of all the actions, which terminated in the death of his fellow mortal. Here lies that malice prepense, which is called murder. This is termed a moral evil, because it exists in a being who is a complete moral agent; and because it is the *cause* of the death of his neighbor. To sum up the whole ; moral good and evil belong to moral agents ; and natural good and evil to natural agents But what is the difference between these two agents ? One has all the properties necessary to render it a proper object of praise and blame, or a *designing agent ;* and the other is destitute of them. But why is not every thing in a moral agent, which may be denominated good and evil, to be considered a moral good or evil ? Because they do not proceed from a primary, active, principle of action. Accordingly, no good or evil is to be considered *moral,* but that which proceeds from the *heart of man ;* because this is the only primary principle of action. The heart then, and its various operations, constitute the only class of moral good and evil. Every other good and evil belongs to the class of natural good and evil.

It is a general opinion, that *exercise, action, activity,* &c. are essential to vice and virtue. Hence voluntary exercises have by many been considered as holy or sinful, because they have been viewed as being exclusively *active.* Since it is proved, that the mind is endowed with that faculty called the taste or heart ; and that this is the only primary, active, principle in men or moral agents ; all, who consider *activity* essential to vice and virtue, will now see why the heart is the only moral faculty ; and why it with its operations include all holy and sinful exercises, by considering the subject in connexion with what is advanced in this Essay. Such are, hence, desired here to give the subject a reconsideration.

❊❊❊❊❊❊❊

ESSAY XX.
On the nature of moral evil, or sin.

1. John, 3, 4. Whosoever committeth sin transgresseth also the law ; for sin is the transgression of the law.

The moral law is the rule of duty, given by God to man. It is a perfect rule ; and binding on all intelligent, created beings. It never can be repealed or disannulled, any more than either moral good or evil can cease to exist ; or their natures, in the

U

present system, be so altered, that virtue may become vice, and vice virtue. Hence the moral law is immutable, and will be eternal in all its requirements and prohibitions. In this passage, sin is expressly declared to be a transgression of the law. Of course, every transgression of this law is a sin. And the moral law, according to scripture, extends to the heart, as well as life and conduct. It will be natural then,

I. To inquire what may be considered as a transgression of the moral law.

This law contains two general branches. 1. *Requirements.* And—2. *Prohibitions.* The first respects what we ought to do ; and the second what we ought to omit doing. *Thou shalt love the Lord thy God with all thy heart, and thy neighbor as thyself.* This contains the sum of all that is required of men. *Thou shalt not do any evil.* This contains all that is prohibited. These two constitute the whole rule of duty given to men. Here it is proper to consider how this rule may be transgressed. And,

1. How may the *requirements* of the law be transgressed. So long as men have in their hearts and lives all that is required of them, they certainly do not transgress this branch of the divine rule. If they love God with the whole heart, and their neighbor as themselves, they fulfil all that is required in their hearts. They have the heart and the affections required of them. On this ground they cannot be blamed. For they do not transgress. The only way then by which men can transgress divine requirements is by *defects*, by omitting to do what is required. When the heart is destitute of love to God, that temper and affection are wanting, which are required. Here is a deficiency, a want of the thing required ; a defect. The person does not come up to the rule of duty, but falls short of it. Is not a total want of love to God a great imperfection ? Is it not a transgression of the law ? Who can deny it ? It is then evident, that this *defect*, this *privation*, this *want* in the heart of what is required, is a sin, a transgression of the law. Hence any deficiency in this particular is a sin. We are required to love God with the whole heart. Nothing short of this comes perfectly up to what is required. Accordingly, if a person has love in his heart to God, so far as he comes short of the measure required, or of loving with the whole heart, there is a *want* in him of the affection required. This want is a sin. And so far as any holy affection, whether it be love, repentance, humility,

or any other grace, is wanting in strength or in equalling the power we have for such affections, it is deficient; there is a want of more life, and a greater measure. And this defect of strength in any holy affection, is a sin, a transgression of what is required. So far as this want prevails, the christian character is deficient, or imperfect. Hence a total want or deficiency, in any holy affection, is a sin. And this is the *primary imperfection* in every moral character. Did not this in the first place exist, there would be no irregularity, no sin in the heart or life of any moral agent. This will be proved in its proper place.

But as many deny there is any sin in a mere want, deficiency, or defect in the moral character of man, it will be necessary to attend some further to this subject.

Suppose the heart and life of a person is perfectly what it ought to be, in all respects but one; and that is a want of holy affection. Would not this want be considered a great imperfection in his character? Would it not be viewed as sinful? Could he be considered as keeping the law perfectly? Would not the divine law condemn him? Could he, without any love in his heart to God, supposing every thing else be right, be admitted into heaven? And when he stands at the bar of God for trial, destitute of any love, would not his Maker blame and condemn him? The answer to these questions is easy; and proves that this want is a sin.

Again. Do not all christians feel worthy of blame, so far as they know there is a deficiency in them? Do they not consider the *want* of more love, more humility, greater conformity to God, and more intense desires after holiness, a sin in them, a moral imperfection? Do they ever expect to be perfect, until every grace arrives to perfection in its measure? And is not this want a grief and burden to them daily? Does not this accord with the experiences of all christians? And fully prove that this want, in their view, is a sin? This want is the very thing intended by stupidity, and barrenness. And for this want of more love, zeal, fervency, engagedness, and fruitfulness, they are condemned in the sacred oracles. Why do they cry, my leanness, my leanness; why are they condemned for their stupidity in scripture, if such a want be not a sin? Holy affections are the fruits of the spirit. And so far as these are wanting, there is a want of fruit; and so far as christians are wanting in fruit, they are barren. And so far as their affections are wanting, they are wanting in life, zeal, and fruitfulness. And so far as they are wanting in life, and zeal, they are stupid. And for such stupidity and barrenness, which we now see is only a want of a greater measure of holy affection, they blame and condemn themselves ; and also the word of God blames them. Why else are they condemned for their barrenness, stupidity, and deadness ? This fully proves, that this want or deficiency of holy affection is a sin, in the view of christians, and according to the word of God.

Further. In what way can divine requirements be transgressed, but by a deficiency ? Nothing but a want of what is required, can be a transgression of requirements. Need any thing more be said to make it evident, that this want of right affection is a sin ? In like manner, all external neglects of duty are sinful. We are required to pray. If this be neglected, the thing required is not done. This neglect, which is nothing but an external deficiency, is sinful ; is so considered by men generally, and is thus represented every where in the word of God. The same is true of all external neglects of duty. A neglect of any duty is a deficiency in a person's life, a want, a defect. And there is no way by which a person can live contrary to divine requirements, only to neglect to do what is required. If a person neglect to give to the poor, when it is his duty to give, he has omitted a duty, and has done no more ; fo he has not stolen from the poor. Hence a neglect of duty implies no more than a mere want. But if he steals from the poor, when it was his duty to give, he has both omitted his duty to them, and done what is prohibited. Hence all acts, which are forbidden, imply a breach of the whole law in its requirements, and prohibitions. But omitting a duty is a transgression only of what is required ; it does not imply a transgression of what is forbidden. It is now evident, that a want or deficiency in the heart, and a neglect externally of what is required, are each of them sinful, a breach of what the law requires. But as love is the sum of all the law requires, it may afford some light to reflect on what the term implies. Love certainly implies a *pleasedness* with the object beloved. To say we love an object, is saying we are pleased with it. Pleasure is an agreeable sensation. But what is the foundation of this pleasure ; or what is it, which is pleased ? It must be something. For we can no more conceive how pleasure, or any affection, can exist without a subject, than we can conceive of an action without an agent. If it be said the agent is the subject of the pleasure, and of every affection; still this is not sufficiently definite. For every moral agent has faculties, different in their nature. The understanding is one faculty. And all agree it is not a feeling faculty; therefore, it is not the subject of pleasure. And the taste, or heart is another faculty; and the only feeling one, which belongs to the human mind. And the sensations of this faculty are always antecedent to voluntary exercises. This faculty then is the subject of that pleasure, which is ever implied in love. As we are required to love God, and this love implies a pleasedness with his character, and such pleasedness cannot exist without a *disposition* or heart to *be pleased*, God requires us to have this disposition. Indeed, that we ought to have a disposition or heart to be pleased with the divine character, is a truth so evident, it is presumed no one will deny it.

Another thing implied in love, is a *desire* for the honor and happiness of the person beloved, and a desire to enjoy his society. This all know to be a fact by experience. Do not all wish well to the object beloved, and wish to possess and enjoy it? Now, when God requires us to love him with all the heart, he requires us to have a disposition at all times to be pleased with his character; and he requires us to be pleased with it, and to have desires for the glory and honor of his name, and to enjoy him forever. For as God requires love, he requires every thing implied in it. But a disposition to be pleased with him, and to desire his glory, and the enjoyment of him, is love. This shows how much is implied in the command, to love God with all the heart. And I here make no other distinction, than what is made in the command itself, by him who knows all things. He considers the heart a distinct thing from love, and antecedent to it. Thou shalt *love*, with what? With thy *heart*. The heart then, or what I mean by disposition, is distinguished from love, which is only an operation of the heart. Hence, to require us to love with the heart, is requiring us to have a heart or disposition to love, if we have it not.

And if men have not a disposition to love God, the most essential thing in the requirement is wanting. And if this is wanting, the command is violated; and the person never will love his Maker, till this disposition is created in him. And this want of a disposition to love, or be pleased with the character of God, is the *primary imperfection* in the moral character of men. I am now ready to attend,

2. To the *prohibitions* of the moral law.

There are many affections of heart, which we never ought to indulge or gratify ; and many external actions, which we ought never to perform. Such as anger, revenge, lying, stealing, and hating God or man. If we have and indulge those passions, which the law forbids, or perform those actions, which are sinful, we transgress the prohibitions of the law. In doing this, we go beyond the rule of duty, there is *excess* in us, as well as *defects*. It appears, then, that we transgress the rule of duty in two ways. 1. By not coming up to it, or not doing and having all that is required ; and 2. By going beyond it, or having and doing what is expressly forbidden. And is it not as great a sin, not to live up to the rule of duty, as to go beyond it ? Are not defects as really sinful as excesses ?

Why are positive acts of transgression sinful ? If it be answered, because they tend to destroy the happiness of the moral system ; for the same reason such defects are sinful. For nothing tends more to destroy the system. For if all the members were destitute of that love the law requires, the system is ruined. Nothing but wars, contentions, disorders, and desolations would prevail in it. But this consideration belongs to another part of the subject, where it will be attended to more at large. I have now shown what a transgression of the law is, and of course what sin is. To elucidate this subject more fully, a number of other things must be taken into consideration. I proceed therefore to attend,

II. To the principles of action in the human heart.

Every agent possesses a principle of action. There must be something inherent, abiding in him, which will move and excite him to action, or he is not an agent, and will never act. He may be a subject to be acted upon, and used as an instrument in the accomplishment of many things ; but he is nothing more than a passive subject or instrument. As every being must have a principle of action in himself, to be an agent, it is a matter of importance to attend to this in particular.

One thing is self-evident, that a principle of action must be something susceptible of feeling. And as nothing is a feeling but sensations and emotions, which are pleasant or painful, something must exist in man, which is susceptible of pleasure and pain. And it will be granted, that the faculties of understanding and will are not the subjects of sensations. The heart is the subject of all our pleasant and painful sensations. The heart is the only principle of action in moral agents, as has been already proved. The next inquiry is, whether it be a simple, or complex principle of action. On examination it will be evident it is a complex principle.

Here let us attend to facts and experience. Is not benevolence a principle of action? Is it not pleased with divine things, and disgusted at sin? Does it not excite to action, and move us to keep the law in all its parts, and make us active and zealous in the service of God? It in fact operates in this manner, in all who possess it. Then it is a principle of action.

Do not hunger and thirst excite to action? Is not the appetite pleased with food and drink? Does it not move men to use all the means, necessary to a supply of bodily wants? Then it is a principle of action.

Are not natural affections, such as the parental, filial, and conjugal, principles of action? Do they not operate as powerful principles, and excite to innumerable actions? Then it is a fact, which agrees with experience, that in the heart there are several distinct principles of action; principles, which excite men to pursue very different objects. Benevolence will lead to seek the glory of God; hunger, to seek food; thirst, to seek drink; and other principles, to seek their respective objects.

These principles are so many distinct appetites. Benevolence, hunger, thirst, natural affections, are so many distinct appetites. And these, collectively considered, constitute the heart. Hence the heart is a complex faculty, composed of a number of appetites united; which prepare us to be the subjects of all the sensations we ever experience, and to perform all the actions which ever belong to us as agents. This point has been clearly established in the essay on the appetites. Inquire,

III. Why all vice and virtue must have their seat in the heart. The reason is, because this is the primary fountain from which all good and evil proceed. The appetites of the heart are the principles of action, which set all the wheels in motion. They govern the understanding, and the will, and all our external actions. Take these away, and men would not be agents, and good and evil could not be imputed to them.

When we see in men external conduct, good or bad, we are to trace back, and find from whence it all proceeds. In running back, we find the external actions proceed from the will; and the will from the heart. Here we come to the original fountain, from which all good and evil proceed. Here then is the seat of all vice and virtue. Here are the principles of action, which are the causes of all the good or evil ever done by men, considered as agents. Their moral character, then, is according to the nature of the heart. The heart is either virtuous or vicious ; and all its operations, or affections, are of the same nature with itself. For streams are like their fountains ; and fruit, take the nature of the tree which bears it. For the reasons now given, nothing can be more evident than this ; that vice and virtue must consist in principles of action, and must have their seat in the heart of all moral agents.

Here it may be well to observe, that as the appetites of men, in the sense explained, are the principles of action ; so some of them may be lost, and then again restored. This is in fact the case, with respect to benevolence. Adam lost his disposition to love God, at the fall ; and if he became a good man, it was again restored. And all men are born destitute of it ; and when any are regenerated, it is implanted in their hearts. And other appetites, as well as this, may be lost and restored. And this often in fact appears to be the case. Still this does not affect the subject of moral agency. For when an appetite is lost, others, which are principles of action, still remain ; and men are as active agents as ever. Though it does not affect agency, yet it will cause a great alteration in men's conduct. That appetites may be lost and restored, is one thing of importance to be considered in relation to this subject. I shall now,

IV. Show that vice and virtue are not in themselves good or evil, but only in a relative sense. This has been proved in the essay on good and evil. This point being made plain and established, we may now observe, that the same thing may be good at one time, and evil at another, just according to its circumstances and connexions. For instance, when poison is taken in such quantity as to destroy life, it must be considered as an evil thing ; but when taken mixed with other ingredients, or alone in a proper quantity, it produces health, and is esteemed a good medicine. Fire, when under our government, is a great blessing. But when it rages uncontrolled, it is a very great evil. The sun is a very great blessing, when connected with a supply of rain. But without rain, it proves the greatest evil ; for then its tendency is to destroy life. If the earth should lose its projectile force, it would directly be swallowed up in the sun ; and every thing on its surface would be destroyed. We might multiply instances to show, that a great blessing in one state, might prove a great curse or evil in a different condition.

These remarks may serve to show, that the same principles of action in the heart of men in different circumstances may have a very different tendency. I shall therefore now consider,

V. How some principles of action in the heart may and will tend to produce happiness in one state, and misery in a different state. Adam, we are informed, was created in the image of God, both natural and moral. He was therefore created with a heart to love his Maker supremely. And this was the governing principle of his heart. It was an active principle. He had also other principles of action implanted in his heart. Such as hunger, thirst, a love for his wife and children, a desire for knowledge, a principle of self preservation, and others enumerated in Essay 9th.

Now as long as Adam was governed by love to his Maker, all the principles of action in his heart would be subordinated to the glory of God, and kept in due regulation. If he ate or drank, or gratified any other appetite, it was with a view to the glory of God. He would not neglect any duty, the law required of him; nor perform one action, which the law forbade. There would be no *defect*, or *excess*, in his heart or life. He would not fall short of the rule of duty, or go beyond it; but live according to it. And so long as he did this, he was perfect. All the feelings of his heart, and the actions of his life harmonized, and centered ultimately in the same end. Nothing but obedience, order, regularity, and harmony prevailed in paradise. Both natural and moral evil was unknown. And in this perfect manner every thing would have proceeded, had he not been deceived by his adversary the devil, and then violated the divine command. Under this deception he believed, that good, and not evil, would result from his eating the forbidden fruit. Being deceived he ate. And then, according to the divine appointment, he forfeited and lost his benevolent principle. The moment this was done, he was in a state of spiritual death. One of the greatest changes took place in his moral character. He was no longer a saint, but a sinner. He had lost the moral image of his Maker. Every thing the law required of him was wanting. He had no benevolent disposition to govern him, or to be gratified. He had no love for the happiness of others; no love for the law of God, and nothing to prompt him to seek his glory, or the good of his kingdom. He was in the view of the law a sinner. Because every thing the

V

law required of him was wanting ; and by the law he was condemned.

Now all this is true, considering only what was *wanting* in
Adam. Is not that character morally imperfect, which is destitute of all holiness both in principle and action ? Is it not a
sinful character ; such as the law condemns ? Then a mere
want, and privation of holiness is a moral imperfection ; it is a
sin, or a transgression of the law.

This sentiment demands the careful attention of the reader.
It will surely be granted, that as long as a moral agent is perfectly benevolent, or loves God with the whole heart, and this
principle governs him, it will be impossible for him to do any
thing in a moral sense wrong, or to commit sin. It is evident,
then, the first sin in a moral agent must consist in the *entire*, or *partial* want of benevolence. For so long as benevolence is perfect,
and he is governed by it, he cannot sin. There is no way, then, by
which he can become a sinner, but by the loss of benevolence
wholly, or in part. If entirely lost, he has no moral goodness
remaining. If it is diminished, and he should not love God half
so much as he might and ought ; then there is a partial defect.
Hence the first sin in a moral agent must be an *entire*, or *partial*
want of benevolence. The first sin must be a deficiency, privation, or imperfection. There is no other way conceivable by
which a perfect, moral agent, can become imperfect or sinful ;
or by which sin can enter, or begin to exist. Could saints in
heaven, whose benevolence is now perfect, become imperfect or
sinful, unless by a perfect or partial want of benevolence ? Of
course the *primary* existence of moral evil must consist in a deficiency, or want of benevolence, in whole or in part.

This benevolence is all that Adam lost at the fall. All his
other principles of action remained the same. He had the same
appetites of hunger, thirst, self preservation, conjugal and filial
affection, and desire for knowledge. This fact is undeniable.
But now the great inquiry is, how will these principles of action
operate, where there is no love in the heart to God ? One
thing is certain ; these principles of action will have the sole
and entire government of the man. For he has no other principles to govern him. Now these principles will never lead a
person to seek any objects, but those he loves. And he loves
no objects, but those of a worldly nature. Hence the world, in
some shape or other, will be the only object of pursuit. The
world now is his idol, and only portion. These principles of

action, where there is no love to God to regulate and govern them, will lead men astray from God. Instead of serving him, they will serve only the creature and themselves. These principles are all of the same nature, and will produce nothing but evil. They fix on the world with supreme affection, lead men astray from God, and keep them travelling the road to death ; and thus tend ultimately to a state of misery. This is their only tendency. They must then be viewed as sinful, or morally evil. The primary fault, however, is not in these principles, but in the want of benevolence. This is the primary, original fault in the character of men. The consequence of this fault is, that all the other principles will have no tendency, but to misery. Just as the tendency of the sun is to destroy life, when there is no rain; or of the earth to fall into the sun, if it has lost its projectile force. But this will appear more fully, by attending particularly to their operations.

Let us suppose pride to be a principle of action, which we bring into the world with us. Honor, or applause is its object. Then some honorary office or station is the object it will seek. How will this principle operate, in a person who has no love for God or man ? Its first operation will be, desires to obtain the object, the honor which is pleasing. Secondly, desires will arise for all the *means* necessary to possess and enjoy the object. If other persons aid him in his pursuit, he will be much pleased with their conduct, and appear to be very friendly to them. But if they oppose him in his schemes to reach his end, and thwart and disappoint him, from his pride will arise hatred, malice, anger, revenge, or a desire to retaliate on them for the injuries he receives. If others rise above him in honor, he will envy them ; and if he encounters great and continued opposition, his envy and revenge will become a rooted hatred and malice. This is the worst passion, which can exist in the human heart; and when excessive, it seems to exclude the common affections and passions. And as he has no other love for God or man, he will use any means which promise to secure his end, whether they are lawful or unlawful, good or bad. Nothing restrains him but the fear of punishment or disgrace in this world. This is the way in which pride operates in every natural heart ; although it does not always reach this enormous degree.

Let us now attend to the operations of some other appetite, as hunger for instance, in a person who has no love to God or man. The object of this appetite is food. From this appetite will arise desires for the object ; and also desires for all the *means*, which are necessary to obtain food in variety and plenty. Then will follow desires for land, money, and many other things useful in procuring food. Persons who favor his wishes will be regarded as friends ; and opposition will lead to the same results as in the former case.

We will next attend to selfishness. This many suppose is a principle, by which all men are governed, and the root of all sin; indeed the only sinful principle in the human heart. We will grant, for the present, this opinion is true. Let us see how this will operate in men, who have no love to God or their fellow creatures. Self is the object or end of selfishness. To please self, is the end ultimately sought. From this principle will a-rise desires for every object, which is pleasing to it ; and also for all the *means* by which those objects can be obtained. And the person will use all the means necessary to this end, as far as he is able ; whether they are lawful and just, or unlawful and unrighteous, as far as is consistent with safety. He also will be gratified with such persons as favor his plans ; and will have his malignant passions excited against those who oppose him.

Let us now attend to the operation of the same principles of action in the heart of a person, who has a benevolent principle, invariably governing him in all he does. The end or object of benevolence is the happiness of others, or the highest good of God's kingdom. If he is governed by benevolence invariably, he will do every thing with a view to this end. Let us see then how the other appetites implanted in him will operate.

They will certainly be subordinated to the object he ultimate-ly seeks. He will never suffer them to lead him astray. He will never do one wrong thing to gratify them. And in some of his pursuits these will harmonize with benevolence, and prompt him to do the same thing. Benevolence will prompt him to feed the poor ; and natural pity will move him to do the same thing. Here, and in other instances, they will harmonize. This man will seek his end by no other, than lawful means. If others aid him, he will be pleased. If they oppose him and his great object, he will view them enemies to God and man. But he will not be angry with them ; no hatred, or revenge, or envy, or malice, will arise in his heart. But he will pity, and pray for them; and labor to bring them to repentance. For he loves them as he does himself. And he will sacredly regard the rule of duty in all he does ; and never go beyond it, or fall short of it. In this man, who is invariably governed by benevolence, his other appetites do no hurt ; and sometimes aid him in his pursuits. They produce no evil, but are perfectly under the government of benevolence. While he is governed entirely by benevolence, no principle of action in his heart can ever lead him one step astray. He will act as perfectly, as Adam did in a state of innocence. No principle of action can ever lead him astray, or harm him, unless it becomes stronger, and operates with more force ; which can never be, so long as benevolence is entire and governs.

I have now given a just view of the operations of all the principles of action in the human heart. These principles are the laws of our nature, by which all men are as invariably governed, as the planetary system is by the laws of attraction and gravitation. And did we understand this subject, and know what principles of action would govern a man at any given time, and the exact circumstances in which a person would be placed, we could ascertain how he would act, as accurately as we can calculate an eclipse. We must now admit the following conclusions. 1. A benevolent appetite is the only principle, which will lead men to seek the good of God's kingdom, or the happiness of others. 2. All other principles of action are implanted in us, with a view to have them stimulate us to seek those things which are necessary to the life and comfort of the body, and of society, while in this life. And as they will not be needed by saints in heaven, and there cannot be of any benefit to them, they will either be eradicated, or cease to operate forever. 3. That if men in this life were always governed by benevolence, other principles of action in the heart would never do any hurt, or produce any evil. 4. That where benevolence is totally wanting, all the other principles of action will in their operations lead men astray from God, to transgress his law, and to perpetrate all the crimes, to which circumstances and temptations lead them. 5. That all the principles of action in a natural heart are equally sinful. One in its tendency is no worse than another. Hunger, thirst, pride, natural affection, and selfishness will equally lead natural men astray, and their tendency is equally to final misery. 6. That if those principles of action were never opposed by God or man, and should meet with no obstacles in their operation, but were assisted, we should never see the passions of hatred, anger, envy, revenge, or malice rise in the human heart. For these passions are always excited by opposition made to such principles of action, in their operation, by God or man. 7. That principles of action are not good or evil in themselves considered ; but are good or evil according to their tendency to produce happiness or misery ultimately. 8. That the primary fault, or imperfection in the character of moral agents is a want of a principle of benevolence. Where this is totally wanting, all other principles of action tend to misery ultimately ; and when this is in the heart, and has the entire government, they do no hurt, and their tendency is not to misery. Hence—9. A benevolent appetite is the only law of our nature, which will cause all other principles to operate regularly, and prevent confusion, disorder, and evil. It is therefore in this case similar to other things governed by uniform laws.—Things are so planned and ordered, both in the natural and moral worlds, that they operate in connexion with each other. Of course, if one important thing should cease to operate, the operation of other things would, in consequence of this, produce nothing but disorder, confusion, evil, and misery. The system is perfect, if all the parts operate in harmony together, as they were first created. But if one part should be destroyed and be wanting, and the other part continue to operate, disorder, evil, and misery are the consequence. Hence the most fatal consequences may follow from a mere want or privation. As I have already observed with respect to the operations of the sun, if there was to be no rain ; and of fire, when it is not under a master ; and of the earth, if it should lose its projectile force ; and also of the whole planetary system, if one planet should be annihilated ; or in case they should be deprived of their gravitation. A privation of one thing in such cases would be followed with the most fatal consequences.

So when all the laws of our nature operate in connexion with each other, as they did in Adam before the fall, their tendency was to nothing but happiness. All was order, and harmony. But at the fall, one of these laws, that of a benevolent appetite, was entirely lost. In consequence of this, all the other laws of our nature in their operation tend only to disorder, evil, and misery. This world became the supreme object, the idol of the heart. And this will be their operation, until a benevolent appetite is restored, or again implanted in the heart. Where this is done, as it always is in regeneration, then every thing begins to operate regularly; and when this appetite in saints shall have the entire government constantly, perfect order, obedience, and regularity in their conduct will prevail ; and the tendency of every thing in them, and their conduct will produce nothing but happiness. It must then be plain, that the want of a benevolent principle is the great, and primary fault, or imperfection, in the moral character of moral agents. It is the want of this, which turned holy angels into devils, and our holy progenitors into sinners.

We now see what sin is. It is a transgression of the law. And the law is transgressed by *defects*, and by *excesses*. As it is a rule, which extends to the heart, as well as the life ; every thing wanting in the heart and conduct of man, which the law requires, is a transgression of its requirements. And every thing in the heart and life, which the law forbids, is a transgression of its prohibitions. And these two classes of transgressions, of the requirements and the prohibitions of the law, are innumerable.

Let it be granted for a moment, that there is an individual principle of selfishness in men, which is the root of all sin in them, and the only fountain from which all wickedness proceeds, as some contend ; and now let us attend to its operations. We may first ask, what is selfishness ? Is it self love, a love to self; and love for our private, individual interest ? In whatever way defined, I suppose it will be granted, that such a degree of love to self, or to our private interest, as we ought to have for others, is right. To love our neighbor *as* ourselves, implies, that a degree of love to self is a duty. And if we love ourselves no more in proportion, than we do others, we are not guilty. Such a degree of love to self is not sinful. Hence, it is not sinful, until we love ourselves *more* than we ought. This principle, then, is not sinful in itself. It is no sin to love self as much as we ought to love others. The sinfulness of it, then, conists, not in a degree of love to self, but in loving self *too much*. Its sinfulness we see consists in an *excess* of love to self. This is precisely the case with hunger, considered as an appetite, and principle of action. There is no sin in loving food. But it is a sin to love it more than we do God. This must be granted. But all unrenewed men love food, *more* than they love God. So the sinfulness of this appetite consists, not in loving food, but in loving it *too much;* it consists in an *excess* of love to food.

Here the case is parallel with that of selfishness ; and for the same reason we must view selfishness sinful, we must consider the appetite of hunger sinful.

Again, to indulge or gratify self to a certain degree, is a duty. But to indulge self beyond a certain degree, is sinful ; it is indulging self too much. Here its sinfulness consists in an *excess* of indulgence. So it is no sin, to indulge hunger to a certain degree. But to indulge it beyond this degree, is sinful. And its sinfulness consists in an *excess* of indulgence. Here the cases are parallel. And for the same reason we view selfishness sinful, we must consider the appetite of hunger sinful.

Again. When a principle of selfishness is indulged, in using unlawful means to obtain the objects which are agreeable to self, it is sinful. Here its sinfulness does not consist in using lawful means to obtain its desired objects, or ends ; but in using unlawful, unjust means. So it is not sinful, for hunger to use lawful means to get food ; but when it uses unlawful means, it is sinful. Here the cases are parellel.

Again. Will selfishness give rise to a thousand desires, such as a desire for money, cattle, land, elegant houses and furniture ? And will a multiplicity of such desires take off the attention too much from religion, and place it too much on the world ; and is this sinful ? In like manner, hunger will give rise to a train of such secondary desires for money, land, cattle, and every thing necessary to procuring food, and enjoying it in an elegant manner. These desires will perplex, take off the attention too much from religion, and place it too much on the world. Here again the cases are parallel.

Again. If a selfish man is opposed in his pursuits by others, this will produce in him anger, hatred, revenge, and such malignant passions ; a principle, which will give rise to such malignant passions, is sinful. In like manner, if others oppose a man in his pursuits to gratify his hunger, the same malignant passions will rise in his heart. And if selfishness is sinful, because it will give rise, if opposed, to such malignant passions ; then the appetite of hunger is sinful ; for it will operate in the same manner, and give rise, if opposed, to the same passions. And this is what we daily see in fact. So that here the cases are parallel.

And there is no light in which this subject can be viewed, I believe, but we shall find that every reason, which can be assigned to prove selfishness to be sinful, but what will equally prove the appetite of hunger to be sinful; and every other appetite, or natural affection, with which we are born.

I have under this particular granted, for the sake of light, that there is such a principle of selfishness in all men, as many contend for, which is the root of all sin.—At the same time, I do not believe in such a principle. I suppose every appetite with which we are born is selfish. The man, for instance, who is governed by the appetite of hunger, has no other or higher end in view, than the gratification of this personal appetite. In doing this, he has no regard to the happiness of other persons, unless near relatives whom he considers as part of himself. Whether others are benefitted or injured, he will gratify himself by indulging this appetite. And can we conceive of any thing more highly selfish than this? In like manner, every other appetite in men is selfish. So that selfishness does not consist in one single individual principle of action. It may be predicated of every appetite, with which we are born. They are all in this sense selfish, that men under the influence of them will not seek any higher good than the gratification of their appetites; and in doing this they have no regard to the happiness of others; and will, by unlawful means, injure them to gratify their appetites. And this is proved by daily and numerous facts.

Furthermore. If a man had a principle of self-love in him, according to the opinion of many; at the same time was constantly governed by a principle of benevolence, his selfish principle would never be gratified in any of the above cases to an *excess*, and no further than it ought to be indulged. This is certain, if he is governed in all he does by benevolence. In this case his self-love would not do any hurt, or produce any evil effects. And the same is true of all our appetites, so long as we are governed by benevolence. Hence, no appetite will produce any evil effects in any man, until benevolence is wanting wholly, or in such a degree as not to be all the time the governing principle. So that the privation of holiness wholly, or in part, must take place, before any principles in men will produce any evil effects; except in cases where they are so far deceived as to believe that is right, which is wrong.

It appears to me that enough has been said to show what sin is; or in what total depravity consists. And according to the doctrine advanced in this essay it is evident, that the depravity of the heart consists—1. In the entire want of a principle of

W

benevolence, or holiness. And this want is the primary deficiency, or imperfection in the moral character of man. And this privation of holiness must take place, previous to the existence of any positive acts of sin, except in cases of deception. And—

2. In the existence and operation of those appetites with which we are born. The tendency of these is to sin, to excesses in all the ways described, where there is no principle of holiness. Then these appetites prefer this world to God and heavenly things ; lead men to indulge them to an excess in the objects they love ; and to the use of unlawful means to obtain such objects. And these two principles, the want of holiness, and the appetites implanted in us, will account for all the sins and crimes ever perpetrated in this world. And this scheme is fully taught and supported by the word of God. Why will not men come to Christ? Because they see no beauty in him to attract them; and because they love this world, and prefer it to Christ and to heaven. Why will they not come to the gospel supper, when so often invited ? Because that supper contains nothing which is agreeable to any other, than a holy heart. They refuse to come, and go after the world, their farms and merchandize ; because those objects please and gratify their appetites. They serve the creature, and not the Creator, for the same reasons. And with this representation the whole word of God harmonizes. So that we have both scripture and reason, to vindicate the sentiments advanced in these sheets.

This manner of accounting for the passions and actions of men, is more satisfactory to my mind than the scheme which imputes to man a principle of positive malignity. Disinterested malevolence ; or that disposition which takes pleasure in the misery of others, independently of our own interest, is too diabolical to be admitted as existing in the human breast. It is the perfect opposite of the spirit of holy and disinterested benevolence. And when the love of God and man is wanting, all the other principles of our nature become devoted to transgression, and arrange us on the side of rebellion, and lay us under wrath with the devils themselves. But it is not necessary to suppose, that a cruel and fiend-like disposition is the ruling principle of fallen man. Departing from God, he becomes selfish ; and all his affections are indulged for the gratification of selfishness, and contrary to the divine prohibitions and requirements. Meeting with opposition in his favorite pursuits, both from his fellow men, and from the providence and word of God, his passions become malignant, and he indulges in deeds of injustice, cruelty, and revenge. This mode of accounting for such malignancy appears to me to agree with facts that pass under our observation, even including the deliberate cruelties of savages and of despots.

✳✳✳✳✳✳✳✳

ESSAY XXI.

On the subject of praise and blameworthiness.

We ought, in the first place, to have clear and distinct ideas of what is implied in praising and blaming persons.

If a person sustains a *good character*, we say he is *worthy* of *praise*. What does praising him imply? It implies—1. That we judge his character to be what it is, really good. This is an act of the understanding. This is the faculty, which judges concerning truth and falsehood, right and wrong, good and bad characters. 2. That we approve of a good character, justify it, are pleased with it. This is an act of the heart. It is the heart, which likes, or dislikes, is pleased, or displeased. So it comes to pass often, from the influence of a bad heart, that good characters are disliked. 3. That we treat the person *well;* so that our conduct corresponds with his real character. To treat him well, is to make him happy as far as we are able. This is not always done; good characters are often treated very ill. But this is a great inconsistency. If we *judge* a character to be good, which really is; and *approve* it; and *treat* the person accordingly, we do every thing implied in praising him. In this sense God the Judge will praise good men at the judgment day. He will judge their characters to be what they are, *really good.* He will approve them, and love them. And he will treat them well, or make them happy. This is praising and honoring them before an assembled universe ; greater honor cannot be done them.

Blaming is the reverse of this. If a character is really *bad*, a sinful character, it *deserves blame*. And judging it to be what it really is, disapproving or hating it, and treating it according to what it is, is blaming the person. In this sense God will blame the wicked at the judgment day. Their characters are bad ; he will judge them bad ; he will disapprove and hate them ; he will make them miserable. This will be blaming them in the highest sense. Greater censure cannot be shown a person, than to pronounce him wicked, hate him, and treat him accordingly. These are the things implied in praising and blaming men.

And now the question arises, what properties are requisite, to render a being a proper object of praise and blame, in this sense ? For we do not consider all beings, or existences, worthy of praise and blame. The sun may be termed a good being. It is daily doing good in many ways, and diffusing happiness through the world. But we do not consider the sun a proper object of praise. We consider a pestilence, or plague as a great evil. Yet we do not consider it a proper object of blame, or censure. But we consider good men as proper objects of praise ; and bad men as objects of blame or censure. Why do we make this distinction ? Because we view man as endued with every property, necessary to render him a proper object of praise or blame. But the sun, and the plague, we consider as devoid of all these properties ; and hence they are not proper objects of praise and blame.

Then we ought to inquire, what properties are necessary to render a being a proper object of praise and blame ; and why they are requisite ? This we have done in previous lectures. In order to have them now distinctly in view, it may not be a- miss to enumerate them. These properties are the faculties of the *understanding*, *taste* and *will*. It has been shown why each one of them is requisite, and the reasons have been assigned.

To be brief in a recapitulation ; the understanding is necessa- ry, because it is the only *perceiving* faculty, the eye of the mind, and its only eye. This faculty can see *ends*, and *means*; it can arrange, and connect means, in the best manner adapted to the end we wish to seek ; or it can form plans of operation ; show us the right and wrong way ; and thus prepare us to act with *aim* and *design* in all we do ; and it can discern the wis- dom or folly of every being's conduct.

The taste is a faculty which feels ; is the subject of all our sensations, whether pleasant or painful ; so it must be *active* in its nature ; and is the only primary principle of action in men. It governs the whole man ; is the seat of all virtue and vice ; and is the only faculty, which renders us capable of rewards, whether good or evil. Hence without it man would not be an *agent ;* nor virtuous or vicious ; nor capable of any reward. Hence it is the most essential property, to constitute a being worthy of praise or blame.

The will is an executive faculty ; by this all the effects are produced, needful to execute any plan, and obtain the ends we seek ; it thus renders *visible* the characters of men, that all may know them, and see what they deserve. When we see any being endued with those properties, we cannot so much as form a conception of any other faculty, as necessary to constitute him a proper object of praise or blame. For it has been shown that those faculties, in their several operations, include every thing meant by *conscience,* or a *moral sense ;* by a capacity for pleasure and pain ; and by immanent and imperate acts.

Accordingly when any creature exists, & we find he has each of these faculties sound & entire, we say he is a perfect, complete moral agent ; a proper object of praise or blame. Suppose a person, when born, is possessed of all these properties, though they have not as yet begun to operate ; we should say he is *prepared* for all the operations or exercises of the understanding, taste, and will, when they shall be developed. As we say of a clock when finished, before it is put in motion, it is a complete machine of its kind ; it has every wheel, and part, necessary to a clock. So here we say of this being, who has all these properties ; he has every thing necessary to constitute him a complete, moral agent.

The next inquiry is, whether he deserves praise or blame. To determine this we have to examine what his *character is ;* is it *good* or *bad ?* If we find he has a good, benevolent heart, we pronounce him worthy of praise ; if his heart is bad, wholly depraved, we declare him worthy of blame or censure. We view him worthy of every thing implied in praising or blaming any one, as soon as we know what his character is. We have no occasion of making any further inquiry ; and men generally, with respect to them, never do make any further inquiry. As soon as we find any person is benevolent in his heart, we pronounce him good ; if he is proved guilty of malice prepense, he is pronounced a murderer.

But however useful the sun may be in diffusing happiness, or however destructive the plague ; as each of them is destitute of all the properties which constitute moral agency, we never think of praising the one, or blaming the other, or of rewarding them with any thing good or evil.

And whereever we find any being endued with the properties or faculties men possess, we only wish to learn their moral character, whether they have benevolent, or depraved hearts, in order to pronounce them worthy of praise or blame, and of rewards, good or evil. And here, in relation to this subject, our inquiries ought to terminate ; and here, after all a fruitful imagination can say, they must and will forever end. And here they would without any doubt have terminated, with full conviction and satisfaction, had man continued holy. But his depraved heart is ever searching for some plea, to justify him in his rebellion against God. Hence, here arise the various reasonings on this subject, which, instead of reflecting light, have only served to involve it in greater darkness. Either with a view to justify or condemn the fallen race, some have invented a self determining power ; some have made a distinction between natural and moral inability ; and some have contended for a *creating power* in man, in order for them to be considered as worthy of either praise or blame. And all the different opinions, which have been adopted and warmly defended on this subject, appear to me to involve only one question, which is this ; *how much power* is necessary to render men worthy of praise or blame ? Concerning this, I have already given my views in these essays. I have shown that men are agents ; have a primary principle of action implanted in them ; and are able to carry all their plans of operation into full execution ; and in this way to obtain their ends at which they aim, and to gratify the desires of their hearts. And more power than this is not requisite, to render men proper objects of praise and blame. But many contend that more power is necessary. Of course it becomes us to pay some attention to the power they contend for ; and show that such a power does not relieve any difficulty, nor reflect any further real light on this subject.

They contend for a *creating power*. They seem to suppose, that for men to be worthy of praise or blame, they must have a power to alter the nature or temper of their hearts, as readily and easily as we can move our hands or feet. So that they can change a good heart into a bad one ; and a wicked heart into a benevolent one. If this be a fact, that such a creating power is necessary, it will effectually exclude all praise and blame from the universe.

Let us view this idea in relation to God. All grant he is an eternal, self-existent being. His existence had no beginning; was never produced or created. It is also granted he is a perfectly holy being, worthy of praise. Hence his holiness is as necessary as his being. And he *cannot* change his heart from holiness to sin ; for this plain reason, that he has no disposition to exert his omnipotence for such a purpose. And let power be defined as it may, it is an attribute which in all beings will be exercised, according to their prevailing and governing wish or temper. Now then God did not create his own holiness, or that benevolent heart which he possesses ; and he cannot alter, or change it. He is necessarily holy, and by the same necessity will forever remain the same. Hence, according to the sentiment we are combatting, God is not holy, or he is not worthy of praise.

And according to this opinion, no created beings can be considered as holy, or worthy of praise. For it is absurd to suppose any being ever created himself. For this implies that he existed before he did exist. He is created by some other agent, by Jehovah. When God created man, he must create him with all the faculties we now have, or he would not be man in his image. Of course he must create in him a heart, or the faculty of taste. As this is an active principle in man, it must have a *nature*, either to be pleased with the character of God, or displeased. It must therefore be holy or sinful. An active principle cannot be created, which is neither sinful nor holy. Because, as an active principle or faculty, it is, and must be, capable of *feeling*, capable of pleasant or painful sensations ; it cannot be in a state of indifference ; it must be either pleased, or displeased, with the character of God, and divine objects. In that case it is either sinful or holy. And at first, Adam, and all other rational beings were created with holy hearts. They came from the hand of their Creator, perfectly pure. Adam and the fallen angels became sinners after their creation, and in consequence of some act of their own.

Now men could not create themselves ; they are produced by God ; and to be moral agents they must have the faculty of taste, as we have seen ; and this faculty must be sinful or holy. This we see is a fact. And Adam was created with a holy heart. But, according to the sentiment we are confuting, he was not worthy of praise ; because he did not create his own heart, and because his holiness was necessary. And if he and his posterity had continued holy to this day, men would not be worthy of any praise, for the reasons just assigned. And the holy angels in heaven are not praise worthy ; for they are necessarily holy ; they are what God made, and continues them to be. Hence, if the sentiment be true, that a power to create, alter and change the nature of the heart, inherent in men, or any other being, is necessary to praise and blame ; then all praise and blame worthiness, both in God and all rational beings, is forever excluded from the universe. This, I think, is sufficient to convince all, that such a power is not needful to render beings worthy of praise and blame.

But let us look at the subject in another light. The power they contend for does not consist in the nature or disposition of the heart. For it is a power of *changing* the heart from holy to sinful, and from sinful to holy, which they contend for. So the *power*, and the *subject* to be changed, must be as distinct as a cause and an effect are. For they make their power a *cause*, and the alteration of the heart from good to bad, or from bad to good, the effect it is to produce. Hence their power they contend for is an attribute, which a person can use or exert, as he pleases, to alter the nature of the heart. As they can exercise it as they *please*, it is in fact under the control and government of the heart. Now a perfectly holy heart would never exert this power, if possessed of it, to change the heart into a sinful nature. For it would never be its *pleasure* to change the heart, that is, to change itself, from holiness to sin. And if the heart is perfectly sinful, as satan's is, it would never be the pleasure of the heart to exert this supposed power to make it holy. For it loves sin, and hates holiness ; so it could never be its pleasure to exert this power to produce an effect it hated, and to destroy a present temper in which it delights. Hence, on the supposition men had such a power, they would never exert it to change their heart from holiness to sin, or from sin to holiness. Accordingly this power, if they had it, would be of no use to them. They would still remain what they are, whether holy or sinful.—Also, how can any being, in the exertion of his power with a good design, produce a sinful effect ; or, with a bad design, produce a holy effect ? It is absurd to suppose it. For it implies that a person, with a good design, exerts his power to change it into a wicked design. The design of his

heart is good, and he exerts his power to change this good design into a bad one. This is acting directly against his design,
which is impossible. Hence it would not be possible, if men
had this supposed power, for them to exert it in changing the
heart from what its nature is, whether sinful or holy.

To look at this subject in one more light ; we shall find, if
men had such a power, still they would be sinful or holy for the
same reasons they are without it. That this may be clearly
seen, keep in view the reason why every thing is called good or
evil. Every thing is good or evil according to its nature, or
ultimate tendency. Hence to determine whether any thing is
good or evil, sinful or holy, we never search for its cause, but
for its *nature*. If the sun had created itself, still it would be
considered a great blessing, not because it produced itself, but
because it promoted happiness. If any particular poison produced itself, it would be viewed as an evil thing, for the same
reason it now is ; not because it created itself, but on account
of its nature or tendency.

Hence, to determine whether any thing is good or evil, we
have no occasion of searching after its cause, or the power
which produced it. By whatever power or cause any effect is
produced, whether by a power inherent in itself, or by some foreign agent, yet if its ultimate tendency is to promote happiness,
it is good ; and if to produce misery, it is evil. By the cause,
which produces an effect, we can never ascertain the *nature* of
the effect ; this we learn only by its ultimate tendency. It is
therefore futile, and needless, to inquire after the power, or cause,
by which any thing is produced, to determine what its nature
is.

Hence if men had the power supposed, and should in fact often change their hearts from holiness to sin, and from sin to holiness ; they would not be viewed as worthy of praise or blame,
because *they* produced these changes ; but for the same reason
they now are—because the effects, which they did produce, tended ultimately to promote or destroy happiness. Accordingly,
their having, or not having, such supposed power, would make
no alteration in the nature of their character. They would be
viewed and treated according to their moral character, whether
holy or sinful, as they now are. Such supposed power would
effect no change in the subject of praise and blame. All the
good it could do them would be only this, that they would be
able to do many things which now they cannot do. If men

X

were able to fly, or create worlds, still their character would be estimated according to its *nature*, and not according to the degree of their power.

God is holy, because his heart is benevolent, and not because he is almighty. And whether men are weak or strong, dependent or independent, they must be viewed as worthy of praise or blame, according as their hearts are, whether sinful or holy. If they were omnipotent, they would still be viewed as worthy of praise or blame, according to the nature of their hearts.

There is one idea to which mankind are not apt to give much attention. It is this ; that every thing, which has existence, must have a *nature*, or a *tendency* to good or evil. And when we take a review of individual existences, we cannot find one single thing which has no nature. Every thing, the moment it exists, has a *nature ;* and its nature must be *good* or *evil ;* it must tend to promote or destroy happiness, ultimately.

God is an eternal being ; had no beginning, and is uncaused, or self existent. And his *nature* is eternal. It is love, or infinite benevolence. And angels in heaven, as soon as created, had a nature, or a heart, or taste ; and their nature was holy. So Adam when created had a nature, or the faculty of taste, and it was holy. If he had not been created with this faculty, he would not have been a moral agent. But the nature of this faculty must be good or evil, sinful or holy. Hence, a moral agent, as soon as he exists, must have a heart either sinful or holy. And all moral agents created by Jehovah have had a holy heart or taste. They come from his hand holy, pure and upright. The sentiment then which some have embraced, must be false. The sentiment is this, that moral agents, when they first exist, are neither holy nor sinful, and have no *nature* in them, either good or evil. Hence in this state they deserve neither praise nor blame. And they suppose such agents make themselves holy or sinful. Accordingly, when angels were created, some of them produced a holy nature in themselves, and others produced a sinful nature ; and then they deserved praise or blame, according to the nature they gave themselves. This sentiment is certainly erroneous, if moral agents must have a nature either sinful or holy, as soon as they have a being. And such a nature they must have the moment they exist, as every one will see, who has any just views of the properties or faculties necessary to constitute a moral agent. It is therefore very evident, that a *power* in a moral agent to create in himself a holy

or sinful nature or heart, is not necessary to render him an object of praise or blame ; or, if such a power is necessary, then
there is no being in the universe, who is worthy of either praise
or blame. For no being, in fact, has this power for which
many so earnestly contend. The holiness of the Deity is unproduced ; the holiness of angels, and of Adam before his fall,
were not produced by them, but by their Maker. Yet all view
their Maker as worthy of infinite praise. They view angels
also, who are holy, worthy of praise. And indeed all holy beings are worthy of praise. Hence it is not considered by any
one as essential to praise worthiness, that an agent should have
power to make himself holy.

If any being has all the faculties which constitute a moral a-
gent, and is holy, he is viewed worthy of praise. Whether he
created his own holiness, or whether it was produced in him by
some other agent, never comes into consideration in determining whether he is worthy of praise. All that need be known
is, whether he has the faculties of *understanding, taste,* and *will ;*
and then whether his heart is holy. If he has these faculties
and is holy, he is worthy of praise.

But we ought to remember, nothing more is needful to render a being worthy of blame, than to render him worthy of
praise. If any being has all these faculties, and is sinful, he deserves blame. And as no other faculties or powers are necessary, to render beings proper objects of blame, than are needful to render them worthy of praise, how shall we account for
the existence of the opinion, that something more is requisite to
render a being worthy of blame, than to make him deserving of
praise ? This sentiment, without any doubt, is the fruit of a
disposition in man to justify himself.

Mankind are a fallen depraved race of beings, and deserve
censure. But we do not love to admit this. Hence their in-
vention has been exercised, to find some way to justify themselves ; and if they can, to render themselves so far independent of God, that their future state shall be determined by their
own pleasure, and not by the pleasure of God. Hence men
have labored to make themselves believe, that a *power* to create
in them either a sinful or holy temper, is necessary to render
them proper objects of praise or blame. For they feel thus ;
if we have such a power, then we are not dependent on God for
a moral character ; we can make ourselves holy or sinful, at
any time, just as we please. But we have seen, men do not pos-

sess such a power ; they have no power to *create* any thing. We have also seen it is not necessary to render men proper objects of praise or blame. And this is further evident from this consideration ; that after all their reasonings, such persons cannot wholly divest themselves of a consciousness of blame. Their consciences, at times, accuse and condemn them. This they cannot prevent : because it is *so evident* that they are, even without this power, proper objects of blame. They cannot reason themselves out of it ; the conviction still abides.

And if mankind had never sinned, but had continued perfectly holy to this day ; such a power as is now contended for, would never have been demanded. There would have been no use for it. We should have seen, with the greatest clearness, that beings endued with the properties we have, being holy, are proper objects of praise. Concerning this there would have been no doubt. And being holy, and free from blame, there would have been no occasion to invent a way to justify themselves, and free themselves from censure and punishment. But as men are sinners, they now wish for power to gratify all their desires with impunity ; or to render themselves independent of God. Hence they have labored to make themselves believe, that they have such power ; or, if they have not, that they are not worthy of blame.

That this sentiment is true, is evident from this ; that we are ever ready to blame and condemn *others*, for the very things we *allow* in ourselves. If our fellow men injure us in any way, we blame, censure, and condemn them. And their plea, that they could not help doing as they did, has no weight ; we still blame them. Mankind never make the plea of inability to justify any but themselves. If a person's disposition to rob, steal, and murder, is so strong that he cannot resist it ; he is so much the more depraved in our view, and deserving of censure. As we do not admit the plea of inability to have any force to justify others, it is evident it would never have been made, if men had not become depraved. It would sound harsh indeed, if any person should plead that he was not worthy of praise, because his nature was *so benevolent*, he could not help being benevolent. And we have never heard such a plea made. And the stronger a person's benevolence is, so much the more worthy of praise we view him. And the more strongly we find persons inclined to evil, we blame them so much the more.

On the whole, when we find any being endued with the faculties of the understanding, taste, and will, we consider him a complete moral agent; a proper object of praise and blame, and of future rewards. Then, if we find such a being is holy, we praise him; if sinful, we blame him; and are ready to justify God, in distributing rewards according to persons' characters. And though we have sinned, yet a way for our recovery is revealed in the sacred volume. Now instead of spending our time in inventing some plea for our justification, which serves no other end than to blind and deceive us, and in this way keep us in a state of fatal security; it is our wisdom to spend our days in securing an interest in the great salvation. We should cry unto God to renew our hearts, and in this way raise us from the ruins of the fall to a state of purity and bliss. For though depraved and justly condemned, we are capable of being reclaimed, and sanctified, and exalted to the highest seats of felicity in heaven.

To give conviction to gainsayers and cavillers, so as to satisfy them on this subject, is impossible. No more can be done, than to exhibit the truth in the most convincing light. Nothing short of a power, sufficient to change their own hearts at their pleasure independent of divine control, will satisfy them. For all power short of this, it is granted they possess. They have all the faculties necessary to repent and love God supremely, and nothing is wanting, but a heart or disposition to love and obey. A power to produce this disposition, is what they contend for earnestly. This would be to endue them with *creating power;* a power to do as they please, independent of God. And still they will not see nor feel the absurdity this implies. A power of this kind is always used by an agent, according to his prevailing inclination. If he has an inclination to use his power to renew his heart, that he might serve and glorify God; his virtue in this case is in this inclination, which is distinct from the new heart he creates, and antecedent to it. And it must ever be holy or sinful, according to the end he aims at in using his power to change his heart. There is no virtue in the exertion of his power to change his heart, unless the effect produced is of a holy *nature*. If the effect produced is of a sinful nature; then the inclination, which moved him to use his power in producing this effect, is sinful. This clearly proves that his inclination, which excites him to create something new in his heart, is holy or sinful, according to the nature of the effect produced. But how came he by this inclination? According to his own scheme, it cannot be praise or blameworthy in him, unless he produced it. To account for this he must have another inclination distinct from this, and prior to it, which led him to exert his power in producing it. And in this manner he must, on his principles, run back forever, and never arrive to a first cause of all the changes he has produced. This all grant is the greatest absurdity. But there is no way for him to avoid it, unless he grants there is a first inclination or cause, which is unproduced, self existent. But to grant this, is overturning his whole system. It would be granting the heart is holy or sinful according to its nature, whatever be its cause.

ESSAY XXII.

On the first principles, upon which the Arminians and Calvinistic systems of divinity are founded : and the primary difference between them.

Rom. 9, 19. Thou wilt say then unto me, why doth he yet find fault ? For who hath resisted his will ?

Paul, in the preceding part of this chapter, had brought very clearly and expressly into view the holy and absolute sovereignty of God. To his doctrine the objection stated in the text was made. If God does according to his pleasure, then his own will is done; and if done, how are men blameable ? They are not ; for no one hath resisted, or can resist his will. The meaning of the objection is this. If God is an absolute sovereign, as Paul preached, mankind are no more than machines ; and of course not subject to blame.

Paul was what is called at this day a Calvinist ; and the objector is what is now termed an Arminian. The same objection was then made to the Calvinistic scheme, which is now, and ever has been made to it by Arminians. The Calvinistic and Arminian schemes have ever been at variance. All schemes or systems are founded on some first principles. And a difference in opinion concerning first principles, is the foundation of different systems of divinity. This difference is the primary cause of the existence and prevalence of these two systems.

My object is, to examine the primary difference between the Calvinistic and Arminian systems of divinity, and then attend to such remarks and inferences as the subject affords. Arminians and Calvinists have ever been agreed with respect to some things. They believe there is a God, and divine providence, and that men are moral agents, accountable for their conduct. They agree that all men enjoy liberty; but with respect to the nature of that liberty, which is considered as essential to vice and virtue, praise and blame, they widely differ. This difference is the primary ground of their respective schemes of divinity. This, I think, may be made very evident by stating their sentiments concerning liberty.

And, I. I shall consider the *Arminian* system.

1. Arminians say that necessity, both natural and moral, is inconsistent with liberty and destroys it. Their notion of liberty is such, that freedom from necessity is essential to liberty. So far as men act under the influence of necessity of any kind, so far they are not free. They are not governed by liberty of choice, and of course are not free. Hence they say, to be free, men must never act under the influence of the least degree of necessity.

2. They say, perfect indifference is essential to liberty. By this they mean, that men must not have any inclination, for or against any object of choice, previous to choice. If an object is pleasing and agreeable to a person, antecedent to choice, if he has any inclination towards it, this impels him to choose it. This impelling force is necessity; and he does not choose freely. For the same reason he must not be disinclined, an object must not be disgustful to him, before choosing it. For this would impel him to reject it. Hence, to act freely, a person must be in a state of perfect indifference. If he has a thousand objects of choice presented to his view, they must never please or offend him, they must not give him any pleasure or pain, previous to choice. He must be destitute of any feeling whatsoever, as much so as a stone is, till he has made his choice. Such is the indifference they contend for. And if the least necessity is inconsistent with liberty, they are right. For so far as persons choose under the influence of any previous inclination, for or against any object, so far they are governed by necessity.

But as this wholly excludes motives and their influence, to be free, persons must not be governed by motives. If a person is in a state of perfect indifference when he chooses, he can give no reason, why he prefers one object to another. He must not say one is agreeable, and another disgustful ; for if this be true, he is not in a state of perfect indifference. If objects of choice neither please nor offend ; no reason can be given why one is chosen, and another rejected ; and there is no room for objects, considered as motives, to have the least influence. And indeed they must not have the least influence, before choice. For if they have, so far they operate as necessity operates ; so far there is a reason and necessity, of choosing one and rejecting another. Hence the doctrine of indifference wholly excludes the influence of motives.—How then can any one account for the existence of choice ? To do this—

3. Arminians say men have a *self determining power.*

By this power they determine their wills, or produce volitions. Then ask them why they choose one object and reject another, they answer, because it is their *pleasure.* This is the way by which they account for the existence of volitions in a state of perfect indifference. So Arminians do every thing by a self determining power. Ask them to define this power, or to describe it, or in any way give others an idea of it ; and they are non-plussed. For there is no such power in existence ; hence no one can give another any idea of it. For that which has no existence, cannot be defined or described. It is not volition ; one volition does not produce another ; for this would run us back, in an endless train of volitions, and lead us into obscurity. And if it be not this, it can be nothing, unless a previous inclination. But this would destroy indifference ; of course it cannot be any such inclination. And hence it can be nothing, it is a word without any meaning.

We now have a clear view of that liberty, which is essential to the existence of vice and virtue, praise and blame. Liberty, according to their idea, must not be under the influence of any necessity, natural or moral. In order to this, a person must be in a state of perfect indifference when he chooses, uninfluenced by motives ; and have a self determining power, that in this state he can choose and refuse. Hence Arminians commonly define liberty, to be a power to act, or not to act. When persons are in that state of indifference described, and have a power to choose or not to choose, to act or not to act, then they are free.

Then they consider such beings moral agents, possessing genuine liberty, and accountable for their conduct.

It will now be easy to see what that system of divinity must be, which is founded upon, and is consistent with this theory of moral agency and liberty. And all that will be necessary to keep in view, as we proceed, is their notion of liberty, a freedom from necessity, and a state of indifference.

1. To be consistent, they must deny original depravity, or original sin. For if an infant is born with any corrupt or holy principle in his heart, he is not in a state of perfect indifference. If a man or an infant is perfectly holy, he is inclined to walk in the way of holiness; or if wholly corrupt, he will choose nothing but forbidden paths. So far as he is influenced by holy or sinful inclinations, so far he is necessitated to pursue the course to which his inclination leads. Hence to be indifferent, and free from the influence of necessity, a person's heart must not have any holy or sinful propensity. His heart must be like clean paper, on which there is no impression, no mark whatever. And this is what all consistent Arminians believe. They say Adam, when created, had a heart which was neither vicious nor holy. He was in a state in which, by his self determining power, he could make himself holy or sinful. Also infants are born in the same state, with hearts clean as paper, neither virtuous nor vicious. To allow that men are created holy, is as inconsistent with their scheme, as for them to be created sinful. For if men are holy, they are no more indifferent, nor free from necessity, than they are if made sinful. Hence, to be a consistent Arminian, a person must believe that Adam and all his posterity are created with hearts, which are neither holy nor sinful. This and this only is consistent Arminianism. Accordingly, all moral agents make themselves holy or sinful, by a self determining power.

2. To be consistent, they must deny total depravity. For if men are totally depraved, they are not in a state of indifference or freedom from necessity. This is very easy for any one to perceive. Hence all consistent Arminians do deny total depravity. They say, when men make themselves sinful, yet there remains in them a good, and holy principle. And if this were properly cultivated, it would become a ruling principle, and then a person might be called a good man. This however is their belief, that even the most vicious men have some moral

Y

goodness remaining in their hearts, and therefore are not totally depraved. Still they are not consistent with their first principles. For when a moral agent has made himself sinful, he is no longer in a state of perfect indifference; and the same is true, if he makes himself holy. Neither are they in that case free from the influence of necessity. For so far as they are sinful or holy, they are under a necessity of acting as a holy or sinful inclination leads. To be perfectly consistent with the Arminian notion of liberty, a moral agent must never become sinful or holy. To be in a state of indifference, he must forever live without any inclination to vice or virtue. And as soon as he is either holy or sinful, his liberty is then destroyed, and he is not a moral agent ; he is not accountable for his conduct, or rewardable. However, not to dwell on this absurdity here, I only add ; that to be consistent, Arminians must deny total depravity. This they do deny without any hesitation, if they understand themselves. And we see why they must deny it,to be consistent with their notions of liberty. So they hold, that all men have some moral goodness in their hearts ; and are inclined to good as well as to evil.

3. To be consistent, they must deny regeneration by the power of God. For if God by his power creates in the heart a holy principle, man cannot prevent it. He is the subject of an absolute necessity, which destroys liberty. In regeneration he is not free, and exercises no liberty ; he is what God is pleased to make him. Accordingly we find they do deny regeneration by the power of God.

They hold to regeneration ; but it is in this sense. All men have some moral goodness remaining in them. This moral principle they ought to cultivate. If they cultivate it properly, it will increase ; and when it becomes stronger, than the remaining corruptions of the heart, so as to govern men in their conduct, and make them act like good men, then they are regenerated. According to their scheme regeneration is a progressive work, and effected by themselves, and not by the almighty power of God. In the sense in which Calvinists explain the doctrine of regeneration, they utterly deny it ; and must deny it, to be consistent with their notions of liberty. This is so plain, that any attentive person may see it.

4. To be consistent, Arminians must deny the saints' perseverance. Calvinists say, the perseverance of saints does not depend on themselves. If left to themselves, they would immediately fall into

sin. It depends on God. He has promised to keep them by his power unto salvation. He will therefore work within them both to will and do, and promote the work of sanctification till they arrive at perfection. According to this, the Arminian says they cannot help being holy ; they are constantly under the influence of necessity, which destroys liberty. For this reason, to be consistent with their ideas of liberty, they must deny the perseverance of saints. They do deny it ; and labor to prove that saints may, and often do, fall from grace. Hence every one may see why they deny saints' perseverance.

5. To be consistent, they must deny divine decrees.

The doctrine of divine decrees implies the highest degree of necessity ; and is perfectly opposed to the Arminian notion of liberty. Hence they deny it ; and also, for the same reason, they deny the doctrine of personal election to eternal life. There are no doctrines which they abhor more than these ; or to which they manifest a greater opposition. Because no doctrines imply a greater necessity, or more effectually destroy their liberty ; and because no doctrines so fully manifest the divine sovereignty, which they violently oppose. The absolute sovereignty of God is perfectly inconsistent with their notions of liberty, as well as opposite to the pride of the human heart.

6. To be consistent, Arminians must deny divine fore-knowledge. If God fore-knows what will be, the events fore-known are certain. They will and must take place. To say a being knows an event will be, and yet it may not take place, is a contradiction ; it is saying it will exist, yet it may not exist ; it is certain, yet uncertain. There is the same necessity that events fore known should take place, as there is for the existence of events decreed. Fore-knowledge implies the same, and as great necessity, as decrees imply. Hence to be consistent, Arminians must not only deny divine decrees, but also divine fore-knowledge. If they do not, they destroy their own system of liberty. This is so bold, and so contrary to scripture, and the character of God, but few of them dare deny it. But every Arminian, who means to be consistent, does deny the foreknowledge of God ; and those, who do not, are inconsistent with themselves.—We now see what Arminians must deny, to be consistent with their notions of liberty. They must deny original sin, total depravity, regeneration, saints' perseverance, divine decrees, the doctrine of election, and the foreknowledge of God. For the same reasons they deny one of these doctrines they

must deny them all. This any person may see with great ease, as soon as he understands the Arminian notions of liberty and moral agency. On the other hand, consistency requires them to believe, that Adam and all his posterity are created with hearts, which are neither sinful nor holy ; and have in them as they grow up a principle of moral goodness, which men can and ought to cultivate, till they become perfectly holy and fit for heaven ; and then their salvation is effected by themselves. They must believe that men act independently of God. All he has to do is to preserve men in existence, and leave them to the exercise of their liberty, and the powers they have as moral agents, to fit themselves for heaven or for hell ; and he can never interpose, without destroying their liberty. And when men have produced events which tend to destroy the universe, he must prevent it as well as he can, and overrule their evil conduct for good as far as he is able. But after all that God can do, men by their rebellion produce so much evil, that in the final result there will not be so much happiness by a great amount in the universe, as there would have been if mankind had not abused their liberty. And there is no way by which God can, consistently with human liberty, prevent this great diminution of happiness in the moral world, or in the universe. God does not reign as an absolute sovereign, doing according to his pleasure ; but men reign, and by their self determining power, destroy all order, peace, regularity and happiness to an awful amount, and it is not possible for God to prevent it. All he can do is to patch up the system as well as he can, after men have destroyed it. He must not interpose, by a general or particular providence, to order and direct all events ; because this would destroy liberty and moral agency.

He is not a holy, absolute sovereign, doing according to his pleasure ; but is dependent on the will of men ; and cannot determine what to do, till men have first accomplished their will and pleasure. Such is and must be the Arminian scheme, as far as men will be consistent with their first principles concerning liberty and moral agency. I will now,

II. Define, state, or describe the Calvinistic ideas of liberty. To show what that liberty is, which all mankind experience, and with which they are satisfied, does not require any deep metaphysical investigation. It consists wholly, according to the common opinion, in a person's choosing and acting as his pleasure is.—When a person has been long sitting, and feels the need of exercise, the question with him is, what kind of exercise he shall use. Among the various kinds contemplated, no one is so pleasing to him on every account, as walking the room. Here then it is his pleasure to walk the room. This, every thing considered, he prefers to any other exercise. He chooses to rise and walk. He finds he is at liberty to choose according to his pleasure. His will is not bound; there is nothing to prevent his making a choice, which corresponds with his pleasure. Therefore he enjoys perfect liberty of choice. In case he found any thing opposing, and preventing his choosing as he wished, he would say liberty of will is destroyed. But if no hindrance is in the way of choosing according to his pleasure, he enjoys all the liberty of will he desires. When the choice or exertion is made to rise and walk, he finds nothing to prevent his walking, he then enjoys liberty of action. If any thing, at that time, restrained him from walking ; or any thing constrained him to walk in directions contrary to his choice, he would say that his liberty of action was abridged and destroyed. But if he found no impediment in the way, and walked according to the exertions he had made, and of course according to his pleasure, he would confess he enjoyed all the liberty of action he desired. In the case now stated a person enjoys perfect liberty of *choice* and of *action*, as great as he desires ; and so great, he cannot conceive of more perfect liberty, than what he experiences. And what is liberty here ? It is the *total absence of every thing*, which might prevent his choosing and acting according to his pleasure.

According to this description of liberty, there is a *connexion* between a person's *pleasure* and *choice* ; and between his *choosing* to act, and his *actions*. Pleasure is first, choice next, and actions are the result. If an object is *disgustful*, and we wish to avoid it—with this disgust choice is connected, and with choice actions are connected, the actions necessary to shun the disagreeable object. And here also a person acts according to his pleasure. And one thing here to be carefully noticed is, that the greater, or more certain the connexion is between our pleasure and volition, and our volitions and actions, the more certain, and the greater is human liberty. In the case above stated, it is a person's pleasure to walk. I will now suppose there is no connexion between his pleasure, choice, and walking. Suppose choice will not follow his pleasure ; and if volitions exist, and actions or walking do not follow these ; or suppose volitions and actions to follow, which are directly opposed to his pleasure, would a person feel himself in the possession of liberty ; would he wish to exist in such a condition ? Again ; suppose a person knew he might have his wishes gratified, concerning the liberty he should desire to enjoy. Would not any wise man say, let me have liberty to choose and act as I please, or according to my pleasure—let volitions be connected with my pleasure, and let actions be connected with my volitions, so that I can have my pleasure done? This, he would say, is the liberty I wish. And let this connexion be so firm, so certain, that nothing can ever dissolve or destroy it ; then I am sure of acting according to my pleasure at all times. Such liberty I desire, and I desire no other kind, or greater liberty. For I cannot form a conception of any liberty greater than this.

It is now evident that such a connexion as the above is essential to liberty. For without this there is no certainty that any volitions or actions will ever follow our pleasure ; or if any follow, there is no certainty they will be of that kind, which will gratify our pleasure. Hence without it, there cannot be any such liberty enjoyed, as a wise man would wish ; and with this certain connexion established, a person enjoys liberty in the highest perfection. Accordingly, such a certain connexion is not inconsistent with liberty, but essential to its existence. This connexion between our pleasure and volition, and between volition and those actions which accomplish our pleasure, is what is meant by *necessity*. Whether this be a natural or moral necessity, will make no difference, as it respects liberty. Every one, therefore, is at liberty to call it natural, or moral, as he pleases.

This shows that this necessity, all the necessity I contend for here, does not destroy liberty ; but is essential to its existence. So that liberty and this necessity agree, they are consistent with each other. This is the Calvinistic idea of liberty. Though they may explain it in different ways, yet all their explanations will be found to be contained in the description here given ; so far as they differ from the Arminian notion of liberty. For all consistent Calvinists agree, however they may explain themselves, that liberty and this necessity are consistent with each other. And it will in the end appear, that those, who essentially differ from this description of liberty, are not consistent with themselves, if they profess to be Calvinists ; and that in fact, they are neither consistent Calvinists, nor consistent

Arminians, but partly both, and inconsistent with themselves. The only material fault any Calvinist can find with this description of liberty is, that it makes a distinction between our pleasure and volitions. It does not grant, that the pleasure or disgust which objects afford us, is nothing more or less than a volition ; but maintains, that they are antecedent to all volition. This dispute has been attended to in other essays, to which I refer the reader at this time. Here I shall only observe two things ; first, that those, who consider this pleasure as a volition, must admit the Arminian doctrine of perfect indifference, as has been proved in previous essays, or be inconsistent ; and secondly, that on the Arminian plan there can be no such thing as liberty, only in theory. For let a person be in a state of perfect indifference, a state in which he has no inclinations, no feelings, no desires, any more than a stone or block. Ask him what kind of liberty do you wish to enjoy ? His answer must be, that he does not know ; for he has no idea what you mean by the term liberty. He does not prefer one thing to another, for he has no preference. He is indifferent. And one thing is as agreeable to him as another ; because nothing pleases or disgusts him. He must answer, it is all one to him what kind of liberty he has, or whether he has any at all. In this state it is impossible for a person to choose or to act. For there is nothing in the universe exciting him to action. And without excitement there can be no such thing as choice, or action of any kind. And if he could choose in that state of indifference, and by this choice destroy his indifference, and now have a preference of one thing to another in future, he would by this devest himself of all liberty forever. For he would no more be in a state of perfect indifference ; and as indifference is considered essential to liberty, he can no more enjoy any liberty, after he has, by making one choice, overcome this indifference. Being overcome by the choice he made, he is no longer indifferent; he prefers in future one object to another, and therefore has no liberty.

I have now described the idea of liberty, which is entertained by Calvinists. On this ground it appears, that liberty and necessity agree ; that the latter is essential to the existence of the former ; and that the greater the necessity is, or the more certain the connexion is established between desires and volitions, and between volitions and actions, so much the more perfect is our liberty. God has established this connexion, and thus has endued moral agents with liberty. This connexion he will continue to preserve, and thus grant his creatures all the liberty they can desire.

If it be their pleasure to rebel against him, they are at liberty to do it ; and they do abuse their liberty for that purpose. If it be their pleasure to serve him, they are at liberty to do this ; and all, who have this pleasure, do serve him.

We may now easily see, that if any of the doctrines contained in the bible imply a necessity, however great, they are not on this account inconsistent with the Calvinistic idea of liberty. Any doctrine revealed, however great the necessity it implies, Calvinists can consistently admit and believe with their ideas of liberty. All therefore they have to do is, to go to the word of God, and there learn what are the doctrines which God has revealed and taught. Has he there revealed that Adam was created holy ; and was not indifferent, whether he served the Lord or not ? He was strongly inclined to obey his Maker ; and, so far as inclined, he was under a moral necessity of doing his will ; it was his pleasure to serve the Lord only, and according to his pleasure he acted, till he sinned. All this the Calvinist can consistently believe ; but the Arminian cannot admit it. It is revealed that infants are born with corrupt hearts, inclined to evil only ; and that all men are totally depraved, inclined to forsake God and live in rebellion. So it is their pleasure to serve satan, and disobey their Maker. And according to their pleasure they live, till they are renewed. These doctrines Calvinists can consistently believe ; for they harmonize with their ideas of liberty ; but Arminians, to be consistent, must reject these doctrines. It is revealed that men, who are saved, are born again ; have a relish of heart given them, which inclines them to forsake sin and serve the Lord, and according to their pleasure they live. Calvinists can consistently believe this doctrine ; but consistent Arminians must reject it.

Calvinists can consistently believe all that is revealed concerning the christian warfare. According to which they have the old and new man in their hearts, and sometimes do the pleasure of one, and sometimes of the other, just as one or the other has the ascendancy. This agrees with the Calvinistic idea of liberty ; but not with the Arminian notions on that subject.

It is revealed that God has decreed all things, and has chosen some from the fallen race to be the heirs of life, and has determined to renew & sanctify them and bring them home to heaven. All these decrees perfectly harmonize with liberty. For the first in the train is, that men shall always act according to their pleasure. Hence to have men act freely, and divine decrees be accomplished consistently therewith, all God has to do is to produce such alterations in the feelings of men, that it shall always be their pleasure to act as he has decreed.

Hence Calvinists can, consistently with their ideas of liberty, believe in the doctrines of divine decrees and personal election, as they find them revealed. But Arminians are obliged, to be consistent, to expunge from their creed all doctrines which imply any necessity. Hence Calvinists can admit into their creed every doctrine revealed in the bible, however great the necessity which it may imply. And Arminians, to be consistent, are obliged to reject all such doctrines.

This shows us the fundamental and primary difference between Calvinists and Arminians. They first differ in their sentiments concerning human liberty ; that liberty, which is supposed to be essential to vice and virtue. This lays the foundation of their different systems of divinity, as has been shown. And if the several parties are consistent with their own ideas of liberty, they must form opposite systems, which are subversive of each other. All this must now be as evident to an attentive mind, as noon day light. And both systems may be understood readily, as soon as a person has clear ideas of the Arminian and Calvinistic ideas of liberty.

And when we take a view of the two systems, can any one be at a loss, to determine which is most agreeable to the word of God, and to common sense ? The Arminian has to explain scripture to support his system. To do this, he has to put forced, unnatural, and false constructions on the word of God. If he construes scripture according to its plain, and most obvious import, it confutes his system. He is obliged therefore to be constantly forcing, and wresting the meaning of scripture, and to go contrary to common sense and the experience of mankind.

But the Calvinist has formed such ideas of liberty, as harmonize with the word of God. Hence he goes to the bible and reads the word, and becomes acquainted with the doctrines there taught, and finds they agree with his sentiments concerning liberty and moral agency ; and has no preconceived opinions to bias his judgment. He only has to construe the word according to its plain import, and the dictates of sober, unbiassed reason ; and every page adds to his knowledge, till he forms a system from the word of Jehovah, which is of course supported by it. He can therefore with ease, with the bible in his hand, support his system. These things are evident from the writings of Arminians and Calvinists. It is now clear, that the primary difference between these two denominations, consists in different opinions concerning liberty and moral agency. Here they differ so widely, that, if each is consistent with himself, they must form systems of divinity, which are ever at variance with each other ; systems so essentially different, that they never can harmonize. Hence every person must be an Arminian in length and breadth ; or a Calvinist, with respect to all the essential doctrines of the gospel ; or be inconsistent with himself. What I have further to say will be included in remarks and inferences.

1. *Remark.* There are but two systems of divinity in christendom, which are consistent with the fundamental principles on which they are founded. These two systems, which include all others, are the Arminian and Calvinistic systems.

There are, it is true, a great variety of sects and different denominations in christendom. Let any one take pains to examine them candidly, and he will find they are either purely Arminian ; or Calvinistic ; or composed partly of the one, and partly of the other, and of course are full of contradictions, inconsistencies, and absurdities. To be fully convinced of this, let any one be at the trouble of examining the systems, which are now embraced by different sectaries. For instance, a person believes in the Arminian notion of liberty, yet believes in the doctrines of original and total depravity. If he does believe the latter, he is perfectly inconsistent with his first principle concerning liberty. For the fact is, if the Arminian notion of liberty is true, his whole system founded on this is true. And if the Calvinistic idea of liberty is just, his system founded upon it, if consistent, is true. And these two sects can never agree, unless they can agree in their ideas concerning liberty. Were they agreed here, and consistent with themselves, they would have but one system of divinity. For the primary dispute between Arminians and Calvinists respects liberty and moral agency. Did they agree in this, and were they consistent, they would agree in every thing essential. But with respect to liberty, their views are essentially different ; and this is the foundation of their different systems. And the reason why Calvinists in their system agree with the word of God is, because their ideas of liberty are such as the bible teaches. Hence if these parties ever do agree, and dismiss their disputes, they must believe alike concerning human liberty.

And as every essential doctrine must harmonize with that idea of liberty which is consistent with necessity, or destroy it ; all men must, if consistent, embrace the doctrines of Calvinists, or Arminians. And all the essential doctrines of every denomination must therefore agree with the Calvinistic, or the Arminian system, or a person must be very inconsistent with himself. Hence there are but two systems, which agree with first principles, the Arminian and Calvinistic; and these two include all other systems, by whatever name they are called ; or else some embrace a system, whose parts are forever at variance with each other.

2. We learn the importance of understanding the subjects of moral agency and liberty, in order to be correct and consistent divines. Moral agency and liberty, are the foundation of every system of divinity. The ideas men form of divine and human agency, and liberty, lay the broad foundation on which systems of divinity are formed. And as no man can form a consistent system, unless he clearly understands the foundation on which it rests ; it is evident the first principles must be understood.

And it is owing to the want of a knowledge of moral agency and liberty, that there are so many divines in our land, whose minds are inconsistent and confused. Here then is the place, where the study of divinity ought to begin. Every candidate ought to begin with the study of moral agency and liberty, in God and in his creatures. And if he understands these subjects, and is capable of founding a system upon them, the parts of which agree with each other, he will have a consistent scheme, and one which will agree with the word of God. But if he is unacquainted with these fundamental subjects, he may have what he calls a system ; but it will be composed of heterogeneous materials, partly Arminian and partly Calvinistic, without any consistency. And this is the lamentable state, in which many divines are at this day involved.

And now the cry against metaphysics is so great, that the first principles of divinity are overlooked, neglected and never brought into a candidate's view. Hence the reason why we have so many candidates at this day, who are so inconsistent, so unable to defend their systems, and unable to make any progress in divinity. They have no foundation laid, and of course have nothing on which to build; and know not when they are consistent, or inconsistent with the word of God. Hence it is the duty of all, who teach students divinity, to begin with the subject of moral agency and liberty. This would lead to the discussion of a number of distinct questions. The first in order would be this; what properties must a being possess to be a proper subject of vice and virtue, praise and blame, and future rewards? And then inquire whether men have these properties; and reasons ought to be given why each particular property is necessary to constitute such a moral agent. By such a method, a candidate would obtain a clear and consistent knowledge of the subject of moral agency and liberty; and see not only the several parts of this subject, but their agreement with each other, and the reasons why each property of the mind is necessary. Then he has a foundation laid to form consistent views of all the doctrines, and parts, which constitute a complete system of divinity. And in this way only, will any person ever see clearly the consistency of all the parts, which compose a system of divinity. This shows the importance of the previous essays on the faculties and operations of the mind.

3. On supposition the heart is not a faculty, and is nothing but those exercises, which many call immanent and imperate in succession, it is very evident on this ground, that men must be in a state of indifference previous to choice, and the influence of motives is excluded. To be convinced of this, we have only to go back to the first exercise of the heart. Previous to this there is no heart. For the idea of a faculty, antecedent to an exercise, is denied. Hence there is nothing on which motives can operate, or have influence. There is no such thing as pleasure or pain, experienced by a man. All objects are alike to him. And on supposition he has a clear perception of objects, of truth and falsehood, and sees their adaptedness to their respective ends; yet, antecedent to the first exercise, they do not affect him agreeably or disagreeably; they excite no sensation, no feeling of any kind. He is in a state of perfect indifference towards every object. In this state the first exercise has existence. Whether this exercise be an agreeable or painful sensation, or an immanent or imperate act, still it is a volition according to the defenders of this scheme. This first exercise is an effect, and must have a cause. And it is produced in a moral agent at the time, when he is in a state of perfect in-

difference. And if choice can exist in such a state of mind, it is agreed by all opposed to Arminians, that motives cannot have any influence.

Hence the defenders of the exercise scheme and Arminians must agree in two particulars. First, that voluntary exercises may exist, when the mind is in a state of perfect indifference ; and secondly, that motives have no influence in choosing ; or that the influence of motives is wholly excluded. And of course the only difference in this particular, between Arminians and those on the exercise scheme, respects the cause of voluntary exercise. The former say, it is produced by a self determining power in man ; the latter say, it is produced by the immediate agency of God ; and which of them is most consistent, I leave for others to determine. But to make this subject more evident, it may be observed,

That by indifference is meant a state of mind, in which a person has no inclination for or against an object of choice ; or is totally destitute of any feeling for or against an object. He is then in a state, in which objects of choice make no impression, excite neither agreeable or disgustful sensations. He has no sensations, no feelings of pleasure or pain.

By the influence of motives is meant, that the object of choice moves or excites a person to choose or reject it. If motives do not this, it is hard to conceive how they have any influence. To say a motive is nothing, but the object or end chosen, or on which choice terminates ; and to say this object is neither a-greeable nor disagreeable, antecedent to choice, is to deny the influence of a motive entirely. To objects of choice the term motive is applied. And why ? Because some objects are supposed to *move*, incline, or excite the will to choose one object rather than another. And so far as an object pleases or disgusts a person, so far it moves him to choose one object in preference to another. But if it does not excite in him any feeling of pleasure or of pain, it does not move him. For this is the only way, by which an object can move or incline the will to choose or reject. Hence to say, antecedent to choice objects excite neither pleasing nor painful sensations, is denying the influence of motives, and defending the doctrine of indifference. And if, antecedent to choice, there is nothing in the mind or heart which objects of choice can affect, please or disgust ; then certainly, at the time choice does exist, the person is in a state of perfect indifference ; and the object chosen did not move or create in him that choice ; it had no influence. It is then very clear, that the exercise scheme agrees with the Arminian notions of liberty, in two important particulars. It supports their doctrine of perfect indifference, and wholly denies the influence of motives. And to evade this reasoning by saying, that motives have influence after the first choice exists, is very futile. For how can they have influence then ? Certainly they had no influence in the production of the first choice. For the influence of a motive is too late, after the choice has existence. And it can have no influence in any future choice, any more than in the first. For the first choice, as soon as it exists, is *past*. It is fugitive ; it is gone, as much as an exercise a person had ten years since ; and can no more be a *something* on which motives can have influence, than exercises a person had ten years before. Hence every future succeeding choice must exist, when the mind is in a state of perfect indifference ; and of course, motives cannot have any influence.

And to say there is in every moral agent a capacity for pleasure and pain, antecedent to choice, and must be, or the existence of choice can never be accounted for, is giving up the exercise scheme wholly ; and granting all those contend for, who are opposers of the scheme. For this is granting that a capacity exists, which is a *feeling* capacity, and the foundation of all our pleasures and pains ; that the mind is never in a state of indifference antecedent to choice : and that motives have influence, by exciting in this capacity pleasing or painful sensations. And this capacity must in its nature be moral ; either vicious, or virtuous. For when the divine character and divine truths are exhibited to view, they must please or offend this capacity. If they please it, does not this prove it is virtuous or holy in its nature ? And if they offend it, does not this prove it is vicious or sinful in its nature ? Certainly no one in his senses can deny this. This capacity then for pleasure and pain is the very thing, which we call a faculty, or by the name of taste. Its nature and operations are the same. Hence they yield all we contend for. How a person on the exercise scheme can grant this and be consistent, is hard to conceive. On the whole, the exercise scheme, to be consistent, must agree with the Arminian scheme in two fundamental points ; by admitting the doctrine of indifference, and by excluding the influence of motives. And how such can be consistent Calvinists, is beyond my power of conception. This shows more fully, how important it is for all candidates to study the subject of moral agency. For it is the foundation on which every consistent scheme of divinity must rest.

4. The Arminian notion of liberty destroys vice and virtue, accountability and future rewards. Because, if moral agents are either sinful or holy, they are not in a state of perfect indifference. And if not in a state of perfect indifference, they are not free, but governed by necessity, which Arminians say destroys liberty. And if they are not free, they say they are not moral agents, any more than clocks or other machines. And if not moral agents, they are no more virtuous or vicious, or accountable, or proper subjects of future rewards, than mere machines are. Hence, according to the Arminian notions of liberty, there cannot be any such thing as vice or virtue, praise or blame, accountability or rewards, in the universe. Thus the Arminian notion of liberty, with one bold stroke, excludes all vice and virtue, and rewards and punishments, from the moral system.

5. If any persons contend for the Arminian notion of liberty, yet admit the doctrines of total depravity, and regeneration by divine power, they are perfectly inconsistent with themselves.

A person totally depraved is inclined to sin only. This inclination is a strong, moral necessity, causing him to depart from the living God. And as this necessity is inconsistent with liberty, how is he free? And if a person is renewed by divine power, how can he help being holy, and inclined to virtue? But as he is thus inclined, he cannot be free. So that all, who admit these doctrines, must either relinquish their notions of liberty, or be forever inconsistent with themselves.

Indeed there are but two schemes of divinity, the parts of which can agree with each other. These are the Arminian and Calvinistic. Hence all divines, and all other men, to be consistent, must be entire Arminians or Calvinists. And if they admit some Arminian, and some Calvinistic doctrines into their systems, they are always inconsistent. For these two schemes are forever at variance ; there neither is or can be any agreement between them, because their first principles are contradictory to each other. We now see the reason why there are but few divines, in any land, who are consistent. There are but few, who do not admit into their systems some Arminian, & some Calvinistic sentiments. So far as they do this, they are inconsistent with themselves. It requires much study and close in-

vestigation, to understand clearly the foundation, the first principles of Arminianism, and Calvinism. And but few, on either
side, clearly understand the first principles on which these two
schemes are founded. Hence the reason why they are so apt
to be inconsistent. This shows the vast importance of having
the first principles, or the subjects of moral agency and liberty,
taught to theological students. With this study they ought to
begin, and lay the foundation right ; and then they may erect
consistent schemes thereon. And if what is here written shall
awake attention to this subject, one great end aimed at in this
Essay, will be obtained : that all may see the reason, why so
many contend they are not to blame, saying, who hath resisted
his will ?

****

ESSAY XXIII.

On the decrees and prescience of God, and their consistency with each other.

Acts 2, 23. Him, being delivered by the determinate counsel, and foreknowledge of
God, ye have taken, and by wicked hands have crucified and slain.

These words assert the crucifixion and death of Christ.
They contain three propositions, which respect this event. 1.
That the death of Christ was determined or decreed by God.
2. That it was foreknown by him. And—3. That his enemies
acted *freely* in putting him to death. Each of these propositions is true ; and, of course, they do not destroy, but are consistent with each other. They teach, that divine decrees, foreknowledge, and human liberty consistently harmonize. This
many deny, and say they destroy each other, and hence they
cannot all be true. And many grant they are truths, which a-
gree ; but to show their consistency is beyond the powers of the
human mind. Others believe that their agreement and consistency may be seen and demonstrated. Such diversity of opinions prevails concerning this subject. There can be no harm
in attending to it, and the light and evidence which may be re-

flected upon it. This is my object at this time.

I. Let us see what reason teaches concerning the decrees and foreknowledge of God.

It is certain that all created things had a beginning. Hence there was a time, when nothing existed, but that being who is eternal, and acknowledged to be the uncreated, and infinite Jehovah. As he was the only being in existence, before any thing was created, He was the only being, who could create. He must be the first, efficient cause of all things. But can any being act, or create, without determination? If God was neither determined to create, or to forbear, he was indifferent, whether any thing should exist, or not, except himself. If God had determined never to create any thing, then certainly nothing would ever have existed. For he could not exert his power to do what he was determined never to do. He would never exert his power contrary to his will. Hence he must be determined to create, previously to giving existence to any thing. This is only saying, that determination must precede action; and must precede the exertion of power.

Whatever definition may be given of power, this much is certain, it is an attribute of a moral agent, which is exercised to accomplish his determinations. Hence it will not be exerted, till there is a determination to exert it. And it will always be exercised according to the determination of the agent. A man may form in his mind a complete plan of a house. He may have a clear view of all its parts, with all their arrangements and connexions. Such an entire plan of a building may exist in his mind. He may then determine to erect, or not to erect, such a building. If he determines not to erect such a building, and never alters his mind, such a building will never be erected by him. But if he determines, and does not alter, to erect such a building, then his power will be exerted for such a purpose. And his power will be exerted to prepare all the materials, to bring them to the spot, to arrange and connect them together just as he had determined, till the building is finished according to the plan he had formed. And if he has power to do any thing he determines, and is certain his mind will never change, and knows there is no being able to prevent his carrying all his determinations into execution; then, when he has formed the plan of a building, and has determined to erect it according to his plan, he knows perfectly before hand, what kind of building will finally be erected.—For as the whole depends on his deter-

A2

mination, and he has determined what to do from step to step, till the building is finished ; and knows what his own determinations are, which no being can frustrate ; he from that moment knows what will be done, and can tell, before he does one thing, what he can, and what he shall do. All this is true respecting any plan, and every thing done by moral agents, supposing them to be able to accomplish their determinations, and that they will never change their mind. These observations lead us to several important and interesting conclusions.

1. That a wise agent, such as God is, will form a plan of operation, before he acts, or does any thing. Indeed we cannot conceive it to be possible for a being to act, without a plan previously formed. Because, without a plan, he could not know what to do. Could any being form such a creature as a man, or create a world, or a vegetable, or a fly, or any thing else, without any plan of it previously formed in his mind ? Every one sees it is impossible, and what a wise agent would never attempt. This shows undeniably, that a plan of every thing existed in the divine mind, previously to his creating any thing whatever. Also, that when God does create or accomplish any purpose, he acts according to the plan he had previously formed. In this sense, God might have a knowledge of a thousand different plans, and know which among the whole is the best to attain the end he designs ultimately to reach. This knowledge of plans is a knowledge of what *might be*, or of what is *possible*. For he knows he is able to carry any plan, among ever so great a number, into execution. But this is only knowing what might be done, or is possible ; it is not a knowledge of what *will be*, only of what *might be*. This forming of plans, and having a perfect knowledge of them, which is necessary previous to action, is only a knowledge of what is possible, but not a knowledge of what *will* have existence.

2. By what has been said we see, that a determination to act must *precede* action. If God has formed a plan of creating the world, and of governing it when created ; still nothing will be done, till he has *determined* to carry his plan into execution. A man may form the plan of a house ; but he will not build, until he comes to a determination to execute the plan he had formed. And when any being has formed a plan, and has determined to execute it in all its parts, then he knows what he shall do. And if an agent has determined to carry such a part of a plan into execution, at such a time, and knows no one can hinder his act-

ing as he has determined ; he could tell beforehand particularly every thing he should do, and every thing which would be
done. He could sit down and write a history beforehand of
what would be done from day to day, even to the smallest mi-
nutiæ, till his whole plan should be perfected. God formed a
plan of the creation, a plan of government, and had a perfect
view existing in his mind of every part of his plan, from the
greatest part to the least, even the falling of a hair to the ground.
And forming a plan, we see, was necessary previous to action.
Then he determined to execute it, in all its parts, according as
it existed in his mind. And such determination we see is necessary, previous to action. Then the divine being could foretel
every thing which would be done, from the beginning of time
to the final conclusion of all things. Because he knew what his
plan was, and what his determinations were ; and that all things
depended upon him, and that no being could frustrate his designs.

God is an eternal being, and all his determinations are eternal.
So that one thing is not before another, in the order of time.
But in the order of nature one thing is before another. Though
a sun and light may, and must exist at the same instant, yet we
must conceive of a sun as being previous to light ; and a cause
as being previous to an effect, though an effect may exist instan-
taneously with the cause. In forming clear and just conceptions of the divine being, we must view one thing as being
previous to another in the order of nature.

Hence we must conceive concerning God, that he forms a
plan of every thing he means to do, in his own mind, previous
to his effecting any thing. This plan formed is a knowledge of
what *may be.* Then he determines to carry the plan in all its parts.
into execution. This determination is also previous to action.
Then, as all things depend on his determination, he knows
what he shall do ; and can predict every event that will take
place, if he pleases, from the beginning to the end of time.
This is a knowledge of what *will be.*

Now a knowledge of what may be is previous to his determinations. But this is not foreknowledge. For foreknowledge
is a knowledge of what *will be,* whereas this is only a knowledge of what *might be.* But when he has determined what he
will do, then he knows before hand what will have existence.
This is *foreknowledge.* This is *subsequent to his determinations,*
and founded upon them.

It is like this. A man forms the plan of a building in his own mind, which he knows might be erected. But he does not know that it ever will be built, because he has not as yet determined to erect such a house. The plan then he has formed, is only a knowledge of what might be done. When he has determined to build a house, exactly according to the plan he has formed, and as the erection of it depends solely on him, he then knows what will be done. And all this he knows before he does any thing. Now a foreknowledge of a house exists in his own mind. This foreknowledge is founded on his determinations.

We now now see what reason teaches concerning the divine being.

1. That divine *determinations or decrees must precede action.* God neither did nor can do any thing, but what he has decreed to do ; because no being can act without determination. This establishes the doctrine of divine decrees, which is taught in the bible. It proves that he did decree to make such a world, in all its parts, as we see exists ; and to govern the universe according to his plan ; and that no events can or will take place, but as he has decreed. As every thing depends on him, and as he cannot act without determination, nor otherwise than he has decreed, so the existence of this world, and every event which takes place, must be according to, and an effect of his determination.

2. We see that *two kinds of knowledge exist in the divine mind ;* one is a knowledge of plans, or what *might be,* and is antecedent to his determinations ; the other is a knowledge of what *will be,* and is foreknowledge.

3. That *foreknowledge is different from a decree, and founded upon it, and subsequent to it.* Hence if God had never decreed any thing, he could never have foreknown any thing. This is a most obvious truth. For if any thing depends wholly on my determination, it is impossible for me to know what I shall do, till I have determined what to do. When I have determined what to do, as all depends on me, then I know what I shall do, or what will be done. Hence if any deny divine decrees, they must, to be consistent, deny also the divine foreknowledge. Thus much reason teaches concerning the divine character, and proves the decrees and foreknowledge of God, as clearly taught in the text. Now let us see what the bible teaches concerning the decrees, and prescience of God.

1. Both are expressly asserted in the text. Also the bible

says, he worketh all things according to the counsel of his
own will ; that he doeth according to his pleasure in heaven a-
bove, and on the earth beneath ; that he is of one mind, and
none can turn him ; that the counsel of the Lord shall stand ; and
that all the counsels formed against him shall be frustrated, turned into foolishness, and be carried headlong ; that all things
are his, and he hath a right to do according to his pleasure ;
and many other passages, too numerous to be mentioned. The
evident language of scripture is, that God has decreed all things ;
so that a sparrow is not sold, and a hair does not fall to the
ground, without his notice. And every one will admit this to
be the language of scripture, when they reflect, that it is impossible for God, or any agent, to act without a previous determination ; or that the determination of an agent is the cause of
every thing done by him.

2. The predictions in the bible prove the decrees and prescience of God. The present state of the Jews was predicted
by Moses ; that they should be scattered, and be a by-word, and
a proverb, among all nations. The ruin of Babylon and Tyre
was predicted by Josiah and Jeremiah ; the coming, the birth,
the life, sufferings, death, resurrection, and ascension of Christ,
were all predicted by the prophets, long before he made his
appearance on earth. No one can deny, that the bible contains many important predictions ; and that the book of revelation contains predictions of all the leading and important events
and revolutions, which are to take place from the days of John
to the end of the world.

And it is granted by every one, that no being can look into
futurity and predict events, but Jehovah. The predictions
then, contained in the bible, are a standing proof of the divine
foreknowledge. But how does this prove his decrees ? Only
keep in view what hath already been said, and every one will
readily see, his foreknowledge proves his decrees. His foreknowledge is founded on his decrees. If future events depended solely on any of us, we could not tell what we should do, until we had determined what we would do. We must determine
then what we will do, before we can tell what will be done. If
then we infallibly foretold any event, this proves we had determined, or decreed, that such an event should exist.

The existence and downfal of such a nation as the Jews, and
of such a city as Babylon, depended wholly on God. How
then could he know such a nation would rise and fail, and such

a city, if he had never determined such events ? His foretelling their rise and fall, proves he had decreed it. Thus we see the bible proves, what reason dictates, concerning the decrees and prescience of the great Jehovah.

Now only go on this plan, that God never has decreed any thing, deny this doctrine wholly, and then look at events which have taken place, and see how the divine character must appear. Angels did rebel, and there was war and confusion in heaven. Men have rebelled. Sin, disorder, and confusion have prevailed in this world. Satan has reigned as the god of this world, and done unspeakable mischief. The Son of God has come into this world to destroy the works of the devil ; he has suffered reproach, shame and a cruel death on the cross. His followers have been persecuted, tortured, and cruelly slain. These, and many other such events, have taken place in God's dominions. Was he determined they should take place ? No. Was he determined they should not have existence ? No : say those who deny divine decrees. What then ? He was perfectly indifferent concerning them. What character was that, which was perfectly indifferent concerning such events in his kingdom ? Can any king sustain a more odious character ? Opponents may say, he was determined against their taking place ? Why then did he not prevent them ? Because he could not, consistently with the liberty he had given to his creatures. But is that being wise, who makes creatures, and endues them with such liberty that he cannot govern them ; creatures who will perpetrate the most horrid crimes, and destroy all the order, peace, and happiness of the world he had created, yet he cannot prevent it ? Would it not argue the greatest folly in a man, to make such a clock as would destroy the peace, government, and happiness of his family, and he knew it would, and yet knew he could not prevent it ? Would he make such a clock ? And would God make such creatures, who would do so much unspeakable mischief, and he knew it, yet knew he could not prevent it ? Thus, they who deny the decrees, either make God an indifferent being concerning the most interesting events that ever existed, or make him so weak, or so unwise, that enemies may destroy his kingdom, and it is not in his power to prevent it. But,

II. Let us attend to human liberty, the other proposition contained in the text.

Every person knows by experience what liberty is. It is the

privilege of acting as we please, without restraint, or constraint. This supposes that we have inclinations or desires, which we wish to gratify. If we had no feelings, objects would neither please nor disgust us ; they would not affect us, any more than they do stones. For without feeling, we should be insensible as stones. But mankind have feelings ; they have appetites, inclinations, and desires. Many objects are agreeable, and others are disgustful to us. We wish to obtain and enjoy those things, which are agreeable to us. It is our will or pleasure to possess and enjoy them. And if there is nothing to prevent or hinder our obtaining and enjoying the objects, which are a-greeable, we enjoy liberty ; we feel that we act freely. If a person has a strong inclination to take a journey, to visit a dear friend, it is his will or pleasure to take it. If nothing prevents his making such preparation as he wishes, and nothing hinders his journeying as he wishes ; or if nothing hinders the obtainment of his end, which is making the intended visit ; he acts according to his pleasure, and enjoys all the liberty he wishes. But if he is by some power restrained from taking the journey he wishes, or is constrained to go another way contrary to his desires, in this case his liberty is infringed and destroyed ; for he does not act according to his pleasure. In all that mankind ever do, they always have some object or end, which they wish to attain. And to act as they please, and to act freely, is to pursue and obtain their object or end, without any thing to hinder or prevent. In such cases they act freely ; and they cannot conceive of any greater liberty than they enjoy. For no one can conceive of any greater liberty, than to act free from all restraint and constraint. Then men always act as they please, and follow their inclinations whithersoever they lead them.

Now do mankind wish to live in a condition, in which it is very uncertain whether they shall enjoy liberty ? And to have it very uncertain, whether, if they act, they shall obtain the end they seek ? No person would wish to live in such a state. Then there are two things, which men desire. One is, to have it made certain, that they shall always act freely, or enjoy liberty ; and the other is, to have it made certain, that when they act, they shall always reach the end they seek. And if it is made absolutely certain, that they shall always enjoy liberty, and always succeed in reaching the ends they seek, the more pleased they are. They wish to have it *certain* that they shall act freely, in the management of all their temporal and spiritual concerns ; and they wish to have it *certain*, that if they sow, they shall reap. Mankind then are friendly to the idea of *necessity*, when it agrees with their wishes ; and never oppose it, only when contrary to their wishes. Now all see what liberty is ; it is to act as we please, or as our inclinations lead us to act, free from all restraint and constraint from any external agent. Can you conceive of any greater liberty ? Are you not conscious that you enjoy this liberty ? Do you not daily act as you please ? Do you not rise in the morning, and thro' the day follow your inclinations and desires ? Is there any external agent, who restrains you *from* acting as you wish ; or who constrains you to act *contrary* to your wishes ? If not, you are perfectly free.

III. Inquire whether divine decrees are inconsistent with human liberty. Some say they are, and destroy it. Some say they agree, but it is beyond the power of mortals to show their consistency with each other. All I shall attempt is, to show what the decrees of God are with respect to human liberty. This perhaps will show clearly their consistency.

Previous to the creation of man, God formed the plan of such a being in his own mind, as he intended to create. Then he created him, according to the plan he had formed. Hence he formed a plan of a human body, of all its parts, and connexions. He also formed a plan of the soul, or immortal part, he meant to create. He formed a plan in his mind to agree with his own image. The model formed was this ; that the soul should be endued with certain faculties ; such as an understanding, to perceive objects, to reason, to judge, to remember, and to reflect. Also man was to have that faculty given him, which in scripture is called the heart ; the philosophical name for it is *taste*. This was a faculty capable of pleasure and pain, of loving, hating, desiring, and of all the affections and passions we ever experience. He was to have given him a will, to enable him to choose and refuse, and to carry the wishes of the heart into execution. According to the plan formed, man was to be a free agent ; and always act as he pleased, or to follow and gratify the inclinations and desires of his heart, without any thing to hinder or prevent. Such soul would resemble God, and be in his likeness and image. This soul, when made, was to be united to the body ; and this union was to continue until death. This is the plan formed. And we have shown that a plan of operation must be formed, previous to determination ; because determination respects the plan. For the determination is, to accomplish the plan formed, in all its parts. And this determination must precede action, or the exertion of power to execute the plan. Now when God had formed a plan of a man in his mind, as we do of a building, such a being as man would never exist, if God did not determine to give him existence ; as we should, never erect a house, till we determine to do it. God did determine to make such a being as man, and to create him exactly according to the plan he had formed in his mind. Man is created according to the plan formed, and according to the determination, or decree of God. And we find it is a fact, that all men have bodies, and souls, which are alike. They all have an understanding, a heart to feel, and a will to choose. They do in fact enjoy liberty. Here observe, every part of a man is the effect of the decrees of God. God said, that is, decreed, let there be light, and light was ; the existence of the light was the effect his decree produced. God said, or decreed, let a man exist, with the faculties of understanding, heart, and will, and with the privilege of always acting freely, or as he pleases. Such a man exists. And every part of his existence, all his qualities, properties, and powers, and his liberty are the effects of the decrees of God. And if God had not decreed to make such a being as man, such a being would have never existed.

Now all you have to do is, to inquire whether the decrees of God destroy the liberty of man. So far from it, they are the cause of his existing, and acting as a free, moral agent. Did God's decreeing the existence of light, destroy, impede, or hinder its existence ? Did his decreeing to make a man, who should always act as he pleased, or freely, destroy the idea of liberty ? Why does man exist ? Because God decreed it. Why does he reason, feel, will and act? Because God decreed he should. Why does he follow his inclinations, and act as he pleases, and free from restraint and constraint ? Because God decreed he should always thus act. Then the decrees of God, so far from infringing, or destroying the liberty of moral agents, are the cause of all the liberty enjoyed. The perfect liberty of man is the effect of his decree. And it is as certain that man will always act freely, as it is that the decrees of God will never alter. Take away this decree, and man, together with his liberty, would immediately

3

cease to exist. The decrees of God are the foundation and cause of the existence of moral agents, and of perfect freedom, and of the continuance of their existence and liberty. Now every one may judge, whether decrees are inconsistent with human liberty. And it seems all must see, that so far from infringing liberty, the decrees of God are the foundation, on which the liberty of moral agents wholly rests for its support.

Remarks. 1. Did not Joseph's brethren act freely in selling him ? Did they not act as they pleased ; did they not follow their own inclinations ? At one time it was their aim to kill him ? After that it was more their pleasure to sell him ; and this they did. Why did they act thus freely ? Because God decreed they should act freely in all they did. While acting thus freely, they did what God had decreed, and were fulfilling his decrees. But did they mean this ? No, they meant to gratify their revenge, & did it ; & God meant by what they did, to promote the glorious ends, which were accomplished by Joseph's living in Egypt. Did not the Jews act freely in crucifying Christ ? Why did they ? Because God decreed they should follow their inclinations. And they gratified their hatred and revenge, in putting him to death ; & in doing it they fulfilled the decrees of God. It was not their object to fulfil his decrees, or to do his will ; but to please their own hearts. But God's object was to promote his own glory in the salvation of men. Here we see men may act freely, and in so doing perform what God has decreed ; and in the same events men and God have totally different ends ; and men may be wicked, and God righteous.

In this manner all men act. They always act freely ; yet are always doing what God has decreed. What men aim at is, to do their will, to gratify and please their own lusts. While they thus live, they do the will of God, contrary to their intention. Hence men act just as though nothing was decreed. Because they act just as they would, if nothing ever had been decreed. Hence it is easy to see how men may do their own will, and be very wicked, and yet without meaning it, do the will of God. A person's inclination may lead him to do something you wish to have done. He does it to please himself, not you ; yet he has done the very thing you wished. In this case you easily see he is as deserving of blame, as he would have been, if the thing he did had been something contrary to your wishes ; because his end is the same in both cases. Men never act with

a view to fulfil the decrees of God ; they are never influenced
by his decrees, neither can be ; because they never know before hand what they are. Yet while they are doing their own
will freely, without meaning it, they are fulfilling the decrees.
And their wickedness, and blameworthiness are the same they
would be, if no decree had ever existed.

2. Sinners travel the road freely, which leads to hell, and
saints walk the path freely, which leads to heaven. The very
life the wicked live, is the road to death. Why do they live
this life ? Because it is their pleasure, agreeable to their inclinations. And they complain, when they are so restrained that
they cannot gratify their feelings. As you prefer this road,
how can you justly complain, if you land in hell ? Has a man
any reason to complain, when he reaps the same seed he freely
sowed ? Eternal death is the wages, the fruit of sin. While
you sow the seeds of corruption freely, have you any ground
to complain, that you reap corruption and death ? Saints also
act freely. It is their pleasure to serve God; their inclinations
lead them to it. And they never serve God any further, than
their hearts prompt them to do it. All who come to Christ,
come freely. For they never do come, till their inclination
leads them to him. Hence all men act freely, and all act as
their inclination leads them ; and all do their pleasure, as far
as their power extends.

3. Men never find fault with the divine decrees, only when
they cross their feelings. God has decreed that men shall always act as they please. This decree they approve. He has
decreed that the truly virtuous and benevolent shall be forever
blessed. This they like. He has decreed that the husband-
man shall reap what he sows, that all seeds shall produce their
own kind ; that seed time and harvest, summer and winter shall
succeed each other. Such decrees they approve, and a thous-
and others, which accord with their own feelings. God has also decreed, that the wicked shall lie down in hell. This they
dislike ; for they wish to live a wicked life, and yet be saved.
They wish to serve satan while they live, and at death be admitted into heaven. And because God has decreed they shall,
after death, live and suffer with the master they served through
life, they are provoked. They do not find fault with this decree, because it is unreasonable ; but merely because it is contrary to their wishes.

But it is the nature of fallen man, to find fault with every thing which is opposed to his wishes and feelings. Men are often angry with themselves, because they cannot gratify all their desires. One loves money, and loves a life of intemperance ; loves honor, and hates poverty and disgrace. His feelings are so opposite to each other, that he cannot gratify them all. His love for spirits is his strongest inclination ; and he freely indulges it, till poverty like an armed man comes upon him, and he is covered with shame and disgrace, and his family is ruined. Then he murmurs, frets, and finds fault with himself for his folly, and with every one around him. Go where he will, it appears to him every one dislikes him; this he cannot endure. If he enters the sanctuary, and hears the word preached, it seems to him that all he hears is aimed at him ; because he is in such a state, that almost every truth is against him. Now he leaves the house of God, provoked, and angry with his Maker. How many besides drunkards often by their own misconduct plunge themselves into such a state, that they cannot please themselves, or gain a reputation with the virtuous and pious. In this state they are peevish, turbulent, and do nothing but make themselves and others around them unhappy.

What would men have, if they could ? They would have power to gratify all the inclinations of their hearts ; and they would do all this with impunity, without ever being called to an account, or punished for any of their deeds. In order to this they must be omnipotent, and exalted above God himself, so as to be independent of him and all other beings. In this they never will be indulged. Hence they never will, or can be gratified, while they remain enemies to God.

4. What is meant, when persons say, they cannot help acting as they do, because every thing is decreed, and that they cannot counteract the decrees of God ? The thing meant is, they cannot help acting as they please ; for this is what is decreed. And it is true that persons cannot act contrary to their pleasure. Are they any the less worthy of blame for this? This is the very reason why they are blameable when they do wrong, because they *have* acted as they pleased. It was their *pleasure* to do wrong, and they do it. And who can shew a worse spirit than a person does when he says, in murdering a man, I did my pleasure. So all sinners act, and in all their wickedness they only do their pleasure? It is their pleasure to act wickedly ; and they cannot help it while they remain wicked, for they must act according to their pleasure. That is the vilest heart,

whose pleasure it is to be always living in rebellion against God, rejecting his Son, and refusing offered mercy.

5. To be happy, men must submit to the will of God.

When their hearts are united to the happiness and glory of God's kingdom, then it will be their desire that all things should promote these ends, and terminate in the highest felicity of God's friends. When they learn from the word of God, that no events shall take place ultimately to injure his cause ; and that every event necessary to advance it shall take place ; and are assured that all this is made certain by the unalterable decrees of God, then they feel safe and happy. The accomplishment of his decrees is doing his will, which is the highest glory of his kingdom. As his decrees assure them of the accomplishment of all their desires, they are the foundation of their peace, safety and joy. Whatever may take place, they rejoice that God reigns. They submit to his will. Take away his decrees, their foundation of joy and safety is removed. Hence no subject is more pleasing to the christian, than the divine decrees. And no subject is more disgustful to the wicked. Can any characters then be more opposite, than those who love, and those who hate the decrees? And if those who love them are saints, how can those be saints who hate them? This is a test, by which to try and know the hearts of men.

※ ░░░░░░

ESSAY XXIV.

Containing arguments from scripture, that the sentiments advanced in the preceding essays are true.

Here it is necessary for the reader to recal to mind the sentiments which have been advanced, and which I propose to substantiate by scripture. Otherwise he will not see the relation of arguments to the points to be established, nor feel their force.

The leading sentiments advanced in the essays written are these; that the taste, or heart, is a faculty of the mind, separate and distinct from the understanding and will : that it is a moral faculty, containing all the *primary* principles of action in moral agents ; and is the seat, or fountain of all vice and virtue. So that when we trace back all the actions ever performed by men, with a view to ascertain their original and primary source from which they all proceed, we shall find, that according to scripture, the heart is this fountain. If this be a truth taught in the bible, then the sentiments advanced in these essays are true, bible sentiments ; otherwise they are not. For the whole system these essays contain is founded on this principle, that the heart or taste is a distinct faculty.

All the operations of the human mind, of which we are conscious, or of which we see indications in others, are included in three general classes. First, *perceptions*. And the more any person examines the subject, the more he will be convinced, I am confident, that all the operations of what are called *reason*, *memory*, *judgment*, *conscience*, *imagination*, or simple *apprehension*, are nothing more or less than *perceptions* of objects, differing from each other in the manner which has been described ; which difference is the reason of dividing them into several specific classes.

Secondly, *affections* form another general class of operations. An affection or passion is a compound of either painful or agreeable sensations, with desires to avoid the painful, or obtain the agreeable object. These have the same generic, or general nature. The more they are examined, the more evident this will appear. These affections have a specific difference, and ought accordingly to be divided into specific classes as has been attempted.

Thirdly, *volitions* constitute another general class of operations. A volition is an exertion made by an agent, with a view to produce external effects, for the purpose of gratifying the affections or desires, or doing our pleasure. These have the same general nature, without any specific difference ; and are not divisible into specific classes.

The first class are the operations of the *understanding* ; the second class, operations of the *heart* or *taste* ; the third class, operations of the *will*. These three classes contain all the operations of the mind of man. We experience no other, we see no other ; of course we never hear any person say or write any thing concerning any other operations. And I believe every person, who has candidly read the essays on the operations of the mind, must be convinced, that there is as real a generic difference between the affections and volitions, as there is between either of them and the operations of the understanding. Hence, for the same reason that all correct writers have considered the mind as having *two* distinct faculties termed the understanding and the will, they must admit a third called the heart or the taste. Perceptions and volitions are so different, it is agreed, that they cannot be operations of the same faculty. And the sensations and desires, or the affections and passions, are a class of operations so different from perceptions, they cannot belong to the understanding ; and they are so different from volitions, that they cannot belong to the will ; of course, they must be the operations of another faculty, which is properly called the heart.

Now if the bible teaches that all moral good and evil proceed from the heart ; that the affections are operations antecedent to volitions, and contain all vice and virtue ; then it proves that the heart ought to be considered a distinct faculty, of which the affections are its operations. If the bible establishes this sentiment, it proves the system explained in these essays to be according to the mind of God. This is the point to be proved, to which I shall now attend.

I will begin with our Saviour's answer to the question of the scribe. He answered, thou shalt love the Lord thy God with all thy heart, and thy neighbor as thyself. Here Christ makes a plain distinction between the heart, and love ; the former is a faculty, and the latter an operation of it. Here he brings into view the person, the agent, *thou ;* and the faculty, which is to be exercised to its utmost strength, the heart ; and the exercise, or operation of it, called love. Thus viewed, the language is correct, and makes good sense. If a person was commanded to reason with all his understanding, the ideas we should receive would be these ; the person as an agent is to reason, not with the heart, but understanding ; this is to be exercised to its utmost strength, and reasoning is its operation. Such modes of expression make good sense, and agree with our common understanding. But to construe the passage to agree with the opinions of some, would be nonsense, and vain tautology. They say the heart and love are the same thing ; love is the heart ; we know of nothing antecedent to love. To construe the passage to agree with this sentiment, we must read it thus, thou shalt love the Lord thy God with all thy love. If love is the heart, this is its sense, and proper reading. But who can agree to this sense, if free from prejudice? Here then our Lord plainly distinguishes between the heart as a faculty, and its operations. On this ground and no other, the words are intelligible. Again; Math. 7. 15—21, Christ teaches that as we know trees by their fruit, so we are to know men by their fruit. This passage exhibits the same sentiment with the former.

What do we learn from the fruit a tree brings forth? We learn its *nature*, whether it be good or corrupt. It is an opinion universally prevalent, that every being has a *nature* peculiar to itself; and its fruit will be good or bad, according to its nature. Hence by its fruit we learn its nature. It is on this ground our Lord uses the similitude in this passage. If men have not a nature, different from their fruit, by their fruit we learn nothing. To say men have no nature distinct from and antecedent to their fruit, is destroying the force of our Savior's reasoning in this passage entirely.

Here then we must inquire, what that fruit is by which men are to be known. He is speaking of false teachers, and says they come to men in sheep's clothing, but inwardly are ravening wolves. By their fruits ye shall know them. But their external actions, words, and conduct are good. These constitute the sheepskin, with which they externally clothe and adorn themselves. They outwardly manifest great love, humility, and zeal in the cause of Christ. To judge them by this fruit, we should say they are what they appear to be, real sheep, friends of Christ. But when we look farther, we find that their inward feelings are against the truth. They show a hatred of truth, a proud, self-conceited spirit, a self-righteous temper. They manifest a want of humility, of love to Christ, and to the self-denying doctrines of the cross. These internal affections seen in them are the fruit, by which we learn their nature, and detect their hypocrisy; and by it are convinced they have the nature of a wolf, though they have on externally sheep's clothing. It is by the affections of the heart we learn what men are. If we wish to know whether a person is renewed or not, we labor to learn what his inward feelings or affections are. If we discover love to God, repentance for sin, a humble, and teachable spirit, faith in Christ, love to the truth, resignation to the will of God; if we see evidence of these inward affections, we infer from them that he has a new heart. Indeed, such internal affections are the fruits by which we know men. These are the fruits of the Spirit, as they are enumerated by the Apostle in

Gal. 5. 22, 23, and in many other passages. If we do not discover such affections in a person, we have no evidence that he is born again ; though outwardly his life may be regular and inoffensive, and though he may manifest much joy, fervency, and zeal in the cause of Christ. It is by such fruit false teachers are detected. It is by our internal feelings or affections, we judge ourselves as well as others. And these are the fruits of the Spirit, and the fruits by which our Lord would have us judge of men in the passage under consideration.

But what are we to learn by this fruit ? We learn the moral nature or character of men. Every being has a nature. Of this we have no intuitive view, we cannot see it as God does. We learn it by their fruit. From the fruit which we see, we infer what the nature of any being is. Where we see rational operations and exercises, we infer from them that the person has a rational faculty, called the understanding. From voluntary operations or exertions, we infer the man has a will, a willing faculty. And from those operations which we call affections, desires, or passions, we infer that men have a heart, the faculty called by this name. And from these fruits, when we see them, we infer what the nature, the temper of the heart is, whether it be good or bad. In this way we learn there is a great difference between the hearts of different persons, and between the heart of man at one time, and the heart he has at another time.

But on supposition man has not such a faculty as we call the heart, which is antecedent to its operations, and distinct from them, then from the affections or fruits we see in man nothing can be inferred, and the whole force of our Savior's reasoning is destroyed. But in the ground I have taken, his reasoning is full to the point, and conclusive.

All men believe trees have a nature, something in their constitution which prepares them to bear different kinds of fruit. What the nature of the tree is, when they approach it, they know not. Nature is something beyond the direct view of men ; and something which we cannot ascertain, only by its fruit. And if we admit this principle as just, that every tree will bear fruit according to its nature, then from its fruit we safely infer its nature. It was on this principle Christ at all times reasoned, when the nature of any thing was to be learned. Hence if men have no such thing as a nature, no faculties distinct from, and antecedent to their operations, from their fruits nothing is to be

4

inferred, and the reasoning of our Lord has no force. But if there are faculties belonging to the mind, which are antecedent to their operations, and which are known to men only by their operations or fruits ; then our Lord's reasoning is conclusive. Hence, when we see what kind of affections men have, whether they are holy or sinful, the fruits of the Spirit or of the flesh, then we know what the heart of man is. From their fruit we infer two things—1. That they have the faculty called the heart, which is antecedent to all affections, the foundation or fountain from which they rise. 2. We infer the moral nature of this faculty. In some we find it is altogether corrupt. In others we learn it is holy in part, though not perfect as yet. Such are the sentiments taught by Christ in this passage. And when the temper of the heart is known, then we know what a person's moral character is, whether good or bad. For not his *fruit*, but his *nature*, constitutes his moral character. And if we could have an intuitive view of the heart as God has, we should know what every person's nature or moral character is, and what fruit he would bring forth, without having first seen the fruit. We should know *certainly*, by an intuitive view, what their nature is ; but to judge by their fruit, we may form an erroneous opinion. This passage, then, proves the sentiments it is brought to establish, conclusively. There is no fair way to evade the force of the argument.

Another passage of the same import is in Math. 15. 19. For out of the heart proceed evil thoughts, murders, adulteries, fornication, thefts, falsewitness, blasphemies. The sins here mentioned are internal, such as sinful desires, affections, and passions. If it be admitted, that those external actions called by those names are included, yet the internal desires of the heart are also intended by our Savior. And he undoubtedly had his eye expecially fixed on such evil desires within. For Christ has taught that the desires of the heart are sinful. If a man look on a woman, to lust after her, he hath committed adultery with her already in his heart. Lust is a desire. This desire to commit the unlawful act, is adultery ; and this is a sin of the heart. The heart here is the fountain, from which such evil desires proceed. Also John saith, he that hateth his brother is a murderer. Hence hatred is expressly called murder. And the moral law extends to the heart, and condemns all sinful desires or affections. Indeed, when desires exist to murder, to steal, to commit adultery, or perpetrate any crime, the person is then in the sight of God guilty of these crimes. This the word and law of God clearly teach.

Such evil desires, our Lord says, proceed from the heart. He makes here a clear distinction between the heart and its operations, or desires. Such desires defile the man. He represents the heart here as a fountain, and desires as the streams proceeding from it. And by these streams, or desires, every person may know what his heart is, whether holy or sinful. This passage, with the former which has been explained, expressly leads us to view the heart as existing antecedent to its desires or operations, and as constituting the moral character of man.

Another text spoken by Christ, of the same import, is in Luke 6. 45. A good man out of the good treasure of the heart, bringeth forth that which is good ; and an evil man out of the evil treasure of the heart, bringeth forth that which is evil. This passage is in connexion with what Christ said concerning trees, that they are known by their fruit, and that men are known by their fruit. Hence the good treasure of the heart, or the heart itself, which is the same thing, is the nature which is known by the good or evil things which proceed from it.

Every person has what is here called a good, or an evil treasure ; and from this all good or evil, both internal and external, proceed. If we see in false teachers or any other persons, such evil desires or affections prevailing, as hatred of God, envy, revenge, pride, anger, selfconceit, and the like, we should pronounce them wicked men, and say their hearts are full of evil. Mankind do not consider such affections as constituting the primary, and real character of man ; but as evidences of his real character. That every man has a heart, either sinful or holy, which is antecedent to its operations ; and that every person's moral character is what this heart is, is evident from the manner in which persons uniformly express themselves, in conversation and writing in relation to this subject. Their manner is to say that the *heart hates, loves,* and so on. They never say, that *hatred hates,* and *love loves ;* which they ought to do, in case love and hatred, or the affections, constitute all that is ever meant by the heart. To say the heart loves, when in fact love is the heart, is ever calculated to convey erroneous ideas. Hence if there is no heart antecedent to affections, a radical change ought to take place in the use of language. It is needless to multiply passages, which are of the same import with these already explained. Every one may now easily see that every passage in the bible, where a distinction is made between the heart and its operations, the heart and the affections and fruits which proceed from it, are direct proofs of the sentiment they are adduced to establish. Such passages are very numerous, and need not here be quoted.

One method is taken to evade the force of such passages. Writers make a distinction between *immanent* and *imperate* acts of the will. They then say, by the heart with which we love, from which good and evil proceed, and the good treasure of which Christ speaks, are meant *immanent acts;* & the *imperate* acts are the fruits which proceed from them. In their view immanent acts constitue the heart, & imperate acts are the things which proceed from it. Hence they say, there is nothing, no faculty, no heart, antecedent to immanent affections; and these and imperate acts are both of them exercises of the will; or in fact, their immanent acts constitute the will, and imperate acts are the operations of it.

In answer to this objection, several things may be observed.

1. Their *immanent acts* are what are called the affections and passions. These are called immanent, because they do not immediately produce any external actions. Love may exist, yet not appear outwardly in any actions. Still it remains there, and never will become visible, till imperate acts are exerted. According to this distinction and this scheme, immanent acts give rise to imperate acts ; and imperate acts produce external and visible fruit. Imperate acts proceed from the immanent, as streams from the fountain ; and from the imperate acts proceed external actions and fruits. This is their scheme, if I can understand it. Hence when it is is said that out of the heart proceed evil thoughts, and from the good treasure men bring forth good things, they say immanent affections are the heart, and imperate acts and external fruits proceed from them. On this sentiment it is proper to remark.

1. That all virtue and vice must consist in these immanent affections. If love to God may exist in any degree antecedent to any imperate acts, it may exist in a perfect measure. A person may be said to love God with the *whole heart*, and in this respect be as perfect as any saint in heaven. This love may exist and remain in his heart an hour, without any other acts proceeding from it ; and if an hour, it may remain there a month, or a year, without producing any imperate or external actions. This is certainly possible. In this case the person may be, and is, all this time, a perfect character, perfectly holy and benevo-

lent in the sight of God. Hence his virtue primarily and essentially consists in this immanent affection. And as this may, so other immanent holy affections may exist in perfection for days, months, and years, without giving rise to any imperate acts, or producing any external fruit. This also is possible. In like manner, immanent sinful affections may exist in their full strength for days and months, without producing any imperate acts or external fruits. This is also certainly possible. According to this scheme a person may be a perfectly holy, or a perfectly sinful character, for days and months, without having one imperate act, or performing one external action. This shows to a demonstration, that on this scheme immanent affections constitute the moral character of every person. Those affections comprise all virtue, or vice, which ever exist in men. This I think is now evident ; and I wish it to be carefully noticed and kept in view.

2. From the preceding demonstration it follows, that imperate acts are no more of a moral nature than external actions, are not considered as criminal, and constituting any part of murder. These imperate acts, or voluntary exertions, which immediately produced these effects, are not murder, nor do they constitute any part of it. They are only the fruit of a murderous heart. The person's hand, which holds the dagger, and thrusts it, is not an active principle, nor the primary cause in the agent of this murder. This hand acted, as it was moved by the agent. This is the reason why the hand is not blamed. And those imperate acts which produced those effects, are not a primary principle of action in this case. They are such as the heart, or immanent act, produced ; they obeyed the command of the heart, just as the hand obeyed these imperate acts. And for the same reason the hand is not worthy of blame, these imperate acts are not worthy of it. Again, murder had a complete and full existence, previous to those imperate and external acts. Hatred, or what is called *malice prepense*, constitutes the agent a murderer ; and this hatred is an immanent affection, and the primary principle of action in the agent, which gave rise to those imperate and external actions. Hence, there is the same difference between immanent and imperate acts, as there is between acts which are virtuous or vicious, and those which are not ; or between virtuous or vicious actions, and external actions.

3. It follows, that imperate acts are not affections. They

are mere voluntary exertions, to produce some bodily motion and some external action or effect. The immanent acts are the affections. Love and hatred, and every other affection, has complete existence before imperate acts arise, or any exertions are made to produce external effects. A voluntary exertion, therefore, is not an affection, nor an affection continued, any more than the motion of the hand is an affection continued. And it seems to me that every person is conscious of a difference between love when he feels it, and voluntary exertions. If a person experiences a warm love for an absent person, and then by a voluntary exertion puts his body in motion to go and visit the beloved object, is he not conscious of a difference in those operations ? Does he not perceive as real a difference, as he experiences between an affection and the exertion of strength to raise or move a heavy body ? Imperate acts, or voluntary exertions, are mental strength, exercised to obtain the object of an affection, or to avoid it. This voluntary exertion is not a sensation of pleasure or pain, nor a desire ; but both of these together constitute an affection. Volition is a mere simple exertion of the mind, or rather of the will, to gratify an affection in obtaining possession of its object. It does not, therefore, partake of the nature of an affection.

Imperate acts are internal operations of the mind, as really as immanent acts are. They are internal and invisible, until seen in the external fruits they produce. Hence they are not called imperate acts, to distinguish them from those which are internal. Why then are they thus termed ? It is, as I suppose, because they command the existence of external actions; they regulate and govern the external conduct of all men. But they are inferior commanders. And whence do they receive their orders ? From the immanent affections, as the abettors of this distinction allege. Hence they are the only servants to their master, who in fact governs the whole man.

These observations are sufficient to show, that there is a wide moral difference between immanent and imperate acts. Immanent acts comprise all vice and virtue, and are the primary principle of action in moral agents. But imperate acts are neither virtuous nor vicious ; are not of a moral nature in any other sense, than external actions are ; nor are they primary principles of action. They are in fact only servants to the immanent affections ; they are not affections, and nothing more than simple exertions, whose end is to gratify the affections.

No operations of the human mind differ in their nature more widely. Can any candid person then say, that they are operations of the same faculty; and differ from each other in no other sense, than the first and all successive acts of the same series differ from each other? We might with as much reason say, that our perceptions or rational operations, and affections, are of the same nature, and differ in no other sense than the first and successive acts of the same series differ. They so widely differ in their nature, that they must be the operations of different faculties. And as the advocates of this scheme say, that imperate acts are operations of the *will*; the immanent acts, or affections, must be the operations of some third faculty. They cannot be the operations of the understanding, and for the same reason they are not the operations of the will; of course they belong to some other faculty, and we say the heart is this faculty. And if there must be a third faculty, to which the affections belong, our opponents would not object against attributing them to the heart.

Though they sometimes admit the existence of faculties, yet at other times they deny it. If we meet them on this ground, they must acknowledge the existence of *three distinct classes* of operations, belonging to the mind. One class includes all our perceptions or rational operations. A second class includes all the affections and passions. And a third class comprises all our volitions, or exertions to produce external actions. And we may reduce these classes to one, with as much reason, as to reduce them to two. Therefore, when this distinction of our opponents is fairly examined, it makes nothing in their favor, nor in the least evades the force of the texts adduced to support our system.

For now, to be consistent, they must grant, that by heart in these texts is meant that faculty called in these essays the heart; or if they deny the existence of faculties, they must grant, that the second class of operations, called the affections, constitutes the heart. Then this heart, which we call a faculty, and which on their scheme must be considered a distinct class of operations, is the heart intended in scripture; which includes all moral operations, all vice and virtue, and from which as a fountain all good and evil fruit proceeds. And this is the point for which we contend; and the sentiment they mean to undermine by their distinction between immanent and imperate acts. But their distinction fails them on examination, and is devested of

232

all its force. Hence the scriptures adduced retain all the evidence contended for, to prove the sentiment for which they were
adduced.

✻✻✻✻✻✻

ESSAY XXV.

Objections against this system, stated, and answered.

Objection 1. It is said this scheme represents vice and virtue, as consisting in principles which are inactive and dormant;
which is contrary to all our ideas of vice and virtue ; and according to which we may as well suppose, that sin and holiness
may be as rationally predicated of inactive matter. No principle, say they objectors, can be holy or sinful, unless it is active. Activity is essential to their existence. And as there is
no action, or activity but in volitions, or such exercises ; vice
and virtue cannot have existence in any thing else. This is one
objection in its full force, so far as my knowledge extends.

Answer. It is evident the person, who makes this objection, for some reason or other, has not understood the sentiments to which he objects. I have labored to prove there are,
and must be, different and distinct principles of action in the human heart. There is no other way to account for the effects it
produces, and to accord with facts, and the experience of all
mankind. But I have no where said, that these principles are inactive, and dormant. If I have, it is a great oversight. Again,
the scheme advanced in these essays, is fully proved by the
scripture account of the christian warfare. According to the
word of God, saints have in their hearts what are termed the *flesh*
and *spirit ;* the *law* of the members, and the *law* of the mind ;
the *old* and *new man* ; so that when they would do good evil is
present with them.

These opposite principles abide and remain in them. They
do not succeed each other, as volitions do, but are permanent.
They are in the same man, at the same time. According to the
word, they are very *active, operative* principles ; and the affec-

tions proceeding from them are as different from each other, as sin and holiness. Also they oppose each other at the *same time.* The flesh *lusteth* against the spirit ; and the spirit *lusteth* against the flesh. The law in the members *wars* against the law of the mind ; and the law of the mind *wars* against the law in the members. From one of these fountains proceed sweet, and from the other bitter waters ; and the old and the new man are constantly at variance. In the opposition of these two active principles to each other, consists the christian warfare ; that inward war, which all real saints experience. This is the scripture account of this warfare ; and it is perfectly similar to the description of the heart given in these essays. It has been shown that the heart of man is composed of several distinct appetites, from which proceed different and opposing affections, both in saints and sinners ; so that sinners experience a warfare at times, as well as saints, though of a different moral complexion. For the warfare of the sinner is between one sinful and another sinful affection, which arise from distinct appetites, or inclinations. But the war of the christian is in the opposition of holy, and sinful affections. And this, it is believed, is the only scriptural and rational description, which can be given of the christian warfare. And as this is agreeable to these essays, the word of God, by giving the same view of the subject, fully establishes the leading sentiments advanced in them.

If we take the ground of some, that all vice and virtue consist in voluntary exercises ; and that two of these do not exist in the mind at the same time, but are constantly succeeding each other ; a warfare seems to be impossible. For a war necessarily supposes two parties, opposed, and contending, at the same time. Though holy and sinful volitions are different and opposite in their *nature ;* yet they cannot in that case contend or fight with each other, because they are never on the ground, or in the mind, at the same time. How can two armies fight, if not opposed to each other in the field at the same time ? If they come into the field in succession, so that one has left the ground before the other occupies it, there cannot be any *actual fighting* between them. Also, on the scheme that men have but one volition at a time, and that all vice and virtue consist in volitions, saints must be perfectly holy, or perfectly sinful, through every moment of their existence in this world. For the same simple volition cannot be partly holy, and partly sinful ; and this is granted by them. Hence, when they have holy volitions

5

they are perfectly holy, and when they have sinful volitions, they are perfectly sinful. Hence they fall from grace, and are renewed again, perhaps a thousand times every day. Such ideas are too absurd to be admitted. Yet they necessarily follow from the sentiment now opposed. If it be admitted, to avoid such absurdities, that the heart is a faculty, which exists antecedent to any of its operations, and is the seat of all vice and virtue ; yet if it is a *simple faculty*, how is it possible to account for the christian warfare ? It is very inconsistent to suppose that a simple faculty, or the same simple principle of action, should contain in itself two different and opposite moral natures. Yet it must, in order to account for its sending forth both sweet water and bitter, at the same time, or to account for the existence of sinful and holy affections at the same time. Of course, on this ground a warfare cannot exist. This simple faculty must be perfectly holy, or sinful. And if saints have both sinful and holy exercises, this faculty must be changed in its nature from holiness to sinfulness, and then back again, as often as they have sinful and holy affections. This is as absurd, as to suppose sinful and holy volitions succeed each other, and of course that persons may be perfectly holy and perfectly sinful many times in a day. And there does not appear to be any way to avoid these absurdities, and to account for the christian warfare of which the scriptures inform us, except on the ground taken in these essays.

Hence the sentiments advanced concerning the heart or taste, as a compound faculty, containing different, active principles, which may and often do oppose each other, are rational and scriptural. It agrees with the experience of Paul, and all christians in every age, who have ever found one law in them warring against another, the flesh and spirit contending, so that when they would do good evil was present to oppose them.

For it has been my design to show, that they are in their *nature* the most active principles in existence ; and the primary cause in moral agents of all the effects ever produced in the universe.—Hence I see no way but one, by which any persons could have received such ideas, as are contained in the objection. These principles have been considered as existing in the order of nature, or of time, antecedent to their operations. So from this, the objector might say, if they exist prior to any operations one second, they might a year, and during that time remain inactive and dormant. But does this prove they are *in-*

active in their *nature* ? It is thought not. The objector, it is supposed, will grant there are such things as *causes* in existence, and causes which are active in their *nature*, and which exist in some sense antecedent to the effects which they produce. Will it follow from this, that all causes are in their nature inactive, and dormant, and of course that there are no *active causes* existing in the universe ? He may as well draw this inference, as the former. Suppose the objector should say, that active causes are always operating. Grant it. Does this prove they did not exist in some sense, previous to the effect they produce ? If it be said, they exist previous to their effects in the order of nature, but not of time : and may not active principles, which are in reality causes, exist in the order of nature previous to their operations ? This he must grant, or boldly say, the operations of the human mind have no cause, but are accidental. For if these causes do not exist in the human mind, they must exist some where. If it be said that God is the immediate cause of all mental exercises ; still this cause existed previous to the operations of the mind, or the operations it produces.

Hence the existence of effects, and all operations of the human mind, prove the existence of active causes and principles ; and that these exist previous to the effects and operations, which they produce. If this be not true, then effects and operations have *no cause*. But this is the principal thing, which I labored to prove ; that active principles do exist in the mind, antecedent to the operations which proceed from them ; antecedent in the order of nature, or of time, or both. And now is the objector prepared to say, that active causes or principles are always operating from the instant they exist, and never cease to operate for one second ? He may assert this ; but can he prove it ? Perhaps he would find he has a task to perform, greater than he supposed, or will be able to accomplish. It is the nature of water to run to the centre. But is it always running ? It is the nature of lightning to deprive man of life. But is it always lightning ? Is this fluid always in operation ? It has been proved, and the objector must grant, or deny the existence of any causes, that active principles do exist previous to their operations. They do produce love, hatred, anger, and a great variety of affections and passions. Is the same person always hating, always loving, always angry ? If not, where is the principle, which produced anger, but is not *now* producing it ? Is it always operating, or producing its proper effect? If so, why is not the same person always angry ? And the saint, who has an active principle in him, operating in love to God ; is he always loving God, and to the same degree ? The objector is a person who is apt to say, that man cannot have but one exercise at a time ; also that he has some sinful exercises; of course, he is not always loving God. Hence, the principle which produces love is not *always* in operation, producing the same affection. If the objector says, when it is not operating in love, it is operating in hatred, and in this sense is *always* operating : but can the same principle produce both love and hatred ? This the scriptures expressly deny. Hence the principle, which operates in love to God, is not operating in the same person, while hatred or some other affection is there. Perhaps it is not easy, or possible, to prove that active causes are always in operation. To say a cause is active in its nature, does not prove this, nor necessarily imply it. If not, then causes or principles may be active in their nature, yet not always be in operation. And to say they are so, a person would involve himself in difficulties, from which he could never extricate himself. By an active cause, active in its nature, no more I believe is generally meant than this, that it produces an effect by its own energy ; or, that it is the primary and only cause, in a person, of a given effect. Love, and all the affections of men, proceed from some primary principle implanted in them. We do not mean by it, that the cause or principle of action is, or is not, always in operation. But when an effect exists, we search for the cause ; when we have traced it to a primary principle in man, so that we find in him nothing antecedent as a cause, we consider this the proper, primary, and real cause in him of the effect. And we call it *active*, because we cannot conceive it possible for any thing to be the real, only cause of an effect, unless it is in its nature energetic, active, capable of operating. This we call an active cause. Some of them may be *always* operating, as we may suppose the benevolence of God has been ; and some of them may not be always in operation. For this idea is not necessarily implied in causes or principles, which we say are operative or active in their nature. However, by primary active causes in men, I do not mean causes which operate independently of God, any more than other *secondary causes* do.

The appetites or principles of action, which constitute the heart, are not dormant, and inactive. Some of them, at certain times, may not be in operation. Whether this is the fact, it may

be impossible to ascertain. But granting they do not all operate at the same time, this no more proves that they are inactive
principles, like inert matter, than that causes are not energetic
in their nature, when they are not producing their respective
effects. These principles of the heart are the only principles
in the universe, of which we have any knowledge, which are active in their nature. And they are the primary cause of all effects which exist ; at least this is my belief. Being active in
their nature, and the primary cause in men of all the good and
evil of which we as agents are the authors, they must be virtuous or vicious. To view them in this light, it is not necessary
every principle should be considered as constantly operating.

To determine whether any thing is good or evil, we wish to
know two things ; what the *nature* of a thing is, and what the
tendency of its nature is. Mankind believe all things have a
nature. Yet many carp at the word, and ask, what is nature ?
By it is generally meant the internal form or construction of a
thing. By the nature of a clock, a vegetable, a tree, is meant
its internal structure, or organization. As these structures are
different from each other, therefore, things are viewed as having
different natures. And we learn what the different natures of
things are, by the various fruits and effects they produce. If
any ask what is meant by the nature of an active principle in
the heart ; the answer is, a particular something, of such a construction, by whatever name it may be called, which is susceptible of *pleasure* and *pain ;* and when either of these is felt, the
principle operates and produces effects. If the fruits or effects
it produces *tend,* or in their *direct course* and *connexion,* if not
prevented, will ultimately destroy happiness, or promote it, it is
good or evil. This is the way, by which we learn what the nature of a thing is. When the divine character is seen by two
persons, if one is pleased with it, and the other displeased, we
are sure they have *different* hearts. If one is good, the other is
evil. But which of them has the good heart, and which the
evil ? This we learn from the ultimate tendency of their operations. If the operations of the heart, which is pleased with
the divine character, promote happiness ultimately, it is good,
or virtuous ; and if the operations of the other destroy happiness, it is evil, or sinful. It is in this way that we learn, that
hatred is an evil, and love to God, a good, affection ; or that
the former is sinful, the latter holy. If love should produce the
effects of hatred, and hatred those of love, ultimately ; then

hatred would have been viewed as holy, and love a sinful affection.

When an object of choice is presented to view, one person
chooses it, and another rejects it. We then know their volitions are not the same in their nature ; and if we say the volition of one is holy, and the other sinful ; yet we cannot determine which of them is holy, and which sinful, till we learn what
is the ultimate tendency of each volition. Hence it is evident,
that those volitions are not sinful or holy, merely because they
are *exercises*, or what is called *action* and *activity*. If they
were, each of them would be sinful or holy ; for each of them
is an *exercise*. The only reason, why exercises, action, activity, energy, is considered essential to vice and virtue, is this ;
nothing else can ever produce effects, and ultimately promote,
or destroy happiness.

If, then, what we call principles or appetites are operative,
active, and will produce effects, which will ultimately destroy
or promote happiness, they have the quality which is necessary
to denominate them sinful or holy. It is said vice and virtue
must consist in *exercise*, and cannot consist in any thing else.
And why ? Plainly, because nothing else will produce effects,
and ultimately promote or destroy happiness. Volitions are
exercises of this kind ; hence they only are sinful or holy. But
it has been proved, that there is, and must be, something antecedent to volitions, which in fact produce or give rise to them ;
or there never would nor could exist such an exercise as a volition. And this something, which we call the heart, composed
of principles of action, is antecedent to voluntary exercises.
And these principles, appetites, or inclinations, are *operative, active*, and do produce volitions, and by this medium external effects and fruits, which ultimately promote or destroy happiness;
and of course are virtuous or vicious. And whether they are
sinful or holy, we must determine in the same way by which
we ascertain the moral nature of volitions ; and that is, by their
ultimate tendency. Seeing such principles do exist in the heart,
whether each of them is operating constantly or not, they are
with the same propriety termed sinful or holy, that the advocates
for the exercise scheme say that all *volitions* are sinful or holy.
And as those principles, whether called principles or immanent
exercises, are antecedent to volitions, or what they denominate imperate exercises, vice and virtue must be primarily seated
in these principles ; these are the fountain, from which all good

and evil in men flow or proceed. And what has now been said is a sufficient answer to the objection.

Here I will put a case, and then proceed. A certain tree produces excellent fruit. From this we infer it has an excellent nature. And by nature here we mean its particular structure, which is the cause or foundation of its producing such good fruit ; whether this nature be active or not. We find this fruit puts an end to misery, wherever it is eaten, and produces nothing but pure constant happiness. Hence its nature is to destroy misery, and promote happiness forever. We therefore call it a good tree ; and its goodness consists primarily in its nature. But we say, it is good in a natural, but not in a moral sense. Suppose this tree should be endued with a faculty of understanding, and could perceive, reason, judge, remember, accuse and condemn. Also had a heart given it, which would be pleased or disgusted with every object seen; and should now become very active and operative in affections ; then in volitions, by being endued with a will ; and in this way produces daily innumerable fruits, which will forever destroy pain and promote happiness. I now ask, would not its nature be good, for the same reason it was before called good ? Would not its nature be good in a moral sense ? And would it not be a moral agent, and a proper object of praise, and of a blessed reward? You answer, yes ; but say, it is no longer a tree ; it is formed into a moral agent. Very well ; but do you not now see all that is necessary to constitute any being a moral agent ; and do you not see that the moral character of such an agent is just what the *nature* of the tree or the heart is ? That his heart, or nature, constitutes his moral character ; and not those volitions, which you call imperate ? And why does the heart constitute his moral character ? Because here are the primary principles of action ; the fountain, from which all good and evil proceed. In this his *agency* consists. Without such a heart, he could not with propriety be termed an agent, and especially a moral agent, any more than a tree.

Objection second. Some say this scheme is Arminianism : that it represents men as acting without motives, governed by a self determining principle, and as being morally good or evil according to their work ; and that it is directly opposed to Calvinism.

Answer. How this objection can arise from the principles advanced in these essays, is beyond my power to conceive. It is not possible for any sentiments to oppose others more directly, than these do the Arminian scheme, if I know what that scheme is. And whether I do understand either the Calvinistic or Arminian scheme of divinity, every one may judge for himself after he has read the essays, and particularly the essay in which the two schemes are stated, and the difference between them illustrated. The essays themselves contain as full an answer to this objection as can be given ; and I will not tire the patience of a reader by adding any thing more, than merely this ; that the person who makes this objection, I am confident, does not understand my sentiments ; and he is advised to study them till he does understand them ; then he will no more make this objection.

Objection third. Some say this scheme tends directly to fatalism ; representing that the universe is governed by an invincible necessity, and liberty is forever excluded.

Answer. It is taken for granted, that the Arminian scheme, and that of the fatalists, are directly opposed to each other. How then can it be accounted for, that when persons read those essays, some should say, it is Arminianism ; and others, it is fatalism ? Can this be accounted for, if all who read them understand the sentiments advanced ? It is thought not. Would it not be well for every person to understand what he reads, before he makes objections against it ?

In these essays it is said, that men are *agents* ; that their agency consists in the active principles of the heart ; that by these principles all men are invariably governed ; that mankind are endued with liberty of will and of action ; and with all the liberty they can conceive of or desire ; and it is shown why such liberty is necessary and for what purpose ; also that men are not only agents, but *moral* agents. It is shown what properties are necessary to constitute complete moral agents, and why they are requisite ; and that men are proper subjects of praise or blame, and of future rewards, according to their moral characters. Is this fatalism ? If so, I have never known what fatalism is. I have always supposed that fatalism excludes all the ideas above stated ; inculcating that men are not moral agents, are not free, are not deserving of praise or blame, or future rewards of any kind ; indeed, that there is no real difference between men and trees.

On the whole, if any person clearly knows what fatalism is, and understands the sentiments I have defended, he will confess that the latter are opposed to fatalism as directly as light to darkness.

Objection fourth. Some say, the scheme advanced in these essays is perfect selfishnesss. That all men seek objects and ends for the same reason, because they please them ; and they seek them to gratify their desires, so that all their pursuits terminate in personal or self gratification; that men seek the glory of God, because it pleases them ; just as men seek their own honor, because it pleases them ; and this is pure and perfect selfishness.

Answer. According to this objection, to avoid selfishness, and be benevolent, a person must choose and act without motives. He must not prefer one object to another, because it is agreeable to him. If he chooses any object, because it is agreeable, he is selfish. Now when objects are presented to the view of the mind, they must please or disgust us *before* they are chosen, or in this way affect us *subsequent* to choice ; or, on the other hand, must neither please nor displease us, *before* or *after* they are chosen. One or the other of these hypotheses must be true.

1. If objects do not please or disgust us before they are chosen, then, if they are ever agreeable or the contrary, it is subsequent to choice. This necessarily implies three things—1. That no reason can be given why an object is chosen ; or, in preferring one object to another, motives have no influence. When objects of choice are before us, and they are not, and must not be, either pleasing or painful, we shall feel in a state of perfect indifference towards them ; and it is in this state we are to make our choice, according to this scheme. When one object is preferred to another, no reason can be given why we preferred it. We cannot say, because it was more pleasing to us. If we say we preferred it because it was our duty, or because it was more valuable than the object rejected, still we are not influenced by any motive. For we are in a state of perfect indifference ; neither the object, nor duty, nor the worth of the object can have any influence. For no object can influence an agent, if it do not affect, please, or pain him. For if we are influenced by either of these considerations, we are *inclined* towards the object previous to choice ; and this the objector calls selfishness. And surely if no considerations move or incline us to prefer one object to another, we are in a state of perfect indifference ; and in this state motives have no influence. If we are governed and influenced by motives, objects must

6

affect us previous to choice ; if they do affect us, we are either pleased or disgusted by them. Because, if they neither please nor offend us, they do not affect us. Hence, according to this scheme, previous to choice we must be in a state of perfect indifference, wholly unaffected by any consideration whatever. And then, if we are pleased,

2. Our pleasures must be subsequent to our choice. One of two things must be true, if objects ever please or displease us ; they must have this effect previous, or subsequent to choice ; unless we say that pleasure and pain are volitions, which is absurd. If they do not excite agreeable or painful sensations previous to choice, they must subsequent to it. If this be true, then our happiness and misery depend on our pleasure ; we can produce either pleasure or pain at any time. For all we have to do is, merely to choose or reject an object. All men love pleasure, and hate pain. Why is it, then, that any suffer themselves to remain in a state of pain one moment, when by a single choice they can render themselves happy? Do any believe that our happiness or misery are produced by us ; that they depend on our pleasure ? If this were true, would persons continue to suffer the pains of disease ; or would sinners remain in a state of torment in hell ? This, however, is the very essence of the Arminian scheme. Bishop King, on the origin of evil, says, that pleasure and pain are subsequent to choice, and we create our own happiness and misery. And he is a consistent Arminian. For objects must please before or after they are chosen, if ever ; the former he denies, as every consistent Arminian must ; and the latter he defends. And all on this ground have embraced the essence of Arminianism. And objects must forever please us, *before* or *after* they are chosen, or

3. They will never afford us any pleasure. This is so evident, it is impossible for any one to deny it. Which, then, of the three hypotheses is true ? If we say, that objects previous to choice never affect us, never excite any pleasing or painful sensations, no not in the least degree ; and this is not, and ought not to be, the reason why we choose one and reject another object ; then we must say, that pleasure and pain are subsequent to choice, and created by it ; or that we never experience either of them. The latter is contrary to daily facts and experience. If we embrace the other hypothesis, we are always in a state of perfect indifference, when we make a choice, and are never influ-

uenced by motives ; and to be consistent, ought to be Arminians in length and breadth. Also, seeing all men hate pain and
love pleasure, why is it that there is any pain, in this world or
a future, since it depends wholly on our pleasure ? Is it not
now evident to every one, that objects must and do affect us, do
please or displease us, previous to choice ; and that this is
the reason why we prefer one to another, because it is more
agreeable to us? And if this be true, then motives govern and
influence us. So far as an object affects, pleases or disgusts us,
so far it *moves, inclines* and *induces* us to choose one and reject
another.—But it is said, this is selfishness. According to this,
saints and sinners are influenced by the same motives, governed by the same reasons.

But I ask, is it wrong, is it sinful in me, to be *pleased* with the divine character ; with the character of Christ ; with the glory & happiness of his holy eternal kingdom ; with the law and service of
God ; & with praising and exalting his name ? If not ; is it sinful
in me, for this reason, to choose God for my portion ; Christ
for my savior ; his law for my rule of duty ; his service to be
my yoke ; and his holy kingdom to be my eternal residence ?
Is this selfishness ? If it is, it is surely a glorious thing to be
selfish.—This objection evidently arises from erroneous ideas
concerning selfishness and benevolence. Every being, who is
destitute of a heart to be pleased with the happiness of other beings, is selfish in all he does. Hunger, and every other appetite in him, is selfish. He seeks every object to gratify his appetite ; and if he destroys the happiness of the universe by feed-
ing this personal desire, he cares not ; because he has no love,
no feeling for the happiness of any but himself.

But if a person rejoices in the happiness of other beings, or
the happiness of God's holy kingdom, this will be the object of
his ultimate pursuit, and he will sacrifice and subordinate every
thing to it. And this is benevolence. To determine whether
persons are selfish or benevolent, we have to learn what is the
ultimate object in which their hearts delight, and which they
seek. Is the happiness of God's holy kingdom, or his glory in
which their hearts delight, is this their ultimate end ? Then
this is the end which they will seek, and to it they will subordinate every thing, and for it they will labor, and patiently suffer every thing necessary to it, even death itself. Can any thing
be more benevolent than this ? Is it a sin for them to rejoice
in the happiness of others, or the glory of God ? No, it proves

a benevolent heart. Is it sinful for them to choose and prefer this as their ultimate end, because it is more delightsome to them, than any other ? Who, if he understands, can see any selfishness or sinfulness in this ? How is it possible for any moral agent to possess a heart more benevolent, or more friendly to God, and the universe ?

On the other hand, if a moral agent has no appetite or relish for the happiness of others, or the glory of God ; if such objects afford him no delight. and he has no love for them, he certainly will never seek them. If at the same time he has a relish for worldly objects, for riches, or for worldly honors, or for any sensual pleasures and amusements ; if such objects please and delight him, he will prefer them, and seek them to gratify the relish and desires he has for them. And to such pursuits he will subordinate every thing, and sacrifice the happiness of millions to please his heart. He will commit any crime, if he dare, to gratify his desires. This I call selfishness, and wickedness. For it is sinful in him to delight in such objects *supremely*, and sinful to prefer them to the glory of God, and good of his kingdom ; sinful to seek them as his portion, and subordinate every thing to them.

But it may be objected, what harm is there in loving bread, or riches ? I answer, as I have labored to prove, that the primary fault, or imperfection, or sin, in the character of men, does not consist in a love to these objects ; but in a want of all love to God, and his kingdom ; or in the total want of all benevolent feelings, or relish for God and his glory. In this want his imperfection primarily consists. If he loves God supremely, if he has far greater delight in his glory and the happiness of his kingdom, than in any worldly objects, he will subordinate all his desires to this supreme delight of his heart ; if he then love food he will seek it no further, nor by any other means, than are consistent with the glory of God, his supreme delight. Deprive him of this love, of this relish for God and his kingdom ; and at the same time let his love of food remain the same, neither increased, nor diminished ; his greatest, supreme delight is in food. Now his heart loves and prefers this object, above God and his kingdom. This is certain ; for he has no love for God, and has a love for food. Hence this object is preferred by his heart to every thing divine and heavenly ; and his conduct will comport with it. And then let his heart be renewed, and a relish for the glory of God be restored, and yet he delights in food as he ever had done. He has now an object in which he experiences far greater pleasure than in food, and therefore will never gratify his love for food in any way inconsistent with the glory of God. All this is plain and evident ; and clearly shows, that the moral characters of men are affected, or changed from holy to sinful, and from sinful to holy, as often as they loose all relish for God, or have it again restored, though all their other appetites or inclinations, implanted in them by their Maker, remain the same through all the changes.

The fact is this, there is in man something, by whatever name it may be called, which is antecedent to, and distinct from, all our volitions ; or there is not. If there is not, then moral agents must necessarily be in a state of perfect indifference, at the same time they make a choice. It can be nothing but a volition, which puts an end to their indifference, respecting any particular object of choice. And if in a state of indifference, then motives do not, neither can, have any influence, as has been clearly shown by many. This plan, then, wholly excludes motives ; and of course wholly destroys moral agency and liberty. It is taking Arminian ground in length and breadth. If they do not, they are inconsistent with themselves.

On the other hand, if it be admitted that the heart is a distinct faculty from the will, and the subject of all the pleasures and pains we experience ; then, to be consistent, a person must adopt the system advanced in these essays. Hence the great question to be decided is this ; whether the heart or taste is a distinct faculty from the will ? Those who deny this must be Arminians, or be inconsistent with themselves ; and those who believe this, must embrace the sentiments advanced, or the Calvinistic scheme and system ; or else be inconsistent with themselves. It is the primary ground concerning which, in reality, Arminians and Calvinists differ ; and where they take their departure from each other, and embrace different systems of theology.

And all who mean to be Calvinists, and deny the heart to be a faculty, are inconsistent with themselves. They have but two ways to maintain apparent consistency. One is, by admitting what they call a capacity for pleasure and pain. This has been shown to be the same thing with the heart or taste. Hence they have to admit, under another name, the very thing they deny. For, their capacity for pleasure and pain is the very thing we mean by the heart or taste. If there be this capacity, not only pleasure and pain, but all the affections or desires, must be its operations, distinct from, and antecedent to, volitions.

Their other way to support an apparent consistency is, by making their distinction between *immanent* and *imperate* acts. According to this distinction, all the operations of the mind are formed into three distinct classes—*perceptions, affections*, and *volitions*. Then, if they deny the existence of faculties, yet they are obliged to admit three distinct classes of operations or exercises. And these are so different from each other, that the class, which they call *immanent acts*, which includes all our affections or desires, includes also all vice and virtue, and all the principles and springs of action. Hence, on their own ground, they make all vice and virtue, and the moral character of man, to consist in operations or exercises, which are antecedent to that class, which they call *imperate acts*. In this way the only grand difference between them and us is this ; we admit faculties, to which these classes of operations belong ; and they deny their existence. For if they admit faculties, they must embrace our system ; or refer classes of operations, very different from each other even in their moral nature, as well as in other respects, to the same faculty. This is very unphilosophical, and creates confusion in the study of the human mind. In fact they have no way to maintain a plausible consistency, only in some form or other to admit the very fundamental sentiments, for which we contend ; yet, while they in fact admit them, they in words deny them. Whereas, if they only granted the existence of such a faculty as the heart, distinct from the will, they might then with ease and consistency be on Calvinistic ground.

Objection 5th. Some may say. the system advanced in these essays represents the appetite of hunger, and all the appetites with which we are born, as being in their nature sinful, in all who are unrenewed, and even in christians. But this cannot be true. For almost every person, in every age, has considered such natural appetites as innocent and harmless. Hence the system advanced must be radically erroneous.

Answer. The particular ends and purposes, for which these appetites were created and implanted in us, has been already shown. Hence there is no need of repeating here any thing to answer the objection. Something also has been said which is connected with this subject, in the essay on the nature of sin.

Accordingly, but few observations more are needful, to answer the present objection.

It will be necessary for the reader to keep steadily in view the idea often expressed, what constitutes the primary imperfection in moral characters. That is, the total privation of the moral image of God, or of all supreme love to God, and that love to our neighbor which the law requires. A character, perfectly destitute of that love to God and man which the law requires, is an imperfect, sinful, character. In this sin *primarily* consists. For, until there is a want of this love, in whole or in part, it is impossible for sin in any sense to exist in the heart of man ; unless we consider as sinful those seeds or principles, which may become corrupt, when the moral image of God is lost.

It will be well also to reflect, that every thing is good or evil in its nature, according to its tendency. Hence, although a particular principle, in one condition, does not by its tendency produce any evil ; yet in a different condition, and under different circumstances, its tendency is to evil daily. When this is the case, if we judge correctly concerning the nature of things by their tendency, we must consider that principle to be sinful, which tends daily to a transgression of the law. If no rain were to fall and water the earth, and the sun should continue shining with all its burning rays, would you predicate good of it ? Would you say, a sun in this condition was a great blessing, or a great evil ? If no water replenished the earth, heat would tend to the production of evil. Here, the primary fault consists in the want of rain.

Before Adam sinned, his appetite of hunger was under the influence of benevolence, or love to God. It would, then, never be indulged to *excess* in eating or drinking, nor in using any unlawful *means* to obtain food. Hence its operation would be harmless, and harmonize with the influence of benevolence.

But when he was wholly deprived of the moral image of God, then food was one of the supreme objects of his heart's desire. Food now occupied the same place in his heart, which God had filled, when his supreme affection was set on him. Now hunger has the entire government. He seeks food for no other end or purpose, than to remove the pain of hunger, preserve his life, and enjoy the pleasure which eating affords. He has nothing to restrain him from eating and drinking to *excess*, or from using *unlawful means* to obtain food. For, however much he may dishonor God, or injure men, in gratifying this appetite ; yet this does not restrain him, or give him any uneasiness, in case he can do it with impunity. For he has no love for God or man ; and hence no desire to honor his Maker, and do good to men. So far as other appetites do not interfere, and fear of future punishment in this world do not restrain him, there is nothing to prevent his eating to excess, and using any means however unlawful or injurious to others in obtaining food, which is now the supreme object of his heart, and his god. And while men continue in this condition, with hearts unrenewed, the tendency of this appetite is to evil only, to excess in eating, and the use of unlawful means to obtain food. And how often has it, in fact, prompted one to steal ; another to rob men on the highway ; another to commit murder to get money ; and another to lie, defraud, and oppress, when the end has been no other than to obtain food to eat, and feast this appetite. So long as he lives within the bounds of temperance, and uses only lawful means to acquire food, this appetite in its operations is innocent and lawful. But the appetite itself will never keep men, long at a time, within such limits. Its tendency is to exceed them, and indulge itself in riotous living. As it does in fact operate in this manner, where there is no love for God or men, who can say it is not sinful, but always innocent in its nature? And the observations now made, with regard to this appetite, will apply to all the other appetites with which we are born. They all seek their respective objects as their supreme good, and seek them often to great excess, and by unlawful means ; so they are daily transgressing the divine law, and disturbing the peace and happiness of society.

These sentiments must be received as true; or we must admit, that when Adam lost the moral image of God, He created in him a positive, sinful principle, such as some term selfishness. Let it be admitted this was the fact, for the present. What will be the tendency and operations of this selfishness? Will it love and regard self supremely, and place its affections supremely on this world? This is the very fact with respect to our other appetites. Will it seek this world as its only portion? This is true of our appetites. Will it seek the world to excess, and by unlawful means? Thus our appetites in fact operate. Will it move a man to commit crimes, crimes of the deepest stain? This our appetites move us in fact to do. View this selfishness in what light we may, its tendency, nature, and operations are the very same with the tendency, nature, and operation of our appetites, as has been represented. Its nature then is the same ; and there is no difference between the two, only in words. Call then our appetites principles of selfishness, as they really are ; and then these appetites constitute the only selfishness we are in fact acquainted with, or any where see in operation. Hence the only difference between the systems advanced, and a principle of selfishness for which some contend, is merely concerning the nature of selfishness. And concerning this, from what has been said, we see there is in reality no difference. And is it not more consistent with the moral character of God, to believe he created in Adam all the principles of action he would need, and all he ever designed to create in him, when he first gave him being; than to suppose, that when the image of God was lost, He then created in him a sinful, active principle? Our system supposes no alteration took place in Adam, but the loss of the divine image ; in consequence of which, all his other appetites were placed supremely on this world, and led him and his posterity away from God the living fountain of waters. If this be admitted, then the objection before us is fully answered. I have now replied to all the objections, worthy of particular notice, which have come to my knowledge.

****

ESSAY XXVI.

An Examination of the ideas of Rhetoricians, concerning a Taste for beauty, novelty, & grandeur.

Rhetoricians commonly define Taste, to be a power of deriving pleasure or pain from objects of nature and art ; and consider beauty and sublimity to be sources of the greatest pleasures afforded to it.

I believe they have never considered this power, as they call it, a distinct faculty of the mind ; nor attended to its operations in this light. When we read what authors have said on this

7

subject, their taste, and what we call taste or the heart, are evidently the same property of the mind. Pleasure and pain,
emotions, affections, passions, desires, are the operations of what
they call taste. In this they agree with us. To me it appears
very clear, that their taste, and what is called by the same name
in these essays, are the same power, property or faculty. They
have reflected great light on this branch of intellectual philosophy. But they have treated the subject, as it appears to me,
in a too restricted and limited sense. The deficiencies of writers on the subject of taste, as far as my reading has extended,
it is proposed here to point out.

1. They have not attended to it as a distinct faculty of the
mind, with sufficient precision. Hence a reader, after he has
perused all they have to say, is ready to ask such important
questions as the following ; do they consider taste to be one of
the faculties of the mind, as they do the understanding, or not?
Do they consider it a *power* belonging to some faculty ? If
they do, to what faculty do they view this power as belonging?
The reader might say, I find no answer to these questions so
definite as to afford conviction, and still have doubts concerning the answers they would now give to them. This deficiency clouds the subject with greater or less obscurity. They exhibit a train of thoughts connected with each other, but to what
general system do they belong? How can I connect them with
other branches or parts of intellectual philosophy, so as to retain them, and see the place they occupy in a system ?

The several parts or branches of any particular science, form
one general system. And when all the parts are so arranged,
that the place each part occupies, with their relation to, and
connexions with each other from the beginning to the end, are
easily and clearly seen, then the whole appears more plain and
convincing, is far more easily remembered and reviewed, when
occasion requires it, and lays a foundation for a further improvement of the system. Taste is one branch of the philosophy of the mind. In order for us to see its connexion with
the other branches of this subject, so as to have our ideas systematically arranged, it seems to be necessary to determine
clearly, whether taste is, or is not, a faculty of the mind. This
point not being fully settled, presents a deficiency, which must
render all that is said by writers, in certain respects, very obscure. And this will appear more evident, as we pass along
in our observations.

2. Another great deficiency, in writings on the subject of taste, is this ; they leave it uncertain, whether they consider all our pleasures and pains, and all our affections and passions, to belong to it or not. This is left, as far as my knowledge extends, in a state of great doubt.

It is true all the pleasures and pains afforded us, and all the affections excited in us, by objects of beauty and sublimity, and many others, do belong to this power or faculty. But with respect to many of our pleasures, and pains, and affections, whether they are the operations of this taste, or not, is uncertain.

Our pleasures and pains, affections and passions, are more or less acute, lively, strong, and powerful. In this respect they differ, from the very least and faintest, to the greatest or most lively, and sensible. Some objects affect us so little, we are unable to say whether they give us any pleasure or pain; we feel almost indifferent in view of them. Others affect us more sensibly. And some objects make very deep impressions, please or disgust us in the highest degree ; and excite in us the warmest affections. Though they differ in all these respects ; yet they have one general, or *generic nature.* Pleasure is pleasure, and pain is pain, every affection is an affection, whether little or great, faint or lively ; almost insensible, or very discernible. Having the same generic nature, they ought to be viewed as forming one general class of operations or exercises ; and as belonging to the same faculty. If they have not the same generic nature, it ought to be proved ; if they ought to be formed into several generic classes, this ought to be done ; and if there are several powers or faculties belonging to the mind, to which such generic classes of operations belong, they ought to be distinguished, and their different natures illustrated, so that their differences from each other may be perceived. This is certainly necessary to a perspicuous, systematic view of the mind, and of its faculties and operations. And so far as this is wanting, intellectual philosophy remains in a state of obscurity and darkness.

Whether only one, or several powers of receiving pleasure and pain from objects, belong to the mind or not, we are not informed ; and whether all our emotions, affections, or passions, are operations of one faculty or of several, we are not told. At least the reader is at a loss to know, in what light writers intend to consider those things in these respects. This deficiency leaves the subject of the mind in a state of great obscurity.

To me it appears plain that the mind has but one *feeling* faculty. To this faculty all our pleasures, and pains, and affections, belong ; or are its operations from the most faint to the strongest. Though these operations form but one general class, because they all have the same generic nature, yet such differences are discernible among them, that they ought to be divided into several specific classes. This renders the subject of mind more clear and systematic. This is wanting, in all the writers I have read, on the subject of taste. Hence, though they have said many excellent things, and reflected much light in relation to many subjects, and especially the subject of criticism, yet great obscurity prevails.—To dispel this darkness, is one thing greatly needed.

3. Another deficiency, in writers on taste, is this ; whether they mean to consider their taste a moral power or faculty, the primary seat of all vice and virtue. This, as far as my reading extends, is left in a state of uncertainty. And so far as they say any thing, which might determine what their opinion was ; yet by comparing what they have written in different pages, there seem to be inconsistencies.

Taste is, or is not, a moral faculty. If moral, it is, in its nature, either vicious or virtuous ; or it partakes partly of the nature of each, so that sometimes its operations are virtuous, and at other times vicious. If all vice and virtue have not their primary seat in this taste, then there must be other moral faculties belonging to the mind. But whether they consider their taste as the only moral faculty, the only primary seat of all vice and virtue ; or as the fountain of some vices and virtues, while other moral acts belong to some other faculty, are points which I do not find clearly decided.

But is it not very necessary, in order to present the subject of intellectual philosophy in a perspicuous systematic light, to determine and show distinctly, that taste is, or is not a moral faculty ? To show to what faculty all vice and virtue are to be referred as their fountain ? And if the mind has more than one moral faculty, should it not be made evident ?

If the mind has only one moral faculty, and is the primary seat or fountain of all vice and virtue, and this is proved, we shall certainly have a far more clear understanding of its operations. Or if it have several such moral powers ; and some virtues and vices belong to one, and some to another ; if this were proved, and illustrated clearly, we should on this ground have more distinct views of its operations. My view of this subject, I have endeavoured to give in previous essays.

4. Another deficiency in their writings on this subject is this ; they do not determine distinctly, whether taste is a *simple*, or *compound* power, or faculty. Some things written would lead us to conclude, they considered it simple in its nature ; and other things would lead us to a different conclusion. This is a point, which ought to be clearly and fully decided. For if two persons should agree, that taste is the only *feeling* and *moral* faculty of the mind ; yet one should view it as *simple* in its nature, and the other as *compounded*, they must differ in their opinions in some things connected with the subject, and take different methods to account for some facts. It is a fact that some objects, which are highly pleasing and entertaining to some, are very disgusting to others. This is a fact with respect to the idolatries and superstitions of the heathen ; and also, with respect to the doctrines of the gospel. Many of these doctrines, which the apostles of Christ loved, the Jews hated. How can such facts be accounted for, if taste is a simple faculty? It is certain that two persons, who embraced different opinions concerning taste, whether it is a simple or compound faculty, would take different ways to account for such facts. And both of them cannot be in the right.

This is sufficient to show that it is a matter of importance, to have this point decided, whether taste is a simple or compound faculty. Such deficiencies as have been mentioned, without adding more, are sufficient to show, that the philosophy of the mind must be in a state of less or greater obscurity, until those deficiencies are removed. They can be removed only by the reflection of greater light, and by giving a more systematic view of the mind.

The subject of taste has generally been investigated no farther, than it respects objects of *nature* and *art*. Its operations, with respect to the wide field of objects which theology opens to view, have not been much attended to by writers. Yet this is the field in which we shall see the operations of taste, and their nature, and be able to reflect more light, and to better advantage, than we now do by confining our investigations to subjects of nature and art.

The faculty of taste is the most important property of the mind. It is the seat of all our pleasures and pains ; contains all the principles of action, which govern men ; it is the fountain of vice and virtue ; and according to its nature such is the moral character of men and of all intelligent beings ; and according to its nature when we bid farewell to life, such will be our endless state beyond the grave. Hence our usefulness, our happiness, here and forever, the honor, and respectability of our characters, our friendship with God, our enjoyment of him, the society of all holy beings, and all good, depend on the temper of heart which we cultivate. If its sinful lusts and desires are gratified, cultivated, and nourished till death, we must then associate with the shameful, degraded, characters of the wicked, and sink deeper forever into disgrace and misery. But if holiness of heart is cultivated on earth, and we die conformed to God, we shall rise, and associate with holy, dignified, exalted, and glorious characters, and with them triumph over all evil, and sing the song of victory over every foe with enraptured delight forever. That which will distinguish men finally, is not riches, or honors, or dignified titles, or the greatest acquired knowledge ; but the nature and character of the taste or heart. Hence the rich man in the gospel, if he had with his riches been an emperor, and swayed the sceptre of the world, and had acquired a knowledge of all the arts and sciences in the greatest perfection, and had died as he did with an evil heart, he would have sunk in endless infamy, disgrace and misery ; while the beggar, notwithstanding his poverty, the neglects with which he was treated, and the disgrace in which he was held, and the misery he suffered here, would be exalted, to the highest honors, glories, and felicities in heaven. Hence every thing good, great, honorable, glorious, and blessed ; and every thing evil, despicable, degraded, shameful, and miserable, depend on the nature, and cultivation of the taste, which is implanted in every man.

Had writers on taste considered the subject in this interesting light, would they have confined their observation chiefly to the effects produced on it by the works of nature and art ? The moral world contains objects of beauty, grandeur, and sublimity, infinitely exceeding any thing of this kind in the natural world, or the arts in which men have excelled. Had they extended their criticism to the moral world, as they have to the natural, and to the arts, they would have rendered far greater service to the best interests of men. Their defects do not pertain to what they have done; but to their neglects. They have done well, as far as they have proceeded in the path of truth, observation, and experience ; and they would have done far bet-

ter, and more for the happiness of men, if they had proceeded
to examine critically all the beauties and sublimities in the moral world, and shown the effects they would produce on a correct and delicate taste ; or on one destitute of these qualities.

When this truth is established, that all men have that faculty called taste, which is the subject of all our pleasures and
pains ; then it is easy to see, that all objects, natural and moral,
and works of art, would produce in the taste pleasant, or painful
sensations, whether we call them emotions, affections, or passions. They would also find, that no objects in the natural
world afford so much pleasure and pain, as the most beautiful
and sublime. This they have found is a fact. Then had they
proceeded to the moral world, they would have seen objects of
greater beauty and sublimity, and objects of greater deformity.
What objects in the universe are so beautiful and sublime, as the
character of God, that *love* displayed in the work of redemption,
the holiness the gospel enjoins; the love, the zeal, the fortitude,
the useful services, the exalted praises, and fervent prayers, of
the apostles and all saints ? What objects in the natural world
are so beautiful and sublime, as the character Christ displayed
on the earth, the doctrines he taught, the wonders he wrought,
and the fortitude and love he manifested on the cross ? What
deformities can be found in the natural world so great, as the
deformity of a sinful, rebellious character, such as the proud
Pharisees displayed in the days of our Lord ? Let the beautiful and sublime, the hateful, degraded, and depraved characters
in the moral world be examined ; also the sensations, emotions,
and affections they produce ; and all would be convinced that
the tastes of men, as to their moral nature, are very different.
The result of an examination of these objects, and the affections
they produce, would have been a full conviction, that taste is a
moral faculty, the primary principle of action, the seat of vice
and virtue, and the foundation of endless felicity or misery.

This must have impressed on the mind the importance and necessity of cultivating a holy taste.

It has been one great object of these essays, to convince men
that they have the faculty called taste by many writers, to describe its nature and operations, and to shew what part it occupies in a correct system of the mind, and its connexion with the
other parts the understanding and will ; and to show that these
properties of the mind constitute men complete moral agents,
who are worthy of praise or blame, and endless rewards. And

as they are virtuous or vicious, and must be forever happy or miserable according to the nature of their taste, which is capable of changes ; that their chief, great and daily attention ought to be given to the cultivation of a holy taste : a taste, which will not only be pleased with the beauties and sublimities, discernible in the works of nature and art ; but also with the far more beautiful and sublime objects, which exist in the moral world.

And in writing these essays, it has been the determination of the author to admit no speculations as true, but those which agree with *facts, observation*, and the *experience* of men. The design has been, to advance no sentiment, which is not founded on facts and experience.

*** *****

ESSAY XXVII.

On total Depravity.

Admitting the views which have been given of the human mind to be true, the doctrine of total depravity, as explained by the orthodox, is a just inference. And one reason, why the advocates and the opponents of this doctrine have not agreed, is, because they have not begun with first principles, nor reasoned from them, in relation to the mind. If any person is well acquainted with the first principles relating to moral agency, he cannot, if consistent, deny this doctrine. But to prove this doctrine, we must in the first place explain it, that all may know how much it contains, as we understand it.

By total depravity is meant, a heart destitute of moral virtue or holiness. No trace of the moral image of God, or true benevolence, remains in the heart. Real holiness is wholly wanting. In consequence of this, all the operations, or affections of the heart, are sinful. Yet it is granted, that the totally depraved have all the faculties, with which Adam was created, still remaining. They have all the faculties, and the liberty, which are necessary to constitute a complete moral agent.

257

They have the same faculties of the understanding, heart, and will, which Adam had before the fall. By his sinning, no direct alteration took place in him, or his posterity, except in the faculty of the heart, or taste. When he ate of the forbidden fruit, he was deprived of that moral image, or benevolent appetite, with which he was created. He was then spiritually dead, destitute of all moral goodness, or totally depraved. Then all the other appetites with which he was created became sinful. Hence, when we say man is totally depraved, the meaning is, he has no moral goodness, remaining ; and every operation and desire of his heart is sinful, in a moral sense evil. Yet all the faculties he ever had, or which constitute a moral agent, remain entire ; and are not, except in a moral sense, in the least impaired. This explains my view of this subject. But a few things are necessary to establish the truth of this doctrine

1. The faculty termed the taste or heart is essential to moral agency. To avoid repetition, the reader is desired to peruse carefully and candidly the description given of this faculty in the 8th and 9th essays, on taste and the appetites.—According to the description there given, the heart is the only faculty which *feels*, or is the subject of pleasant or painful sensations. It is the only primary, active, principle, in moral agents ; and is, also, the only moral faculty. And it is so essential to moral agency, that without it, men would not be *agents ;* could not be *virtuous* or *vicious*, or *subjects* of final *rewards*. Also this faculty is always in its *nature* sinful, or holy.—For the divine character, and all moral objects, must afford it pleasure or pain. Or in view of divine objects, every person's heart will experience delight, or disgust, in a greater or less degree. Being pleased with divine objects, proves the heart to be holy ; and if displeased, this equally shows, that it is in its nature sinful, depraved. These are truths, which have been proved in the essays to which we have referred.

This shows with a moral certainty, that a moral agent cannot exist, and at the same time be neither sinful nor holy. If a moral agent, he has the faculty called the heart ; and this is, in its nature, always sinful, or holy. It cannot exist in any other condition. Hence the sentiment which some advance, that the hearts of men when born are like clean paper, without any marks of vice or virtue, is certainly false. And if any feel inclined to view this as a whim, or an absurdity ; they are desired to undertake to show, how it is possible for any person to exist, and be neither sinful, nor holy, yet be a moral agent. If he is a moral agent, he has the faculty of taste. And if any person should labor to show, this faculty may exist, and be clean as paper, in its nature neither sinful nor holy, he will soon find his labor is in vain.

He may deny the existence of this faculty. If he does, he must admit the existence of a faculty similar to it, or grant men are not moral agents. If he should say, we have not the faculty of taste ; but we have a capacity for pleasure and pain, and this constitutes us moral agents ; this is only another name for what is termed taste ; and the nature of this capacity must be such, that the character of God will please, or offend it ; and in either case, this proves it to be sinful or holy. Call it by whatever name they may, they must admit it is susceptible of pleasure and pain ; or grant we have no active power or principle in us ; and of course are not moral agents.

If it be granted, that men are moral agents, it must be admitted, that we have that faculty, which I call the taste or heart ; and if any give it a different name, yet this does not alter its nature. It will, therefore, remain an eternal truth, that as men are moral agents, they have a faculty, the nature of which is similar to the description given of it, in the essays on taste and its appetites. Hence the sentiment, which some advance, that we are born with hearts as clean as white paper, neither sinful nor holy, is a dangerous falsehood ; a sentiment, which can never be supported, and men, at the same time, be moral agents.

2. Adam, when created by his Maker, was perfectly holy. The moral image of God was instamped on his heart, perfect and entire. He came from the hand of his God perfectly holy. He was made in a moral sense upright, created with knowledge and holiness. God created in his heart the same benevolent appetite, which in Himself is termed *love* or holiness. In this respect he perfectly resembled his Maker ; having the same benevolence in *kind*, though not in *degree*.

God, also, created him with all the other appetites, which are enumerated in the 9th essay, on the appetites. These prepared him to live in this world, to preserve his life, propagate his race, support them in infancy, relieve them in distress ; and for every other purpose needful to his comfort in this life, in case he should lose his benevolent appetite, as God knew he would. Thus Adam, as first created, was endued with all the faculties necessary to make him a complete, moral agent ; and

being perfectly holy, he was prepared to serve and enjoy his
Maker, here and forever; and he endowed him with every other
appetite requisite to answer the ends for which they were given,
if he should be deprived of his moral image, which at last proved to be the fact.   This shows what our first parents were, when
they came from the hands of their Creator.   Accordingly, when
they were deprived of the moral image of God, they still had
all the other appetites remaining, which were necessary to answer the ends for which they were implanted in them.   Such
were our first parents, when created.   They were moral agents;
being perfectly holy, they were prepared for the enjoyment of
God ; and their other appetites qualified them to live in this
world, even when sin should enter it.

3. When they ate the forbidden fruit, they were deprived of
the moral image of God ; of that benevolent appetite, with
which they were at first created.   They were now in a moral
sense dead, and had no holy principle remaining in them ; and
were in a moral sense also, imperfect, and sinful.   In one word,
they were in a state of total depravity.   For by total depravity
is meant, an entire want of a holy principle of action.   No
trace of holiness remained in them, after they ate, unless their
other appetites were, some of them, holy ; which it will be
shown was not the fact.—There are only two ways at present
conceivable, by which this truth can be evaded.

1. It may be said by some, that Adam, after he had eaten,
was not *wholly*, and only in a *partial* sense, deprived of the holy
image of his Creator.   It may be said, he had some supreme
love for his Maker still remaining ; and of course was not totally depraved.

All this may be asserted.   But assertions, without proof,
have no weight.   What evidence can be adduced, to prove
that Adam was but partially deprived of God's moral image ?
The word of God is directly against this opinion.   If Adam by
the fall was only in part, and not wholly, destitute of love to
God ; then all his posterity have some love to him, when born.
If this be true, why does the bible represent all men as going
astray from the womb, and as by nature children of wrath, condemned already ; conceived in sin, and born in iniquity ? Will
God condemn, and send to hell, those who love him supremely ?   There is not one passage in the whole bible, which represents unrenewed men as having some supreme love to God,
remaining in the heart.   But they are repeatedly said to be his

enemies, as hating both the Father and the Son ; and in a state of rebellion, robbing their Creator. Till proof from the bible is produced in support of the assertion, that all men have some supreme love remaining in their hearts, since the fall, or until renewed by grace; the assertion ought to be rejected as a dangerous error.

Again. The assertion we reject as unfounded is contradicted by *facts*, and the experience of men in all ages. If men, since the lapse of Adam, have some supreme love for God remaining, there is no special difference between them, and those called christians, or saints. For christians do not love God with the whole heart ; in this respect they are deficient, and imperfect ; and complain daily of the want of more love. Unrenewed men, then, are really saints, holy in part, and having the same character in reality, with those who are called by the pen of inspiration the friends of God. If this be true, why does the word of God divide mankind into two classes, saints and sinners ; the unrenewed, and renewed ? Also, if this be true, mankind do not need the change called regeneration. They are renewed, as really as saints are. For when they are born again, they have a heart given to love God ; but this love is imperfect. Indeed, if the assertion is true, there is no difference among men, in a moral sense, but this ; some may love God more than others ; but all love him, and all will be saved. For God will send none to hell, who have some supreme love to him.

But does the assertion we oppose agree with facts ? Do all men, in fact, appear to have some supreme regard for their Maker ? Did the body of the Jews, in the days of Christ and his Apostles, manifest any true love for God, and the religion then taught ? Do the heathen appear to know and love the true God ?. Or do all men, in our day, manifest a supreme love to Him ? If, for an example, we select those men at this day, who are the most moral, honest, and upright, yet unrenewed ; what spirit do they manifest, when sorely afflicted ? If they were to be stripped naked, as Job was, would they say as he did, with a sincere heart, the Lord hath given, and taken away, and blessed be his name ? Would they not rather display the temper of Job's wife ? Is there not reason to believe this from the fretful, murmuring, and complaining spirit, which they frequently manifest, when providences are crossing and afflictive ? We know men will manifest much of what is called good nature, when all events agree and harmonize with their desires. But what spirit would they show, if afflicted, and treated as Job was, and persecuted like Paul ? Would they sincerely adopt Paul's words, these light afflictions shall work out for us a far more exceeding and eternal weight of glory ?

Again. Can all men say sincerely, that they daily *experience* that spirit, described in the beatitudes of Christ, Math. 5th chapter? Can all among us say, they experience daily, that poverty of spirit, that mourning for sin, that purity of heart, that hungering and thirsting after righteousness, that meek and lowly spirit, that love of peace, and that blessedness in their souls, which is given to those who have such a heart ? Do they know by experience, what the spirit and blessedness are, described by Christ ? If they have some supreme love in their hearts for God, they certainly know by experience the nature of that spirit, and the blessedness held up to view in that chapter, and in other passages of the new testament. But those who converse much with unrenewed men on experimental subjects of religion, will always find, that, instead of their being acquainted experimentally with such subjects, they are perfect strangers to them. Inform them that those, who love God in some measure, groan daily under the weight of remaining sin; that they never lie so low before God as they ought, and wish ; that nothing they see, in this or any other world, is so lovely as holiness; that they long more earnestly to be freed from sin, and made perfectly holy, than for their daily food ; that they pant after God as their only portion, and that it is their *chief* concern to grow in grace, and ripen for heaven. Such feelings are so distant from any thing they experience, that they would say, if all who love God feel thus daily, we have no love for Him. And such language would appear so strange to them, they would be ready to say, that persons of this description were superstitious, fanatical, hypocritical, blind, and deceived. Yet this is the language of all who love God, according to the bible ; and those who love God understand such language, their own experience accords with it. Indeed the bible, facts, and experience, unitedly testify, that unrenewed men have no love in their hearts for God. And to say, they have some love remaining, or are not totally depraved, contradicts the scriptures, and is opposed to facts, experience, and observation. And this is so evident, but very few pretend to say, that Adam's posterity have any of that supreme love to God, which he had before his fall. Instead of saying all men have some supreme love to God, to evade the truth, they generally take other ground, and say,

2. That all men have remaining in them some natural pity, and gratitude, and other natural affections, which they call virtuous or holy ; hence men are not totally depraved. And it is true, if any of the appetites implanted in Adam, when created, and which remained in him after he ate, are virtuous and holy, men are not totally depraved. For if men have any thing remaining in their hearts of a *holy nature*, the doctrine of total depravity must be rejected.

Here the reader is desired to attend carefully to a few observations. One is, that when God created Adam, he not only implanted in his heart a benevolent appetite, or a disposition to love him supremely ; but he created in him every other appetite, which he had and manifested after his fall. Another remark is this, that at the time Adam ate the forbidden fruit, and was deprived of his benevolent appetite, there was nothing created in him, which he had not before his fall. Some have seemed to think, that when Adam ate, and lost the moral image of God, that then God produced in him an evil, sinful disposition, which they call a principle of selfishness ; that he never had this, till after he ate. If this be true, then there was a *new something*, very sinful, created in him, at the time he fell. This sentiment is without any foundation. There is not so much as a hint given in the bible, which I could ever find, that something new, and sinful, was then created in him. And such a supposition answers no purpose ; it will not help to account for the sins, which have prevailed in the world, which may not be as easily accounted for without it ; nor does it shun any difficulty ; but it produces one hard to be solved, or reconciled with the moral character of God. Let it, then, be carefully noticed, that at the fall there was nothing new created in Adam, unless a new heart ; and none suppose this took place at the time he ate, and lost the moral image of God. The truth is this, according to scripture representation, that when God gave Adam existence, he created him with all the faculties he ever had ; created in his heart all the appetites he ever had ; created him perfect in his own likeness, both natural and moral. And his moral likeness consisted of that benevolent appetite, which the word calls a spirit of righteousness and true holiness. This is all he lost, when he ate. All the other appetites or propensities, with which he was at first created, remained in him entire, after his fall. And now, to avoid repetition as much as possible, the reader is requested to peruse carefully what is written concerning the appetites and their operation, in the essays on the appetites, and on moral good and evil, and particularly on sin.—Then but few remarks here will be necessary, to establissh the doctrine of total depravity.

Now let the reader take a careful survey of Adam, after he had eaten the forbidden fruit. He has lost the moral image of his Maker. He has no benevolent appetite left, no love for God. His glory is departed. He has none of that love for God, and men, which the moral law requires. But all his other appetites remain unimpaired. Here consider, what are the objects, which these appetites respectively love and seek? For what purposes and ends were they implanted in him? When you have read those essays to which you have been referred, you will see they were implanted in him to be active principles, stimulating to all those exertions necessary to preserve life, propagate his own species, to support and nurse men in infancy, to relieve the distressed, in a word to promote the good of society, and the happiness of our race as long as we continue inhabitants of this world.—There you will find, that his appetites are not placed on any other, or higher, or better objects, than those of a worldly nature. They will never move him to seek any other or higher good, than worldly good, till fear of eternal death is excited. Hence they are sinful.

For, let me say, his appetite or love of property is idolatrous. He has no love for God, but he loves property, or riches. This love for riches is supreme ; it prompts him to seek this object with an ultimate regard to his personal gratification, without any regard for the happiness of the human family. For remember, he has no love for the happiness of others. In pursuit of riches, if he injures others, defrauds them, and transgresses the law, he will not care, if he personally suffers no evil by it. Is not that love, which is placed supremely on this world, when there is no love for God, sinful ? Is it not loving and serving the creature, and not the Creator ? Does not this world stand higher in a person's heart, than God, when it loves the world, and at the same time has no love for the Creator? Is not this idolizing the world, having another god and portion, distinct from the true God ? Will not this love for this world, where there is none for God, lead him to seek it as his portion ; to forsake the fountain of living waters, and go after a broken castern ? Will it not lead him to reject Christ, and turn his back upon the gospel supper, when he finds to embrace the Savior, and come to the supper, he must give up, and deny all the supreme regard he has had for this world ? And is not this, in fact, the way in which mankind do treat gospel provisions ? Now what I have observed concerning this appetite for property, is true with respect to all other appetites. They move men as active principles to seek their respective objects, to gratify them without any regard for God, and the happiness of men. But as those, who deny total depravity, have much to say concerning the virtues of natural pity, gratitude, and some other natural affections, it may be well to give some more particular attention to these appetites.

Natural pity claims our first attention. This affection is a compound of a painful *sensation*, and a *desire* to remove its cause. It is excited by objects of pain and distress. God has so formed us, that the distress, and calamities of our fellow-men shall excite in us a painful sensation. The appetite, which we call pity, is given to all men ; and its nature is such, that the calamities, which befall men, shall give us pain. The reason of this is apparent, when we consider the aim and design of pity. It moves us to relieve others in their distresses. And the end obtained by offering help to objects of distress, is the removal of the pain in us excited by the evils others suffer. This presents to our view the *cause* of the pain we feel. It is the evil, calamity, or affliction, which we see others are suffering. It, also, presents to our view the object of pity, this is the entire *relief* of the sufferer. And the reason why we afford them relief is, that the pain we feel, when they suffer, may be removed. As soon as we are relieved of the pain excited by distress, pity ceases to operate. Our desire to help, and do them good, subsides. This is pity, and such are its operations. And it is easy to see why God has implanted this appetite in us. Many in a distressed, helpless state, would die, if no one assisted them. And as men in a fallen state have no benevolence to influence them to afford relief to sufferers, and God knew this, he implanted this appetite to answer the end of benevolence in this particular way. Still it is very unlike benevolence in its nature. For benevolence delights in the happiness of others, and desires to remove pain in others, because it is inconsistent with their happiness ; and at the same time to promote their positive happiness, and especially that which is durable and eternal, or which consists in the enjoyment of God. Hence its operations are wholly different from those of natural pity, except in one particular, which is the mitigation and removal of pain in a sufferer.

Natural pity moves us to afford relief to a sufferer, and remove his pain and distress. As soon as this is done we feel relieved, our pain is removed, which his calamity excited. Here, then, we stop, and are now satisfied. And then probably we shall invite him to some place of merriment and vanity, to drinking and feasting, that he may forget his sufferings. This is certainly enticing him to spend his time and money in unlawful ways. And if we have business to transact with him, some bargain to make, we shall, if possible, take the advantage, and defraud him. It is certain there is nothing in natural pity, which will prevent our enticing him into sin in many ways, or which will keep us from injuring him in his character, property, or person. This is proved by facts. For if we see others, towards whom we have always been inimical, in a distressed, helpless, dying state, natural pity will excite us to relieve them. And as soon as they are relieved, and our pain excited by their sufferings is removed ; we pursue our former course of hostility towards them. Hence it is not their happiness, which pity aims at ; it aims at nothing further, or better, than a removal of the pain we feel, when we see others in a calamitous, helpless state. When pain is removed we shall treat them as we do ourselves, after we have recovered from a state of dangerous sickness. Then how often it is, that men proceed in the same sinful courses, they had followed previous to their sickness. So we shall treat men, whom we have assisted in distress, as we always had done, previous to their calamity. If we had always been enemies to them, we shall continue to injure them, as soon as the pain is gone, which their distress excited in us. A thousand facts might be adduced to prove this truth.

But benevolence, which ever aims at the happiness of others, will not only remove calamities others suffer ; but when they are removed, will seek to promote and increase the person's happiness in every consistent, possible way. Benevolence is not satisfied with a mere removal of distress in another ; and will never be satisfied with any thing short of their entire happiness. This shows, that the object and aim of benevolence and natural pity, are as different as light and darkness, except in one particular. One aims at the happiness of others in af-

9

fording them relief, when in distress ; the other aims at nothing higher, than its own relief from the pain which the sufferings of others excite. As they cannot mitigate their own pain only by affording assistance to sufferers, they assist them. And as soon as their pain is removed, they will treat the person they had helped as they always had before done.

Again. It is a known fact, that natural pity may be almost wholly eradicated from the human breast, by a very frequent repetition of calamity and suffering. Hence soldiers, by daily beholding death and carnage, and hearing the cries and groans of the wounded and dying, become so hardened, that such scenes of suffering excite scarcely any emotion or pity. They see the wounded and dying, hear them cry for help, yet pass on without affording them any relief. So when epidemical diseases prevail in a place, and many die every day, in a short time the living are so hardened they pursue their own ways, free in a great measure from every painful emotion. This is a fact, though it is not my design to enlarge upon it, or show why it is thus ordered.

But the more frequently instances of calamity occur, and the greater they are, benevolence, instead of being hardened at the sight, becomes more engaged to remove distress, assuage grief, and listen to the cries of sufferers. Every thing will be done, which can be done, to remove every evil, and promote happiness. Is it not now evident, that there is a wide difference between benevolence, and natural pity ? As they differ so materially in their nature, all, who will grant that benevolence is a moral virtue, or holy appetite, will say that natural pity is not. They will grant it is a selfish appetite. And that the person, who is possessed of it, aims at his own freedom from pain, the peace and quietness of his own breast, in relieving distress ; just as he aims at removing the painful cravings of hunger, and his own personal happines in seeking and eating food. In this he does not aim at the happiness of others ; and whether they are happy or not is a matter of indifference to him, if he can remove his own pains, and promote his own good by eating. So a person influenced by natural pity, feels no concern for another's future good and happiness, if he can by assisting him in his present distress remove all the pain he feels, and quiet his own breast. As soon as this is done, he has no feeling for the future happiness of his fellow mortal ; and instead of promoting it, in many ways he injures him, as facts prove many have done. Hence natural pity, where there is no benevolence, is selfish in all its operations ; yet it answers the end in many cases for which it was created in the heart. And as soon as any one has a clear view of the human mind, and is acquainted with the laws of our nature by which we are invariably governed, and sees for what end they were created in us ; he will then see readily, that natural pity is wholly unlike benevolence, and is selfish in its operations.

We may next attend to natural gratitude. What is it? A pleasant sensation is experienced ; and a desire which corresponds with it, according to the nature of the object which excites the pleasant emotion within.—A pleasant, agreeable sensation, with an attendent desire, constitutes the affection of gratitude. The difference between natural gratitude and benevolence may be easily seen. The object of benevolent gratitude is the divine goodness. This is the object, which excites in the heart of the benevolent man pleasant and delightful emotions. His desire is to enjoy the divine goodness more sensibly, to have his pleasant emotions continued and increased ; and to have the goodness of God displayed, and diffused to the highest possible degree. This is desiring the glory of God.

In natural gratitude, delightful emotions are excited by the temporal blessings enjoyed. Worldly prosperity is the object and source of the pleasure felt in this case by the selfish man. And his desires, which arise from his pleasant emotions, have for their object the continuance, and increase of worldly prosperity ; that the pleasure this affords him may be continued and increased. Here we clearly see, that the objects which excite agreeable sensations, and the desires attending them, are very different in their nature. Worldly prosperity is the object which pleases in natural gratitude, and divine goodness the pleasing object in benevolent gratitude ; and the desires of the former are for the continuance and increase of temporal blessings ; and in the latter the desire is for the display and greatest diffusion of divine goodness. Hence these affections are very different in their nature. One is benevolent, and the other is selfish. What is explained and asserted as truth shall now be proved.

1. The vilest men have natural gratitude. They commonly have the most of it ; and all have it in proportion to the love they have for this world. The more they love the world, the greater will be their delight when their goods increase. Yet

the more they love this world, so much more they transgress the law of God in amassing wealth. They are in the same proportion forgetful of God, and their duty, and engaged after the world as their portion. All this is verified by facts daily. Who idolize this world? Who are most apt to forget God, restrain prayer, defraud, and oppress? Surely those, who love this this world most, and are most pleased with earthly good. Now can that gratitude, which is most delighted with worldly blessings, and has the strongest desires after them; and which invariably forgets God, and seeks things below as a portion; have any thing morally good in it? Is not such gratitude evidently selfish and sinful?

2. Compare the man mentioned in the gospel, who pulled down his granaries to build greater to contain his goods, with the apostle Paul, who relinquished all earthly good, and laid down his life, for the sake of diffusing the goodness and love of God through this world in the salvation of souls. And remember the rich man had a great share of natural, and Paul of benevolent gratitude. Then ask, was the gratitude of these two men similar in its nature? Did it not operate in Paul as differently from the operations in the rich man, as light is from darkness? If in Paul it was holy, such as the rich man had was unholy and selfish. But it may be said, that we have not given a right definition of natural gratitude. It may be said, that the object, which excites a delightful sensation, ever implied in gratitude, is not worldly good, but divine goodness. If this be true, then there is no difference in nature between natural and benevolent gratitude, they are entirely similar. Why then do those, who deny total depravity, go on the ground, that natural gratitude is distinct from benevolent; so that, if men naturally have no benevolence, yet they have natural gratitude, which is holy, so they are not wholly depraved? In my illustration I have endeavored to show what gratitude implies, give it what name we may. And if natural and benevolent gratitude are not the same, but are distinct affections; the definitions given of them are just. And if just, then natural gratitude is an unholy, sinful affection, as proved.

But those who deny depravity, to maintain their ground, will say natural gratitude does delight in God. The evidence they bring for this is, that when a person takes a view of the numerous blessings he enjoys, and reflects they are given him by his Maker, he cries, oh how good God is, how kind to me; blessed be his name for such displays of his love. They say, is not this the feeling and language of gratitude ; and are not such feelings holy? Answer. Any person, who takes it for granted, that all such feelings when expressed are surely holy, has no just views of human nature, and may in many ways be imposed on and deceived. Let us put a case. A certain neighbor has ever been a bitter enemy to you. To let him know that you indulge no ill will towards him, and as you know he is a great lover of money, you make him a present of thousands of dollars. In that case how will he feel, and express himself? Will he not be highly pleased with the gift ? Will he not thank you for it, in language which will express much friendship for you ? Would this be inconsistent with his feelings of hatred towards you ? For he expresses no more, than a high pleasedness with the gift. All this he might do, yet to morrow curse you, if you should in any way oppose him. Not only so, but watch an opportunity to steal money from you, which he knows you have by you. I have shown in the essay where the affections are formed into distinct classes, that if you gratify a person's primary, and secondary feelings, he will appear to love you, and view you as a friend ; yet if you oppose him in his pursuits, he will hate you. So it is with men in their conduct towards God. If he bestows plentifully on them those blessings, which they love, they will manifest many feelings, which appear like love and gratitude ; yet if in his providence he should sorely afflict them, as he did Job ; they would murmur, complain, and act like bullocks unaccustomed to the yoke, as the Jews did in the wilderness. They would give full evidence, that at the time they expressed so much gratitude, it was not God with whom they were pleased, but solely on account of the blessings given them. Then their seeming gratitude all disappears. Hence when the definitions given of natural and benevolent gratitude are attended to, and the argument brought to prove the difference there is in their nature, every person will grant, that natural gratitude is a sinful, selfish affection. For if this gratitude has the nature of benevolence in it, it does delight in the goodness of God, in his character as just, as well as merciful, and will delight in the happiness of others. If this be a fact, why do not all men, who have it as our opponents say, seek the glory of God, obey and serve him, and do all in their power to promote the happiness of man, and have their whole conduct harmonise with the nature of an affection, which is placed supremely on God? Instead of living according to the nature of the gratitude contended for; they live in opposition to it, and just as all men would, if they highly valued the blessings given them, yet had no love for God, or their fellow men. Those, then, who assert that natural gratitude is a holy affection, ought to prove it does delight in the whole character of God, and in the happiness of others, whether friends or foes ; and that the conduct of all men does correspond, in some measure, with this love to God and man. Till they have proved all this, their assertions have no weight, and this gratitude is only a love for self, and the blessings necessary to its gratification.

It is also contended, that natural affections are holy, such as the mutual love of husbands and wives, parents and children, brothers and sisters.

If any persons had a clear view of the nature of holiness, or benevolence, how could they assert, that natural affections are holy in their nature, and so men are not totally depraved? The nature of holiness has been described in the essay on that subject ; I shall, therefore, repeat no more than what is really necessary in this place. It has been shown that benevolence, which comprises all holiness, delights ultimately in the happiness of others, or in the greatest felicity of God's kingdom : and that this is the ultimate object of all its desires : and that the lives of all who have benevolence, will agree more or less with that good, which is ultimately loved and desired for its own sake. It will, therefore, as readily incline such to seek the happiness of enemies, as of friends; and the happiness of all men, as well as that of relations. This is the nature of holiness ; and no affection is holy, unless it has this nature, and will operate in this manner.

But have natural affections this nature ; do they operate in this manner? Do such appear to regard, and seek the happiness of all men ; of enemies as well as friends, and of all those, who are not by blood or descent related to them? No. Natural affection does not embrace all men ; and extends no further, than to the circle of a few relatives. Beyond this circle natural affection manifests nothing of the nature of real benevolence. It is a known fact, that husbands and wives may love each other with ardent affection, yet live at enmity with all around them, for years, yea their whole lives ; and instead of desiring and seeking their happiness, may, and often do, act a part hostile to them, and calculated to lead them on in the ways of sin, and to final perdition. Is this benevolence? God has created in all men natural affections; or an appetite, which is an active principle, and which operates in love to all near relatives. His design in this is very evident. It is a principle, which inclines men to propagate their own species, to nurse persons in infancy; to seek each other's comfort and happiness, and promote harmony and peace among relatives. If all men were perfectly benevolent, that principle would incline them to promote these objects; and then there would be no need of natural affections. But God knew that man would, after the fall, be born without any benevolence; and that some other active principle would be necessary to propagate, and promote the peace and happiness of the human species, so far as to render their existence here somewhat comfortable. The principles, called natural affections, were created to answer these purposes, and no others. Hence they never move men to seek the good of any, but their relatives and particular connexions. How can any consistently view natural affections as holy in their nature, which are so limited; which never incline them to promote the happiness of more than one in ten thousand of the human family?

This is not all. Natural affection does not oppose the reign of sin, which is the final ruin of our race. It does not oppose the prevalence of sin in relatives, any further, than it militates against their worldly prosperity. Hence the reason parents in fact do, in a thousand instances, set an evil example before their children; justify them in those vain amusements, which lead to their final ruin; and exhort them to follow the customs and fashions of this world, as far as is consistent with their temporal support; and say, or do, little or nothing to turn them from sin to holiness, or from the service of satan to the service of God. Indeed, notwithstanding the influence of natural affection, it is a fact, that thousands of parents travel the broad road to final ruin, and by their example lead their children after them in the same way, without any remorse or compunction. And if all the parents in this world were to live and die destitute of that benevolence, which loves God supremely, and ultimately seeks the highest happiness of his kingdom, it is certain they would perish forever, and their children with them, if they followed their example. How can there be any thing of the nature of holiness, or benevolence, in those affections which will incline men to travel the road, even to death, which will land them in hell ? This would be a new and strange kind of holiness.

It is a fact, that natural affection is not hostile to the reign of sin in our own hearts and lives, or in those of our relatives, and in the rest of the world, in any instances in which it does not oppose worldly prosperity. Hence natural affection inclines no person to listen to gospel invitations, to renounce the world as a portion, and come and put their trust in Christ for eternal life. It does not incline any person to do this himself, or to persuade his relatives and others to do it. Hence, although all men have natural affections, yet the world is filled with sin and misery. Would this be the fact, if all men had real holiness, or benevolence ; and were influenced as much by it, as they now are by their natural affections ? No, if this were the fact, we should see the fruits of love, friendship, and righteousness every where prevail. Mankind would lead lives as different from those they now live, as light is from darkness. Indeed we cannot view this subject in any true light, in which it will not appear very evident, that natural affection has nothing of the real nature of holiness in it. And all that can be said is this, that in one or two particulars it has the resemblance of it ; but not its nature. If all would, with candid and unbiassed minds with the light they have, form a just opinion concerning natural pity, gratitude, conjugal, parental, filial, and fraternal affections ; they would say, these active principles are necessary to the temporal happiness and prosperity of man, in a world destitute of the principle of holiness, and in some good degree answer the end for which they were implanted : yet they have not, in their nature and operation, any thing of the real nature of holiness or benevolence. Hence these natural appetites or principles are no arguments, disproving the doctrine of total depravity. Men may have these principles, yet be totally depraved. In fact these principles are so far from being holy in their nature, they are sinful, and do in thousands of instances influence men to commit sin. How often has the love parents have for their children led them to defraud, and oppress their fellow men, for the sake of acquiring property to bequeath to their children when they die. The nature of their love is such, it will lead them to do any thing however sinful to promote the credit, the honor, and the wealth and worldly prosperity of their children, as far as is consistent with their own honor and safety; and in fact have done it.

It was the love Jehu had for his children, which, as one principle, led him to commit all the sins he did commit to gain the crown of Israel, and secure it to his posterity. Love to children was one principle, which led Jewish parents to persuade their children to live in idolatry. The love the Pharisees had for their children was one principle, that led them to entice and persuade them to reject Christ as the true Messiah. The love heathen parents have for their children, leads them to initiate them into all the superstitions of heathenish idolatry. And love to children is one principle, which induces parents to lead their children into all the errors and sins in which they have indulged themselves. Would real benevolence lead men to embrace errors, and live in a course of wickedness and rebellion against God, and persuade their children to do the same? No, benevolence enlightens the mind, hates every error and sin; and leads all governed by it to shun errors, fight against sin; and persuade, if possible, their children to do the same. It appears, then, that natural affections are so far from being holy, that their operation is sinful in all, in whom benevolence is wanting. Hence, as Adam when he ate lost the holy moral image of his Maker, and had no principles of action remaining in him, but those appetites which were necessary to his well being in this life, and of which mention has been made; and as it now appears, that these have nothing of the nature of real holiness in them, but are sinful in their operation in all destitute of holiness; the doctrine of total depravity is proved, and established on a permanent foundation.

Those who deny the doctrine under consideration, proceed on this ground, that men are endued with several distinct, holy principles of action. According to their reasoning, natural pity is one; gratitude, another; natural affection, another; and the harmless good nature, which children manifest, another. And according to this we possess several distinct, individual principles of action, each of which is holy. This mode of reasoning clearly proves, that such persons have not a distinct, and just view of the true theory of the mind. For if they had they would be convinced, that no beings with whom we are acquainted have more than *one* individual, holy principle of action. Holiness is comprised in one, simple, uncompounded principle of action. An appetite, or disposition to be pleased with happiness as an absolute good, is holiness. Happiness is the only absolute good in the universe, which is delighted in, and sought for its own sake. And a disposition of heart to be pleased with it, and seek it, and desire it, for its own sake, is holiness. This is the ultimate end of real benevolence. This will incline all beings, who have it, to seek the highest possible measure of happiness in God's holy kingdom.

This is the only principle of holiness in God. He is love. He rejoices in the happiness of other beings. He esteems happiness as a good in itself, an absolute good. His love to it inclined him to create beings capable of happiness; and to give his Son to redeem sinners. In a word, it is this love, which moved Him to display all his attributes, and diffuse and communicate all his fulness perfectly and entirely, for the sake of producing ultimately the greatest possible measure of happiness, in that holy kingdom which is to exist forever in heaven. And let it be remembered, there is every reason to believe, that the happiness of this kingdom will be eternally increasing ; and in this view we may consider his attributes in the highest degree displayed, and his fulness perfectly diffused, or communicated. This love, or simple uncompounded disposition in God, viewed as an eternally *active* principle, is sufficient to account for all the actions of Deity, appearing in his works, or his word. All he ever *did*, or *said*, may be traced back to this active, self-moving principle. Hence every thing is from him as the self-moving cause. And we do not read in the word of God of any other principle, which influences and governs Him in all he does. God is love ; he *so loved* the world ; he first loved us ; herein is love ; so every where love is the first, moving cause ; all things are ascribed to it as the eternal fountain of good. And there was no necessity for the existence of any other holy principle in God. This one is sufficient to account for every thing he ever said, or did. This moved him to employ his wisdom in forming a plan of operation, and his power, or will, in carrying it into full execution ; which plan includes all his works, and words.

Holiness in angels is a disposition of the same nature. And they need only this one, simple, active principle, to incline them to seek the greatest happiness, and serve God with all their might. And holiness in men, in saints, is the same love, or disposition which delights ultimately in happiness, and inclines them to desire and seek it as the greatest good. Hence all holy beings have the same holy appetite, or disposition ; they all seek the same object as their ultimate end ; and of course they will agree, and harmonise, in all they *say* and *do,* which proceeds from this principle. According then to Christ's prayer, they are and will be forever *one ;* one with each other, one with God, and with Christ ; they will be perfect in *one.*

Now one simple, uncompounded, holy principle of action is sufficient. No being needs another to render him perfect. For there is but one absolute good in the universe ; but one ultimate end, which ought to be sought ; which is the greatest happiness of God's holy kingdom. Accordingly, no being we ever heard of has any more, than one holy principle in him. This is all the law of God requires. Thou shalt *love* the Lord with all thy heart, and thy neighbor as thyself. This love, if perfect, is all the holiness the law requires. And the word of God uniformly speaks the same language. Hence all holiness consists in one simple, uncompounded, active principle, which I have for the sake of perspicuity called a holy *appetite*, to distinguish it from all other appetites with which men are evidently endued.

All the appetites of men, holiness excepted, are created in them to answer particular distinct ends, or purposes, while they live in this world, and are destitute of holiness. Thus the appetite of hunger was created in us, to prompt us to seek food for the nourishment of the body, and to relish it while eating it. As far as food is obtained, this appetite is gratified, and its end is answered. It never moves man to seek any thing else as an end. It inclines him to use all the *means* necessary to his end.

The sexual appetite is created in men for the propagation of our species. As far as this end is obtained by it, its end is answered. Hunger does not incline us to seek this end ; nor does the sexual appetite incline men to obtain food. They are appetites, which incline men to seek different, and distinct ends.

Natural affection, or an appetite in parents to be more pleased with their own children than with others, is given to move them to nurse and provide for their children in infancy, and through life. And the love children have for their parents inclines them to obey them, and support them when old ; and their love for each other is necessary to unite their exertions in promoting the peace, prosperity, and happiness of the family. As far as these ends are obtained, natural affection is gratified. Such affection never moves them to seek the good of any but their relatives, unless the good of others is necessary to their own. And natural pity is an appetite created in us, to incline us to help and relieve each other in calamity and distress. And this is requisite to the preservation and comfort of the human race. But when persons in an afflicted, helpless state are relieved, then this appetite is gratified, and its end obtained; and it seeks nothing further, and will cease to operate, until another object of distress meets the eye, and excites pain in the beholder.

And all the appetites created in man, however many, are designed to move us to seek these particular distinct ends, necessary to our being and happiness in this world. But not one of them delights in happiness as an absolute good, or seeks it as an ultimate end. And if the human family were all as perfectly holy as Adam was at first, or as saints are in heaven, these appetites would not have been needful, nor have been created in us. For benevolence would have inclined all men to seek all the ends, which these appetites incline us to seek. But as God knew that holiness would be lost, he created those appetites in Adam and all his posterity, to supply the want of benevolence in some measure, while we live on this earth. Hence they will not be needed in heaven, where all are perfectly holy; and there they will never operate, if they exist.—It is very evident, then, that not one of these appetites partakes of the nature of holiness or benevolence. Hence our having them is no evidence of holiness in us, or any objection to the doctrine of total depravity. While Adam was perfectly holy, and governed entirely by his benevolent appetite, those other appetites would be regulated by it; and never be indulged to *excess* in any thing, or in the pursuit of their respective objects in any *unlawful way*, or in any manner inconsistent with the end and desires of benevolence. They would be so regulated and governed, as never to lead him to do any thing contrary to his benevolent designs and desires. Hence they would do no harm. Such order, and harmony prevailed in Paradise previous to the fall.

But when Adam ate the forbidden fruit, he forfeited the continuance of his benevolent appetite, and was deprived of it. Then he had no holiness existing in his heart, and was a sinner, spiritually dead, and totally depraved. For as holiness is the only holy principle existing in any being, as we have seen, the moment this was lost, he was perfectly destitute of every trace and operation of a holy principle. And this is the principal thing intended by total depravity.

But his other appetites all remained in full vigor, not lessened, or impaired in the least degree. And all his posterity are born destitute of holiness, with the same appetites which Adam had. For he begat a son in his own likeness, the likeness he had after he sinned.—Now these appetites remaining in him, sound and unimpaired, were the only active principles in his heart. By them he would be governed in all his conduct. They were the laws of his nature, by which he would be as invariably governed, as he previously had been by his benevolent appetite. These appetites would lead him to seek the respective ends, which were pleasing to him. And as these appetites were not pleased, or had any feeling or desire for any other objects or ends, than those of a worldly nature, the world was now his supreme object, his god, and only portion. They inclined him to seek every object which pleased the appetites created in him, and still remaining.

Is it not easy then to see, that Adam and his posterity would love the world, its riches, honors, and pleasures ; and seek them as their only, and highest portion and good ; as we see in fact they have done ever since the fall ? Will not every one go after the objects which please his appetites, without any regard to God's glory, or the happiness of their fellow men, any further than might be requisite to their own personal gratification ; just as we see they have in fact lived from age to age ?—Indeed Adam, or any of his posterity, if they had understood clearly the principles and laws of our nature by which we are invariably governed, might have foretold, *then*, how all men would in general conduct through the whole of their lives, in case no renovation or alteration should take place in the laws of their nature. Adam might have said, my posterity will never seek each other's happiness, or the glory of God ; they will never aim at any other, or higher, or greater good, than what the objects of this world will afford them. The world now is, and will be their god, their portion ; and as such they will seek it. They will disregard the authority of God, his law, and government ; and live in rebellion, robbing him of his due, and of every thing they owe to him. And if God send a deliverer to save them, according to what is implied in the promise that the seed of the woman shall bruise the serpent's head, they will reject him. For they cannot embrace and serve this Savior, unless they renounce the world as a portion, and deny self, and keep his benevolent precepts. They will, therefore, unitedly say, we will not have this man to reign over us. And thus they will live and conduct, each one through his life, and perish. They will never any more return to their allegiance to the king of heaven, unless God should again restore to them that benevolent appetite, which we have lost by eating the forbidden fruit. All this any one, who understood the laws which govern moral agents, might have predicted. And all that is said in the bible, of men in their natural state, harmonises with the general representation.

And now those who deny total depravity are desired to observe carefully, that after Adam had lost the moral image of God, all his other appetites were placed supremely on this world; and the same is true of all his posterity. And if candid, will they not own that a supreme regard for this world is idolatry? And of course that all the operations, all the desires of their appetites, are sinful? They are represented in this light in the word of God; that mankind serve and worship the creature and not the Creator. It is true, that men love food, and all the means necessary to it. But this leads them to seek the world as their only portion. Parents love their children, and this leads them to seek their worldly prosperity only, and as their highest good. And all their seeming gratitude is no more, than their delight in worldly prosperity; and the pity they manifest towards objects of distress, aims at nothing more than freedom from the pain they themselves feel, when they behold distress; so that as soon as they are relieved, they manifest no more concern for their happiness. And as men have no love for God, or for the everlasting happiness of each other, they never aim at these ends in any of their conduct; and aim at nothing higher, than to gratify their personal desires. All their aims terminate in self gratification; and will, until a benevolent appetite is again restored.

Hence no holy principle is to be found in any unrenewed person. And all his appetites prompt him to seek the world as his portion without any regard for God or the happiness of his race; and of course are wholly sinful in all their operations and desires. If such characters are not totally depraved, such depravity cannot exist. And there is no way to evade this reasoning, unless we deny the first principles upon which it is founded. It must be denied, that mankind have that *feeling* faculty, and those appetites, which have been described in these essays. If this be denied, then men are not agents, and of course not moral agents ; our accountability is all a dream, and all vice and virtue, praise and blame, are banished from the world. But if it be admitted, that men have this *feeling* faculty, and such appetites, which constant experience and facts prove to be true; then the consequence inevitably follows, that men, in the sense explained, are totally depraved.

In discussing this subject, I have not quoted those texts which prove this doctrine. The reasons are, this has been often done by others ; and my design was, to establish the doctrine as a true inference from a just theory of the human mind. I feel, that this end is now answered. The subject is, therefore, left to the judgment of all candid readers.

****

ESSAY XXVIII.

On benevolence or holiness.

"Without holiness no man shall see the Lord."

Various and different opinions have been entertained concerning the nature of benevolence ; and each one cannot be true in all its branches. On this subject, as well as others, truth and error are frequently blended together. Seeing opinions are so various, a candid examination of the subject is necessary. And the subject is very interesting and important ; for holiness is a requisite qualification for eternal life. Persons may embrace false views of the nature of holiness and they may have that disposition in which they suppose it consists, and on this ground believe they are the heirs of heaven and with a false hope feel safe and secure. But at death they meet with an awful disappointment. For all men will be rewarded hereafter according to their *real character*, and not according to their *opinions*. Hence, as holiness is a requisite qualification for endless bliss, it is all important to have clear, distinct and just views of its nature.

In discussing this subject, I shall aim at truth, and endeavor to expose some errors concerning holiness, which have been advanced by great names.—I design to consider the subject extensively, and in its several relations. And,

I. Attempt to *describe the nature* of benevolence.—To understand the nature of benevolence, two things are necessary— a distinct view of its *seat* in man, and of its *ultimate end.*—The mind is endued with several faculties. To which of them does benevolence belong ? And ultimate ends may be numerous ; which, then, is the final end of holiness ? To ascertain this is of the last importance. Because we cannot learn the nature of any active principle, until we know in what end it ultimately terminates.

By an ultimate end is meant that *object,* which is sought for its *own sake* ; which is in itself a real, absolute good.—When we seek any object for the sake of another, it is not an ultimate, but subordinate object. An ultimate object is never sought for the sake of another beyond it ; but for its own sake. Our views and affections centre in it ; with it we rest satisfied ; and they never extend beyond it, after some other or better object. When a person has attained his ultimate object, he has reached the end in which all his desires terminate ; here he rests, with this he is satisfied ; and this is the great source of his happiness.

And every moral agent, in this sense, must have an ultimate object or end. If he had not, he would seek one object for the sake of another, and the last for the sake of another further on ; and in this manner would he proceed forever, and never arrive at any final end. This is not, and cannot be the case. There must be some object, which is final, and for the sake of which all other objects are sought. That every moral agent must have an ultimate end in view, which he seeks for its own sake, in which his happiness is placed, is a truth so obvious it is needless to spend any more time in proving it.

The next inquiry then is, what is the ultimate object or end of benevolence ? If this can be certainly understood, the nature of benevolence will appear clear and distinct,—All will agree that whatever is the final end of benevolence, it must be an object which can be sought consistently with the glory of God, and the highest good of his kingdom. For all profess to believe that benevolence is friendly to God, and his holy kingdom ; that it is not in its nature or operations hostile to the highest good in the least degree.

Then what object can be sought on its own account, which is consistent with, and in all respects friendly to the divine glory, and highest good of his kingdom ?—It is believed, there is but one object in the universe, which can be sought as an ultimate end, which is friendly to the highest good ; and this is *happiness*. But that this may be clearly understood it is necessary to observe, that the happiness intended is an object or end, which is sought for its own sake; also, it is not *our own personal* happiness ; but happiness existing in others, distinct from ourselves. The hungry love food, not because it is *their* property, but because it is suited in its nature to satisfy hunger, whenever, and wherever it can be found.—So the benevolent delight in happiness, wherever they see it, because it is in its nature agreeable to their feelings. Happiness in the abstract is the ultimate object of benevolence. Hence they delight in it wherever they see it, whether in young or old, rich or poor, honorable or abased. And happiness cannot exist but in a feeling, sensible being ; and no where is it ever seen, except in rational beings, or beings capable of pleasure and pain. Hence it is the happiness of such intelligent beings, which is the ultimate object of benevolence. Hence, when it is asserted, that happiness is the ultimate object or end of benevolence, it is not *our own* which is sought ; but the happiness of *others*, of God's holy kingdom.

Our personal happiness can never be our ultimate object. This implies an absurdity. For in this case we must be happy in order to, or before we can be happy. We derive our happiness from our ultimate end ; this is the object which pleases and gratifies our desires. Hence the object or source of happiness, and happiness, are two distinct objects. And it is obvious, that the object or source of happiness must exist in the order of nature, and of time, previously to our deriving pleasure from it. It must exist, and be seen, before it can afford pleasure, or gratify our feelings. Hence if our happiness is our ultimate object, our happiness must exist as an object before we can derive any satisfaction from it. Does not every one see, that according to this theory we must be happy *before* we can be happy. If I am *now* happy, and this is the ultimate object of my pursuit ; from whence do I derive this happiness ? From what object or source ? Surely from nothing. For to say I derive it from previous happiness as an object, is running back in a circle forever.—It is plain to all, who reflect, that our

11

own happiness is not the ultimate object of any moral agent. Some may ask, then, why is it so often said, that all men seek their own happiness ? The meaning of this expression is this ; that all men seek objects, and especially an ultimate object, for the sake of the pleasure they derive from it, or take in it. For example ; honey is sweet. It is an object of pursuit. It may be sought for its own sake, and not for the sake of some further object beyond it. If sought for its own sake, it is an ultimate object or end. Why is it sought ? What influences, and prompts a person to seek it ? It is the pleasure he expects to derive from it. He expects it will satisfy his appetite, and gratify the desires he has for it. And by doing this, it is to him a source of happiness ; a source, good in its nature, and on its own account. Hence the proper use of language in this case is, to say, honey is his ultimate object or end ; no end beyond it exists, for the sake of which he seeks it. And the satisfaction he expects to derive from it is the *reason* why he seeks it. It is this, which gives it the influence of a motive. In this sense we seek our own happiness. If we say honey is sought, not because it is agreeable, then it is an object of indifference ; and on this ground we act without the influence of motives. For no object has the influence of a motive, unless it is in itself pleasing. A person who has a taste for honey, yet has never tasted it, does not know it is sweet. Hence he may see it, and pass by it, and never seek it; and never will, until in some way he believes it will afford him pleasure. Then the pleasure expected gives the object the force and influence of a motive. The truth then is this—the object, which is in itself agreeable is an ultimate end ; and the reason why we seek it as ultimate, and not for the sake of some further object, is, because it is agreeable, and suits the relish of the heart. It is in this sense that all men, good and bad, seek ultimate objects. All seek them for the same reason, because they are agreeable. This is the sense in which the happiness of others, or of God's kingdom, is the ultimate object or end of benevolence.

We now ought to inquire, whether the greatest sum of happiness is not the highest good, which all ought to seek. It is generally granted, that the greatest good is the ultimate object of benevolence. Concerning what constitutes the highest good, various opinions have been embraced. Here, I mean to show, in what the greatest good consists ; and then confute erroneous opinions.

What is the highest good ? If we can clearly show what constitutes the highest good of an individual, rational, being, we shall clearly see what the highest good of the universe is. For the greatest good of the universe, is the *sum* of all the good enjoyed by the friends of God. Suppose one thousand to be the whole number of rational beings existing. Add the highest goods of these individuals together, and the sum total is the highest good of this society. This is very evident. Hence, as soon as we learn what is the highest good of an individual, we see at once what is the greatest good of the universe.

And it is so evident, that the greatest measure of happiness any person is capable of enjoying, is his highest good, nothing scarcely can make it plainer. It is nearly, if not really, a self evident proposition. A rational being never does, and never can, set a value on any object whatever, which does not, and cannot afford him the least degree of pleasure, or pleasing gratification. Happiness is in itself, on its own account, a good. It is the only absolute good existing. If, then, we are surrounded with objects, and behold them, yet they neither please nor disgust us in the least degree, we view them with as perfect indifference, and without any emotion, as stones which are incapable of feeling. In this state we should not view objects as good, or as evil ; or possessing any real worth. But, if they excite in us painful sensations, we view them as evil, as hostile to us. If they give us pleasure, we pronounce them good ; we set a value on them according to the degree of pleasure they do, or can afford. If a person possessed all the riches of this world, and its highest honors ; yet if they did not, and could not, excite in him any sensation of pleasure, they in fact do him no good ; he would be as well without them, as he is with them ; and he would treat them as perfectly useless things. If he were perfectly holy, yet this did not, and he knew never would, afford him any pleasure, it does him no good, and is of no value to him. Indeed, to exist, yet feel no pleasure in any thing, any more than stones do, is no better than non-existence. It is of no service to have existence, unless happiness attends it. And to exist and be perfectly miserable, is worse than non-existence. For as happiness is an absolute good, so misery or pain is an absolute evil. And when any person reflects candidly on this subject he must grant, that happiness is an absolute good, and the greatest happiness of which a rational being is capable is his highest good.—This cannot be denied with any consistency.

From this it follows, that the greatest *sum* of happiness is the highest good of the universe.—Here it is well to observe, that rational beings cannot be finally happy, unless they are holy. For it is holiness which prepares them to enjoy God, the only fountain of good. And as all holy, created beings, are finally to live together in heaven ; it is in this society only that happiness will be enjoyed. These holy characters are the subjects of God, and constitute his heavenly, divine kingdom.

And it is the design of God, that in this kingdom, with Christ as the head or king, the greatest possible sum of happiness shall exist. And this greatest sum of felicity, existing in this kingdom, is the highest good of the universe. And the sum total of the happiness of each individual is the highest good of this kingdom, and the ultimate end of benevolence.

I say, the greatest *sum* of happiness is what benevolence seeks. Some have made it a question, whether benevolence aims ultimately at the greatest *sum*, or at making the greatest *number* happy. If the greatest number is the object sought, then benevolence would be constantly creating beings capable of pleasure, and making them happy. But we see in fact this is not the ultimate end of divine benevolence. For God might create millions more than he really does, and might make all of them happy ; yet he assures us some will be finally miserable ; and misery in a great degree does in fact prevail in this world, which is wholly inconsistent with this supposition, that he aims at making the greatest possible number happy. If this were his end, there would be no need of any misery in this, any more than in the world to come. We may then safely conclude, that it is not the greatest number, but the greatest sum of happiness, at which benevolence aims. And this is consistent with the nature of benevolence, according to the dictates of reason. When the happiness of an individual is the object, it is his greatest happiness, which is sought. For if happiness itself is agreeable, and for this reason it is sought, then the greatest sum will afford the most pleasure, and will be aimed at. Hence whatever would destroy, or lessen happiness on the whole, would be avoided ; and whatever, every thing considered, will promote this greatest happiness, will be pursued. Accordingly, if suffering a degree of pain for a time will increase a person's happiness, beyond what it could have been if no pain had been endured, he would choose to suffer this degree of evil. On this ground it is, that men daily suffer more or less pain :

they do it for the sake of greater happiness. Hence in a perfect system of means, when the greatest sum of happiness is the end, so much evil will be permitted as is really necessary to the greatest sum of good finally, and no more. It is in this view only, that evil can be permitted in the universe, consistently with the nature of benevolence ; and it is on this ground that the final punishment of the wicked is justifiable. And as this is the plan God is in fact executing, we may rest assured that infinite perfection knows it is necessary to the greatest sum of happiness, that evil should prevail ; and the degree and duration of its prevalence are determined by Jehovah. It is now evident, that the greatest sum of happiness is that highest good, which benevolence seeks as its ultimate end. And that it is not our personal happiness, but the happiness of God's holy kingdom, which is the object of benevolence. This being the end,a holy being will invariably avoid and oppose every thing, which is inconsistent with the greatest sum of happiness; and diligently pursue objects, and use all the means necessary to this greatest sum. As far as benevolence governs, the means necessary to the greatest happiness will be invariably and constantly used.

Having ascertained the ultimate end of benevolence, it will be easy to see what benevolence is, and where seated in the mind. Benevolence must consist in a disposition to seek the happiness of God's holy kingdom. It is then a disposition or an appetite, to be pleased with happiness wherever it is seen ; and a disposition to seek the increase of it. And it must be an *active* disposition. By this is meant, it must be a disposition which will excite, prompt, or move a person to seek the happiness of God's kingdom. And if it is a disposition, which is pleased, or which takes delight in the happiness of his kingdom on its own account, it will excite and move a person to seek this end with all his powers. For the ultimate pleasure an object affords is the motive, which influences and governs ; it is the spring of action, which puts every wheel in motion. It is then in its nature an active disposition. Its seat must be in the heart. For this faculty is the seat of all dispositions or appetites, good or bad, and of all the affections. I call it a disposition. If it be called a *taste*, or a *relish*, or an *inclination*, or a *preparedness*, or more properly an appetite for seeking happiness ultimately, still it is the same thing in its nature. It is a simple *something* in the heart, by whatever particular name called, which prepares a person to be delighted with the happiness of others, or of God's kingdom on its own account as an ultimate end. And as it prepares him to be pleased with this object, it will prompt or move him to use all his powers in seeking and promoting this end. Because there is no other way by which he can gratify his own feelings and desires. And every agent will seek the gratification of his desires. This is too evident to be denied. And it is self-evident, that where there is no *feeling* there is no principle of action. And where neither pleasure nor pain is experienced, there is no *feeling*. Painful or pleasant sensations are *feelings*, and our only primary, original *feelings*. Hence they are the primary, and original principles of action. And where there are sensations, they must have a *subject* or *something* which feels. This same thing, by whatever name called, is what I mean by a benevolent disposition. And this disposition must be antecedent to action, to every desire, and affection ; it must be the foundation or fountain, from which all actions and affections proceed or take their rise ; as a primary cause must be antecedent to all the effects it produces. So that every effect can be traced back to this primary principle. This is agreeable to all sound philosophy. Hence this disposition is not a *volition*, or an *exercise ;* but the foundation, the fountain of them ; or the primary, original cause in moral agents, from which all their desires, affections and volitions proceed.

We have now ascertained two things—the ultimate object of benevolence, and what benevolence is, and where seated ; and we see it is the primary, original cause or active principle in moral agents from which all their holy affections and actions proceed.

We may now attend to some *objections* to what is here advanced.

1. Some say, it is not the happiness of God's kingdom, but his *glory*, which is the ultimate object of benevolence. They say the scriptures make the glory of God his ultimate end. *Answer.* The truth of this affirmation is acknowledged. For, it is believed, the glory of God, and the greatest sum of happiness or highest good, are one and the same. No one supposes an increase of God's *essential* glory is his end ; but his *declarative* glory is his final object. And his highest declarative glory is no more, than a perfect display of his attributes. Here it ought to be observed, that there is a difference between a *display*, and a *communication*, of the essential fulness or glory of God.

In this display of the attributes of God in the material creation, there is no *image* of him instamped on every thing. But
in the moral world the image or the likeness of God exists.
Man was made in his likeness, both natural and moral. Here
a communication of the essential fulness is made ; and also here
is a display of his attributes. But in the material heavens and
earth there is a display of his perfections, but no communication is made ; we no where see his image existing, either natural or moral. Hence the greatest communication of the divine fulness is the highest and brightest possible display of
his glory ; far exceeding any displays made, where there is no
communication. It is therefore certain, that the greatest
communication of the divine fulness is the brightest possible display of his fulness ; and this is the same with the highest good,
or greatest happiness.

To illustrate this we may observe, that an unrenewed man
bears the natural image of his Maker, but not his moral. In
this state he does not enjoy the highest good. In order to this
he must have the moral image of God instamped on him. This
teaches, that the attributes of *knowledge*, of *power*, and of *holiness*, are necessary to happiness. And men are endued with these
properties, that they may be happy. This is the end. And
this is the reason why regeneration is necessary. God has
communicated his *natural likeness* to unrenewed men. And
to saints he has communicated his moral image. And the glory
of God is displayed with far greater brightness in saints than
in sinners. This clearly shows, that the existence of the natural & moral image of God in man, is necessary to the greatest display of his glory. It is also evident, that the brightest display
of the moral image of God constitutes his greatest declarative
glory ; and the greatest display of his goodness or benevolence
is the brightest display of his glory. It is so represented in the
sacred oracles. But surely the greatest display of divine
goodness is seen in the enjoyment of the greatest happiness.

Now every one may distinctly see, what is necessary to the
existence of the greatest created happiness. 1. The natural
image of God, and 2. His moral image ; Or an understanding
to perceive truth, a will, or power, to perform actions, and a
heart to feel, and enjoy the sources of endless bliss. A created
being with those properties, perfectly happy, enjoys the highest
good of which he is capable ; especially when in view of those
properties, and the attendant happiness eternally increasing.
And the greatest communication, and the brightest display of

the essential fulness of God, are not made, until the society exists in which his image natural and moral, or the greatest happiness, are possessed. This society must be perfectly blessed,
in order to the greatest display of his goodness. Hence a society, in which the greatest sum of happiness exists, is the
brightest display of the glory of God. In this society we behold the greatest display of God's benevolence, in the sum of
happiness enjoyed by it. If this society was ever so knowing,
and perfectly holy, yet not happy ; the displays of God
would be faint and obscure, no greater than what we behold in
the material creation. For the benevolence of God is the
beauty, glory, and excellency of his character ; accordingly
the greatest display of his love is a display of his chief glory,
of his excellency, yea the brightest emanation of the Godhead.
Hence in whatever light the subject is viewed, in the existence
of the greatest sum of happiness we behold the brightest possible display of the essential **glory of** God.

Suppose a vessel **to contain the** most excellent liquid, and a
communication of it to **be its hig**hest glory ; then when communicated to another vessel, **its gr**eatest glory is displayed.
Here the liquid, which is in the vessel, is the highest glory of
the vessel from which it was communicated. The liquid communicated, and the glory of the vessel from which the communication was made, is one and the same object.

God has an infinite fulness of knowledge, of power, of goodness, and of happiness. This is communicated to the heavenly
society, in as large a measure as it can receive ; knowledge,
power, goodness, and felicity, are communicated ; they exist
in this society. And this communication is the brightest possible display of God's essential glory. And as knowledge,
power, and goodness are necessary to happiness, and have no
value only when considered in relation to happiness ; it is evident, that the happiness of this society is especially the brightest ray of his glory. In the enjoyment of this happiness by
this society, he is glorified. And when we consider this happiness as forever increasing, we see his glory more and more
displayed, until it reaches the highest possible splendor. Accordingly the perfect and increasing happiness of the heavenly society, and the declarative glory of God, are not distinct, but
one and the same object. In harmony with this we find, when
the bible speaks of the glory of God as his end, it considers his
his glory as displayed and perfected in the felicity of heaven.

So that the brightest glory of God consists, in making sinful men perfectly and increasingly happy in heaven. Herein is love, the richest displays of his love, which is the sum of all his glory. In no way is God so much glorified as in the displays of his love or grace ; and in no way is his love so brightly displayed as in the final happiness of all the elect in heaven. So his glory, and the highest good, or bliss, are the same object, or final end. In the possession of the greatest sum of happiness, the greatest declarative glory of God consists.

2. Some object and say, that holiness is the supreme good, and the ultimate end of God in all his works.

Answer If it is the supreme, highest good, it is his last end. But it has been already shown, that holiness is not the highest good. And there is no way to make this more evident, unless by some illustrations, which will lead persons to look more candidly at the subject. Those, who consider holiness the supreme good, generally consider holiness and happiness the same, and especially to view them inseparably connected. But facts prove they are not inseparably connected. For Christ was perfectly holy, yet endured much suffering and pain. And any one cannot but see, that if events would finally destroy the highest good, this would give the most pain to a perfectly holy being ; he would be filled with painful grief, while this would occasion no pain to the enemies of God. Nothing would afford satan more satisfaction, than the destruction of all good. Hence they are not inseparably connected. Again. If the perfectly holy inhabitants of heaven were never to enjoy any happiness, why would their condition be better, than a state of non-existence? Without the enjoyment of happiness, it is as well not to be, as to have existence. This shows that holiness without happiness is not desirable, because it could not be a benefit to any one. And though in heaven the holy will be forever happy, yet it is plain they are not the same, and that holiness is not the highest good. And it is needless to spend more time in proving a point so plain. For more evidence would not convince those, who are now unconvinced. This has been proved in other essays.

3. Some object and say, that being in general is the ultimate end of benevolence. They view being, simply considered, as the object of benevolence. This opinion has been supported by many. Answer. What is implied in love to being in general,

12

By those who embrace this sentiment, I do not know certainly, and hence cannot say their opinion is not just.

To determine this point, we must attend to the exercises of benevolence. These are two.—1. A *delight* in the object ; and 2, *desires* for its highest good. When we contemplate simple being, we may view it as incapable, or capable of holiness and happiness. Mere matter is being, for it has an existence. But it is incapable of eithei holiness or happiness. Hence it is no proper object of benevolent affection. Rational beings are capable of both holiness and happiness. When they are considered as being in general, if love to them means a *delight* in their happiness, and *desires* that they may be perfectly and forever happy ; if this is what is meant by love to being in general, the sentiment is just ; or the very same with that of the author. For here the happiness of being in general, is the object of benevolence. Loving in this sense is only *desiring* the greatest happiness to exist, and *delighting* in it. If this be not the meaning of those, who advance this opinion, I know not what they do mean ; and can give no further answer, until they explain themselves so as to be understood.

In connexion with this opinion the advocates of it say, that we ought to love men in proportion to their *quantity* of existence. They say, if another person has a *capacity* as large again as mine, and one or the other must die, benevolence will lead me to surrender life voluntarily, that his life may be spared. And they use many similitudes to illustrate this sentiment.—Hence they insist, that if others contain a greater quantity of being than we do, we ought to love them more than we do ourselves ; and we ought in *practice* to prefer them to ourselves, to die that they may live. This sentiment does not seem to accord either with the laws of God, or his government of the world. The law says, thou shalt love thy neighbor *as* thyself. Now, allowing this to mean that we shall love our neighbor with the same *kind* and *degree* of love, which we ought to have for ourselves ; yet no one can construe it to mean, that we shall love him *more* than ourselves. Also God, in the government of the world, does not exercise love to men in proportion to their quantity of existence. For some of the greatest capacities are taken away by death, and, according to the lives they have led, are made forever miserable ; while others of far less capacity are permitted to live, and are renewed, and made happy. According to this sentiment Paul should have said, for you see your calling, brethren, that not many poor, or despised, or things that are not, are called ; but God has chosen the great, the noble, and those of the greatest capacities.

There is one sense, in which we may be said to love others more than ourselves. Suppose one person out of ten to contain as great a capacity or quantity of being, as all the other nine ; if we wish each of them as much happiness as their capacities will admit, or wish each of them perfectly happy, which is the same, the sum of happiness enjoyed by one is equal to the sum of the other nine ; and we have wished so much more good to one, than to the other. Here we are to observe two things—1, the sum of good we wish a person to enjoy—and 2, the wish or desire itself. We may desire the happiness of ten ; and the desire for the happiness of each one may be the same in fervency ; that is, we have no stronger desire for the happiness of one, than we have for the others. In this sense we have the same degree of love or desire for each one. One is loved no more than the other. Our desire for the happiness of one is no greater or stronger, than for another. Yet if one is capable of far greater happiness, than others, the quantity of good we wish him to enjoy is far more, than the quantity we wish to the other ; keeping in view that we wish all to enjoy as much happiness as their capacities will contain. Here the quantity of good we wish to one is greater, than the quantity we wish to others ; and in this sense we may love one more than others. But when we consider the *desire* of the heart, or of benevolence, we love one no more than others. For our desire for the happiness of each one is equally strong. But I suspect the advocates for loving beings in proportion to their existence mean, that our desires for the happiness of some ought to be stronger, than for the happiness of others. If this be their meaning, their sentiment is erroneous. To make this evident, I will state a case. Twenty persons are in the same room, and their happiness consists in eating oranges. One of the number has oranges with him, and proposes to distribute them according to the rules of benevolence. He has then in the first place to ascertain the quantity of each person's existence, and finds on inquiry, that himself contains more quantity of existence than the other nineteen. He accordingly says, the oranges ought all to be enjoyed by me ; and they all must acquiesce in his decision. He eats and is happy. The others having none, sit without any thing to afford them any satisfaction. Does this look like benevolence ?

Let us now proceed on the ground, that the happiness of others is the object of benevolence. Then the person who has the oranges, hands them round to one & another ; and each one is more desirous that others should eat them, than to eat them himself. And why ? Because each one says, I take more delight in seeing you happy in eating them, than I experience in eating them myself. Here, then, each one is for *giving* to others. In the first statement, the disposition called benevolence leads a person to monopolise, to possess every source of enjoyment, if he can make himself believe he has a much greater quantity of existence than others. And according to the last statement, benevolence is of a *diffusive nature;* it prompts persons to give away, and distribute sources of happiness far and wide as they are able. Because what he aims at is to make others happy. And his greatest happiness consists in seeing others happy. Does not this last disposition look far more like benevolence, than the first ?

Again. The sentiment, that we ought to love and seek the good of men in proportion to their existence, or quantity of being, is impracticable. To be convinced of this, let it be kept in view, that benevolence aims ultimately at the highest good, or greatest sum of created happiness. Now, according to the sentiment we are opposing, to promote the highest good, a person must be able to determine two things—1, who has the greatest quanity of being, and, 2, that to seek the good of those most, who have the most being, is necessary to the highest good ultimately.—But in many cases it will be impossible for us to judge truly, who has the greatest quantity of existence ; and where we cannot determine this point, we cannot know what duty is, and therefore cannot act. And if we could always determine, who did possess the greatest capacities ; yet we could not know it would be most for the general good, to seek and promote their good, more than we do the good of those of far less capacities. For we have reason to believe, that God sees it is necessary to the highest good, that some men of the greatest abilities should be miserable. It is impossible for us to determine with certainty what is, or is not, for the greatest good. Hence we cannot know it would be most for the general good, that we should always in practice seek the good of the greatest, more than the good of others. For aught we know we may promote the greatest sum of happiness ultimately, by seeking here the good of the least, more than we do the good of the greatest men.

We here see this sentiment cannot be reduced to practice. And an impracticable sentiment is certainly erroneous. But if we delight in the happiness of others, and ultimately seek the highest good ; then it will be our object to promote the happiness of every individual, as far as we have opportunity and ability ; and leave it with God to determine, who shall finally be the heirs of endless life. This is practicable. And in this way we keep the law. For we do in this way with the *same*, and with as *strong* a *desire*, seek the good of others, as we do our own good ; and love our neighbor *as* ourselves. This is certain. Because our happiness consists in the happiness of others. In order then to our own greatest gratification, we must seek and increase the happiness of others. Hence our desire to make others happy is the same, and as strong, as the desire we have for our own gratification. Hence a benevolent man in reality always has just as much love for others, as he has for himself. So that when he is cold and stupid, and but little engaged to make others happy, he is but little engaged to make himself happy. This must be the case, so long as benevolence places its own happiness or gratification in the happiness of others. Hence I think this objection is now fully answered.

4. Some object and say, that all love is resolvable into self love. They will not admit, that any other kind of love has existence, and say every species of love is nothing more or less, than self love ; and some distinguish between selfishness and self love ; they admit the former is not benevolence, but contend that the latter is.

Answer. It is impossible here to affirm or deny, until we distinctly understand the term self love. Every species of love has an object ; in loving there is always something loved. And love must always have some ultimate object, or objects, which are loved on their own account.—What then is the ultimate object of self love? Is the happiness of others, or of God's kingdom, its ultimate object ? If it is, then all other objects are sought in subordination to this end. For all agents subordinate every thing to their ultimate end ; every thing is loved and sought with a view to the end, which is agreeable in its own nature. Here then self love, if it has the greatest happiness for its ultimate object, is the same as benevolence.

And if this is not the ultimate object of self love, what is ? If it be said, that worldly property, honors, and the pleasures of time and sense, are sought for their own sake ; then other objects are sought for the sake of attaining these ends. Here suppose the authority and law of God, and the good of his kingdom should be in the way of attaining these worldly objects, in the view of the agent. In this case he will certainly disregard and oppose the law of God, and the interest of his spiritual kingdom. For it is the uniform practice of moral agents to seek whatever is necessary to their ultimate end, and oppose whatever is inconsistent with it. This is the reason why the divine law is so often transgressed ; because obedience is inconsistent with the ultimate pursuits of men. On the same ground civil law is transgressed. Hence if worldly objects, whether riches, honors, or pleasures, are the ultimate object of self love, the agent must oppose the law of God, his cause and kingdom, whenever they interfere with his ultimate pursuits. And the law of God is always opposed to an agent, who makes any worldly object his final end. An ultimate object is always chosen as a portion, is supremely loved, and the highest source of happiness. The law of God, therefore, does not allow any person to make any worldly object his ultimate end ; or any object, but the highest good of his kingdom. And to make any object, except the highest good of God's kingdom, an ultimate end, is idolatry; it is making that *supreme*, and a *portion*, which ought not to be thus regarded. Indeed there are but a few objects, which are ever sought as ultimate ends by any agent. *Riches*, worldly *honors*, and *pleasures*, and the *glory* of God, the greatest *happiness* or *good*, may be sought as ultimate ends. The glory of God, the greatest sum of happiness, and the good of the universe, I suppose, are one and the same.

Now then there are four objects, worldly riches, honors, pleasures, and the greatest happiness, which may be sought as ultimate ends. Can any one name a fifth, which is not included in one of these ? He cannot. If an agent seeks the riches, honors, or pleasures, of this world, either one or all of them, as his ultimate end, then those constitute his portion ; they are the objects of his supreme affection, and of course they are his god ; and he is an idolater. This is directly contrary to the law of God. And while seeking those objects he is constantly transgressing that law. And if these are the ultimate objects of self love, it is evidently the same with selfishness; it is a principle in the human heart, which is, in its nature and operations, contrary to the law of God ; and so far from being of a benevolent nature, it is directly opposed to benevolence.

But if it is said, that the greatest happiness, or the glory of God, is the ultimate object of self love ; then its nature is the same with benevolence ; yea it is benevolence itself ; and it will subordinate every wordly pursuit to its ultimate object. But in this case, why is it called self love ? The advocates of this sentiment may say, because the highest good, or happiness, is sought for the same reasons that we seek every other object, or final end. This is, the pleasure or satisfaction taken in the object. The satisfaction, or delight in an object on its own account, is the reason, or motive, which excites all moral agents to seek any object ultimately. All men, they say, are governed by the same ultimate motives, which are the gratification of our desires by the object sought. So they say it is proper to term all kinds of love by the same name ; and to call it self love, because *our personal* desires are gratified.

Here we ought to observe, that, although all ultimate ends are sought for the same reason, because they please ; yet the ends are very different in their nature. Worldly riches, and happiness, are very different objects. If we seek the former as our end, it will lead us to lessen the property of others to increase our own. For if one possesses all the property in this world, others must be deprived of it, and left to live and die in poverty and misery. Hence in seeking this end we are daily robbing others ; and while increasing our own happiness, we are lessening the felicity of others. But if the happiness of another is our ultimate end, the only way to promote our happiness is by increasing his ; and the more the happiness of God's kingdom is increased, so much the more our own is augmented. Hence if all men possessed this principle, to love and seek the happiness of others, all would be united in mutually promoting each others' felicity or highest good. And this is the only end, which can be sought as an ultimate object, and which can be pursued consistently with the highest good of rational beings ; and this is the reason why it ought to be the ultimate end of all moral agents.—Hence when we view worldly property, and the happiness of others, as two distinct ultimate ends, we clearly see the wide difference between the nature and operations of those principles in the heart, from which love to them respect'vely proceeds. And there is no other way to learn the nature of any *active principle*, but by considering the nature of its ultimate end. So, though all men seek ultimate ends for the same reason, or from the same motive ; yet we see the active governing principles within, are very different in their nature and operation, and ought of course to be called by distinct names. And hence self love is either the same principle with benevolence, or it is of the same nature as selfishness. And as all beings are governed by selfishness or benevolence, those different active principles ought to be distinguished by distinct names.

Having answered the principal objections, which might arise against the description given of the nature of benevolence, which occurred ; I now proceed,

II. To attend to the *operations* of benevolence.

The ultimate end of benevolence is the greatest sum of created happiness ; or, which is the same, the highest possible good. And every thing which exists, whether works, creatures, or events, will be hostile to this end, or friendly to it. It cannot be said of any thing, *this* will never promote nor oppose the general good. For all things, which have existence, have a *tendency* to this end, either *for* it, or *against* it. It is granted, that every thing has a *nature*, which is *good*, or *evil ;* and the nature of all things is according to their ultimate tendency. If their tendency is to the highest good ultimately, they are *good ;* if their tendency is ultimately hostile to the general good, they are evil.

Now benevolence will always love or hate every thing according to its nature. It will be friendly to every thing, which is in its nature friendly to the greatest happiness ; and oppose every thing, which is in its nature hostile to it. Let it also be kept in view, that benevolence is a disposition, appetite, or relish, to be pleased with the happiness of others, or of God's holy kingdom. It is an abiding, permanent, active principle in the heart. It is not strictly speaking an *exercise, desire,* or *affection ;* but a foundation for affections. As it is in its nature exquisitely *sensible,* every object seen affords a pleasant or painful sensation, from which desires or affections proceed. Accordingly desires, or what are generally called affections, are the operations of benevolence. Desires are what we call affections. And every affection has an object. Where there is a desire, there is some object desired ; where there are love and hatred, there are objects which are loved or hated. Hence to have a clear and distinct view of the operations of benevolence, we may now attend to their several objects.—The ultimate object of benevolence is the happiness of God's kingdom. Hence, God will be the first, and supreme object of a benevolent heart. He will be loved with supreme affection. He will have the first and highest regard or place in the heart; for this obvious reason, that he is the source, fountain, and original efficient cause of all good. All happiness is from him, and produced by him. And being infinite, he is the *greatest* and *best* being in the universe ; and accordingly merits the supreme regard and affection of all rational creatures. As he is a being of infinite greatness and majesty, he will be *feared*, and *reverenced*. Being infinitely holy, and excellent, he will be loved; will be an object of the highest delight and affection. As he is the Ruler of the universe, who cannot err, or do wrong, the benevolent soul will put all his confidence and trust in God ; feel safe in his hand, and rejoice that he reigns.—He will be the object of all religious worship, and adoration. Such in brief are the feelings or affections of a benevolent heart towards God.

Next, Christ will be regarded, and honored, equally with the Father. Every affection exercised towards the Father, will be also given to the Son. And here the benevolent person will deny self, renounce all self righteousness, and sufficiency ; and as a sinful, ruined, helpless creature, come and put all its trust and dependence on the *merits* of the Savior, for the pardon of sin, for deliverance, and salvation ; and rely alone on his almighty arm to be preserved by faith to endless life. In this way the saint will come up from the wilderness, leaning on his beloved.

Next in order is the Holy Spirit. All the supreme regard paid to the Father will be given to the Spirit, as equal with God. And as the Holy Spirit, in his office, renews and sanctifies the heart, the saint will look to the Spirit for all spiritual light, peace, comfort and joy, and for the perfection of sanctification. Such affections will be exercised towards the holy Trinity by the benevolent soul.

Another object of benevolent affection is man. According to the requirement of the law, saints will love all men as their neighbors. They will have the *same* love, in *kind* and *degree*, they have for themselves. For it will be their desire, if consistent, that all may be perfectly happy. And they can have no more love for themselves, than a desire for their own perfect happiness. And as they have this desire for all men, if God could consistently save all, they have the same *kind* and *degree* of love for their neighbor they have for themselves. But for real christians they have a brotherly affection. They not only wish them happy, as they do others, but they also love their characters, delight in the holy image God has instamped on them. When men are the objects, such are the affections of benevolence towards them. And here it may be added, that they will have the same affection for holy angels they have for saints.

The moral law, also, will be an object of their love. This law, in all its requirements and prohibitions, tends directly to the highest good. This is evident. For if all men obeyed it perfectly, and never in one instance transgressed it, all would be perfectly happy. Hence it may be pronounced to be holy, just and good ; and all saints with David will delight in it, and esteem it more precious than silver or gold, and sweeter than honey. Thus the law will be loved and regarded by the benevolent.

And all the doctrines of the gospel, as well as its precepts, will be the objects of love. Because they all tend to exalt God, and humble sinful men, and advance the happiness of God's kingdom. They are holy doctrines ; and as food will delight the heart, and nourish the new man. Hence the reason why saints delight in a preached gospel, and are edified, and strengthened, and ripened for heaven.

Again. The service of God is an object of benevolent affection. And why ? Because its tendency is to the greatest happiness. It is a *holy* service, and reasonable ; a service due to God, and the way by which saints actively promote the highest good of God's kingdom. Hence saints will delight in the service of God, and esteem it as their meat and drink to do his will, as Christ did ; yea they will account this yoke of service easy, and this burden light. Such are the feelings the benevolent have for that service and obedience which are required of them. We have now exhibited to view the principal objects of holy affections, in which saints take peculiar delight.

Some objects they will hate: and sin is one. The tendency of every sin is to destroy that happiness, in which benevolence ultimately delights. Hence sin must be an object of their hatred and abhorrence. All remaining sin, the old man in their own heart, they hate. They loath and abhor themselves, and will repent ; will have broken hearts for sin, and be humble, and lie in the dust, ever crying, God be merciful to us sinners. They will also hate sin in others, as they do in themselves. Hence they will be employed in fighting against sin, and satan ; and strive with all their might to have the kingdom of darkness demolished. They will therefore, while in this life, ever experience a warfare within, between the new and the old man ; and carry on a war against all the works of darkness.

This is sufficient to show, in general at least, what objects benevolence will love, and hate ; and to show what are the operations or affections of a holy disposition or relish. By these operations or affections of benevolence, we may know what *our own* characters are, and those of *others*. For these are the fruits of the spirit ; those fruits by which all men are to be known. As the fruits of holiness and sin are very different in their nature ; wherever the fruits of holiness prevail and abound, it is easy to distinguish between saints and sinners. But if the fruits of holiness are few, faint and imperfect, it is difficult to discern between the clean and unclean.

III. Describe the difference between benevolence and selfishness. The nature of benevolence has been already delineated. When selfishness is described, the difference between them will at once be evident. The selfish man has appetites, inclinations, and desires. And he daily seeks to gratify and satiate them. In this his whole happiness consists. The objects he seeks are those which are agreeable, which please and gratify his desires. Whatever they are, he will wish to possess them in such *abundance* as to gratify every desire; not only for a day, but through life ; he will wish for power to obtain, and to increase the supply constantly ; he will wish for power to defend himself in the possession of his treasures ; and for power to enjoy them with *impunity*, even if they were unrighteously obtained. Men, who are daily accumulating property, and use unlawful means to obtain it, are never willing to be called to an account, and punished for their crimes. And they never would suffer themselves to be thus treated, if it were in their power to prevent it. Hence it is very evident, they not only wish for power to obtain whatever they love, but to have power also to possess and enjoy it with impunity. To be in a state or condition, in which they can possess and enjoy every object they love with impunity, they must render themselves *independent* of all beings, and possess power unlimited. This serves to show to what a state selfish men would exalt themselves, if they could do it. And we find all such men hate a state of dependence ; are ever striving to render themselves independent of men; and the more independent they are, the more they are suited. And they would render themselves independent of God, if it were possible. They hate as much to be dependent on him, as on their fellow men. Hence if they could attain unto that state or eminence, which is most desired by them, they would render themselves independent of all beings both created and uncreated. Then they could enjoy all the objects of their pleasure and delight, without any *fear* of being deprived of them, or punished for any crimes they had committed.

They have no principle within to restrain them from seeking this state of independence. For they have no benevolence ; no love for God or for men ; nothing to excite them to seek the glory of God, or happiness of any of their fellow men, except those for whom they have a natural affection, and view as a part of themselves. Being totally destitute of benevolence, they pursue the objects of their pleasure without any regard to God, or the happiness of men ; they care not how often they transgress the divine law, or how much they injure their fellow men, if they can do it so as to avoid punishment. Nothing but a fear of disgrace and punishment restrains them. And they would, if possible, reach a state of such eminence and independence, as to be above all fear of punishment.

Now our inquiry is, of what nature are the objects, which please and gratify the desires of selfish men ? Daily facts prove what it is they love and seek. One object is property. They wish for food to eat and raiment to wear ; and for every other object necessary to their convenience, ease, and comfort. They wish to have property sufficient to satiate every desire ; and to have a lasting store, which will not be expended while they live. Hence they are earnest in their pursuit of riches. And however rich they are, they never have *too much;* yea they never have *enough.* Hence there is no end to their pursuit of riches. Property is not only agreeable to their natural appetites and desires, and is sought for this reason ; but property is *power ;* the more they have, the more *able* they are to acquire more, and also to gratify every desire. As property is in one sense power, they love it for this reason, and seek it. As with property they gratify their appetites, their bodily cravings, it is agreeable to their *primary* feelings ; and as it enables them to acquire more with greater ease, it is agreeable to their *secondary* desires. This shows at once why riches are so agreeable to selfish men, and are sought by them with so much assiduity and zeal.

Another object highly pleasing to them is *honor*, or the esteem of men, and high, eminent stations of office. Why is honor so agreeable to a selfish man ? If pride is a primary appetite or principle of action ; the reason is obvious. Because honor gratifies pride. Then, again, an office is power. A man in office is invested with authority ; he has power to rule ; and with the help of this power he can more readily increase his wealth ; and especially when we consider, that profit is annexed to his office, and is the fruit of it. Again. The higher they are exalted by any office, the more independent of men they feel themselves to be. Now when we consider these facts, it is not strange that *honor* is an object *so pleasing*, and sought with *so much zeal*. And the more a man is esteemed by his fellow men, if he has no office, the more power he has to gratify his desires. For if esteemed, all around him will strive to please him, and aid him in his pursuits. Hence he enjoys a more favorable opportunity to acquire property, than a man does, who is hated by his fellows. This men find is a fact. Hence they love to be esteemed ; because this enables them, with more ease and greater success, to obtain every object agreeable to their desires. Hence we see why worldly honors and greatness are so pleasing to men. And especially why they are pleased with *supreme* power in any state or kingdom. If a person has authority and power to command, to rule, and act according to his pleasure with impunity ; he is so far above, and independent of men. No wonder, then, that men are so ambitious, and have such a thirst for kingly authority, and to possess absolute power. For he, who enjoys absolute power in a kingdom, can gratify all his desires, and can live and act according to his pleasure, with impunity. He has so far attained to that state of independence which all seek, in which he can gratify all his desires with impunity, as long as he possesses this power.—As such absolute power is the most favorable to all the desires of natural men, and enables them to live as they please ; no wonder mankind have sought it with so much zeal ; and have spilt the blood of millions, and filled the world with misery, to obtain it.

Another object highly pleasing to man, is the enjoyment of sensual pleasures or gratifications. The end of a selfish man is the constant gratification of all his desires. In this his happiness consists. So the constant enjoyment of every pleasure is his end ; in this his desires are gratified. Every object he seeks is with a view to this end. And he wishes to live in the enjoyment of every pleasure unmolested, free from all fear of being deprived of them, or punished for any of his unlawful deeds. And if he can possess the riches of this world, and its honors, and rise to such authority as to rule and reign according to his pleasure ; then he has reached the highest pinnacle of greatness, grandeur and felicity, this world affords.—These observations show us, what is the end of a selfish man, what objects are most pleasing to him, and what his life and conduct will be as far as he has power.

All we now have to do, is to compare selfishness and benevolence with each other, and then we shall see the difference between them. The primary operations of selfishness are covetous. Covetousness may, with great propriety, be considered the first operations or exercises of selfishness. If a person is hungry, he covets food ; this is only a desire for it to satiate his appetite. He will also covet or desire a sufficient quantity to satisfy him, not only for a day, but through life. When he obtains it, he will covet power to defend his possession, that others may not rob him of it. And if any should think he had obtained any of it by fraud, and pursue measures to have him punished, he will covet or desire power to defend himself, and to ward off the stroke of justice, and to enjoy his food and all his possessions with impunity, and without fear of being deprived of them. Such are the operations of selfishness. And then, as far as any assist him, and appear friendly to him in the pursuit of the objects of his desires ; he will call them friends, and treat them in a friendly manner, as far as is consistent with his own schemes and desires,& no further. And if any appear unfriendly, and oppose him in the pursuit of his dearest objects, or embarrass him in executing his schemes, this opposition will excite in his heart hatred, anger, revenge, and such malignant passions ; which will lead him to injure them as far as he can with safety, and his own honor.

Hence the selfish man has a disposition, which leads him to accumulate property, and become very rich. He never has enough. The accumulation of wealth only increases his desire after more. His desire is to engross and monopolise all the wealth of this world, and reduce all his fellow men to the condition of *tenants*, except a few who are his children or near relatives, and whom he views as a part of himself. And if he succeeds in acquiring riches, and multiplying the number of his tenants ; then his desire is to usurp power and authority sufficient to defend his possessions, and to enjoy them with impunity, and free from all danger or fear of being dispossessed and punished. So he will covet power, and monopolise to him all authority, that he may rule and reign ; and have all around him revere his name,and submit to his will & pleasure. In such a state of independence he views himself able to indulge himself, and to gratify every desire of his heart ; or in one word, to live, and swim in an ocean of worldly pleasure. And so far he feels himself happy, and enjoying all the felicity this world can afford. In this state of independence he would wish to live forever ; for he has no relish for any other, or higher pleasures, than those he enjoys. To rule and reign independently, and enjoy his pleasures free from all danger and fear, is that high pinnacle of glory and bliss to which his heart has aspired.

Hence we see what the nature of selfishness is, in all its operations. The selfish man is for engrossing, monopolising, all the wealth of this world, and usurping all power, and authority ; and enjoying all the pleasures this world can afford, without any feeling or regard for the happiness of any of his fellow men, except those relatives whom he views as parts of himself. This description of selfishness and its operations agrees with facts, and the word of God. It is evident from the history of men, and what we daily observe, that all natural men pursue riches, honors, power, and earthly pleasures. It is evident, that all men are naturally tyrants ; possessed of a disposition to act according to their pleasure with impunity ; or to live independent, and above all controul. This disposition is apparent in children, and is manifested by their lives, unless they are renewed. And the bible testifies that men have forsaken God the fountain of all good, and have gone after broken cisterns ; that they go astray from the womb speaking lies, and have worshipped and served the creature, and not their Creator.

But benevolence is very different in its nature and operations. The happiness of others or of God's kingdom is its ultimate end. The happiness of God's kingdom is the first, and greatest source of happiness to the benevolent heart. Hence the good man cannot promote his own happiness, only by promoting and increasing that of his fellow men. Hence he will avoid every thing, which tends to the misery of men, and seek every thing, which tends to their happiness. It is the nature of benevolence, instead of monopolising, to *give* and *diffuse* the means of happiness among his fellow mortals. Because the more they rejoice, or the greater their happiness, so much greater is his own joy. Selfishness and benevolence resemble each other only in one particular, which is this; all men seek the objects of their pursuit for the *same reason*, because they are pleasing and agreeable to their hearts. This is the primary spring of action, or motive, which governs all men, good or bad, and which puts every wheel in motion in the moral world.— But as the objects which are ultimately pleasing to them are very different in their nature, their motives differ in their nature, and excite them to different pursuits, and conduct in life, which manifest widely different characters. Their motives lead them to bring forth very different *fruit*, by which they are known and distinguished. The benevolent man delights in the happiness of others. This affords no delight to the selfish man. The latter is for engrossing and monopolising every thing to himself. The former is for giving away and diffusing the sources of happiness among all men, as far as can be consistent with the greatest sum of felicity. The selfish man subordinates religion to his worldly pursuits ; the benevolent subordinates the world to religion. One loves God and all men ; the other has no love for either. One hates sin as the greatest enemy to happiness ; the other loves it, and rolls it as a sweet morsel under his tongue. One seeks heaven as his home ; the other wishes to live here forever. One believes God is perfect, and will govern the world in the wisest and best manner, to obtain at last the greatest sum of happiness ; hence he rejoices that the Lord reigns. The other opposes the character and government of God, because he knows, he will call him to an account, and punish him for all his evils deeds. One submits to the will of God with pleasure. The other opposes his will, and would render himself independent of God, were it in his power. One chooses to be in the hand of God, and at his disposal, and every thing he possesses ; because God knows, and he does not, how every thing should be ordered for the general good. The other cannot endure the thought of being at the disposal of Jehovah. One chooses to be dependent, and receive every gift from God. The other hates dependence, and to be under obligations to his Maker. One delights in prayer, and the service of God ; the other hates to pray, and rejects the service of God, and serves sin and satan, the enemy of God. Thus selfishness and benevolence differ in their *nature* and *operations*. This difference originates from the nature of those objects, which they love and seek on their own account, and as their ultimate ends. According to the nature of the *ultimate end* of a moral agent, will his character and conduct be. We have seen what is the ultimate end of the benevolent man, & of the selfish ; and what of course must be their desires, pursuits, and conduct in life; that they will pursue courses as wide apart as the east and west, and as different from each other, as light and darkness, sin and holiness ; which proves that the primary, active principles which govern them, are different in their *nature* and *tendency*.

IV. Attend to the excellency and glory of benevolence.— The nature of every thing is such, that it will tend ultimately either to good or evil, to promote happiness or destroy it. There is nothing concerning which it can be said, that it exists in vain. Nothing is in its nature indifferent, of which it may be said, this will never do any good, or any hurt. If any thing in its nature tends ultimately to destroy happiness and produce misery, is such a thing useful, beautiful, and excellent ? No, we cannot conceive of any thing, which is more hateful and deformed.—And if any thing tends directly and ultimately to banish misery from the universe, and promote the greatest happiness, what shall we say of it ? Would it not be an affront to common sense, to affirm it was a hateful, deformed thing ? Must not all with one voice pronounce it good, both beautiful and excellent ?

And notwithstanding various opinions and disputes concerning what constitutes beauty and excellency ; all will at least have to acknowledge, that *utility* is *beauty ;* or, in other words, that every thing which tends in its nature to produce the greatest happiness, is beautiful and excellent ; and every thing, which in its nature tends ultimately to produce misery only, is deformed and hateful.

Benevolence tends ultimately to the greatest possible sum of happiness. This is its nature. And as it is the primary, efficient cause of happiness in existence, and the cause, which con-

14

tinues constantly increasing it, and renders every thing subservient to it, and will eternally preserve and increase it; it is evidently the most *useful, beautiful, good, excellent,* and *glorious* quality or attribute in being. Nothing else can equal it in glory ; and without it the universe would be full of darkness and misery. And this it is believed will appear more and more evident in describing the beauty and excellence of benevolence. Having now shown why it is fit and proper to predicate beauty of benevolence, and shown in what it consists, we may attend to a particular description of it.

1. It is the primary, efficient cause of all the happiness existing in the universe. All will grant there must be a first cause, which gives existence to every thing ; and this cause must be in its nature active ; or it must be a primary, efficient cause, from which the existence of all things must proceed. This first cause must have an ultimate end. For every agent must have an ultimate end, as we have seen. And this ultimate end must be happiness or misery. For there is nothing else, which is in its nature, or on its own account, either good or evil. This has been proved. Now as all grant, that God is the *first, efficient cause* of all things, he as an agent must have an ultimate end ; and this end must be the greatest sum of created happiness or misery. And with one or the other of these ends he must be ultimately pleased. Such a disposition or relish he must have. For nothing else, in any moral agent, can be the subject of pleasure or pain. Where there is no disposition, no feeling, nothing can either please or displease. A feeling disposition then he must possess. And he must be pleased ultimately with either happiness or misery. As it is not the object here to prove the moral perfection of God, I shall take it for granted, that God is pleased with the greatest sum of created happiness; this is his ultimate end in all his works and operations. And when we consider how much happiness he has already produced, how every thing is adapted in its nature to this end ; and consider the great work of redemption, no one can have a doubt, but that God ultimately seeks the greatest happiness.

From eternity God saw that the greatest sum of created happiness was possible, and might be produced. This in its own nature was an infinite and sublime source of happiness. Nothing which he could create would afford him so much gratification and delight, as the existence of such a sum of happiness. To please himself, to gratify to the full this disposition of his heart, is what moved and excited Him to produce every thing which has existence. This disposition, in scripture called love, is active in its nature ; is the primary, efficient cause of all things. Why does he create, or produce any event ? To please, or *gratify* this love, this disposition. This disposition, then, moved him as an agent to employ his knowledge, or infinite wisdom, to devise and form a plan for the final attainment of his end. This plan is as extensive as the works of God, both of creation and providence. It includes all the works of creation, and all the events of providence ; and no work will exist, or event be produced, which is not necessary to the production of the greatest happiness ultimately. All things are made by him, and for his *pleasure* they are and were created.

The disposition of his heart moved Him to employ his infinite power, in carrying this plan formed by wisdom into final execution. Hence by his will every thing is produced. He said, let there be light, and light was. In like manner, his will produces every event, and creates every world. He wills, and it is done. In this way his will is operating, and will continue to operate, until his plan is fully executed in all its numerous parts. And this disposition of Jehovah subordinates all things, through the universe, to the greatest happiness. In producing and increasing this, his pleasure is done ; his heart is gratified, and his happiness is infinite.

Hence this love or disposition of God is the primary spring of action, the first, efficient cause of all things. By it all his natural attributes, his wisdom, his power, are exercised and displayed in forming, and executing the best possible plan. His *understanding* and *will*, considered as faculties or attributes, are controlled, directed, and governed by his heart, or his love for the general good. The attributes of God are all comprised in three ; benevolence, knowledge, and power, answering to the faculties in men called the heart, the understanding, and will ; and they constitute a fulness sufficient for the accomplishment of any thing which is *possible*, or which implies no contradiction or inconsistency. They constitute an *infinite fountain* of good. In order to the existence of the greatest sum of created happiness, this fountain must flow forth in streams ; it must be diffused, and communicated. And it is this disposition, which we call benevolence, which puts it in motion ; which diffuses and communicates itself in streams innumerable. This fountain contains in itself an active principle, which diffuses the fountain in the displays of wisdom, power, goodness, and happiness ; so that the perfect diffusion or communication of it is the highest good, or greatest sum of happiness existing *ab extra*, or out of itself. The sun is able to emit rays ; and this emission is the light and glory of the sun, which emanation exists external to itself, or *ab extra*, as some phrase it. So the infinite, eternal fountain of all good contains in itself a self moving, active principle, which emanates, and diffuses the fountain. And this greatest diffusion is the highest possible declarative glory of God; and exists in that holy society of beings in heaven, who constitute the kingdom of God. In this society will be forever seen this eternal fountain, diffused perfectly, and in its endless increasing happiness, the brightest display of all the attributes of Jehovah. So that, as has been shown, the greatest sum of created happiness existing externally in this society, and the greatest declarative glory of God, are one and the same.

Here then we see, that benevolence is the primary, eternal, active, efficient cause of all good, of all the happiness, which does exist, and of all the increasing happiness, which will exist through endless ages. The constantly increasing happiness of heaven through an endless duration, is the end at which benevolence ultimately aimed. Hence its utility is infinite ; its beauty, excellency, and glory are unparallelled. If this active benevolence had not existed in God, no happiness would finally have had existence. If, instead of this, his heart had been malevolent, had delighted in misery, as satan does, all his attributes would have been employed in producing misery, and the universe would have been filled with it. But now we are assured from the benevolence of God, that the greatest happiness will be enjoyed in heaven forever. Thus glorious is benevolence.

2. It prepares created intelligent beings for happiness, and prompts them to seek it.—Until the heart is renewed by the agency of the Spirit, men are totally depraved. They have no moral goodness in their hearts. For benevolence comprises all moral goodness ; but they have a love for this world. Having no love for God, and a love for this world, they forsake God, and live in rebellion. They have no principle within to move them to serve God. Hence they never serve him until born again. In regeneration, a benevolent disposition or relish is created in the heart ; and the sinner becomes a partaker of the divine nature. Then objects which he hated he loves ; and those evil ways, which he loved, he hates. Now

his heart delights in God, loves the Savior as his best friend; he rejoices in the happiness of others, and takes complacency in the holy characters of saints ; he loves God supremely, and his neighbor as himself.

Thus benevolence prepares him to serve God. Now he esteems his yoke easy, and his burden light; and it is as pleasant to him to serve God, as it is to eat and drink. He is a member of the family of God ; his heart is united to the interest of the family ; and the highest good of God's holy kingdom is the ultimate object of his pursuit. He therefore renounces the service of sin and satan forever ; and devotes himself, soul and body, with all his talents, and all the blessings and privileges granted him, to the service of God his Father, and Christ his Savior and friend. Thus benevolence prepares a person to serve God ; and it is the only quality, which disposes men to serve their Maker acceptably.

Again. It is benevolence alone, which prepares persons to *enjoy* God. It is this divine relish. which qualifies them to delight in the sources of heavenly felicity. Without it, if in heaven, persons could not be happy. Benevolence only delights in benevolence, in the service and praise of God. Except a man be born again, he cannot see, that is enjoy, the kingdom of God. And without holiness no man shall see the Lord.—The unholy will be forever excluded from the kingdom of glory. No unclean thing is to enter there.

When we see clearly, that holiness is the only quality which prepares persons to *serve* and *enjoy* God, we must be convinced of its utility, excellency and beauty. It exceeds diamonds, rubies, yea all the riches and most precious things the world affords. Its value is equal to a state of endless, increasing happiness. Its worth equals the eternal blessedness to which it is necessary.—Next to happiness, it exceeds in value every attribute and blessing.

3. Benevolence is moral beauty. Without it no being has any moral beauty, but is clothed with the deformity of sin.— Knowledge is always used to do good or hurt, according to the nature of the active principles of the heart. A benevolent relish will govern, and improve all the information a person possesses, in devising means and ways to promote happiness. And the will is equally under the influence of the heart. Every choice, or exertion, is made with a view of gratifying the heart.

Hence from facts and daily experience we find men using

their knowledge, and exerting their power, to gratify the prevailing inclinations of the heart. The covetous improve all their knowledge and power in amassing wealth ; and the proud and ambitious, in usurping authority, extending their dominion, and reducing the world to a state of subjection. While the fallen angels were holy, every power was exerted to serve their king. But as soon as they were deprived of this disposition, and hatred governed, all their knowledge, subtlety and power have been used in opposing God, defacing the beauty of his kingdom, and destroying its peace and harmony.

Before they sinned they were bright, amiable, glorious spirits ; reflecting divine rays, and shining with the splendors of holiness around the divine throne. But the moment they lost a benevolent disposition, they were stripped of all their glory and beauty, were clothed with deformity, and have been to this day hateful demons. As soon as Adam sinned, his glory departed ; and the divine beauty with which he was adorned is never restored, until benevolence is reinstamped on the heart. Benevolence is the beauty, the excellency, and the only crown of glory, with which intelligent beings are adorned. Without it they are deformed, loathsome, and hateful characters ; and can never be admitted into that world where every member reflects the glorious rays of divinity.

4. Benevolence is the only bond of union and harmony in the moral world. Those who are adorned with this spirit aim at the same ultimate end. They rejoice in each other's joy. Their hearts ultimately centre in the same object. They love God supremely, and are loved by him ; they love their Savior, and he rejoices in his bride ; their love to each other is mutual and strong. Thus by love they are connected with their king and head, and perfectly united to each other.

In heaven, where benevolence is perfect, all are one. As Christ prayed, they are one with the Father, one with Christ, and oneness is perfect among the members. There is no discord there. They are one in sentiment, one in pursuit and action, and one in affection. All hatred, envy, revenge, malice, and every disuniting and jarring passion, is eradicated. Benevolence is the only *active governing* principle in that world. Though the members of the heavenly society are innumerable ; yet they will eternally appear as one united body. Actuated by one and the same spirit, they will move around the throne of God their centre, with perfect harmony and regularity. As one they will bow before the throne, and confess all they have is from God ; as one they cast their crowns at his feet, and acknowledge their allegiance ; as one they will unite in the new song of praise ; and as one will ascribe dominion, power and glory to God, and exalt him forever.

How useful, beautiful, and glorious is that principle of heart, which thus unites millions of millions in perfect bonds of endless affection. Its beauty and glory are so bright, that there is no need of sun or moon in heaven ; and all the hosts above shine as stars of the brightest splendor around the throne, with increasing lustre forever. To have a clear view of the glory of any thing, we ought to survey it in a perfect state. For this reason I have represented benevolence as operating in heaven.

When we consider that benevolence is the eternal, primary, and only efficient cause, of all good existing in the universe ; the only principle, which prepares intelligent creatures to see and *enjoy* God, and all good; the only quality which constitutes the moral beauty of rational agents ; the only uniting principle in heaven; as the light and glory of the universe ; we must pronounce its utility, glory and excellency to surpass all other things in worth and value. Oh how excellent, how glorious is this divine attribute. It is the divinity, beauty and glory of the Godhead. It is the beauty, glory and brightness of all intelligent beings. With it, in a perfect state, endlessly increasing happiness is inseparably connected. It is the glory of the universe, and infinitely exceeds the sun in its meridian splendor, in brightness, and in vivifying, blissful, joyful rays.

Objection. If benevolence is a moral virtue, a holy affection, because it is useful ; then every thing which is useful is a moral virtue. The light and heat of the sun, health, food, and raiment, and a thousand similar blessings are useful, and tend ultimately to happiness. And if utility constitute the nature of moral virtue ; every thing, which has a final tendency to happiness, is of course a moral virtue.

Answer. This objection seems to arise either from ignorance, or negligence, or a wish to conceal and pervert the truth. For by making one plain and obvious distinction, which any one might see, the force of the objection disappears at once. It is only necessary to make a distinction between *natural*, and *moral* good ; a distinction which is made by every one. And why has not the objector made this distinction in this case, as he does in a thousand other instances ? I can give no reason for this omission, but one or the other of the above causes.

It is granted, that utility, or the tendency of any thing to promote happiness ultimately, does constitute the nature of good. For the same reason one thing ought to be called *good*, every thing of the same nature ought to be thus stiled. There is no difference, in their *nature*, between natural and moral good. They are both good, because their *ultimate tendency* is to hapiness. And every thing is evil for the same reason ; because its *ultimate tendency* is to misery. Natural good is not so called for one reason, and moral good for a very different reason. This is not the ground of the distinction between natural and moral good. Moral good is predicated of no action or exercise, but those of moral agents. The light and heat of the sun are not actions of a moral agent ; yet being in their nature good, they are stiled a *natural* good, to distinguish them from the actions of moral agents. Indeed every thing belonging to a moral agent is not a moral good or evil. Knowledge, or the understanding with numerous operations, are not in a moral sense good ; they are not *moral virtues*. Neither is *power*, or the will and its operations. Divines have always made a distinction between the natural and moral attributes of Deity. And the same distinction is applicable to created moral agents. Moral good and evil are not predicable of every thing in exisistence, but of *active principles* and their operations. Nor of active principles, unless they exist in a being, who is a proper moral agent. The reason of it is obvious.

Now benevolence is an active principle, and belongs to the heart, and is the primary efficient cause of all the good or happiness which exists in the universe. This has been made evident. It is then a moral principle ; and all its exercises or operations, which are commonly called the affections and passions, are also moral. And to distinguish all other actions, exercises & operations which are good, they are called natural ; good in a natural sense. Hence, although all things are good for the same reason, because they tend in their nature to produce happiness ultimately, or are *useful ;* yet is it proper for the reasons assigned to distinguish between them, and call some of them a *natural*, and others a *moral* good. This fully and fairly meets and answers the objection. So that we may now say, that benevolence is a moral virtue, because it is useful, or tends to happiness ultimately, And that the light and heat of the sun, and other things similar in their nature, are good, because they tend to happiness ultimately; but they are only a natural good, or natural virtues, if so called. And the ground of this distinction has been made clear and evident ; and the objection is answered.

I have now exhibited my sentiments on this all important subject. And if any understand what has been written, they will consider benevolence to consist in a disposition or relish of the heart ; and view the happiness of others, or the greatest happiness of God's holy kingdom, as its ultimate end, which is sought for its own sake, and not with an aim to any other object beyond it more excellent. In this light they will see, it is the most beautiful, excellent, and glorious disposition, which can exist in any moral agent. They will see it is the original, eternal, efficient cause of all the good in existence ; as the only active, efficient cause, which has put every wheel in motion, and continues them till its ultimate end is obtained. Benevolence is the cause of all the happiness existing forever in heaven ; and also the source of the perfect gratification of every benevolent desire. It is the first cause of all things, and its last end is the highest possible pleasure of benevolence. It is the alpha and omega in causing and attaining the greatest sum of happiness.

*** ******

ESSAY XXIX.

On Regeneration.

What our Savior terms being born again, and generally by theologians is stiled regeneration, is essential to future happiness. It is a subject very interesting and important. The doctrine is very differently explained by the ministers of Christ. And no wonder, when we consider that each one describes it according to the views he has of the mind and heart of man. Regeneration is a change which takes place in the mind, and the heart is especially the subject of it. And if any persons have erroneous views of the heart, they will err in their expla-

15

nation of this change. This, as well as almost every other doctrine of the gospel, requires a distinct, consistent, and systematic view of the faculties and operations of the mind, in order to explain and illustrate it according to facts and experience. And to give an explanation of the new birth, which will agree with the word, with facts, and experience, requires just views of the human heart. No doctrine requires such knowledge more than this. And this will appear more and more evident, as we proceed in a discussion of the subject.

A full and just view of the new birth requires an attention to three distinct propositions. These are the following : Why is this change necessary ? In what does it consist ? And what are its fruits ? If a person embrace false views concerning either of these heads, he lays a foundation for a final deception, and endless disappointment. Feeling the necessity of clear and just views of this subject, and how fatal an error here may prove, I enter upon it with trembling and caution.

1. Why is regeneration *necessary* ? Christ says, except a man be born again, he *cannot* enter into the kingdom of heaven.

That change is amazingly interesting and important, which is necessary to eternal life. And a distinct understanding of its necessity, will prepare the way to a just view of its nature. In a natural state men are unprepared for a heavenly state of existence. The heart is such, if a person were in heaven, he could behold no object which would afford him any delight, or gratify one desire. Regeneration then is necessary, to prepare persons for the enjoyment of the objects and employments of that world. To this end a new creation is necessary. This will be evident, when the necessity of this change is clearly explained.

The word of God represents unrenewed persons as *dead*, *blind*, and *deaf ;* and without one *sense* to delight in divine objects. They have eyes, ears, and life, and all the senses necessary to relish and enjoy worldly objects ; but not one sense to delight in heavenly sources of enjoyment. Being spiritually dead, if they were in heaven, they could not enjoy any object there, any more than a dead man can enjoy the objects of sense in this world. And if the happiness of heaven consisted in beholding the light of the sun, and the numerous colors its rays reflect, and in hearing melodious strains of music, it is evident the blind and deaf would find no object, which could afford them any pleasure. Hence, the enjoyments of heaven are of such a nature, that sinners could no more be happy there, than a dead person could experience pleasure from earthly objects, or the blind from the light, or the deaf in the most harmonious music. Natural men have not one sense, which is a necessary preparation for the enjoyment of heavenly objects. Here then is the inquiry, what has man lost; and what is the nature of his heart, which disqualifies him entirely for the enjoyments of a heavenly state?

The word of God teaches us, that Adam was made upright; created in the image of God, natural and moral. As benevolence, or holiness, or *love*, is the only moral attribute in the divine character; Adam, to be created in the moral image of God, must be endued with the same love, the same benevolent, holy principle. And as an attribute in God is not simply an exercise, but a principle, or relish for the existence of happiness as the only absolute good; so men, to be holy, must have a similar attribute. They must have an appetite, or relish, to delight in happiness as an absolute good, and rejoice in it wherever they see it. Accordingly, Adam was created with this holy appetite or relish. Those who are born with eyes, are prepared to rejoice in light and colors; and those who have ears, to delight in melodious sounds. And we know the five senses of the body are necessary, to prepare us to enjoy all the objects of time and sense. And if we divide all objects of enjoyment in the universe into two general classes, and call one *natural* or *temporal*, and the other *moral* or *spiritual*; then, as our bodily senses are requisite to enjoy the former, so some attribute, or sense must exist in the heart to prepare us to enjoy the latter. All men do or may know, that our bodily senses do not prepare us to enjoy spiritual objects. The only sense, which prepares us to enjoy moral objects, is seated in the heart. It is the heart only, which loves, and delights in spiritual things. And Adam was created with a heart to love God, and rejoice in him as his supreme good.

He was created with a holy, benevolent appetite, relish, or disposition. And this prepared him to love and delight in every divine object; in every object, which is a source of happiness to holy beings in heaven. He had other appetites created in his heart, to prepare him to love worldly objects, and seek them as far as would be necessary to his preservation and comfort in this life. But not one of those appetites ever loves or delights in spiritual things. Thus Adam was created holy, pure and upright; endued with every appetite, necessary to enjoy God as his supreme fountain, and take comfort in worldly objects.

But when he ate the forbidden fruit, he forfeited the moral image of God, and was deprived of it. In that day, in a moral sense he died. And we see a great change had taken place in his feelings. Instead of delighting in God, and running to meet him when he heard his voice in the garden, he now runs from him, and endeavors to hide himself from his sight. He fears his Maker, and trembles before him. Now nothing remained in his heart to love and delight in God. He was as fully disqualified for the enjoyment of spiritual objects, as a person in a natural sense dead, is in that state unprepared for the enjoyment of worldly objects. And as all his posterity are born destitute of the moral image of God, they have nothing in their hearts which prepares them for the enjoyment of spiritual objects. They are as really disqualified for the enjoyment of heavenly objects, as the blind, deaf, or dead, are for the enjoyment of light, colors, and melodious sounds. Hence the reason why they are in scripture represented as blind, deaf, and dead. They have no taste or relish for any objects, but those of a worldly nature, such as property, honor, and sensual delights.

Hence we find it is a fact, that when a door of mercy is opened to sinners by the death of Christ, and provision is made for their entertainment and salvation, and all are invited to come unto the supper prepared for them, and not one will come ; all wish to be excused, and make light of the invitation, and go their ways, one to his farm and another to his merchandise. Why are men guilty of such almost unaccountable conduct? Reason teaches, that when perishing sinners are dying, they would hear the invitation, ' Come, for all things are ready,' with joy ; and that all would flock to the marriage supper of the Son of God, in haste, and with gladness. But no, they prefer this world to the gospel feast, and will not come to Christ for life. And the reasons are, they have no appetite, no relish, for earthly, perishing objects. And as all men are governed, not by reason, but by their hearts, so they will forever act according to the nature of the appetites which govern them. This is the reason, why we see God the fountain of all good forsaken, Christ slighted and rejected, and the gospel supper neglected. This is the reason, why we see mankind so earnest in their pursuits after worldly good. They have no love for God, but they love this world. Hence they worship and serve the creature, and not the Creator.

The supper prepared for sinners in this world is the marriage supper of the Lamb in heaven, upon which saints and angels feast. It includes every source of happiness enjoyed in heaven. And for the reason sinners do not delight in it on this earth, for the same reason they would not enjoy it in heaven. Hence if they were admitted into that blessed state, they would not find one object thereto afford them the least satisfaction. They would take no delight in the marriage supper of the Lamb ; and they would find no earthly objects there to feast and entertain them. So that heaven would not afford them one object of pleasure. But as there they would clearly see, that God was against them, that saints and angels hated their characters, and every thing was opposed to their pride, and self exalting dispositions ; and that they were really only fit to be despised, and treated as enemies to all good ; every thing would be a source of pain to them. Instead of being happy, they would be exceedingly miserable. The reason is, they have no relish for the pleasures of that world. And they will find there no earthly riches, honors, or pleasures, to afford them any delight. As they cannot be happy there they will be excluded, and confined in the prison of darkness, the only place for which their hearts are prepased. There in confinement they can no more disturb the peace and happiness of God's kingdom. We now see, why a change of heart is necessary to heavenly felicity ; we see why a person, unless born again, cannot enter the kingdom of heaven. The reason is, men in their natural state have no appetite, no relish, for any of those objects which constitute the marriage feast of the Lamb, and which are the only sources of felicity after death.

II. Attend to the *nature* of that change, which is effected in regeneration. Regeneration is a *new creation.* There is something created in the heart, which had never before had any existence in it. This is a truth taught in many passages of scripture. The apostle saith, If any man be in Christ, he is a *new creature.* Neither circumcision availeth any thing, nor uncircumcision, but a new creature. And that which is created in the heart, is called the *new man,* the inner man. So we are commanded to put off the old man, and put on the new man.

And as in regeneration something new is created, hence all who are born again are stiled new *creatures*, and are said to be created, to be the subjects of a creation. " We are his workmanship, created in Christ Jesus." This workmanship is a creation. Saints are new men, created after God in righteousness and holiness. And have put on the new man, which is renewed in knowledge after the image of him that created him. So they are called new born babes.

As regeneration is evidently, according to scripture, a *creation;* we may ask, what is created? An appetite, relish, or disposition to be pleased with divine objects, is what is created in the heart. By creating this relish, the lost moral image of God is restoted; the holy image with which Adam was created. " Put on the new man, which after God is created in righteousness and true holiness." Here the new man created is *after God*, a likeness of God, which consists in righteousness and true holiness. And the new man is said to be after the *image* of him that created him. Such texts make it evident, that in regeneration the moral image of God, which was lost by the fall, is restored. The moral character of God is love, or benevolence. God is love. His moral image in men is the same disposition, appetite, or relish, which is styled love; that love to God and man, which the law requires.

By this we see what the new creation is. It is the creation of that relish, which prepares a person to be pleased and delighted with that class of objects, called moral, or spiritual, or divine. It is an appetite or disposition to be pleased and delighted with the character of God, of Christ, with the law and government of God, with the truths or doctrines of the gospel, with the service of God, with the characters of saints and angels; and all those objects, which are the sources of all the joys and felicity in heaven. Objects of this class infinitely exceed in value, beauty, glory, and excellence, that class which is generally styled earthly, worldly, temporal, and fading. We have shown that no one, antecedent to regeneration, has any delight in this divine class of objects. So far from it, that as they are opposed to the desires and pursuits of men, they excite in the hearts of the unrenewed hatred and opposition. But when born again, with this new relish they are prepared to be pleased with them, to love, and desire them as their portion. This new appetite created in the heart is a spiritual, holy *life;* it is the *eye* of the heart by which it discerns the beauty of divine objects; the *ear* by which they hear with pleasure the voice of God in all his doctrines and precepts; the sense of *smelling*, by which they smell the sweet odor of divine things; the relish, or *palate*, by which they taste superlative sweetness in spiritual objects; and the *feeling* or *sense*, by which they rejoice in God with joy unspeakable. This new appetite created in the heart comprises every sense, which is ascribed to saints in the word of God, and which is peculiar to them. Hence,when a person is born again,he is said to have eyes to see, ears to hear, and a heart to realize and love all the beauties and glories of divine objects. He is no longer in a state of perfect spiritual death, darkness, deafness, and brutish stupidity. The creation of this new appetite is bringing persons from darkness into marvellous light. This new relish, created in the heart, is light infused into it. This is the way by which God shines into the heart. And this new appetite is a principle of light in the heart, by which christians shine as lights in the world. They emit rays of light; and these rays are a reflexion of divine light, as the moon reflects the rays of the sun. And by this light they glorify their Father, who is in heaven.

Hence saints are called children of the light, and of the day. They are said to come to the light, and walk in it. They love the light, and hate the darkness in which they once lived. And if they live as they ought, their light shines more and more unto the perfect day. And like stars they will shine around the throne of the Lamb forever, reflecting the light of the sun of righteousness.

When persons are born again they are brought into a new world; as really so as a person born blind, and afterward has eyes given him; or as one born deaf has ears given him to hear; or as one raised to life from actual death, will appear to himself to be in a new world. Now they see beauties, which they never saw before; they hear the melody of God's voice, which they never heard before; and they have *new views, new feelings, affections and desires*, and will live a new life. With them according to scripture, old things are done away; they no longer place their affections on this world, nor seek it as their portion; behold all things are become new. They view divine objects in a new light, and experience now views, feelings, affections, and joys, to which they had always been strangers. We hence see, that creating this new holy relish in the heart, according to representations in the bible, makes them new creatures ; it is giving them eyes to see, ears to hear, life from the dead ; bringing them into a new world, in which the beauties and glories of divine objects excite in them new views, affections, and new feelings of joy and delight. Now they walk in the light, love it, become lights themselves, and shine to the praise of divine grace. This is a great, and blessed, wonderful, and glorious change ; and it consists *primarily* in creating in the heart this new appetite, restoring the lost image of God. They hereby become the children of God, sustain a new relation to him ; and are now prepared to love, serve, and enjoy him here and forever.

Again. Creating this holy relish in the heart, in which this great change consists, is effected by the agency of the Holy Spirit. It is the office work of the spirit to renew the heart, and then carry on the glorious work of sanctification, till saints arrive to the stature of perfect men in Christ. Hence we are said to be born of the Spirit. And we find the great work of renewing and sanctifying the heart, is generally in scripture ascribed to the Spirit, the third person in the Godhead. Hence the reason why saints are called *spiritual ;* why they are led by the Spirit, and by him quickened, purified, and assisted. The sanctification of the Spirit begins in regeneration, and is carried on by his influences to the perfect day. By the Spirit we are renewed, created anew, purified, enlightened, quickened, and filled with joy and consolation. This is a most glorious work of the Spirit, a work absolutely necessary to eternal life. How great, then, is the promise and gift of the Spirit. And as far as any oppose this work of the Spirit, they are said to resist the Holy Ghost, to quench, and grieve the Spirit. And this is one of the greatest, and most dangerous sins ; because there is danger of blaspheming the Spirit, and committing the sin which will never be forgiven.

And this work of the Spirit is *instantaneous.* Creation from nothing, or producing something new, is always an instantaneous work. It is absurd to suppose a thing to be only in part brought into existence. God said, let there be light, and light was. It was not some time rising into real being, it existed instantly. Every person, in a spiritual sense, is either dead or alive. He is not a day, or one moment, passing from death to life. By the agency of the Spirit this new appetite is instantly created. Although regeneration is an instantaneous work, yet the work of sanctification is progressive. This work begins in regeneration, and in an instant; and others it progresses through life. Saints begin to live in a moment; but this life is increased, and invigorated all their days, till they reach heaven.

It will be well also to observe here, a few things more in relation to this change. It appears evident, when all the passages of scripture are carefully compared, and their import is understood, that the only thing immediately done in regeneration, is the creation of this holy appetite in the heart. This is creating anew, and restoring the moral image of God, which was lost at the fall of Adam. If this be true, then some ideas, which many bring into view, are erroneous. Some treat the subject as though they believed the change consisted in altering the nature of sin. As though pride was changed into humility, selfishness into benevolence, and love for this world in a love for heavenly things ; opposition to God into love to him, hatred to men into love for them, and so in relation to other sinful affections ; as though their nature is so altered, that from being sinful they now become holy. But this sentiment appears to be contrary to scripture, to reason, and to all sound philosophy of the mind. Sin may be subdued, and eradicated from the heart ; but its nature cannot be changed. To suppose, that pride can be changed into humility, or any sinful affection can be made holy, is very absurd. Not only so, but this would effectually destroy that warfare, which all christians experience. For to make a warfare on this ground, the same affection, as pride for example, must be partly pride, and partly humility, or partly holy, and partly sinful ; and then the contest would consist in having the same sinful affection fight against itself. The proud or sinful part, fighting against the holy or humble part. This is representing the same affection as having two natures opposed to each other. Every affection is no more than a feeling and desire, simple in their nature. And to represent an affection as having two natures, and opposed to itself, is as absurd as to suppose the same drop of water as having two natures ; one part a fluid, and the other a solid. This is so absurd every one will reject the sentiment, as soon as the inconsistency of it is fairly stated.

Some speak in such a manner as would lead one to suppose, they considered sin as wholly subdued and eradicated in regeneration. In this sense they seem to understand the passage, in which God says, I will take away their heart of stone and give them a heart of flesh. Whatever *may be* the meaning of this passage, it cannot mean, that all sin is eradicated. For if this were the fact, christians would never experience any warfare within. For this warfare consists in the opposition of the flesh to the spirit, or of the old man to the new man. But according to this sentiment, when a person is born again, the flesh, the old man, is subdued, eradicated, no longer has any being in the heart. The scripture every where represents christians as having a body of sin and death remaining in them ; as having flesh, and spirit, an old and new man, fighting against each other. Hence taking away the stony heart, and giving a heart of flesh cannot mean, that sin is all eradicated, and the person is now perfectly holy. To construe it consistently with other passages, its meaning must be. that the power of the stony heart is lessened, has received a deadly wound, will no more reign without opposition, and will finally be wholly subdued, and eradicated. If, then, we make the word of God our guide, we must still view a person who is born again as having every sin, the old man, as still remaining in him. Not one sin is erad- icated. And all the change is this ; a new, holy, principle is created in the heart, which will ever fight against all remain- ing sin, and daily weaken its power, and keep it in subjection, until the day arrives, when the new man will gain the victory, and all remaining sin will be wholly and forever subdued or eradicated. Then the person is perfect, perfectly holy, and has no sin remaining to pollute him, or disturb his peace and happiness.

There are also some, who consider regeneration as immedi- ately affecting all the faculties of the mind. They say, that this change consists in enlightening the understanding, renew- ing the heart, and subduing the will. Hence regeneration does not respect directly one faculty, any more than another. This is confounding things, which ought to be distinguished ; and surrounds the subject with mist and darkness. It is true, that this great change affects all the faculties indirectly ; but the immediate effect produced is in one faculty only. The heart is the subject wrought upon, and affected, as has been shown in all that has been said on this subject. In the heart a new appetite is created. When this is done, a person is pre- pared to be pleased with a divine class of objects. Light in the understanding, and the obedience of the will, are consequen- ces, which follow this change in the heart. The understanding and the will are ever under the influence and government of the heart. Hence as long as the heart continues totally corrupt, all the other faculties will have a wrong direction. But as far as the heart is renewed and right, the other faculties will then have a right direction. A reformation in every person must begin in the heart. And creating this new relish in the heart will incline every person to lead a new life ; and so far as he is governed by this holy relish, all the exercises and operations of the mind will be directed to the glory of God.

When the heart is renewed as explained, a person then delights in the character of God, and in all that class of objects called moral or divine. Now the person will delight in contemplating and studying them. He will, therefore, confine the attention of the understanding to them. Now the understanding beholds new beauties, perceives new sensations and desires, gains clear and distinct views of every gospel doctrine, and will improve in knowledge daily. Previous to this change in the heart, and while secure, he seldom attended to divine objects ; and when he did, the disrelish of the heart to the truth blinded, and prejudiced him to such a degree, he was more likely to embrace errors than the truth. The heart blinded the understanding, and by its influence led him to judge of every thing so as to please the heart. Under conviction, previous to regeneration, persons through the influence of fear turn their attention to divine objects ; and the truth is so obvious, they soon perceive they are great sinners, justly deserve hell, are dependent, and if saved, it must be by grace. This light prepares the way for a change of the heart. Yet they see no beauty in divine objects ; and instead of being pleased with them, opposition is excited ; fear, and the distress which attends it, is a load too heavy to be borne long at a time. But as soon as the heart is renewed, then divine objects please him ; his fears and distress of mind are gone ; he is relieved of his load and burden. And these objects, which before gave him pain, now please him, and afford him great satisfaction. The new sensations, joys, and desires, which he experiences, are new objects of perception. He now knows what the feelings and joys of religion are. In this respect the understanding has new light, which is attained by experience, as the greater part of our knowledge is. Now he will attend to the truth, will make it a subject of study, and will be daily growing in light and knowledge. And his understanding will be more enlightened often, in one month, than it had previously been in many years. But all this light or knowledge is the consequence, the fruit, of the change produced in the heart. Before his heart is changed, a person's understanding is unimpaired, is sound and good. A person in a dungeon with good eyes cannot see objects. But the fault is not in his eyes. So a person in an unrenewed state is kept by his evil heart in darkness ; and many are surprisingly ignorant of divine truth. But the fault is not in the understanding ; its eyes are sound and good. Remove every obstacle which had perverted the understanding, and kept its eyes closed ; then it will perform its office, and judge of divine things according to truth. As the understanding is not impaired by the fall, but is blinded by the heart as our natural eyes are by a thick vail ; so remove this vail, and the aversion of the heart to truth, the understanding will then see objects as they are, and improve in light and knowledge. Hence as the understanding is not impaired by the fall, and, considered as an eye, is in a sound healthy state, it needs no change or alteration. All that is wanting is, to remove the vail which blinds it, which intercepts its sight. This vail is the heart. Renewing or creating this holy relish in the heart, is removing this vail, as far as a person is governed by this new appetite. As sin still remains in the heart, so far as this governs, his understanding will be still blinded ; but so far as his new taste governs, it will see, and judge of things as they are. Hence the light of the understanding is the consequence and fruit of regeneration. So that this change makes no alteration in the understanding ; it respects the heart solely and primarily, and light in the intellectual part is a consequence of it.

With respect to the will, it is always obedient to the heart. It is always exerted according to the pleasure of the heart. The design of every volition is to obtain the object, which is pleasing and gratifying to the heart. Hence the way to subdue the will is to renew the heart. It is said, " Thy people shall be willing in the day of thy power." When that day arrives, in which the power of God is exerted to renew the heart, then the will is obedient. As the heart has a new pleasure, so now there will be a new train of volitions. It is also said, his arrows shall be sharp in the heart of the king's enemies. When the enemies of God see their wickedness and danger, this light in the understanding excites painful sensations in the heart ; sensations keen as those produced by arrows, when they wound and pierce the heart of the body. When Christ says, Ye *will not* come unto me, every one would be ready to ask, why will they not come? The reason is, the character of Christ does not please the natural heart, but is offensive to it. So the will, ever obedient to the heart, rejects him. Renew the heart, then the will readily chooses him as a Savior. Creating a new relish in the heart is the way by which persons are drawn to Christ, and made willing to come unto him for life.

The will viewed as a faculty is not impaired, nor its nature altered, by the fall. After Adam sinned he was just as capable of choosing and refusing objects, as he was previous to his fall. But a very great change took place in his heart. He lost his holy relish, and was no more pleased, as he had been, with moral and divine objects. Now his heart was imperfect, sinful, and corrupt. It now, like a vail, blinded the understanding, and commanded the will to reject God, and choose this world for a portion. But when the heart is renewed, it is again pleased with divine objects ; the vail being removed, the understanding is filled with light, and the will is directed to reject the world, and seek God as the best portion and fountain of living waters. The motion of every faculty will be towards God as its centre, as far as a person is influenced and governed by this new and holy appetite. This is the way in which the understanding and will are affected, in regeneration. The heart or taste is the subject of the operations of the Holy Spirit, and the only subject directly and immediately affected. In this faculty a great and glorious change is effected by creating in it a new and benevolent appetite. In consequence of which the understanding is greatly enlightened, and the will is obedient to the heart, and conformable to the law of God ; and the life and conduct of the person, from that day he is renewed, will harmonise with the doctrines and precepts of the gospel, as far as he is governed by this new relish created in him.

Again. Some suppose regeneration is effected by light, and moral persuasion. They suppose that light and proper motives are sufficient to change the heart, and produce an entire reformation in any person.

But surely such persons have no correct views of the human mind, or of the nature of moral depravity. If they had, they would agree with the scriptures in viewing regeneration to be a *new creation ;* so that all, who are born again, may with propriety be styled new *creatures.* But has light in the intellect power to create something from nothing? Have any motives power to create something new? If any can believe this, they betray great ignorance respecting the nature of light, and the influence of motives, and the faculties and operations of the mind of man. Facts and experience both prove that light, instead of rectifying the corrupt heart, excites its opposition to God and the truth. This is the effect of light on a depraved, corrupt heart, as is daily proved by facts and experience. And no motives will ever influence a person to choose or reject objects of volition, contrary to the pleasure of the heart. The will has no power over the heart. The will does not govern the heart, but is governed and influenced by it. This also is evident, from facts and experience. We may, therefore, as soon expect water will run from the centre of gravitation, as expect light and motives will change the heart, or produce any radical change in the feelings and desires of men. As the will is governed by the heart, motives will never influence the will to choose contrary to the pleasure of the heart. And light will here, as it forever will in hell, excite opposition against God, instead of producing any friendly feelings, as long as the pleasure of the heart remains unrenewed.

If all that has been suggested on this subject is true, and harmonizes with the word of God, and agrees with facts and experience, as has been made evident ; every one must be convinced, that the Holy Spirit in regenerating men does, *immediately* and *directly*, no more than create in the heart that holy relish or moral image of God lost by the fall. And this creation is sufficient to account for all the new views, feelings, desires. and joys, which the regenerate experience ; and for the new life, which they live. And this will be further confirmed and illustrated, by what will be said under the next general branch of this subject.

III. Describe the *fruits* of regeneration.

These fruits are internal and external. When internal fruits appears in the life, actions, and conduct of persons, they are then external and visible. It will be most instructive to attend in the first place to those internal fruits, which all renewed persons experience. It has been made evident, that all the change effected immediately in regeneration consists in the creation of that new, holy appetite, which was lost by the fall of our first parents.

This was created in Adam, when God gave him being. It

constituted one part of his being. This, and the other appetites created in his heart, were active principles, and prepared him for all the exercises and actions necessary to his being and happiness in this life, and the life to succeed. When this was lost, he had no relish for the class of objects styled moral or divine. But when it is anew created in the heart of any of his posterity, then such person is prepared to relish and feed on divine objects.—As the appetite of hunger prepares persons to relish food, and all the different species of it ; so this holy appetite prepares a person to relish and delight in divine objects. And in attending to the operations or exercises of this appetite, we must carefully observe its *primary*, its *secondary*, and its *third* class of affections. For its operations are divisible into these three distinct classes. And by attending to these classes every one will be better able to judge, whether he has ever passed from death unto life. And,

1. Attention will be given to the *primary operations* of this holy appetite.

Every reader will readily see, that no object can affect the heart, unless seen or known ; or unless it is in view of the mind. When a person is renewed, and divine objects pass in review of the mind, he will have feelings and affections correspondent to their nature. When his attention is fixed on the character of God, of Christ, or of saints, he will feel an inward *delight*, what some call joy. They appear to him beautiful, and he never saw them in this light before. And such persons often say, that every thing they see appears *new* to them ; they seem to be in a new world. This is occasioned entirely by a *new sensation*. They never before experienced that kind of delight, joy, or satisfaction in viewing divine objects, which they now feel. As they have a new and most pleasant sensation within, and as they do not reflect that this is caused by a change in their hearts, their first thought is apt to be, that the things they see are altered ; and they are of course in a new world. It may be compared to this. A person, who never delighted in music, but had painful sensations when he heard it, we will suppose has his ear so altered as to relish music. He hears it, and experiences delightful and transporting sensations. He would be apt to say, the music he heard was a new kind, such as he never heard before. And this is the occasion of his new sensations. Yet on reflection he would soon be convinced, that his new sensations arose from a change in his ear. When a person is born again, the first alteration he experiences is a new sensation, which he considers very pleasant ; and so sweet, and different from any he had ever felt, he wishes to have it continued. His pleasure is such, he cannot conceive it possible for him or any one to experience any which would be sweeter in their nature. Now it seems to him that he has found true happiness, which he had been always seeking, but had never found. Now, as Christ said, he will thirst no more ; he will no more thirst after any other species of happiness, or any other water than that which affords him such delight.

But he will desire the continuance and increase of his present pleasure. As he has a new sensation, so divine objects appear new to him. The divine character, the character of Christ, the law and government of God, saints, and gospel doctrines, appear new, beautiful and glorious. Some experience this new and pleasant sensation, in a greater measure than others do. But all feel it in a greater or less degree.—This inward, delightful, satisfying sensation, is the *first primary operation* of this holy appetite. In an active sense the person may say, his heart delights in God, in Christ, in divine objects, as they succeed each other in view of the mind.

From this new sensation a new class of desires or affections will arise. He will *desire* the continuance and increase of the satisfaction he then feels. He will *desire* to have daily communion with God, to have increasing and clearer views of his glory, to serve and glorify him. It will be his desire to put all his trust in Christ, to have a greater sense of his beauty and preciousness, to be one with him, and enjoy him as his beloved. He will *desire* to enjoy the society and conversation of saints, and to unite with them in acts of worship. He will *desire* their growth in grace, and the increase of their happiness. He will desire the salvation of all men, as far as is consistent. It will be his *desire* to have all come to Christ, and feel what he feels. But it is not necessary to be any more particular. Suffice it to say here, that for every divine object, which affords him inward delight, he will have a *desire* corresponding with the nature of his sensation. And these desires will be numerous ; and will constitute what is called in scripture, panting after God, hungering and thirsting after righteousness.— And this new sensation, with the desires which immediately arise from it, and are connected with it, are intended by *love ;* love to God, to Christ, to saints, to enemies, and to the truth.

Such sensations, with their attendant desires, constitute that love which the law requires towards God and man ; that gospel charity, without which nothing can profit us. What other sense can any one affix to the term love to God and men ? Do not those, who have that love for God the law requires, *delight* in his character, and *d, sire* to have him glorified ? Do they not *desire* to be conformed to God, to enjoy him daily, and with increasing satisfaction ? And can any person be said to love God, who does not delight in him ; and who has no desires for his glory, or to be like him, and serve him ? If not, it is certain that by love to God is meant, delight in his character, with every desire correspondent with it. And the same exercises or operations are included in the term love, when any divine things are the objects of it. Hence, in the sense now explained, *love* to God, to Christ, to saints, to all men, and to the doctrines and precepts of the gospel, and the service of Jehovah, is the first, *primary* operation of this holy appetite. And of any persons find they have not those primary exercises, they may rely on it, they have not any of the fruits of regeneration ; and are not renewed in spirit. For they must have the primary, before they can have any of the secondary fruits of the Spirit.

It is proper now to observe, that some objects, which belong to the class of moral objects, instead of affording pleasant sensations, excite directly the contrary. This is true with respect to every species of sin. When a person is born again, when he has a view of sin in others, especially in himself, it excites in him a disagreeable sensation, a sensation more or less painful. A desire immediately arises to have sin subdued, and eradicated from his heart. It appears to him in a new light; as odious, hateful, and one of the greatest or most awful evils that has existence. He feels a decided opposition against it. It is his most formidable enemy, and he views it in this light, and hates it. The reasons why sin is thus hateful to him are many, and it may be he has never reflected on them. He hates it in reality, because it separates between him and God; is an obstacle in the way, which prevents his serving and enjoying Him as he wishes ; renders him unlike his Maker ; removes him to a great moral distance from the fountain of all good; and hardens, blinds and stupifies his heart, and unfits him for the services and enjoyments of heaven. These are the reasons why sin is so painful and hateful. And though he

17

cannot perhaps tell why he hates it, yet he feels this aversion to it. And the more he becomes acquainted with its pernicious nature, on his journey through the world, the more he will hate it, groan under it as the greatest burden, and more fervently desire its destruction. Now the painful sensations sin occasions, and the *desires* he immediately has to be delivered from its power, and to be washed from its pollution, are the primary operations of this holy appetite towards it. These primary exercises are in scripture denominated sorrow, grief, hatred and repentance. By these terms is meant, that to the new born soul sin is a painful, hateful object; the destruction of which he *desires* more fervently than the ruin of any other enemy. And it is thus painful and hateful to him, and an object of his greatest aversion, for the reasons which have been given. Hence, if he knew he should never be punished for sin, yet his aversion to it would be the same, and of the same nature that has been represented. We now see what the primary operations of this holy appetite are. This appetite delights primarily in no objects, but those included in the class of moral objects. These, especially God, it regards with supreme affection. They are to the renewed the sweetest sources of their happiness. They esteem them as their portion; and are ready now to renounce every other object, for the sake of enjoying forever these wells of salvation. Under the influence of the pleasant sensations they feel, and the desires which attend them, they do and will turn about, and tread the narrow path, and seek heaven as their home. Having given this view of the primary fruits of regeneration, we may

2. Attend to the operations of this new appetite.

As every person, when renewed, will delight in divine objects, he will experience a desire for the continuance and increase of the happiness he now experiences. And as these depend on the increase of his appetite for such objects, he will desire to grow in grace. And as the growth of every thing, and the performance of every work, is effected by *means*, so he finds means are requisite to his growth in grace and happiness. Hence from his pleasure in divine objects will arise a secondary class of affections or desires. And these desires have for their object all those things which are the *means* of their advancement in knowledge and grace. Accordingly, every thing which is really a means of a christian's growth in grace, from infancy to manhood, will be an object of his desire. In such means he takes satisfaction, and desires them, not on their own account, but for the sake of those objects which are in themselves pleasant, and are the primary sources of his happiness. A person loves food for the body for two reasons. One is, he finds it is necessary to preserve life, health, the increase of strength, and vigor. Another is, the food suits his taste, and he takes satisfaction in eating; it is one source of his happiness. Then when he finds certain means are necessary to obtain food, and preserve a sufficient supply, he will delight in using them; he will desire them, and attend to them. Hence the reason why men love land, cattle, labor, money, and every other object needful to preserve life and promote their comfort. But these means are not desired on their own account, but merely for the sake of procuring food, and other gratifications for the bodily appetites.

So when persons are raised from moral death to life, they experience a new kind of pleasure, and delight exceedingly in the character of God, the living fountain of waters, in Christ, and in the happiness of all in his kingdom. These objects are in themselves very pleasant and delightful. They know these objects are a fountain of bliss; they know that their essential excellencies cannot be increased; but they very soon learn that their glories may be displayed, and that their happiness in them may be increased; and they find the increase of their happiness depends on the appetite, the relish they have for them. Hence the increase of this relish, their growth in grace, and conformity to God, is by them fervently desired. And as *means* are appointed by God for them to use, and to promote their growth in grace, these *means* are objects of their desire and love, not on their own account, but for the sake of promoting their conformity to God, and happiness in Him.

The means which God has appointed for the growth in grace of his children, are, the doctrines and precepts of the gospel; a preached gospel, by which doctrines and precepts are explained and enforced; the holy Sabbath; all divine ordinances; religious conference and society; meditation on divine subjects; prayer; watching; self-denial; maintaining the christian warfare. These, and similar things are the *means* by which the growth of grace is promoted, till we reach a perfect stature in Christ. These means afford satisfaction, are objects of fervent desire, for the sake of attaining unto perfection in holiness and bliss. And till persons love God, they have no love or desire for these means of grace, which are holy. But as soon as they love and delight in God, then we find these secondary desires operate. Now they love the word of God, its doctrines and precepts. Now they love the preaching of the word. They love prayer, have fervent desires to come before God and supplicate for mercy. They earnestly desire religious conference and society. The Sabbath is their delight. They love all ordinances, and all the means of grace, and desire the enjoyment of these means and privileges, and will diligently use them, and cry to God for a blessing to attend them, that they may promote their growth in grace, and delight in God, and prepare them for a heavenly state. Before persons are renewed, they have no real love for the Bible. Hence they seldom read the word, seldom pray, or use other means. And as far as they do use them, they are either influenced by fear, or custom, or some other selfish and unhallowed motive. But as soon as persons are born again, and have once tasted that the Lord is good, and experienced new and ravishing delight in Him, they then have a new class of feelings, and of desires for all the appointed means of grace. Now they love to read and meditate on the word of God, it is more precious to them than silver or gold, sweeter than honey ; they delight in the Sabbath, in hearing the word preached; one day in God's courts is better than a thousand spent in sin and worldly pursuits. Now they love their closets, and enter them to converse and commune with God. Now they love to meet with the saints of God, for religious conference, society and prayer. They love to draw near to God in all his ordinances. They love to watch, deny self, fight against sin, and press forward towards perfection. This love for the means of instruction and grace, and their desires to enjoy and use them diligently, are fruits of the Spirit. They are properly *secondary fruits;* because if they had not the primary fruits, such as delight in God, they would not have this secondary class of desires and affections. The secondary are inseparably connected with the primary; and so united, that their satisfaction in the use of means will never be greater than this delight in God. And, indeed, in proportion as a person's relish for the living fountain of waters and his delight in it varies, at one time strong and fervent, and at another weak and faint; in the same proportion he will find his satisfaction and diligence in using means will vary ; and in his attendance on means, he will be alive and engaged, or cold and formal, just as his relish is, either strong, or faint.

Hence these secondary fruits of the Spirit are real evidences of grace, as well as the primary fruits. If then persons find they do not delight in reading and meditating on the word of God, nor in hearing it preached, nor in prayer, nor in divine ordinances, nor in religious conference and society, nor any of the appointed means of their salvation; they may rest assured they have never passed from death to life. If they say they have tasted, all things have appeared new to them, they have been greatly elated with joy, and felt more happiness in an hour, than in all their life before; yet after this do not fervently desire the means of their growth, and do not take satisfaction in them, and are not careful to use them with diligence; they may conclude all the pleasures they have experienced, and concerning which they have so much to say, is no more than the experience of stony ground hearers, or of those mentioned Hebrews vi, who fell away, and drew back unto perdition. All may rely on it, that if they do not experience the secondary fruits of the Spirit, they have never had the primary fruits; and if they still retain this hope, they are deceived, and will hear Christ at last say, I never knew you. Hence it is all important to be well acquainted with the secondary, as well as the primary fruits of the Spirit, in order to judge correctly concerning our spiritual state. If persons have the secondary fruits of the Spirit, they will labor as earnestly for the bread of life, as men of the world do for bread for the body. For their whole work in this life consists in their using the means God has appointed for their growth in knowledge and grace, and ripeness for heavenly mansions. And their desires for these means, that they may grow, are so fervent, they will prompt them to use them diligently. It will be their daily work. Hence they persevere, hold on and hold out to the end, and finally conquer, and receive a crown of life. But those who have not these secondary fruits, soon lose their first counterfeit relish; and then, though various motives may induce them to lead a moral life like the Pharisees, yet they will be formal, cold and barren in religion, without ever manifesting the life or power of it. And some will not persevere in this cold, moral, formal course, but return again to their former mode of living, and wallowing in the filth of sin. Wherefore, let all examine whether they have these secondary fruits of the Spirit.

3. There is one more class of holy desires and affections to be considered, as the fruits of the Spirit, or new birth.

To understand this part of our subject distinctly, it is necessary to remark, that Christ the King in Zion has enemies, and these are enemies to his kingdom, and to all his subjects and friends. They are determined, violent, numerous and powerful enemies. Their aim is, to dethrone Christ if possible, destroy his kingdom, all his subjects and disciples. These enemies are satan with all his legions, all remaining sin in the heart, all infidels and unrenewed persons, the charms and flatteries of this world, powerful temptations, all errors in doctrine and practice. These are inimical to Christ, to his cause, and to his real friends and followers. They are constantly opposing Christians, fighting against them, and aiming at their destruction. Can real Christians view these enemies with indifference? Will not their opposition to every thing which the saint loves, highly prizes, and seeks as his treasure, excite feelings and desires in their hearts of some kind or other? But what are the feelings and affecions which opposition from such enemies will excite? The word of God teaches how we shall feel towards them. We should hate them, feel a holy indignation against them, experience strong desires to have them defeated, destroyed, bound and confined, that they may not injure the blessed cause in which we are engaged.

We shall hate sin in our own hearts, as well as in others; and feel a decided opposition to it. We shall fight against it; never feed or indulge it; nor make peace with it, or ever rest contented with any thing short of its perfect eradication from the heart. We shall be opposed to Satan, to all his works, and all his temptations. We shall resist him, and fight against him, and never give place to him. We shall desire the day to come, when he shall be bound, and confined forever, and wholly defeated. We shall desire, that even enemies to God may be renewed and become his friends. And if they continue enemies, we shall desire to have them defeated and confined with devils, that they may no more disturb the peace of God's kingdom. We shall resist every temptation, and guard against the allurements of riches, honors and vain pleasures. We shall oppose every error in doctrine and practice, and contend earnestly for the truth. We shall fervently desire the day to arrive, when Christ will triumph over his and his people's enemies, when we shall gain an endless victory, when death will be destroyed ; and all enemies, and evils of every kind, shall be forever banished from the holy kingdom of Christ; when peace, and love, and harmony, shall forever prevail; and all the friends of God enjoy perfect good, without any enemy to disturb or interrupt their enjoyments. Such feelings and affections the opposition of enemies will excite in the hearts of all who are born again.

Those who make a portion of this world, if they are opposed in their pursuits, view their opponents as their enemies. Their opposition to them in the pursuit of objects which they love, produces in them hatred, anger, revenge, and such passions, towards their opposers or enemies.

So in this case, all beings and things which are opposed to the happiness, glory, purity, and peace of God's kingdom, will be considered by saints or enemies, opposed to the objects of their supreme delight. And such opposition to all their primary and secondary feelings and desires, and to their pursuit of the highest good of Christ's kingdom, will excite in their hearts a decided opposition to such enemies. And these are holy desires, such as we ought to have, and are the fruits of the Spirit, or the effect of regeneration.—If we do not experience them, we have no ground to hope we are born again. If we do not feel a hatred to sin, and strong desires to overcome it ; if we do not hate and fight against satan, and resist his temptations ; if we do not hate sin in others, and desire to reclaim them ; if we do not hate every error, and guard against the allurements of this world ; if we do not fight against such enemies, desire to overcome, and be crowned with victory ; what evidence have we that we are born again ? If remaining sin is not a grief to us, and our greatest burden in life ; if we are not warmly engaged in the christian warfare ; if the abounding of sin, and the success of satan on the earth, are not hateful ; if our desires for a final victory over all evil are faint ; we have little or no ground to hope we are christians.

Here then is another class of affections, which all will experience who are born again. By them we may try and examine ourselves.

I have now described the fruits of regeneration, or of the Spirit ; and have divided these fruits into three distinct classes, to help all to form a correct judgment of their real character. In the first class is included a new, holy, spiritual appetite ; which delights in the character of God, of Christ, in the happiness of his kingdom, and desires for the continuance and increase of those pleasures. The first pleasures and joys of renewed persons, with their immediate desires, when every thing appears new to them, form the first class of holy affections. From this will arise desires for the continuance and increase of grace, and for all the *means* God has appointed for our improvement in knowledge and growth in grace. Those desires constitute the second class of holy desires or fruits of the Spirit. And from these will arise a hatred of sin, of every spiritual enemy ; and desires for them to be subdued, and a final victory gained. These desires to overcome all spiritual enemies form a third class of holy affections. All these are those fruits of the Spirit, by which we may know what our characters are. But one thing more remains under this head, which is to show,

4. That those who have these fruits will manifest them, in a life and conduct agreeing with their nature.

Every person's external and visible conduct, is under the influence and government of the heart, or affections. The heart is the only primary active principle in man, which produces all the visible fruits in person's actions and conduct. The heart is every persons' moral nature ; and his external conduct is the fruit this nature brings forth. Hence the reason why Christ compares men to trees. He says trees bring forth fruit, according to their nature ; and he says, that men will do the same. This is the way by which we learn what the nature or moral character of man is. We infer his nature from his fruit, as we judge of the nature of a tree by its fruit. In this way every person must learn his own nature or character. Here we take into view a person's internal, as well as external, or visible fruit. We may then adopt this as a true maxim, that if our external fruit does not agree with the word of God, we are not christians.

A person's external conduct may exhibit negative and positive evidence, that he is a saint. By negative evidence is intended mere morality. If a person's life is immoral, it gives positive evidence that he was never born again. If he is strictly moral, he gives negative evidence of piety. His actions and words agree with the rule of duty. And we may have no evidence to support us, in saying he is not a real saint.

By positive external evidence, is meant those actions and conduct, which manifest a real benevolent spirit. He not only abstains from evil, and avoids immoral conduct ; but he goes farther, and manifests love, kindness, and other holy affections, by his actions and conduct in life.—So Christ represents the final trial. I was sick, and ye visited me ; to another he says, I was sick and ye visited me not. Here one gave positive evidence of love to Christ ; the other gave only negative evidence. And we learn, that negative evidence is not sufficient, if positive evidence is wanting. For one is by Christ blessed, and the other condemned. Yet the one condemned is not accused of any immoral conduct.

When a contribution is proposed to send the gospel to the heathen, one professor says nothing against, and does nothing to prevent it ; but though able he will not give any thing to promote the object. Another, no more able to give, encourages all to give, and gives freely and liberally himself. One gives only a negative, but the other positive evidence of piety. This shows us that those who give no more than negative evidence of piety, do not bring forth the fruit which gains the charity of others. Any person unrenewed may do all this ; he may live a moral life, so that no person can have any reason to speak evil of him, or charge him with any crime. But christians are to do more than others ; and must, in order to gain charity. They must not only avoid sinful courses, be careful not to cast stumbling blocks in the way, or do any thing to hinder the salvation of souls, and the advancement of Christ's kingdom ; but they must be actively engaged in affording assistance to fellow travellers, and in promoting the kingdom of Christ. A christian must not only avoid every thing, which may prevent his brother's rising, when he falls or stumbles ; but he ought to help him rise. He should not only refrain from every thing which may prevent his return, when he goes astray ; but go after him, find him and bring him back to the fold, if it be possible. He must not only refrain from evil, but do good ; not only avoid works of darkness, but shine as a light in the world. Some trees are full of leaves, and bear evil fruit ; others have leaves, but no fruit ; and others are full of leaves and laden with good fruit. So a good profession is like a tree with leaves ; and if such are only negatively good, they are as trees full of leaves, which bear no fruit. But a real saint is not only beautiful with the leaves of a profession, but is more or less laden with good fruit. This may show what of external visible fruit we must bring forth, to give evidence of real friendship to God. If professors are not negatively holy, are not

18

moral, but immoral, it is very certain they are not christians, however good their story of experiences may be. If they are moral, and thus negatively good, and profess a change of heart, we have not sufficient ground to say they are not saints. But if they exhibit only this negative evidence, our charity for them will be faint.

But if their relation is good and they bear fruit positively good, they gain our charity at once; and we shall have warm and full confidence that they are what they profess, according to the measure of good fruit which they bear. Now whatever we have felt inwardly, even though we have been elated seemingly to heaven with good feelings, yet if our visible life and conduct do not harmonize herewith; if we have only a negative, but no positive evidence; we have not ground to support that hope which purifies the heart. Hence, to have that fruit which the word of God describes as good fruit, we must experience all those internal affections, which have been illustrated; and our external conduct and life must agree herewith; otherwise we have not the fruits of the Spirit, which we may rest on with safety.

After all, persons may be deceived. They may exhibit much positive good fruit externally, yet not be christians. Because all those external good things may be performed from bad motives; from pride, or a desire to appear well, and gain an honorable name in the world. This is clearly taught by Christ and his apostles.

Our Lord says, that some at the great day will plead, they have wrought miracles in his name, and eaten and drunk in his presence, to whom he will declare that he never knew them. And Paul signifies, that persons may speak with the eloquence of angels, feed the poor, work miracles, and give their bodies to be burned, yet not have charity; and if they have not charity, they are nothing. And this agrees with his description of certain characters in the 6th of Hebrews, and with what Christ observes concerning stony ground hearers. And it agrees with the dictates of reason. For however good and useful actions and words are, if they are not performed with right motives, and do not proceed from a benevolent principle of heart, they cannot be pleasing in the sight of that God, who looketh at the heart, and requires sincerity in the inward part.

I have now exhibited to view those fruits of the Spirit, or of the new birth, which all will bring forth, more or less, who are born again. It is by these fruits we are to form our opinion of others, and judge concerning our own characters. For Christ has given the same rule, by which we are to judge ourselves and our fellow men, whether we and they are indeed the children of God. By their fruits ye shall know them ; and by our fruit we must know ourselves. For we have no intuitive view of our nature, any more than we have of the nature of other persons. And of course we have no way to know ourselves, only by our fruits. How important, then, that we should form consistent views of the nature of gospel fruit. For if we are wrong in this particular, we may form false opinions of our own hearts and moral characters.

Reflections. 1. No person can tell the minute, or hour, or day in which he was born again.

Regeneration is the creation of a new nature, or a holy, benevolent, active principle of action, or appetite. And there are but three ways, by which we can know whether such a principle is created in us. One is by intuition ; another by feeling the operation of divine power, at the instant the creation is performed ; and the last is, by the fruits which will follow. We certainly cannot tell this by intuition. To have a naked view of the heart, is the prerogative of God only. And it is as certain, that no person can know this by feeling the agency of the Spirit. The agency of God is constantly operating upon christians, in preserving life, in sanctifying the heart, and in many ways. But no person feels this agency ; no one has a conscious feeling of that power, which causes his lungs to heave, and his blood to flow in his veins. It is then only by the fruits, which the new nature will bear, that we can have a knowledge of this great change. To learn by the fruit, there must be more or less time intervene, before we can infer that we are renewed.

It is granted, persons may know the hour and place in which they experienced a change in their feelings ; when things appeared new to them ; when they felt other joys, and sensations, and desires. But those feelings are not the change itself; they are only the fruits of it. A new nature or appetite must precede these sensations and desires. And from them we may infer, that a change has been produced in us, if those feelings are genuine. But we cannot infer from them that we were at that instant born again. It might be at that instant, and it might have been an hour or day previous. How long the heart may have been created anew, before we experience any of the fruits, no person can tell. It is probable, that some experience those fruits more immediately than others ; according to the nature of the objects in view of the mind at the time the change is effected. As it is by the fruit only a person can know he is born again ; and as no one can infer from the fruit the instant when the new creation was produced ; so no one can tell the day or hour, when his heart was renewed. He can tell when he experienced new sensations, desires, and pleasures ; but cannot tell, when that new principle was produced, which brings forth those fruits. And it may be that the fruit is realized very soon after the change is produced ; but not certain.—This corrects and confutes an error, which is often attended with dangerous consequences.

Some persons believe they can tell with certainty the very instant, or moment, when they were born again. And on this ground it is, that they are positive and certain that they are new creatures. Hence, whatever their feeling and fruits are afterwards, they are still confident they are saints. They will say, I know I am renewed ; for I know the moment, when this was done ; and if grace cannot be lost, I am still a renewed man. So they maintain their hope, though their present fruit condemns them. While a person, who says he cannot tell whether he is born again only by his fruit, will doubt concerning his state so far as his fruit will not warrant him to hope. He can say, I know the very hour when a great change took place in my feelings, and I had some hope then that I was a new creature. But as all my feelings then may have been spurious, and false ; so it may be I was not then renewed, or have been since, seeing I do not bring forth the genuine fruits of a new heart. If my feelings were genuine on which I first built my hope, I should still bring forth good fruit. As my fruit is not such as the bible represents christians as bringing forth daily, I have reason to fear my first fruits were false, only such as stony ground hearers experience ; and hence the reason why I have generally been so barren. Thus different will be the reasoning of persons, when one is certain he knew the moment when he was born again, and the other relies not on this, but on the fruit he bears, as the only sure evidence of a change of heart.

Persons of the former class are generally antinominians ; they maintain their hope firm, when their daily fruit condemns them. How can they do this, only on the principle that per, sons may have a saving faith, yet not bring forth good fruit ? There is reason to fear many have been deceived to their final ruin, who have imbibed the erroneous idea of which I am speaking. While those who depend on their fruit as an evidence of a real change, according to the direction of Christ, will doubt, examine themselves, and feel assured no further than their fruit witnesses in their favor. And they will make it a business to live holy lives every day ; while those of the other sentiment will give very little attention to the fruit they bear. For their hope from day to day is not founded on their fruit, but on the certainty that at such a moment they were renewed.

2. Great transports of joy are no certain evidence of a change of heart. Some lay great stress on such joyful sensations. As soon as they feel them, they are sure of a change of heart. Yet perhaps there is no feeling, no affection, which satan can more easily counterfeit, than this. For according to the known laws of our nature, by which we are always governed, it is certain that joy will attend a deliverance from danger or distress, whether it be *real*, or existing only in the *belief* of the mind. For if a person believes he is delivered from the danger, the enemy, or the evil, which he greatly dreaded, his deliverance is in his view *real ;* and will be attended with the same joyful feelings as a real salvation, though in fact he is deceived, believing he is safe when he is not.

Satan is a cunning and subtle adversary. His object is the ruin of souls. To effect this he will, if possible, keep sinners in a state of peace and security all their days. If at any time they are alarmed with a sense of their danger, he will try every method he can to lull their fears asleep again. If he cannot effect this, his next step is to *deceive* them ; and make them believe they are real saints, when they are not. And this is the most dangerous ground, upon which he can bring them to rest. For it is seldom any person is brought to renounce his *hope*, though it be false. Many secure souls are alarmed and renewed, while not one hypocrite is brought to see his deception, reject his hope, and build anew. It is by deception satan brought sin into this world at first ; and it is by deception he has ever since maintained his kingdom. This is the grand means by which he ruins so many souls. To this end, we are informed, he may and often does transform himself into an angel of light. And when he does this, there is no angel in heaven, who manifests a greater zeal for religion than he. He then labors to have sinners attend to religion with great assiduity. For a proof of this we may produce as witnesses the Heathen, the Jews, and Mahometans. How zealous they are in religion. But their systems are such as satan has invented for them to embrace. Satan finds that mankind in general cannot rest easy, unless they have what they call religion. He accordingly forms systems for them, and persuades them to embrace them; and the more engaged they are in supporting their religious rites, the more safe and secure they feel, and so much the more satan is pleased. For if by such ways he can blind, and deceive, and ruin souls, he is satisfied. He then is their god, and is full of religious zeal himself.

Now in a christian land satan has to take a different course, in many respects. While men admit the bible, he persuades them to embrace damnable errors, and support them with all the zeal, and false learning and reasoning in their power. If any remain orthodox in head, and he cannot ruin them by dangerous errors in sentiment, he will bring them to believe they are christians when they are not, and so rest on a false hope. Hence, when sinners are alarmed and exercised in mind, and even have a genuine conviction of sin, he will persuade them to believe, that remarkable dreams, visions, bodily agitations, texts of scripture occuring suddenly, and in a way unaccountable to the mind, and such like things, are sure evidences of a change of heart. He sets them to reason in this way. 'This dream, this vision, this bodily feeling, this text of scripture, is no part of my agency. I cannot produce such things, nor prevent them. They are produced by some invisible agent, and this agent is the Spirit of God. For satan cannot, and if he could, he would not, do these things. They must be from the holy Spirit, and by them the Spirit informs us we are born again.'

Now it is easy for satan, if permitted, to produce such strange dreams, visions, and bodily affections; and whisper texts of scripture to their minds. He quoted scripture to Christ; he had great power over men's bodies in that day; and he can raise storms, as in the case of Job, and do many such wonderful things, when permitted. When, therefore, men are persuaded to believe, that such wonders are always produced by the Holy Spirit, and are sure signs of a change of heart, he has them in his power, and can deceive them at his pleasure. And persons who believe thus may rely on it, they will have visions and revelations, more or less.

And some, who profess to be ministers, know so little concerning human nature, and the deceitful workings of satan, that they do, by laying much weight on such appearances themselves, persuade many to believe in them, and rely on them. Hence in places where such things are preached and believed, if there is any revival, persons experience these things very often. One has had a dream; another a vision; another a text occuring he cannot tell how; others have felt great weakness of body, so as to lose their strength, and apparently their life. Converts are multiplied very fast; almost every one has a dream or vision, or some such wonder to relate, and then is pronounced converted. Thus satan deceives many. While in other places where there are revivals, and persons are taught differently, and do not believe in such things as signs of conversion, it is very rare that they occur among the converts. Why not? Because satan knows, that he cannot deceive such persons in this way. Such works therefore do not answer his end; and of course he does not produce them. Hence the reason why the weak, the ignorant, and those most likely to believe in such strange things, are most apt to experience them. Because in such persons satan is more likely to succeed in deceiving.

Now when persons are under serious impressions, and have a sense and conviction of sin, satan will deceive them, if possible. He will lead them to settle down on a false hope. And if, in this state of mind, they have an idea that they are born again, whether they obtain this by dreams, visions, or any other way, they will experience an alteration in their feelings. As soon as they believe they are renewed, whatever may occasion this belief, they will feel joyful; their burden will leave them, and their mind will become in some degree tranquil. And those feelings are occasioned by the idea, or the belief they have, that their heart is renewed. And the joy they feel, their relief of the burden they had experienced, and the consequent peace of mind, confirm their belief; and this again increases their joy, and this increase satisfies them still more fully that they have passed from death to life. So in this way they soon have a settled and confirmed hope. Yet their hearts remain unrenewed; and this great change in their feelings was occasioned wholly by their being led to entertain a belief that they had become new creatures. If a person views himself, as he really is, in the greatest danger, and even exposed to eternal death ; if this view excites fear, anxiety, and distress, and sinks him under the burden ; if, by any means, he gains belief that he is delivered from danger, and the death he feared, his fears, and distress, and burden, will leave him. And this deliverance, which he considers as real, will excite in him greater or less joy and gladness of heart. Yet he is deceived ; no such deliverance has been wrought for him, as he believes. But with him it is a reality, and produces the same effect it would in case it had been real. And his relief of his burden, and joy of heart, he will view as evidences of a real deliverance ; and of course will increase and strengthen his previous belief or hope.

Thus how easy it is for satan to deceive persons, when they embrace such erroneous ideas of evidence of conversion. It was in a way similar to this, the stony ground hearers were filled with joy, and their joy confirmed their hope. Similar to this was the joy the Jews experienced at the Red sea. The day before they were burdened with fears and distress, occasioned by their enemies. As soon as they had safely crossed and saw their enemies overwhelmed in the mighty deep, their burden left them ; and their hearts were filled with joy, which they expressed in songs of praise to God their Savior. Yet their hearts were full of rebellion, which they manifested a few days after, in murmurs and complaints.

Hence joy is no sure evidence of a change of heart. And false joy is commonly greater, than that which is genuine. And it is dangerous for persons to place much dependance upon it, especially when they first obtain a hope. And generally, if not always, if persons find on examination, that a hope they had met with a change *preceded* their joy, they may conclude that this hope is the cause of their joy and the relief they feel, and not the fruit of any real change of heart. Where there is a real change of heart, attended with joy and a release from their burdens of mind, it is commonly some time before persons do or can consider this a warrantable evidence of a saving change. Hence if their hope precedes their joy, they ought not to rely on it as an evidence of grace in the heart. It may also be well to observe, that gospel ministers, instead of teaching people to pay attention to dreams and visions, bodily feelings, or the remarkable occurrence of scripture texts to the mind, ought to show them the great danger of laying any weight on such things, and warn them to guard against being deceived by such delusions. This particular may be closed with the following observations.

Within the course of my ministry, which is now forty-three years, I have been particularly acquainted with a number of revivals among my own people, and also in towns adjacent ; and have frequently noticed two kinds of converts, whose first experiences have been different. One class is composed of those, who have manifested a great and sudden alteration in their feelings. They have suddenly experienced great joy, and entire relief of their burden, and manifested much warmth of affection, great zeal in the cause of Christ, and almost a full and sure confidence of a saving change free from doubts and fears. The other class have manifested a lively sense of the great depravity and sinfulness of their hearts ; after a season their burden, as they call it, has left them ; they have felt a pleasedness with the character of God, inward satisfaction in his sovereignty, a willingness to be in his hand and at his disposal ; but, on account of the great sinfulness of their hearts, cannot for a considerable time persuade themselves, that they are new creatures. They begin at last to entertain a hope, with fear and trembling ; yet at no time have they been much elated with joy. This class of converts have generally persevered in the christian course, and given increasing evidence of real, and genuine piety, shining with greater light from year to year ; and it is seldom, that one of them finally proves to be a hypocrite. While numbers of the other class, after a few days, begin to decline, grow cold, and finally, like stony ground hearers, under trials fall away, and embrace dangerous errors of some kind, or return to their former course of life ; many of them give decided proof of hypocrisy. And those of this class, who do persevere and support a christian life, after a few days or weeks from the time of their change, manifest but little of the joy they first felt, lose their confidence, and begin to doubt, whether all they have experienced is not a delusion. They begin to become more and more acquainted with their remaining corruptions, and complain of their depravity, coldness, and stupidity ; and then, with humility and trembling, they persevere in working out their salvation. Hence converts, who are elated with joy at first and on this account have great confidence and assurance, who are warm, forward, and full of zeal, are not very promising, and there is much reason to fear they will prove no better than stony ground hearers. But those, who have a deep sense of their depravity, and obtain a hope by slow degrees, and with many fears ; who show great tenderness of heart, lest they should wound the cause, and many fears that they are deceived ; these are persons, who shine brightest on their journey to the heavenly land. And with this representation, it is believed, ministers who. have been much acquainted with revivals, will agree. Let us then learn not to consider great and sudden joy, confidence, and boldness, so great evidences of piety, as many seem to do, and especially those, who are less acquainted with the operations of the Holy Spirit.

3. All persons, who believe the entire depravity of the heart, and the necessity of a change by the agency of the Spirit, to be consistent, must embrace the doctrine of particular, personal election.

It is the depravity of the heart, which leads men away from God, to travel the broad road to death. This path they will continue to travel, till they are renewed. And if not renewed, all will perish. And regeneration is a change wrought by the creating agency of God. Also it is a plain truth, that no being can act without determination. A determination to do a thing, to produce an event, must precede, in the order of nature, the event to be produced. Indeed the heart of every moral agent must be in a state of perfect indifference, with respect to any action to be performed, or must be determined against it, or for it. For we cannot conceive of any other state in which the heart can be. If God is perfectly indifferent whether any one is renewed or not, he will not exert his agency to renew any heart. If determined not to renew one soul, then he never will save one. It follows then, that he is determined to renew a person's heart, previous to effecting the change, and then his agency is employed in producing it. It is plain a determination to do any particular thing must precede, in the order of nature, the performance of it.

Again. As we see, that a divine determination to renew and save a soul, must precede the exertion of power for this purpose ; so it is as obvious, that God is determined to renew the hearts of all men ; or not to renew the heart of one ; or to renew the hearts of a part only. No other supposition can be admitted. It is certain from his word, that he will not save all men ; and as certain, that he will renew and save some. Then the determination of God is to renew and save some, a part, of the fallen race of men ; and leave the others to act their pleasure, and embrace or reject Chirst. And we know they will reject him forever. Suppose God is determined to exert his agency to renew some heart, the present hour ; must he not have in view some particular person, whom he designs to renew ? Or will his agency be exerted to renew a heart at random, or as chance may direct?

Is such a view of God's agency consistent with wisdom, and love ? God never acts in this manner. If he is to renew some heart this day, he knows whose heart it is, and where he lives. Hence it is evident, that as God is determined to renew the hearts of some only of the human race, he must and does know the particular persons to be renewed. And this Christ teaches. He says he knows his sheep by name, and can call them by name ; this you will learn by reading the 10th chapter of John. If God must know, who the individual persons are, whose hearts he is determined to renew and save, he knows them by name, where they reside, and in what age of the world they live. These are truths, which all must admit to be consistent, who grant men are totally depraved, and must be renewed by the creating agency of God. And if they believe these truths, they embrace the doctrine of particular, personal election of individuals to eternal life. For by the doctrine of election all that is intended is, that God is determined to renew and save some of the fallen race ; and he knows who the individual persons are, whom he will save, and when and where they live. These are all the ideas contained in the doctrine of election, with this belief that this determination of his is eternal. Those then who deny this doctrine, yet believe in total depravity, and the need of creating power to renew the heart, are very inconsistent. But if persons only see clearly the truths expressed under this particular, and are capable of comparing, and seeing their agreement, they must admit the doctrine of election. And if a person has not a knowledge of these truths, or is not capable of comparing them. and seeing their agreement and consistency, he is either so deficient in knowledge, or weak in intellect, as to be unfit to teach others the doctrines of the gospel, and the way of salvation.

4. Is it by our fruits only we can know what our moral characters, and the characters of others, are ? Then, if we would avoid deception, and form a correct judgment, we must have clear and distinct views of gospel fruit. If we err in this, we

may judge a tree to be good, which is evil ; and a tree evil, which is good. How important then it is for all, and especially teachers, to study the scriptures, and acquire a clear and consistent knowledge of all the fruits of the holy Spirit, or of a new heart. To obtain this knowledge, let all with prayer for light and instruction read the beatitudes of our Savior, Math. 5th, and what the apostle says in Galatians, where the fruits of the Spirit and of the flesh are enumerated, and other passages in all of the epistles. And every professor is not only requested to obtain right views of gospel fruit ; but compare himself with the truth, and candidly examine himself. Deception is ruinous to the soul. And it is with fear and trembling, we are to work out our salvation. We cannot give too much attention, to make our calling and election sure. And to attain unto assurance, is one great privilege and blessing. Let us then examine daily, with candor and impartiality, to learn whether we are trees of righteousness, which are laden with the glorious fruits of the gospel.

5. The children of God are under the greatest obligations to bless and serve God, in return for his infinite love to them.

God not only so loved you, as to give his Son to die for you ; but when you despised the offers of life, and set Christ at nought, and were in the road to final ruin, he so loved you that he interfered, renewed your hearts, and saved you from eternal death. You are born of God, are his sons and daughters, heirs of God, and jointheirs with Christ to all the riches, glories, and joys of his heavenly kingdom. In this God has manifested far greater love to you, than he would, had he given you all the kingdoms, crowns, riches, and glories of this world. His love to you is inconceivably great, precious, and unmerited. For, instead of deserving such gracious treatment, you justly merited his endless displeasure. You have been the objects of unmerited, and unlimited love and grace. You are infinitely indebted to your gracious sovereign. You owe him all the love, gratitude, praise, and service you are able to render him. And you can never repay fully the debt of love, praise, and service.

Do you feel these truths ? Is it your constant and earnest desire, to render to God according to benefits received ? Is your life daily devoted to God ? Do you daily glorify him, by reflecting the rays of his glory ? Oh make it your studious watchful and prayerful endeavor to shun every sin, to grow in grace, and ripen for heaven. You are born from above, are the sons of God, members of his family. Then place your affections on things above, seek heaven as your home, and earnestly desire to join the general assembly above in their songs of praise for such boundless love and grace. Pray for, and assist each other on your journey ; with zeal seek the salvation of souls, and the extension of Christ's kingdom through this world. Live in actual readiness to meet death, to stand before your Judge, to be acquitted there, and welcomed forever into the joy of your Lord. Then, as a star among innumerable stars, you will shine around the throne of the Lamb, and as one body with perfect harmony tune your voices, and loud as thunder shout his praise for redeeming love.

6. What madness reigns in the hearts of all, who yet reject the Savior of sinners.

The impenitent are desired to reflect, and consider how vile their hearts are ; how rebellious their lives, and how inconceivably stupid, blind, and mad they are. You are deaf, naked, blind, and dead in trespasses and sins. You travel the road to hell with pleasure, and every day are treasuring up wrath against the day of wrath. Christ has died for you, is able and ready to save you, and calls unto you, Come unto me, I will not reject you ; turn ye, for why will you die ? But you turn a deaf ear. When your danger is set before you, you remain unmoved, and stupid as beasts that perish. Why do you thus despise Christ and his blood, and pursue a course which you know will ruin you ? Why do you act this part of folly and madness ? To excuse and justify yourselves, you often say you cannot help it. Yet nothing but attention is wanting, in order for you to see your vileness, your danger, your just desert of death, and your dependence on sovereign mercy. And if you saw all this, could you live a secure, quiet life ? If a person found himself in a pit, into which he had plunged himself, and saw that there he must die, if he remained, would he feel easy in that condition ? If he knew he was unable to deliver himself, would this quiet his fears ? Would not this dependence on another for help, and the uncertainty of being assisted and saved, increase his fears, and cause him to cry aloud for mercy? Look then, and learn that you are deaf, blind, naked, dead and lost ; and are dependent on Christ for help. Then you will begin to beg and cry for mercy, and not till then. Then, like the sick, the lame, the deaf and blind, in Christ's day, you will come and cry to him, as they did, Lord Jesus, have mercy on us. And till you do thus see your ruined state, your dependence on unmerited grace, and do come and cry for mercy, there is no hope you will escape death.

****

ESSAY XXX.

A Summary View of the system, advanced and illustrated in these Essays.

Every science is founded on what are generally called *first principles.* And as far as persons differ in their views of these, they will embrace different systems. And yet first principles are commonly self evident propositions.

Mathematicks is a science founded on first, self evident propositions or axioms. And all, who reason correctly from them, agree in their results and conclusions.

Theology and Ethics are founded on first principles. And so far as persons distinctly perceive and understand the first principles, if they reason correctly and consistently, they will be agreed in the system of sentiments resulting from them. For the process of reasoning is only inferring one proposition from another. How then is it possible to form a true system of sentiments, unless we are acquainted with the self evident propositions on which they are founded ?

Every science has a *beginning.* To understand and teach it correctly, we must start from the beginning, or self evident propositions. When we trace sentiments back, to learn whether they are well founded, we shall come to first principles from which they follow as inferences ; or continue to run back ad infinitum. And in reasoning and proceeding forward, we must begin with a self evident proposition from which we infer a second, from that a third, and in this way progress in the field of science. Unless we reason in this manner we proceed in the dark, or reason in a circle.—When truths are thus inferred one of another from self evident propositions, every step in the process is demonstrated. By this mode of reasoning, a finite mind in the boundless field of knowledge may progress forever and ever. And how transporting is the thought, that our limited minds may improve in knowledge through an endless duration ; and especially in the science of Theology, which exceeds all others in sublimity, to which other sciences are only hand-maids, if rightly improved, and which contains the most refreshing, delightful, and joyful food for an immortal spirit.— If we can ascertain the first principles of Theology and Ethics, and reason correctly from them, different persons will harmonize in sentiments. To proceed directly to the subject before us, it may be asserted,

1. That happiness is an *absolute good*, and this is one first principle in Ethics. As happiness is considered a good in itself by all rational beings ; and as no one can give a reason, why he thus esteems it, the proposition is self evident. And,

2. That pain or misery is an absolute evil, is another self evident truth. All fear and dread pain, and no one can give a reason why he does. These are two of the self evident propositions, on which the whole system is founded. It is well known that self evident propositions admit of no proof. As soon as they are distinctly stated, and perceived, if a person does not give his assent, he must be left to wonder ; for conviction cannot be produced in him by any thing more evident ; for nothing can be more evident, than a self evident truth. Such truths may be illustrated and explained by other propositions with which persons may be acquainted, but can never be proved.

Some pretend to make a distinction between *pleasure*, and *happiness*. But when nothing more is taken into view, than their *simple nature*, who can show a difference between them ? Happiness, pleasure, in their simple nature, are nothing but agreeable, pleasant *sensations*. A pleasant sensation, emotion, or feeling, is happiness, and it is pleasure. Though all pleasant sensations are alike in their simple nature ; yet they may differ in degree, and intenseness, and may be excited by objects differing much from each other. The objects which please are very different from each other in many respects. And it is granted, that no objects or sources of enjoyment can afford as durable, satisfying happiness, as full as our capacities will admit, but those which are infinite and eternal. The happiness derived from such objects may be styled true, real, and substantial ; while pleasures given us by fading, fleeting, and uncertain objects, can never fill or satisfy the mind.

If we ask any persons whether they esteem happiness a good thing ? All will answer in the affirmative. Ask them to assign reasons, why they thus esteem it ; they can give none. Do you wish to enjoy any greater good, than perfect, uninterrupted happiness ? They must answer, no ; for they cannot conceive of any greater good to be enjoyed than this.—Hence the greatest sum of happiness, which rational beings can enjoy, is the highest good any individual, or society can possess. As societies are composed of individuals, and as the greatest happiness an individual *can* enjoy is *his* highest good ; so the sum total of the perfect happiness of the individuals constituting a society, is the highest, the greatest good, which can exist in it. This is so evident, no one can consistently deny it.

Let us then reason correctly from the propositions, which have been stated as self evident, and we cannot err respecting the nature of right and wrong, good and evil, both natural and moral, or concerning praise and blame. This will be clearly seen very soon. But here let it be observed, that to the existence of happiness a

3. Proposition must be admitted as self evident, which is this, that a feeling faculty capable of pleasant and painful sensations existing in a rational mind, is absolutely necessary.

This cannot be proved, because it is self evident. But it can be explained and illustrated, and made clear to every person. Can a stone, a tree, or any part of the inanimate creation, enjoy, or be the subjects of happiness ? And why not ? Because they are not endued with a feeling faculty, are incapable of all pleasant and painful emotions. And as such a faculty is necessary to happiness, to the existence of the greatest good, so but one faculty of this nature is necessary in the same individual. We therefore find, that man is endued with only one feeling faculty. The understanding can see, or perceive objects, their properties, qualities, relations, and connexions ; and the will can choose, and execute the pleasure of the heart ; but neither of them is the subject of pleasant or painful emotions. All pleasant and painful sensations must exist antecedent to volition. Were not this a fact, volitions could never have any existence in the mind, as it is hoped has been fully proved. These explanations show, it is self evident that a feeling faculty is requisite to the existence of happiness.

And if the other faculties of the mind and liberty are not considered truths in relation to happiness, yet it must be granted they are essential to it, when all things are considered, which are needful to its existence. No one will deny, but what the existence of objects, not only to please, but to afford the greatest satisfaction, is necessary to the highest good. To be happy there must be objects of enjoyment, each of which may be termed a *source* of happiness. And the faculty of the understanding to perceive objects is requisite. For objects cannot please unless seen or known. As our bodily palate never sees the food it relishes ; so our mental taste is not a perceiving, but a feeling and relishing faculty. And as objects unknown cannot please, they must exist in view of the mind by perception, to affect the heart. Hence without this faculty objects could never be enjoyed, and happiness could have no existence.

Again. The will, if not requisite to the being of happiness, is surely necessary to the increase of it. For objects, when perceived, may please, or appear agreeable ; yet to a full enjoyment of them we must have have possession of them. By the will, producing external actions, we get possession of the objects of our desire; and by it we select the pleasing, and reject the painful. By this faculty we use the means adapted to the attainment of sources of happiness. All will readily see, that when we have a view of future and distant objects, and wish to enjoy them, and form our plans to obtain them, it is by the will our plans are executed, and desires are gratified. Also, if we did not enjoy liberty we could never accomplish our pleasure. If we acted continually under restraint or constraint, we might not be able at any time to follow and gratify our desires. We might be made, by some foreign power, to go directly against our pleasure and inclinations. Liberty, freedom from restraint and constraint, to follow the way our desires lead us, and perform the actions conducing to our pleasure, it will be acknowledged, is necessary to our highest good or happiness.

Do not these remarks make it evident, that not only a faculty for pleasure and pain, but also a faculty to *perceive* objects, and a faculty to *choose* and *refuse*, and perform actions, and *liberty*, or freedom from restraint, are each of them essential to the existence of happiness ? And a being, endued with these faculties, is an entire moral agent. Such a being man is ; for he is possessed of these faculties. And do we know, or can we invent, any other or more properties, necessary to constitute a

20

complete moral agent, or requisite to as great a measure of happiness as our nature will admit ? We now see what things
are essential to the highest felicity, or misery of man, according to the nature or inclination of his heart. And these truths
are so evident that when clearly stated, and explained, who can
deny them, or withold his assent from them ? Now,

4. Another proposition may be advanced as self evident ; or
if not, the nearest akin to it ; which is, that happiness, being
the only absolute good, *ought* to be the *ultimate end* of every
moral agent.—This does not need proof, so much as it does
explanation. Indeed, when distinctly illustrated, enough will
be said to gain the assent of candid minds.

Can any one see any difference between existence and non-
existence, in relation to good enjoyed, if no happiness is experienced ? Though a society might be formed of innumerable
individuals, and each of them be perfectly holy, yet if they
should never feel one pleasant sensation, experience no pleasure, no happiness ; would existence on this supposition be desirable, or preferable to annihilation? It must be granted, that
happiness is the only final good, which renders existence desirable. This being granted, there is no greater good, which
can be sought. And when happiness is obtained, we have
then arrived at an ultimate end, to the last exertion in our pursuit ; and here, in the enjoyment of this good, we rest satisfied.
And as this is an absolute good, and the greatest good, we
ought to delight and rejoice in it, wherever we see it existing.
But here an important inquiry presents itself ; whether our
own personal happiness, or the happiness of other rational beings, ought to be our ultimate end of pursuit. In attempting to
reflect some light on this subject, a distinction ought to be made
between an *end* and the reason or *motive*, which influences us
in seeking it. Every one does not at once discern this distinction. Yet it is very important to distinguish properly between
the *nature* of *selfishness*, and that of *benevolence*.

Here then it may be observed, that our personal individual
happiness ought not to, neither can be, the ultimate object or
end of our pursuit.

For the reader to apprehend this aright, let us suppose a being created with all the faculties or powers requisite to constitute him a complete moral agent, as was in fact the case with
Adam. Suppose for a time his faculties are not in operation,
no exercises are excited. He does not feel one pleasant or

painful sensation. In this condition it is not possible for him, on supposition his understanding were in operation, to have any idea of happiness, or of good, or of evil, in any sense. In this state *his own* happiness cannot be an object of his pursuit ; because it has no existence, and he knows not what it is. At this moment, let it be supposed his understanding has a clear perception of some object ; and in view of it he experiences, for the first time, a very pleasant sensation. This puts all the faculties of his mind in operation. Now he begins to act, and aim at some *end* ? The *object*, which is the source of his pleasure, or the *pleasant sensation itself*, one or the other, must be considered as his end ultimately. The pleasant sensation, or his happiness, cannot be his end. Because the pleasure felt must exist before it can be sought as an end. And when it has existence, it is already possessed? And what propriety is there in seeking that as an object or end, which is already attained, is now in our possession. The truth then is this ; the object which affords the pleasure experienced is his *end ;* and the pleasure it gives him is the *reason* or *motive*, by which he is influenced or excited to seek that object. He aims at it as an end, and strives by proper means to obtain possession of it, that the pleasure it gave him may be increased and continued. And the increase and continuance of the happiness he enjoys, is what gives the object its influence, considered as a motive. The moment he felt pleasure in view of the object, a desire arose to possess and enjoy it. And when it is obtained, and all the pleasure is realized which it is capable of affording, so far his desire is gratified, and his end obtained.

It is in this manner that all mankind are influenced and governed, in all their actions and pursuits. The object which is in itself, and for its own sake, agreeable, is sought as an ultimate end ; no object beyond it is in view ; here the mind rests in the pleasant gratification experienced. And the expected satisfaction it will give invests the object with the influence of a motive. As all will grant, if the object did not please, it would not have any influence as a motive, and would not be an object of attention or pursuit in its own nature considered.

According to this view of the subject, all objects, which are on their own account agreeable, are always sought as ultimate ends ; and those, which are not in themselves pleasant, are used as *means* to the attainment of ends, which on their own account are agreeable. Hence, if a person's heart is wholly destitute of every benevolent feeling ; if the happiness of other beings is not any source of pleasure to him, he will never seek their felicity. He will never aim at any higher objects, than those which gratify his personal, individual desires. All his pursuits will ultimately centre in personal self gratification. This is the true idea of s lfishness. Hence the objects on their own account agreeable, and those he uses as means to his ends, he will engross and monopolize to himself as far as he is able. He would possess all the riches and honor of this world, were it in his power. If other beings are by this means deprived of happiness, and rendered unhappy, this will give him no uneasiness, unless their misery should in some way lessen his happiness. Because he has no feeling for their happiness on its own account, and because their pains will afford him no uneasiness, if his own pleasure is not affected or lessened by it.—In unrenewed men, each individual appetite of the heart never aims at any other or higher end, than its own gratification. The appetite of hunger desires food ; when the food is enjoyed and his appetite fully gratified, his end is answered. He aims at no higher end, than the satisfaction of the appetite. If natural affection governs, and he desires the happiness of his wife, or his children, in the enjoyment of worldly prosperity and greatness, as far as they enjoy those blessings his desires are gratified, and he aims at no higher end. If he covets riches and honors, as far as he is able to attain them, his desires are satisfied. In pursuit of such objects he never aims at any other, or higher ends, than those objects which afford personal gratification. Selfishness then is predicable of each appetite, belonigng to the heart of unrenewed men. For under the government of each appetite his end is to obtain the object or objects, which on their own account afford to each full gratification. This gives, in few words, a general idea of the nature of selfishness ; and it is not designed in this essay to enlarge any farther on this subject. And this representation, it appears to me, agrees with facts, experience, observation, and what the word of God says concerning human depravity.

But benevolence delights in the happiness of others, or of rational beings. And as the greatest sum of happiness is the highest good of the universe, this is the end in which a benevolent heart delights on its own account, and which it seeks as its ultimate end. And from this it is evident that the only direct way for a benevolent person to promote his own happiness, is to increase the felicity of intelligent beings. Their happiness is an object of pursuit, and of delight. This object is his ultimate end, and the pleasure it affords gives the influence of a motive, which stimulates him to promote the blessedness of God's holy kingdom to his utmost ability. Hence while a benevolent person is promoting and increasing the happiness of others, he is augmenting his own. For he rejoices in their joy, and the more they rejoice the greater is his joy. This shows that benevolence is a most excellent and amiable appetite. This view makes it evident, that the greatest measure of happiness will, and ought to be, the ultimate end of benevolence. This explains and establishes the proposition advanced, that the greatest happiness of rational existence *ought* to be the ultimate end of m ral agents.

This will afford conviction respecting the origin of moral obligation. For the sake of brevity and perspicuity, permit me here to *personify* the general good, and represent her as addressing moral agents.

" Happiness is the only absolute good enjoyed by individuals, and by societies composed of them. And the greatest measure of enjoyment is the highest good of intelligent agents. This ought to be sought on its own account, as an ultimate end. And until moral agents learn what this blessing is by experiencing or feeling it, they can form no idea of what the terms good and evil ought, and ought not, to mean. The hour in which they feel internal and joyful sensations, they will say, to be filled with this bliss, is the highest good our nature will admit. And to seek and promote the highest blessedness of rational existence, is promoting the highest good. Then they will know, that every thing tending in its nature to lessen or destroy this good, is *evil ;* and all things tending ultimately to promote and increase it, are properly termed *good.* Then they will clearly perceive what is the meaning of the terms *ought* and *ought not ;* one means, it is a *duty* or an *obligation* of every agent, to seek and increase happiness to the highest possible degree as their ultimate end, and opposition to this is doing what they ought not, or what duty forbids. I therefore command all moral agents to aim at me, as their ultimate object or end, in all their actions and pursuits. If any oppose and transgress this command, they are enemies to me, and as such will deserve to be banished from my presence forever.

For there is no authority above mine to control me, because I am the highest possible good, which can have existence."

Is it not clear from this address, that the greatest sum of happiness being the highest possible good, this is the end, which all are under obligations to aim at and seek ultimately ; yes *ultimately*, because there is no greater good, which can be aimed at or sought ?

The propositions advanced are so evident, as to gain the assent of all as soon as they understand them. They are these :

1. Enduing a being or beings with a feeling faculty, is necessary to the very existence of hapiness and misery.

2. That happiness is an absolute good, and the greatest sum of it the highest possible good.

3. That pain or misery is an absolute evil.

4. That the greatest sum of created happiness, which can have existence in God's holy kingdom,(where alone it can exist,) *ought* to be the ultimate aim and end of moral agents.

With these propositions many other truths are so evidently connected, they will gain assent as soon as they are distinctly perceived. A few of them will now be stated.

1. That every thing which tends directly in its nature to promote the greatest sum of created happiness, may and ought to be called good. And as all things, which have this tendency are *means*, by which happiness is promoted, that may and ought to be termed *relative goods*. And all relative good possesses greater or less value, in proportion to its influence in promoting happiness.

2. Holiness or benevolence is a relative good, and the greatest good except happiness, because none can be truly and forever happy without it ; and because it has the greatest influence in promoting and increasing happiness. No relative good can exist, which is so excellent, beautiful, sweet, and inviting, as a holy disposition.

3. That all things, which tend directly and ultimately to destroy or lessen the sum of happiness, and to produce misery, are *relative evils*. And those evils are greater and less, in proportion to the influence they have in diminishing or destroying happiness.

4. Sin is the greatest relative evil, because its influence is greater in lessening happiness and producing misery, than any othery in being.

From the propositions advanced, many other inferences or

truths will follow. But the farther we proceed in drawing inferences from self-evident propositions, the less evident they are, and require more proofs & arguments to trace their connexion with self-evident truths. But if any person will trace the inferences, which follow from the propositions here stated, in all their branches from the nearest to the most remote, he will in this way form a system of Ethics, and also of Theology. For by following them in their connexions and relations, he will be led to embrace all the leading doctrines contained in the Bible, and in the stupendous work of man's redemption by Christ Jesus.

Here is a proper place in connexion with what precedes to observe, *that in God all good, both absolute and relative, exists in an infinite fulness.*

God is an uncreated, infinite, eternal being. As he is infinite in knowledge, goodness, and power, it is evident he is possessed of the same powers or faculties with which he has endued moral agents. These attributes constitute his *essential glory* and fulness. He has an ultimate end in view in all his operations. This, as may soon appear, is the greatest measure of created happiness. This in itself is pleasant to his heart. This end, by affording him the greatest delight, has the influence of a motive, which induced him to employ his understanding in forming the best plan to reach his end, and his will in executing it ; in the accomplishment of this, his goodness, or benevolence, is infinitely displayed and diffused. Hence, as an infinite moral agent, he is influenced as created moral agents are. The difference between divine moral agency, and created, is this. God is an uncreated, infinite, independent, eternal agent. Men are created, finite, dependent agents. But the agency of each is similar in its *nature* or kind, differing only in *degree.* If God then, is a moral agent, men are.

God is infinitely happy and blessed. He accordingly enjoys *absolute good*, in an infinite measure. His essential fulness, being infinite, cannot be increased. But his fulness can be communicated and diffused. The only sense in which his infinite happiness can be increased, is by *diffusing* it. By a diffusion, emanation, or communication of absolute good, or of his happiness, is meant one and the same. He can diffuse his own infinite blessedness, by creating beings capable of happiness, and by rendering them perfectly holy and happy. In this way he is continually doing good, and displaying, or, which is the same thing, diffusing or communicating his own essential glory and fulness. It seems that Jehovah cannot effect and produce any greater good, than to make a perfect diffusion of his own infinite fulness. Hence the highest possible diffusion of his infinite fulness, is the *ultimate end* of God in all his works and operations. He not only aims at a display or diffusion of his fulness, but at a perfect, and *infinite diffusion*. Then his fulness exists *ab extra*, as some express it. By this infinite diffusion of his fulness, when made, the greatest created good or happiness will be produced, and all his attributes will be perfectly displayed ; which is his highest, declarative glory. When the greatest possible sum of created happiness exists, it will be seen that the highest possible diffusion of his fulness, and the brightest display of his perfections are made ; and this is his greatest declarative glory. Hence the greatest sum of created *happiness*, or *infinite diffusion* of the divine fulness, and the brightest *display of his attributes*, which all consider his declarative glory, are one and the same, viewed as an *ultimate end*. As light diffused by the natural sun is its glory, so a full and perfect diffusion of its light would be its brightest possible glory. As God is light, its highest possible diffusion would be its greatest glory, and this glory would be seen in the light diffused. So we behold, in the greatest sum of created happiness, the highest diffusion and glory of God. Accordingly, when we say the greatest sum of created happiness, or the highest diffusion of his fulness, or the brightest display of his essential glory, is his *ultimate end* in all his operations, the meaning is precisely the same. And as the greatest sum of happiness is God's ultimate end, and as all rational, created beings are finite, we may safely conclude their happiness will be forever increasing. For in no given period can it be said, that the greatest good, or an infinite diffusion, or disply of God's essential glory, has an *actual real existence*. It follows from this, that God will be forever diffusing his fulness, and displaying his perfections more and more, by the constant increase of created bliss. Hence his glory will shine with an increasing brightness through eternity, in view of which saints and angels will have their blessedness augmented. The greatest *sum* of happiness, is the phrase which has been used. Because it is not certain, that in order for the greatest sum of happiness to exist, it will be necessary to make the greatest *number* of individuals happy. Also the word of God assures us, that many of the fallen race of Adam will be forever lost. We may therefore safely conclude, that the happiness of the greatest number is not necessary to the greatest sum of created felicity.

To bring what has been advanced under this head distinctly to view, let it be carefully observed, that the infinite blessedness of God is an infinite measure of *absolute* good, existing in his fulness. And the greatest sum of created happiness is an *absolute* good, and the *highest good* of created beings, and of his holy kingdom. And this greatest sum of happiness, enjoyed by holy created beings, is the absolute good in God ; or his blessedness, diffused or communicated. And when we view the attributes of God in relation to this end, they constitute a sufficient ability in him to *devise* and *execute* a plan of operation however great and extensive, to reach and obtain his ultimate end. When viewed in this light his *attributes*, and all the *means* included in his plan, however many, are in a *relative sense good.* This explains what is intended and implied in saying that the being or fulness of God includes all good, both absolute and relative. He is then the infinite and eternal source of all good. And all the created good, both absolute and relative, which has, or ever will have existence, is no more than a diffusion, emanation, or communication of this infinite, eternal fountain. Hence, God is a being of infinite majesty, excellency, greatness, and glory. He ought, therefore, to be loved supremely, worshipped and served perfectly, by all his intelligent subjects, for his intrinsic excellency and beauty.

From the propositions which have been advanced, it follows, that the moral law is holy, just, and good. That it neither requires or forbids any thing, which the highest good does not either require or prohibit. Also it follows, that the work of redemption, which Christ is accomplishing, is, in all its parts, glorious and excellent. For its ultimate tendency, in all its parts, is to produce the greatest sum of happiness. And the sum of all the gospel requires, is love to God and our neighbor. Hence it harmonizes with the moral law, and tends ultimately to the same end. The gospel contains a glorious system of relative good ; and is a ministration of life.

The propositions explained teach us also, in what sense we ought to understand the terms *fitness* and *unfitness*, on which some place great weight. Some embrace the opinion, that there is a fitness and an unfitness, existing independent of the will of God. And as far as they can be understood, they seem to consider it as the rule or ultimate standard, by which we are to judge what is good and evil, right and wrong. They make it the standard, or origin, of moral obligation. By their reasoning they seem to consider it an eternal, independent, immutable standard, existing antecedent to the will of God, by which he, and all his rational creatures, ought to be governed. On this foundation they erect a system of Metaphysics and Ethics, if they are rightly understood.

Do they mean by it, that happiness is an absolute good, and misery an absolute evil ; and that all things are fit, or unfit, according as they tend ultimately to promote or destroy happiness ? If this be their meaning, then they agree with the scheme advanced and explained in the preceding essays. For it has been made sufficiently evident, that on supposition no happiness had ever been experienced by creatures, they could no more have any idea of good and evil, or of the terms fit and unfit, than a person born blind could have a clear idea of light and colors. If then they mean something entirely different from what has been termed absolute and relative good and evil ; their language either has no definite sense, or their views and system are erroneous, and built on the sand. Hence if the terms fit and unfit have any clear and definite meaning, their sense is, that all things are fit or unfit according to their ultimate tendency in promoting or destroying the happiness of God's kingdom.

Again. Some make *utility* the standard, by which we are to determine what is good and evil. This is a foundation on which some have erected a system of Ethics, if understood aright. Does not the term utility, as commonly used, have reference to some ultimate end ? And do we not call things useful or hurtful, according to their ultimate tendency ? So it seems. For those who proceed on the plan of utility, seem to consider the public good as the ultimate end to be sought, according to their system ; and hence consider every thing as useful or hurtful, as it tends to promote or destroy this end, the public good. If by the public good they mean the greatest happiness of a community, or society of beings ; and if in such society they mean to include God as the supreme head, and all created beings as his subjects, forming one entire whole, or society of beings ; and then say the greatest sum of happiness they can enjoy is their highest good ; and all things are useful or hurtful, as they tend to this end ultimately ; then they agree with the system, which has been exhibited. Then the real difference between us, would consist in the use of different terms. By the terms utility and *inutility* they would mean, what has been called all along relative good and evil. And if this be not their meaning, and their system is essentially different from ours, as has been explained ; then it must be considered as erroneous, like the system of the fitness and unfitness of things.

Before this essay is closed, a few further reflections appear to be necessary. One sentiment, which has already been advanced respecting moral agency, ought to be deeply impressed on every mind. Because it might silence some objections often made against the Calvinistic views of depravity. To bring it distinctly into view, this question may be stated. Did infinite wisdom and benevolence require the creation of moral agents ? All created beings had a beginning. And as the Creator is perfectly wise and good, he would give existence to as many things, as are necessary to the highest good, and no more. On this principle, it is generally granted, it was requisite to the general good a race of beings should be created, endued with all the properties essential to moral agency. In order to the existence of such a class of creatures, they must be endued with a *feeling* faculty, or capacity for pleasure and pain. For, if they have not this property, they are not, neither can be, agents.

It has been made evident, that such a faculty constitutes agency ; and is the primary, and only active principle in moral agents. Divest them of it, and mankind would remain as inactive as the inanimate creation is. Hence, if moral agents are created, they must be endued with that faculty, which is denominated taste. And this faculty must have a *nature ;* by which I mean, it must be *pleased,* or the contrary, with the divine character, and with the whole system of moral or divine objects, whenever they are distinctly perceived and known. As it is a feeling faculty, it cannot be in a state of indifference when objects are in view, and especially such impressive objects as the divine character, and the system of truths God has revealed. Will not this be granted ? Surely it must ; and of course, if a moral agent is created, he must have this faculty, and in view of the divine character he must experience pleasure or pain in a greater or less degree. If the character of God and revealed doctrines, please him, are agreeable to his feelings, he will have a desire to honor Him, defend the truth, and promote the good of his kingdom. If his character is disagreeable to him, his heart or taste is opposed to God, and will lead him to act the part of an enemy. This feeling faculty, if it exists, will be pleased or disgusted in view of God's character and will influence man to pursue a line of conduct, which will ultimately tend to promote or destroy the happiness of God's kingdom ; and this tendency is what is meant by its nature. And if created, it must have such a *nature*, and its nature must be *holy* or *sinful*. For such a nature as described, is necessarily good or evil, sinful or holy, according to its tendency.

Can a tree be created to bring forth a particular species of fruit, without giving it a *nature* to produce it ? Must not all created things be adapted to the end for which they were made, or have a *nature* given them to answer their designed end ? Here is a wide field open for enlargement, and illustration of the subject before us. But I stop with this request to all, to consider whether any thing can be created without a nature, which will have a good or evil tendency, if nothing prevents its operating according to its nature ; and whether we can name one thing, which, in this sense, is not endowed with a nature? If not, then, if a moral agent is created, he must have a feeling faculty given him, and this must have a *nature*, which is good or evil, or which will tend to promote or destroy happiness ultimately.

These observations are made, because some suppose moral agents may be created without any nature, either good or evil, and may have objects in view, and even contemplate the divine character, and remain in a state of *perfect indifference ;* and be inclined no way, to good or evil, or even to remain as they are. In this state they are like inert matter, and have no more feeling. Are such beings agents? No ; and as they are now indifferent towards all divine objects, on this ground they must remain so forever, and never act. They may be acted upon by some foreign agent, as the earth is, but they can never act as agents. Such a view of a moral agent is inconsistent with analogy, with experience, with facts, and the word of God ; and it is as unphilosophical as to say, God has created trees to bring forth particular kinds of fruit, but he has not given them a nature to bear *any kind* of fruit. It is a matter of indifference with them what kind of fruit they bear, or whether they bring forth fruit of any kind ; and of course they never will or can be fruit trees.

As it is now evident, if moral agents are created, they must be endued with a feeling, active faculty, and this faculty must have a nature good or evil ; so we find from revelation, that when God created Adam, he did endue him with this active faculty, which made him an agent ; and this faculty had a good, a *holy nature.* He was made in the likeness of God, natural and moral ; and was as completely a moral agent as Jehovah himself. And we read of no moral agents, but such as were at first endued with a holy nature. This was the fact with respect to all created angels, and with respect to Adam. With this, it is supposed, no one will find any fault. They are willing God should create moral agents with a holy nature. At least all are willing for this, except those who wish to have a race of moral, indifferent agents created; that is to have beings created, who are agents, yet without agency, or active principles. They would have them active, yet all the time in a state of perfect indifference. They wish to have God do what is morally impossible. Many are pleased with God's creating Adam with a holy nature ; yet they cannot peaceably endure the idea of necessary holiness, or sin. Though they are more satisfied with the former, than with the latter. Yet the nature of every thing, if it exist, must be good or evil. As no fault can be found with God, in creating Adam at first as he did, unless it is because he was necessarily holy ; the next inquiry is, whether blame can be imputed to Him for suffering, or permitting Adam to eat of the forbidden fruit ? And then in consequence of this to take from him the holy nature, or benevolent appetite, with which he had been created? That such a change did take place, that holy Adam became a sinner, is generally granted. As God might have prevented it, the question is, whether it was wise and holy for Him to permit this change to take place. As this is a question, which the scheme advanced in these essays does not require me to answer, any more than others whatever their system is, no further attention will be given to it. The author will here only observe, that he has a dissertation on the fall, or introduction of sin, which aims at a solution of the difficulties, which have ever attended this subject. But whether it will ever be laid before the public eye, depends much on the approbation or disapprobation these essays may receive from the community in general.

Furthermore. Some consider the doctrine of total depravity, as explained and defended by reputed and orthodox divines, to be *physical.* And being physical in its nature, the opponents consider it as destroying agency and blameworthiness. Viewing the doctrine in this light, they pronounce it very alarming and appalling. It is not designed here to inquire, whether some have, or have not, so explained it as to imply a *physical defect;* or in what precise sense opponents use the word physical. They scorn to consider *any* defect in the soul, which incapacitates it for holy exercises, to be a *physical* defect. They therefore, in opposition to this, represent our race as born with capacities, which are inclined neither to vice nor virtue, oras destitute of any *moral nature ;* and are, like clean paper, liable to receive impressions, which are holy or sinful according to the influence motives have upon them. In connexion with this sentiment, they affirm men are the efficient causes of all their exercises and actions of a moral class. Is the doctrine of depravity, which has been expressly or implicitly exhibited in these essays, so appalling as represented ? According to the system advanced, it is admitted that Aɒam was created in the moral image of his Maker, or perfectly holy. When first created, he was endued with several distinct appetites or propensities. Each of these was a primary, active principle in his constitution, and constituted him an *agent.* One of those appetites was benevolent in its nature, in which the moral image of God consisted. And his other appetites or propensities were given and implanted in him, as active principles, which prepared him to propagate the human race, nourish and protect them in infancy, to provide means for the support and comfort of the body or the whole man, while he remains an inhabitant of the earth. And while these appetites, inferior in their nature, were under the control and direction of his benevolent propensity, or love to God, their operations would harmonize in a regular course of conduct, and no sin or disorder could prevail in paradise.

But Adam, by eating the prohibited fruit, forfeited into the hand of his benefactor that moral image in which he was created, and which was his glory, and it was taken from him. From that day he had no propensity or love in his heart towards his Maker. All his other appetites remained unaffected and unaltered, as principles of action. Here it may be asked, was he not as really a moral agent after his fall as before? Had he not active principles in his heart, which constituted him a complete agent for action? And when this moral image or benevolent appetite is restored to man in regeneration, is he any more an agent for action, than he was previous to this change? If any man is born blind, or after his birth becomes blind, is he not still a man, as really as those who have eyes? And if eyes are given him, is he on this account any more a man, than before? All that can be said of the blind man he is, not in all respects so perfect, as those who have all their senses entire. He labors under a defect or imperfection ; still he is a man. Adam by eating was deprived of one *sense*, or appetite, with which his Maker had adorned him; yet he was an agent, and had all the properties or capacities, which constitute a complete moral agent. Hence he had all the qualifications, necessary to render him a proper object of praise or blame, according to the moral nature or state of his heart. If opponents consider this loss in Adam a *physical defect*, incapacitating him for holy exercises ; yet it does not in the least destroy, or impair the powers requisite to moral agency, or to render him a proper object of blame. Hence what is there alarming or appalling in this description of total depravity? Though man in all respects is not so *perfect* a moral agent, as before this defect existed ; yet he is as complete a moral agent as ever. He has the faculty of understanding, and of will ; he has a faculty to which active principles belong, and which constitute agency ; and he may and will be influenced and governed by motives, and act with aim and design, as Adam did before his fall, and as men do after they are regenerated, and have this moral defect repaired. This defect, which opponents call *physical*, is in fact no more than a *moral defect*. Hence they give it a wrong name. And it is presumed, that orthodox divines in general will contend for no other defect in man, than the one here described. While this defect continues, man is totally depraved ; or he is destitute of every holy principle of action, in consequence of which all his other active principles will lead him away from God the living fountain, after broken cisterns or earthly enjoyments, which never satisfy the soul. Hence orthodox divines have nothing to fear from the attack, by which they are represented as imputing to man a physical defect, which is in truth no more than a moral defect.

If mankind are born with an *efficient power*, which is not inclined either to vice or virtue, but is in fact indifferent to both : it is believed to be impossible to show how this efficient power can exercise itself, without implying the previous existence of a disposition either to sin or holiness. And if a previous disposition must exist, to put this power into exercise, then all the ends supposed to be answered by it are defeated. But concerning what might have been said to show the absurdity of this scheme, the reader for farther light is referred to essay twenty first. But if, by a sel. determining power, and an efficient power to produce all our exercises and actions, no more is intended than this, that in order for mankind to be agents, they ought to be endued with a *feeling*, *active* faculty, by which the whole man is governed, and from which all his exercises and actions proceed, it must be granted, that men do possess this faculty or power. Then all the actions and exercises of men may be traced back to this faculty, as the primary active principle from which they proceed, or flow as streams from a fountain. And as they cannot be traced back any farther, or to any previous active principle in men, this faculty, which has been denominated the taste, is the *primary active power*, which constitutes agency, and gives rise to all our voluntary exertions and actions. I say, if such a faculty is what others mean by a self determining, efficient power, it is granted ; and some pains have been taken to prove, that mankind are in fact endued with it ; and that without it they would not be agents, and could not be considered as moral agents.

If opponents admit this, then the dispute is ended, concerning the nature and degree of power requisite to constitute a moral agent, and nothing further need be said on either side.

But if they advance an idea of an efficient power, which has no nature, inclined to neither good nor evil, and is in itself indifferent. they are laboring, it is fully believed, to establish and prove the existence of an *impossibility*. For an active power, or efficiency, must necessarily have a nature to be influenced by motives, to be pleased or the contrary with moral objects. And if it have not such a nature, it is no active power, and can never operate in any other way, than an instrument used by some other external and foreign agent. This, it is thought, has been proved in the previous essays.—Before this essay is concluded a few things may be suggested for the notice of the public.

The author is is not so vain as to expect the sentiments advanced will meet with universal, or perhaps with general approbation. Some may think the leading sentiments exhibited are erroneous and dangerous. With this belief some opponent may attempt an answer, and confutation. If any should judge this to be his duty, it is hoped his attention will be confined exclusively to the sentiments, which are considered dangerous. For it is often the case when an answer is written against a book, that much time and labor are spent in searching after, and noticing inconsistencies. And there are but few books of much magnitude, which are entirely free from inconsistencies less or greater. Pointing out these, is not confuting an author. For his leading sentiments may be true, although inconsistencies may have escaped his notice. Showing a writer is inconsistent, is proving his mind to be finite, liable to err, and unable to comprehend a whole system so as to see at one view the agreement of all the parts. But does this show his leading sentiments to be erroneous? By no means. Hence time and labor, spent in noticing inconsistencies, are in a great measure lost. A writer may be consistent with himself in propagating errors, though inconsistent with truth. Therefore, until the sentiments advanced are confuted, a book is not answered.

Every attentive reader will see, that the system exhibited in these essays rests on a few plain propositions, or obvious truths. If these are shown to be false and dangerous, the book is answered. If then, an opponent can make it evident, that a feeling faculty, or a capacity for pleasure and pain, denominated taste, does not constitute agency, but something else distinct from it ; if he can prove that such agency has no *nature*, no inclination or tendency to good or evil, but is indifferent as any unfeeling property ; if he can show that happiness is not an absolute good, nor misery an absolute evil ; and that means or things are not called good and evil according to their ultimate tendency to promote or destroy happiness ; if he can prove, that benevolence is not an appetite or love for the greatest good of God's kingdom, and this is not its ultimate end ; also, that those desires of the heart, which tend ultimately to diminish and destroy happiness, are not evil or sinful ; then it is granted he has shaken the foundation on which the system advanced rests. And if he should accomplish this, it is fully believed he will make it evident, that men are not moral agents, or proper objects of praise and blame, and future rewards ; in a word, that they are not accountable beings, any more than in-

22

animate things. Doing all this, would effectually serve the cause of infidelity.

But if after all his labor these truths shall remain firm, that a *primary active* principle does constitute agency ; and that no property or faculty can be active in its nature, if incapable of feeling, or of pleasure and pain ; and of course that the faculty of taste, as it has been explained, has a feeling nature, is the subject of pleasant and painful sensations, and does constitute that agency which is a primary active principle by which men are governed in all their actions ; if after all it does remain true, that happiness is an absolute good, and misery an absolute evil ; and that other things are denominated *relatively* good or evil, according to their ultimate tendency in promoting or destroying happiness ; and accordingly that benevolence aims ultimately at this highest good, and all the desires of the heart of unrenewed men tend ultimately to misery ; if these truths remain unshaken, and unconfuted ; then the main pillars of the system remain entire and firm, and the building, which rests upon them, is not demolished.

This will be a fact, although an opponent may show some small errors, and some inconsistencies, interspersed here and there in different parts of the book. It is then the earnest request of the author, if it is judged reasonable, that an opponent who may attempt an answer would confine himself to these leading, fundamental truths, on which the whole system rests. This would be keeping to the point, and would sooner bring the dispute to a close. When persons suffer themselves to wander from the real questions disputed, a controversy may be protracted without any conclusion.

The book is now committed to the public, whose property it is. Let it be read with candor, free from every prejudice. If it should reflect any light on the first and leading and fundamental principles of Ethics and Theology, and should give a lead to further investigations, and the enlargement of our knowledge of these important sciences, and the good and prosperity of the Redeemer's kingdom, the prayers of the author will be thus far answered.

ESSAY XXXI.

*On the happiness of heaven, showing in what it consists.

Hebrews, 4. 9.   *There remaineth, therefore, a rest unto the people of God.——* This rest is heaven, a state of perfect felicity.

This is a subject very interesting. For unless we know what heaven is, we can never determine whether we are real Saints or not. The elysium of the heather, and the paradise of the Mahometans, are places of great happiness, as they believe. Still the sources of happiness are such, as described by them, that no change of heart is necessary to enjoy them. Indeed the most voluptuous, and carnal, those most fond of every kind of animal pleasure, may be happy in the heavens they describe.

If a person should form an idea of a country on this earth, where all the inhabitants are perfectly happy ; yet, if he had no knowledge of the particular sources of their felicity, he might conclude, if he lived there he should also enjoy all the bliss of the inhabitants. And from a belief that all in that country are happy, he might have a very ardent desire to remove to it. Yet, when he arrives there, he finds the particular sources of their happiness are very disgustful to him. To him, instead of happiness, it is a place of misery. Had he inquired, and obtained a distinct knowledge of the particular sources of happiness in that land, he might have convinced himself, that he could not delight in such objects. And he would have no desire to remove there, unless his relish could be suited to those particular sources of happiness.

Many by reading the bible learn that heaven is a land of perfect bliss. Being convinced it is a place of happiness, they inquire no further ; but conclude, if they were admitted there they should certainly be happy. As they have no distinct idea of the sources of happiness in that world, or of the relish necessary to enjoy them, it is impossible for them to say whether they could or could not be happy if admitted there. And if they conclude they are saints, merely from the idea that they wish to live there, they may be deceived.

---

*This essay has no necessary connexion with those which precede, to elucidate the author's *philosophical* system. It shews, however, the practical application of his principles ; and as it relates to an important subject, it is here subjoined to make the volume more complete.

All men wish to be happy. And because heaven is a land of pure bliss, many conclude they should be happy, if admitted to live there. But this is false reasoning. To be happy in Heaven we must have a relish for the particular sources of happiness in that world. And we cannot determine with any certainty, whether we are prepared for that country, only by ascertaining in the first place clear, distinct and just ideas of the particular sources from whence all derive their happiness ; and then by inquiring, whether we have such a relish for them, as to prefer them to all other objects of delight. Hence it is a matter of the last importance, to obtain a distinct knowledge of the sources of heavenly bliss. A mistake here may prove fatal.

And all our knowledge of heaven must be from the word of God. No one has lived there, and returned, to give us a description of that world. God in his word has described it. If we can clearly understand the description he has given, we may know what heaven is.

And it is more or less difficult to understand the description he has given. It is given generally in figurative language. One question of importance is, whether we are to understand his description in a *literal*, or *figurative* sense. Many things serve to show they are to be understood in a figurative sense. Then the next difficulty is, to explain the figures according to their true sense.

In order to remove, in some measure, these difficulties, several preliminary remarks are necessary, before we proceed to a particular description of the heavenly sources of felicity.

As the terms, *sources of happiness*, will be frequently used in this essay, it is requisite to show what is meant by them. Three things are requisite to the existence of happiness. First, a relish of heart to feel and enjoy ; or a relish to be *pleased* and *delighted* with objects. 2. Objects to please and delight us. 3. The objects must exist in the view of the mind.

For example. If a person has an ardent thirst for water, he cannot have it gratified, unless he can find water to drink. Water may exist in great plenty, yet he not know where to find it. Hence he may thirst, and there may be water to gratify it, yet he may not have his thirst quenched. He must have a knowledge of it. Then he can drink and be satisfied. Here the water, which satisfies his thirst, is what I mean by a source of happiness.

Of course all the objects in heaven, which afford joy to the inhahitants, are what I mean by sources of happiness. Objects of pleasure, and sources of pleasure are used to mean the same thing. Hence, to enjoy the pleasures of heaven, a person must have a *relish* for heavenly objects ; he must see them ; then while in view his relish is gratified, and in this his happiness consists.

The preliminary remarks to be made are the following.

1. All our animal appetites and natural affections will cease at death, we shall have none of them in heaven.

Our bodily appetites are many. So, also, are our natural affections, such as those termed parental, conjugal, filial, and fraternal. These were implanted in us for certain purposes, such as the preservation of life, the propagation of our species, the relief of persons in distress, and our comfort and well-being in this life.

If we had not conjugal affections, there would be nothing to prompt us to propagate our species ; without parental affection, infants would suffer and die ; without filial affection, there would be nothing to excite to obedience of parents or support of the aged ; without the affection children have for each other, there would be no peace in families ; and without natural pity, there would be nothing to move us to relieve and afford help to the weak, infirm, and objects of affliction and distress. All these natural principles of action are absolutely necessary to the being and comfort of the human race. For mankind naturally have no benevolence, to stimulate them to seek each others' good. These affections are requisite to supply the want of benevolence, while this earth is to be our abode.

These natural principles of action are the fountain, from which all the other affections we have flow. But they will cease at death ; because there will be no use for them, or need of them, in the other world. That they will be eradicated at death in the saints, (and I speak only of them,) is evident from several considerations.

1. After death, saints will be as the angels of heaven. Not equal, but *like* them. *They* have none of these natural affections ; if we are like them, we shall not have them. This teaches, that these natural feelings then cease to exist.

2. It is necessary they should be eradicated, otherwise saints would not be perfectly happy. In that world we are informed they never marry. If the same inclinations prevailed there

as here, as they would not be gratified, they would render saints unhappy. Uneasiness would be excited, without any means of removing it. If they have the same affection there as here, the misery of wives, husbands, and children, would excite more or less painful feelings. It seems, then, to be requisite to perfect happiness, that these feelings should be eradicated at death.

3. The nature of the body, when raised, teaches the same truth. At the resurrection, the body will be raised immortal, incorruptible, and spiritual. Hence it will never hunger or thirst, or be diseased, or weary. Of course, it will never need food, clothing, sleep, rest, or medicine. Hence there will be no use for those natural affections we have here. Also this world will be destroyed. And there will be an end to all labor for food and clothing.

These considerations teach us clearly, that all our natural and bodily affections will be eradicated at death ; or at least that they will never operate, or be felt in heaven. Because there will be need of them there ; and if they were to remain and operate in that world, they would lessen and interrupt the happiness of saints, and render that state imperfect.

And if these natural affections all cease to exist at death, it follows, that in heaven there will not be any worldly sources of happiness. There will be no bread, water, or food of any kind ; because none will be needed. There will be no natural pity, because there will be no objects of distress to relieve. There will be no houses, or lands ; because none of these things will be needed there. No part of the happiness of heaven will be derived from the gratification of such natural affections ; because such affections will not exist there. Hence, from the consideration that all these natural principles of action, which operate here, will cease at death, it is evident the descriptions of heaven in the bible are not to be construed *literally* but *figuratively*. To be convinced of this, is one thing necessary to form just views of a heavenly state ; and to understand the word of God according to its true import and meaning.

How can we form right and just ideas of the happiness of heaven, so long as we know not whether the descriptions given us of that world, are to be construed literally, or figuratively ? We must first know in what sense to understand the description given us of heaven, before we can form any true conceptions of that world. This remark therefore is made, to show that the description of heaven in the word of God must be understood *figuratively*.

2. If the descriptions given us of heaven are to be understood literally, why may not sinners, without any change of heart, be happy there ? If in heaven there will be cities, with walls and gates made of the precious stones ; streets paved with gold ; houses rich and elegant ; rivers of water, and all manner of fruits ; and every thing, which suits the taste and relish of natural men here, why may they not be happy there, as they now are here ? If the descriptions given us of heaven are to be understood in a literal sense, it is a place every way suited to the relish of men of this world who love nothing else. It would suit their pride and ambition, to be made kings and priests ; to possess riches, and inherit a kingdom in the literal sense.

Those objects in this world, which are the most *valuable, precious, beautiful, and delightful*, are represented as being in heaven in a great abundance, and in a perfect state. Those things in this world, which in the most perfect manner, suit their relish, and gratify their love of riches, the pride, and ambition of men here, are to be enjoyed in heaven in a far more perfect, uninterrupted manner, than they are here ; if we are to construe the description literally. If wicked men in heaven should find some things disagreeable ; they would experience many other things, which would afford them great satisfaction. So that if they would not be perfectly happy there, they would be far more happy and contented, than they are here.

But we are given to understand, that the unrenewed would not be happy in heaven, if admitted to live there. Christ says except a man be born again, he *cannot see* the kingdom of heaven. He does not mean that they would not have any knowledge of that world, or of the objects existing in it. This is not what he means by *seeing*. For the unrenewed are capable of this speculative knowledge, and in fact have it in a greater or less degree. He means then, that they *cannot enjoy* the objects of that world, because they are not suited to their relish. But if the descriptions of heaven are to be understood *literally*, they may *enjoy* them there, as well as they do here.

And why is not the description Mahomet has given of heaven in general just, if the descriptions of the bible are to be construed literally, as some contend ; and why may not sinners enjoy it, and be happy there, without any change ?

Hence the bible, by teaching us that a change of heart is necessary to the happiness of heaven, and that the unrenewed would not enjoy heavenly objects if admitted there, assures us that the description given us of that world must be understood, not in a literal, but a figurative sense.

3. Saints in heaven will be perfectly holy, as God is holy. This will teach us, that the descriptions of heaven are figurative, and not literal. By the fall of man all have lost the moral image of God. No trace of his moral likeness remains in man.

We are assured that this moral image is restored in regeneration. We are born of the Spirit. And that which is born of the Spirit is spirit. That which is created in the heart when men are renewed, is spiritual in its nature. The *nature* of the Holy Spirit is produced in the heart. So we become partakers of the divine *nature*, as we are taught. That is, the moral image of God is restored. But God is love. Love, or benevolence, is the moral perfection of God. This is the sum of all his moral attributes

When the same benevolent disposition is created in our heart, then his moral image is restored. This is the new man which is to grow until we arrive to the stature of a perfect man in Christ. Saints in heaven are perfectly holy—this moral image will be perfected in them.

Hence in heaven the only principle of action needed, and the only one which will operate, is benevolence, or love. By this only saints are governed, or influenced, as God is. But the nature of benevolence is such, it does not delight in any worldly sources of felicity. The only objects of its delight are *divine*, *heavenly*, and *spiritual* in their nature. It has no delight in worldly riches, or honors, or pleasure, (which are the only objects of sinners' love,) except as *means* to obtain these divine objects, which are its source of felicity. But in heaven the riches and honors of this world will not be needed, as *means* to obtain spiritual objects and enjoyments. Hence benevolence in heaven has no delight in such worldly objects. It is pleased and gratified with the same divine objects, which are the sources of God's blessedness ; or in which his benevolence delights.

Accordingly the very nature of benevolence is such, which will be the only governing principle in heaven, that no objects will afford it delight there, but those which are spiritual and divine ; such as those in which divine love, or benevolence delights. This serves to show, that the happiness of heaven is not derived from any worldly objects, but wholly from those which are divine. And hence no worldly objects will be needed, or be enjoyed there. And if not, then the description of heaven must be construed in a figurative, and not in a literal sense.

Are not these remarks sufficient to convince every one, that when we find heaven represented in the bible by terms which belong to worldly objects, we are not to understand such descriptions in a literal sense ?

And is it not evident, that we can never have any true and just conception of a heavenly state, of that rest which remaineth unto the people of God, until we know whether the descriptions given us of heaven are to be understood in a literal or figurative sense ? And if not, then every one cannot but see that the remarks made are pertinent, and necessary in order to a just view of the heavenly world. For they serve to convince us we must construe such passages, generally, in a figurative sense. If we can ascertain the true meaning of such figures, we shall then form just conceptions of heaven. It is granted great care ought to be used in construing figures. We must not follow a lively imagination, but attend carefully to their obvious import and meaning. And as benevolence is the only governing principle in heaven ; and of course, as the happiness of that world must consist in gratifying this benevolent disposition ; just views of the nature of benevolence will serve to guide us, and teach us, what the sources of happiness in heaven are. It is then designed

II. To attend to the nature of benevolence, as far as is necessary to understand the sources of heavenly felicity.

This being the foundation of the happiness of heaven, understanding its nature will lead us to a correct knowledge of heavenly blessedness. We may rely on it, that whatever suits, delights, and gratifies a benevolent relish, is a source of happiness in heaven. Every object in the world, which delights and gratifies this divine love or taste, is a source of happiness.

So far as any person's happiness in this world is derived from food and drink, we cannot tell what will make him happy, until we learn what kind of food will suit his taste. Then we know in what his happiness consists, and how to suit and please him. So when we learn in what benevolence delights,

23

we learn in what heavenly felicity consists. Hence it is very important to learn the nature of divine benevolence.

To do this we may proceed to observe, that every moral agent must have some ultimate end in view in all his actions. That ultimate end must be some object, on its *own account agreeable* ; and in which the highest good of the universe consists. For all will agree, that benevolence is friendly to the highest good, will seek it, and rejoice in it. Happiness, not his own but that of others, is the highest good of a benevolent individual ; and the greatest sum of happiness in God's kingdom is that greatest good which he will seek as his ultimate end. And it is the nature of benevolence, whether in God or in men, to seek the highest happiness of the universe as its ultimate end. This truth is made evident in the essay on the nature of holiness or benevolence ; and the remarks need not be here repeated. This prepares the way for us to see clearly and distinctly what must be

III. The positive sources of happiness enjoyed in heaven.

If the greatest sum of happiness is the greatest good ; and the nature of benevolence is such as to seek and delight in it, as its ultimate end, as has been shown, then,

1. The happiness of God's heavenly kingdom, is the first and greatest source of felicity to all who surround his throne.

A saint in heaven, when he contemplates the happiness of that society, beholds each one perfectly blessed ; his own heart will have a feast, and he will experience joys which are unspeakable.

Nothing in this world fills the heart of a benevolent king with so great joy, as to see all his subjects prosperous and happy. And nothing affords benevolent parents so much pure delight, as the happiness of all the members of the family. And children, if benevolent, rejoice in no object in this world so much, as in beholding their parents and all around them completely happy. And what in this world ever gives such pure and great joy to a saint, as to see a sinner, when renewed, rejoicing in God ?

And Paul, when Titus returned, and informed him of the happiness of the church at Corinth, rejoiced greatly. He rejoiced in their joy. Their joy was the source of his joy. And when the prodigal returned, and was joyful in his father's house, the whole family were feasted with joy and gladness, except his elder brother.

Every person, who is a real saint, can testify by experience, that the spiritual joys and comforts of his brethren, is the sweetest source of happiness to himself. Reason, experience, and scripture all unite in saying, that the happiness of others is the greatest source of joy. No other object the saints behold, affords them so great and pure delight.

Let us then in this light take a view of heaven. There saints surround the throne of God and the Lamb. When they contemplate the infinite blessedness of their heavenly Father, what joy they must experience. They love him with all their heart, and to behold the object of their love, and the fountain of all the good they possess, infinitely happy, will fill their souls with joy. Suppose he appeared to them unhappy ; this would fill them with grief and pain. If so, then his perfect bliss must afford them great joy.

When they contemplate the infinite happiness of Christ their friend and beloved, will not this excite in them the sweetest delight ? The joys of heaven, which he was to experience, was the prize set before him here on earth. When they behold him, who for the joy set before him, endured the cross, now receiving his reward in the infinite bliss he experiences, this will fill every heart with joys unspeakable.

All the saints in heaven are the sons and daughters of God, and the bride of the Lamb. And their happiness is the great end God sought, and an object of his delight ; and the Son will rejoice in his bride ; nothing will afford him more satisfaction, than her happiness. In her happiness he sees the fruit of the travail of his soul for her. If the Father and Son rejoice in the happiness of saints ; saints, who have the same heart, will rejoice in the infinite blessedness of the Trinity. To see the Holy Spirit, who sanctified & prepared them for heaven, infinitely blessed, will afford them the greatest satisfaction. Hence the boundless happiness of all the persons in the Trinity, will feast the hearts of saints with joy unspeakable and full of glory.

Again. When saints in heaven behold each other's happiness ; when they see all around them perfectly blessed, enjoying that bliss, which will continue and increase forever, what inward satisfaction they will experience. And the feelings and desires of their hearts will be perfectly gratified. They will rejoice in each other's joy. And the happiness of angels, who ministered to them here, will also be a source of joy to them,

In heaven there is but one society, composed of a head and members. God is the head; saints and angels the members. They are perfectly united to their head, and to each other, by mutual love and affection. The greatest good, which can be obtained, they possess and enjoy; which is perfect, enduring, and increasing felicity. When they see each other in the full possession of this highest good, they will experience the most pure, refined, and sweet delight.

Oh how blessed is that society, where the happiness of others, instead of exciting envy and opposition, as is often the case in this world, is a source of exquisite joy. This is bliss, in the highest possible degree.

2. The *holiness* of others will be another source of happiness in heaven.

When saints enter heaven, they will be perfectly holy. For no sin, or any thing which defileth, is ever to enter there. And holiness is the moral image of God; the beauty and glory of every character. There is no other object in the universe, which equals holiness in beauty, glory, and utility; and no one equals it in *worth* but happiness; this exceeds it in value.

Holiness, tho so excellent, is not a good in itself; it is not loved for its own sake, but for the sake of happiness, of which it is the greatest means. If it be asked, why is holiness so beautiful and valuable? It is answered.

1. Because it *prepares* persons for everlasting felicity. Without holiness no man shall see God. Heaven is a perfectly holy state. None can enter there, but the perfectly benevolent. Hence, without it no person is prepared in the temper of his heart for heaven, or to enjoy holy objects, or to spend his time in holy employments. Without holiness no rational being can be happy. Benevolence, which is holiness, is the only quality, which prepares for a state of endless bliss. Is not that of infinite worth, which prepares a person for eternal felicity? What else, in this view, can equal it in value? If we were infinite in knowledge and power, yet had no benevolence, we should be fit for no place, but hell. It is holiness, and this *only*, which prepares a person for heaven, and the enjoyment of holy objects. Hence it exceeds in value gold, diamonds, and rubies. Nothing can purchase it, but the precious blood of Christ.

It is holiness only, which prepares and inclines persons to be *useful*, to seek and promote the happiness of God's kingdom.

When any have this temper of heart created in them, they delight in the happiness of others, and of God's kingdom. This then will incline and prompt them to promote and increase the bliss of heaven. It inclines them to exert all their powers and faculties, to improve their time, and every blessing of God, in promoting happiness. Paul, before his conversion, did all he could to destroy the souls of men. But when a benevolent disposition was given him, then with a zealous employment of all his powers, he labored to promote the salvation of souls. In like manner it inclines all to devote themselves wholly to the service of God, and the promotion of the happiness of his kingdom. In this view, what is there, which can equal it in worth? It is the most active principle which can exist, and which will forever exert itself in making men happy, and increasing the felicity of heaven. For these two reasons, tho holiness is not excellent on its own account, but merely as a means of happiness, we see its value and glory are infinite. Happiness excepted there is nothing else, which equals it in value. It is this, which inclines God to employ all his attributes in promoting infinite and eternal happiness. It prepares persons for a state of endless bliss; and to exert all their powers in promoting the eternal felicity of heaven. Therefore its beauty, glory, loveliness, and excellency, exceed all description, and conception.

In heaven, the individuals who compose an innumerable host, are perfectly holy. Hence they are perfect in beauty; perfectly resemble their Maker; and as stars shine with the brighest possible rays.

When a saint beholds the infinite holiness of God, sees he is love itself, what joy this will diffuse through his soul. When he contemplates the holiness of Christ, he beholds a sun shining with infinite brightness. This is the glory of the godhead, which is the light of heaven; and which far exceeds the sun in brightness, so that there is no need of sun or moon there. Saints will dwell forever in the rays of this glory.—The rays of divine, infinite holiness, will warm, soften, and quicken their hearts, and fill then with joys pure, sweet, and extatic.

And how beautiful and glorious will saints and angels appear to each other. When one saint beholds another, he sees a star, which shines with a golden lustre, whose rays are mild, pleasant, and joyful. They are beautiful in each other's sight, yea perfect in beauty.

Here on earth, nothing affords greater joy, than to see in another this benevolent spirit. This excites the mutual love of saints, and unites them together by the strong bonds of brotherly affection. They are near, and dear, and precious to each other ; delighting in each other's society and conversation. How much greater will be their joy in each other in heaven, where holiness is made perfect.

Wherever they turn their eyes, they behold the holiness of the Trinity, of saints, of angels, shiring with such beauty, mildness, brightness and glory, as diffuses life and joy through their souls, and fills them with divine pleasures. Here are joys flowing forevermore at the right hand of God, of which they drink their full draughts. Behold what glories fill heaven. Beauties innumerable, perfect, and infinite, employ their eyes, and feasts their hearts, day and night forever.

3. *The glory of God*, will be another source of felicity in heaven.

This is included in part in what has been already said ; but needs some enlargement in one particular. For other attributes, beside holiness, and this in its various operations, will be a source of pleasure.—Indeed, the glory of God, and the highest good of his kingdom, are one and the same. The highest good obtained is the greatest declarative glory of God For in the attainment of this end, all his attributes are displayed, and his fulness communicated ; and the holy society of heaven enjoy this communicated fulness. But here a more particular attention is necessary, to the glory displayed in producing the greatest sum of happiness, which is the highest good.

In heaven all the works of God will be the study of saints. As they delight in studying his works *here*, which are a glass in which he is seen ; much more will they delight in surveying them in heaven. The works of God are a boundless field for saints to explore, in doing which their knowledge will increase, and their capacities enlarge and expand.

In the works of creation they will see the wonderful displays of infinite knowledge and power. They will see clearly the end of all these works. They will see clearly how all the parts, from the least atom to the greatest world, have unitedly promoted the ultimate end of God. For when all the elect of Christ are assembled in heaven, his ultimate end is then attained. Now saints have only to look back, and learn how all his works have been perfectly adapted to his end. They will

see the manner in which they have been arranged and connected, and with united influence have in the best way promoted the happiness of his kingdom. In this way they will have
clear views of his infinite knowledge, power, goodness, and all
his glorious attributes.

When a mechanic is making a clock, we may view the parts,
and see much ingenuity displayed. But when he has finished
it, then we clearly see the end and use of it; we see how all
the parts are arranged, connected, and adapted to their end.
We then see, if one cog in the wheel were wanting, it would
render the whole imperfect. But now we behold and admire
the great ingenuity of the artist.

The created universe is a grand and sublime machine. The
worlds and particles which compose it, are innumerable. God
is now making and putting the parts together ; arranging and
connecting them, with a view to the greatest happiness ultimately. In heaven saints will view them in a finished state.
And the more their knowledge of the parts increases, of their
arrangement and connection, and perfect adaptedness to their
end, the more distinct their views will be of all his attributes.
Now they clearly see, that his boundless knowledge, wisdom,
power, goodness, and every attribute, have been employed in
promoting the greatest possible happiness of his holy kingdom.
They see every part has contributed to this end ; and if one
small thing had been either added or diminished, his works
would have been imperfect. As we see in a clock, if one wheel
had one more or less number of cogs, it would have injured the
whole machine. In thus studying the works of creation, they
will have enlarged and exalted views of the greatness of God ;
and will be filled with wonder, and joy, and ascribe greatness
to him forever. Thus the study of the works of creation will
be a constant source of delightful entertainment, and contribute
to the increase of the happiness of saints.

Then the study of the works of providence will afford them
still greater delight. These works are like a building. God
has been collecting the materials, arranging and connecting
them, from the beginning of time, and will finish it at the
close. Then saints can survey the building in a finished state.
It will be one part of their delightful study, to examine all
the parts, their order, and connection, and adaptedness to their
end. Here they will see the work of redemption is the principal part in this building ; that all the other parts have ref-

erence to this, and are subordinated to it. They will clearly see the attributes of God displayed in these works.

When God was executing the part of his plan, which related to Jacob and his family, every thing appeared dark and mysterious to Jacob ; which made him say, all these things are against me. But now, when that part is finished, we look at it, and behold its perfection, and the wonderful displays of wisdom, power and goodness. From this we learn, that we cannot form correct views of the character of a workman, while he is making his work; but when it is finished, then we can see his design, and the perfection and wisdom of his plan. So it is with respect to the works of providence ; now many events appear dark and mysterious, which gives occasion to the wicked to murmur, to censure the works of God, and pronounce them unwise, and thus blaspheme their Maker.

But when viewed by saints in heaven, in their finished state, they will see, as in a glass, the glorious and astonishing displays of his attributes ; especially in the work of redemption. They will have increasing views of his boundless greatness, majesty, glory and benevolence ; and see that he alone is qualified to fill the throne of the universe, to rule and govern all worlds according to his pleasure. In the same proportion they will see their own comparative nothingness, weakness and dependence ; and forever when they fall at his feet, will ascribe wisdom, honor, power, dominion, and greatness to God, saying wonderful are thy works, Lord God almighty ; and to the Lamb they will say, worthy art thou to receive the same ascriptions of glory ; for thou hast redeemed us with thy blood. In heaven, they will see that all the works of God, both of creation and providence, are parts of one plan, perfectly harmonising in promoting the same end ; and perfectly agreeing with every thing revealed in the word of God.

In heaven, they have the three great volumes, of creation, providence, and the word, open before them. Here they see the same character displayed in *actions* and in *words*. His works are his actions, and the bible contains his words, by which he has revealed and displayed himself.

These volumes contain an infinite fund of knowledge, and open to view a boundless field. Reading and studying them will be one of the employments of heaven ; an employment, which will afford them continual, and increasing joy ; and here is one source of the happiness of that world. This study will be a source of delight, because they see more and more distinctly the displays of the divine glory in them.

Hence the reason why John, when in vision he saw a part of the works of God completed, as the ruin of the beast and his power, he and the heavenly hosts in chorus ascribe greatness, power, dominion and glory to God. Here they saw his attributes displayed, and his benevolence in promoting the happiness of heaven, and defeating all opposition made to it.

4. Another source of happiness in heaven will consist *in praising God.*

Mankind here delight in praising those, whom they love and highly esteem. And it is especially a joyful work to saints, here to give praise to God for his benefits. Much greater satisfaction this employment will afford them in heaven.

Let any one read the revelation of John, especially the 4th, 5th, and 19th chapters, there he will find the heavenly hosts united in praise to God and the Lamb, for his wonderful works and still more wonderful love.

We have seen that one source of pleasure will consist in studying the works of God, the volumes he has written ; because in these works they behold the glory of God. His glory clearly seen is the great source of their joy. They will be continually making new discoveries in their studies of his glory ; and those will be followed with songs and anthems of praise.—So it is represented by John in his visions. For example ; when John in vision saw anti-christ destroyed, he then saw and heard all the heavenly hosts praising God, for the glorious attributes displayed in the overthrow of enemies, for the happiness of his friends.

These predicted events are not all as yet accomplished. When they are fulfilled, and all the elect assembled in heaven studying the works of God, they will see step by step the way in which he has defeated and destroyed anti-christ, and all enemies ; and how in this way he has advanced the happiness of heaven. Through the whole his glorious attributes of power, wisdom, justice, and benevolence, shine with amazing lustre and brightness. They will see the greatness and majesty of God, his unerring perfection ; that he alone is worthy to fill the throne, and sway the sceptre of universal government. Clearly discerning all this in studying his works, they will then unite in one general anthem of praise ; and fall at his feet, and ascribe to him all the glory, which is his due. This employment of praise will fill them with unspeakable pleasure.

As they are constantly studying, and making new discoveries of his glory and greatness ; this will afford increasing matter for praise ; and add fresh, and augmented delight to all their songs and anthems of praise to Jehovah and the Lamb.

This shows us that the *study* of God's works, and their anthems of *praise* are connected ; that the latter follows the former. And as the field of study is boundless, there is room for finite minds to be making new discoveries forever ; and of course there will be new matter of course for ascription of power, dominion, and glory to God and the Lamb. Here study and praise will be forever united ; and these will be distinct employments, and sources of joy to them. And in this way their happiness will be forever increasing.

5. *Performing special commissions and mandates* will be another source of joy.

There is much reason to believe, that saints will be employed on messages to the other worlds ; as many departed saints have been thus employed to this world.

A messenger from heaven is generally called an angel. If departed saints were employed in any business to this world, they would be styled angels. We accordingly find they are so called. One being, employed in relating to John the events which were to take place in this world, is called an angel, in 19th and 22d, chapters. When John was about to worship him he said, do it not—for I am thy fellow servant, and of thy brethren the prophets ; worship God. He thus acknowledges he was one of the ancient prophets. And Moses and Elias appeared and conversed with Christ on mount Tabor.

It is evident from scripture that angels are the ministers and servants of God, who wait upon him continually, and he employs them often on special messages to this, or any other world. And why should not saints in heaven be thus employed, as well as those spirits commonly meant by the term angels ? They may and have been thus employed as messengers, who are styled angels. Hence we have reason to conclude that God employs any of the holy spirits around his throne as messengers to this, and other worlds, according to his pleasure.

And as the worlds created are very numerous, and without any doubt are all inhabited by different orders of beings, towards whom God exercises the same benevolent attention, as he does towards this world, according to their various characters and wants ; we may conclude safely, that holy spirits are sent on special errands to them, as they have been to us ; and that saints will be thus employed.

This will be one part of their employment as servants in his kingdom, to go, when commanded, on messages of love or vengeance to other worlds,as events may require. These errands to other worlds they will perform with great delight. For this is one way by which they may enlarge their knowledge of the works and ways of God.

Undoubtedly angels, who visit this world, and minister to the heirs of salvation, learn much concerning the work of redemption, and works of providence. And by this knowledge are greatly benefitted by God's dealings with men. They are so much benefitted, and interested in what God is doing for men, that the great work of redemption is a subject of their constant study. So it is said, which things the angels desire to look into. And these desires are very strong.

Saints in heaven, when they go on messages from God to other worlds, become acquainted with the characters of the inhabitants ; their conduct, and the dealings of Jehovah with them. And while thus extending their knowledge in this way, their happiness is increasing. And serving their king in this way, will be a source of delight to them.

We are informed that spirits are very active, like fire ; his ministers are like a flame of fire. Also, they serve him in this active manner day and night, and never rest. When we consider that the host of heaven is innumerable, and each servant is thus actively employed, what an amazing amount of service they render every day. What are the services, which this innumerable host perform ? They praise God, we are told. But there are many ways of praising him. One is in doing his will. While employed on errands from world to world, they serve and praise him. And this will be one of their employments. We love to serve our friends, whom we love in this world. We delight in activity when our work is agreeable. So in heaven the active services performed for God will be one source of their happiness, and one great source ; especially when we consider how much knowledge they obtain of God's ways and character in such employments.

What joy it gave the angels to announce to the shepherds

the birth of Christ. With what pleasure they ministered to him in this world, and do minister unto saints on their journey home. With similar pleasure will saints in heaven obey and serve their God. In whatever service they may be employed, it will be a source of pleasure and happiness to them.

6. *The society* of heaven will be another source of happiness to saints.

We know that mutual acts of kindness, conversation, giving and receiving information, and mutual intercourse, are in this world one great source of our daily felicity. The society of a family, of parents and children, and of friends, is one of our sweetest joys. And the society of perfectly holy beings will be unspeakably pleasant. This is represented in scripture by the metaphor of a feast, at which the bridegroom and bride regale themselves. The society of husband and wife is a source of great consolation. Far more delightful will be the communion and social intercourse of the bride with Christ in heaven.

The sweetest joys on earth flow from communion with the Father and Son. Christ rejoices in his bride, and his bride in him. They will be one. This intercourse and intimacy will be blissful, and dear ; like that of husband and wife, in a spiritual, not carnal sense. Their joys will be mutual. And this proves a social intercourse in heaven. For persons afford each other no joy or comfort, if they have no social intercourse. In that case, they would be like persons who live alone, without any connexion or intercourse. Such persons never afford each other any comfort.

But the union and intercourse of Christ with his bride in heaven, is represented by the union of husband and wife here. And when saints are called the children of God, brethren and sisters, composing a family, and enjoying family blessings ; such descriptions clearly teach, that in heaven they will enjoy intimate intercourse, which will afford them the greatest delight. Only consider how much comfort parents and children, husbands and wives, brethren and sisters, enjoy in each other's society.

In heaven saints are the children of God, the bride of Christ, brethren and sisters. Such are the relations subsisting there, in a state of perfection. And their society will be as much more intimate and dear, as their union is more close and perfect, than on the earth.

How great then will be the happiness of the children of God, arising from intercourse with him ; and of the bride in her intercourse with Christ; and of the brethren and sisters with each other. From these relations, and the mutual intercourse and society connected with them, will flow the sweetest joys forever, in ways almost innumerable, and concerning which we have but a faint conception here.

Paul teaches us, that in heaven some will shine brighter than others ; they will differ in this respect, as one star differs in glory from another. Hence some will be greater and wiser than others, and be teachers to those of less knowledge. With what pleasure they will communicate, and others hear and receive instruction ; and in this way assist each other in making progress in knowledge.

Indeed, when we reflect that in heaven a love of benevolence will be perfect, and perfectly unite all to Christ their head, and to each other, so that their harmony will be complete without one jarring note ; that they will be all *one* ; their intercourse and society must be inconceivably pleasant and sweet, But one soul and spirit will animate and govern that innumerable host. So that we may well say with Paul, that eye hath not seen, nor ear heard, nor heart conceived the things God hath prepared for those who love him.

Not to enlarge, those mentioned are so many positive sources of happiness to saints and angels in heaven. And these show that the happiness and glory of that world are so great, blessed and sublime, that in describing them the boldest figures must be used. The description must be taken from objects in this world most highly esteemed for their value, richness, beauty, sweetness, greatness, and sublimity. Such figures are used, which we have endeavored to explain under the several particulars of this essay. Yet they come so far short of a full description, that Paul says eye hath not seen, &c. We now see the description given us of heaven is not to be understood literally, but figuratively ; and these figures we have attempted to explain ; and I would add only one or two more particulars to complete the description.

7. In heaven saints will *love each other as themselves*, and be united in perfect bonds of friendship.

This command, thou shalt love thy neighbor as thyself, has never been perfectly obeyed on earth. But in heaven saints will love each other as themselves. This love will render them true, sincere, and faithful friends. Such friendship rarely exists in this world. A faithful man, who can find, was the complaint of one of the greatest of men. Here men are deceitful, unfaithful, insinsere ; so that they seldom put much trust or confidence in each other. But in heaven it will be very different. No deceit, insincerity, anger, envy, or revenge, or any evil passion, will ever be exercised there. Their words and actions will flow from perfect love to each other. They will have no design to deceive or injure each other, but to increase each others' felicity. Of this they will give full evidence. Hence they will put entire and perfect trust and confidence in each other, and without disappointment. They will believe every word spoken to be *true*, every action designed to do good. Hence a fear of being deceived, and injured by some ill design, will never be realized. They will live together in perfect friendship, striving to contribute to each others' felicity. The sweet pleasures and joys, flowing from such love and friendship, was never experienced in this world. But in heaven, when nothing but perfect love and friendship are seen, when the ties of kindred souls make them one, their intercourse will produce the most refined pleasures. All the pleasures and joys of friendship will be experienced in perfection, without any thing to embitter them. This friendship, consisting in mutual, perfect love to each other, is one blessing Christ often prayed for, and promised to his disciples. He prayed they might be *one*, one in him, one in the Father, one together, as he and the Father are one. This is only praying that their love and friendship might become perfect. Hence Christ called them his friends. He considered this love and friendship to be one source of the most sublime happiness.

8. In heaven, mutual *conversation* will be a source of great and constant pleasure.

The *mode* by which saints will communicate their thoughts, views, and feelings to each other, is not revealed. Whether by words, or some other signs, we know not. But as to the *fact*, that they will converse, there can be no doubt.

Abraham and the rich man conversed. And bodies are not necessary to conversation. For it is a fact that Moses and Elias talked with Christ, and created angels have conversed with man, as with Daniel, John, and Manoah and his wife. They have a way to articulate, and use words as signs of their ideas.

We know that conversation here is one means of the increase of knowledge, one source of happiness, and necessary to the intercourse of society, and our highest good. If we could have no intercourse by conversation, our condition would be very unhappy, As mutual conversation is necessary to the pleasures and perfection of society, there can be no doubt but that this privilege will be enjoyed in heaven, in the highest perfection.

And when we consider, that our minds are capable of improvement in knowledge and bliss, and are daily expanding & enlarging ; that heaven is a place where the mind will grow and enlarge with greater rapidity than it does here ; we may conclude, that Abraham and Moses and others now greatly exceed us in knowledge. They have been for several thousand years studying, and improving their minds, in a knowledge of the works of God.

When a saint enters heaven,by conversation with such characters very important information is soon acquired. The themes of discourse will be innumerable. And it will be the delight of all to give, as well as receive, information. As the works of creation, of providence, of the word of God, and spiritual, intelligent beings, will be the subjects of study ; so concerning these they will mutually convey instruction. In these works God is manifested, and seen ; and the better they are understood in all their parts, the clearer, and more enlarged, will be the views all will have of the character of Jehovah, and hereby their happiness will be greatly increased.

Suppose a rational, benevolent being should arrive in heaven from some other world, who had never had any knowledge of the earth ; and by conversation with saints from this world should obtain a knowledge of this material globe, of the works of providence, of the plan of redemption, and the wonderful things God has done for our race ; would he not have, at once, far more exalted views of God ; and be filled with wonder and joy, and with great delight join with the redeemed in their anthem of praise ? And he might give us a knowledge of the works of God, and the wonders he had wrought for *his* race, in the world from which he came,which would fill us with wonder and joy, and excite us to unite with him in hymns of praise to the great Eternal. Such suppositions will without doubt be realised in that glorious state.

For there is but *one heaven* ; and in that the greatest sum of created happiness is to exist. And Christ is to gather together in heaven all things in one. This and similar passages seem to signify, that as he is exalted above every name in heaven and in the universe, and is made head over *all things* to the church, the blessed society above ; so he will collect together in heaven all holy beings from all the worlds they inhabit, and there make them one ; unite them by the bonds of perfect benevolence. Beings from different worlds, when they meet in heaven, animated by the same spirit and soul, will by their conversation and intercourse, afford each other great delight and satisfaction. By such conversation among pure friends, what information, what new wonders, what exalted views of God, what refined and sublime joys, they will afford each other. As the divine plan of operations is infinite, including all worlds and beings in existence, composed of innumerable parts, all unitedly aiming at the same ultimate end, the happiness of heaven ; the inhabitants above will afford each other amazing assistance in studying, and acquiring a knowledge of it. By their intercourse and mutual help, each mind will make rapid improvements in a knowledge of the divine plan in all its parts, arrangements, and connexions.

When inhabitants from other worlds learn from saints here what wonders God has wrought in every age, especially by the work` of redemption ; and when they see that all the parts of this plan operating here have terminated in the increasing felicity of the heavenly society ; what exalted views they must have of God ;, what pleasure will his character afford, when seen in so many new lights, and displayed in such variety of ways. And equal delight must saints from this world feel, when they see the new and numerous ways by which he has displayed himself in works and words to other worlds ; and when they see all these displays are parts of the same plan, and that all terms note in the same end. Such information acquired by conversation will fill every mind with exalted, and reverential views of God, and with wonder and joy.

9. In heaven *benevolence*,with all its affections and operations, will be *in perfect exercise*.

In that world there will be no darkness to obscure the sight ; no stupidity to cool, and blunt enjoyment ; no sluggish inactivity to interrupt pleasure. The views of every mind will be clear and bright ; they will not see through a veil, but face to face ; their feelings will be acute and strong ; their activity equal to their powers ; every affection will glow like a flame. This prepares them to experience the greatest pleasure from every object and employment.

Their love to God,to Christ, to each other,will be in a flame ; their gratitude glow like fire ; their reverence will be profound ; their joys exquisitely sweet ; yes, the whole heart will display the most lively and active exercises, and prepare them to drink pleasures from every stream, and from the eternal source of bliss. Here the heart is so cold, stupid, and insensible, as to render great enjoyments next to impossible. And in proportion to the lively glow of holy affections, our happiness is increased. How then will the fervid glow and heat of holy affections in heaven, prepare all the inhabitants to enjoy every source in full perfection, and to as high a degree as the powers of the mind will admit. With a heart hungering and thirsting with intense desires, the sublime feast of heaven will afford them perfect bliss and joy.

10. To form some adequate and just views of the blessedness of the heavenly society, we must consider, who is *the author*, with *his design* of that world.

The greatest sum of created happiness, including its endless increase, is the ultimate end of God in all his operations. And this sum of happiness, with its endless increase, is to exist in heaven. And God is the author and cause of all this blessedness. He has but one plan, and this is the end at which it ultimately aims. This plan includes all worlds and beings in existence. And all the innumerable parts of it are unitedly promoting this end, and will terminate in it.

Hence it is the design of God to make heaven a state of such blessedness, glory, sublimity, and joy, as is worthy of himself. So that in the happiness and glory of that world, all the divine attributes of power, knowledge, and love, will be displayed to the highest possible degree. There will be seen the essential, infinite, and eternal fulness of God, perfectly communicated. So that all will say, here as great happiness and glory exist, as the infinite Jehovah was able to produce. There God will be seen displayed ; his infinite fulness displayed and communicated. In the blessedness and glory of that state he has glorified himself perfectly, in the highest possible degree.

When all these things are considered, what must heaven be. What astonishing bliss, what inconceivable glory, what sublimity, what consummate perfection of all things, will there exist, and be forever increasing. In that world, every being will behold all the happiness and glory of the universe concentrated ; and the sight will fill each one with wonder and joy ; and this delightful wonder and joy will increase as the glories of that state will forever shine with greater and greater brightness and splendor.

No wonder then, that the images and figures used in scripture to describe this state, are so various, numerous, rich, and sublime ; and then they fall short of giving an adequate view of it ; so that after all that is revealed, it may be said, that here, eye hath not seen, nor ear heard, what will be realized by all in that paradise of glory and pleasure.

We may now attend to the negative description given us of heaven. We are assured that the body will finally rise, be re-united to the soul, and partake in union with it of the felicity of that world. It will be raised immortal, incorruptible, spiritual, and made like unto Christ's glorious body. Hence it will never be subject to any disease, pain, decay, weariness, or death. It will ever remain the same glorious body ; ever fresh, beautiful, young and blooming. It will be capable of the most refined, and sublime sensations. And by this union it is agreed the happiness of saints will be increased. Otherwise, no reason can be assigned for the resurrection of the body. But if it will add to their felicity, this is reason sufficient.

We are also assured, that there will not any evil, natural or moral, enter heaven. All who defile, or make a lie, are to be excluded. None but perfectly holy characters will be admitted to live there. And if evil, both natural and moral, are to be forever excluded, then no evil or suffering of any kind will ever be there experienced. For the terms natural and moral include all kinds of evil.

But to give us the highest assurance, God informs that there will be no sickness, pain, sorrow, crying, or death in heaven. All kinds of particular evils are mentioned, and declared to be excluded from that world.

There will be no darkness, no night there ; no gloominess or fear, or any thing to excite fear. By the rays of the sun of righteousness, saints will enjoy one bright eternal day. How glorious and perfect is that state, in which no evil is felt ; from which every thing, which creatures dread, hate, and fear, will be forever excluded.

This however, is only giving us a negative view of the glory of heaven. For if saints there, though freed from every evil, could find no objects in existence to afford them pleasure, they would not be happy. Where there is no evil, there is no miseny. So in heaven they would not be miserable, or feel any pain ; yet they would not be happy, unless they found positive sources of good, or of pleasure. Such sources they will find, and we have shown what they are ; and from these all their happiness is derived. If they enjoyed these sources, yet suffered many evils as they do here, their happiness would be greatly interrupted ; it would not be complete and perfect. To perfect, uninterrupted happiness, positive sources of pleasure must be enjoyed, free from evil to interrupt and lessen it.

Hence, though freedom from all evil will not render any being happy, yet this exemption is necessary to perfect felicity.

According to the description here given of heaven ; which accords with the description John gives in the 20th, 21st, and 22d, chapters of his revelation ; how glorious is that state ; that world, which is to be the eternal habitation of God, and his people. According to this description, there shall in no wise enter it, any thing that defileth, or worketh abomination, or maketh a lie.

In that world there will be no deception, no pollution, nothing to excite disgust, fear, or abhorrence. Every sinner, and every sin will be forever excluded. Rebellion will be forever subdued, the trumpet having blown its last blast, and the shout of battle ceased, and destructions come to a perpetual end. In heaven saints will never be assaulted with temptations ; lusts will never operate to disturb internal peace ; there will be no enemies to seduce them. Private interests will be known no more ; the general good will allure every eye, engross every heart, and move every hand.

Peace of minds, harmony of views, union of affections, will be enjoyed by the innumerable host above ; and diffuse an universal and eternal serenity within and around the whole soul.

Here all will, in the most perfect sense, *live.* Death and sorrow, disease and pain, crying and tears, will be felt no more. There will be nothing to destroy, nothing to impair, nothing to disturb. Every being will live the most happy life ; and not merely live, but grow, flourish, and bloom forever.

Life in the sublimest sense, life vernal and immortal, will impregnate every source of happiness, and animate the bodies and souls of the children of God.

What an amazing difference there will be, between heaven and our present state of being. This world is a vale of tears. Evils await and beset us here, in a thousand forms. Without

are fightings ; within are fears. Here we have a thousand ungratified desires ; experience daily disappointments, reproach-
es of conscience, and distressing apprehensions of the wrath of
God. We are subject to hunger and thirst, to cold and heat,
to weariness and languor, sickness and pain, decay and death.
Our friends and relatives suffer with us ; they sicken and die ;
their sins disgrace *them*, and wound *us ;* and awaken painful
apprehensions concerning their destiny beyond the grave.
Wars also spread far and wide the miseries of dismay, plunder,
slaughter, and destruction. Fires, famine, and pestilence often desolate cities, and depopulate kingdoms.

To beings, who suffer here so many great and distressing
evils, how great and wonderful the change they experience,
when the ransomed of the Lord shall return, and come to the
heavenly Zion, with songs ; when they shall obtain joy and
gladness, and sorrow and sighing shall flee away ; when they
enter heaven, the seat of unalloyed happiness ; where beauty,
grandeur, sublimity and glory meet the eye ; where harmony
salutes the ear, and raptures of joy fill the soul ; raptures un-
mixed, increasing, and endless.

Thus far it has been designed to give a clear and distinct
view of heaven, so far as it is revealed in the bible. We see
accordingly, heaven is a world of perfection ; every beauty,
glory, and excellency reign there in perfection. Every character is perfect, beautiful and divine. The employments of
that world are study, obedience, and praise. And endless, increasing happiness, without any interruption from evil of any
kind, will dwell there, and render all the inhabitants inconceivably blessed. It will be a state as glorious as an infinite author can make it.

I shall, therefore, conclude with an exhortation to all to prepare for that world without delay. You now see clearly the
prize which is set before you. All you can acquire or enjoy,
in your pursuit after worldly good, is vanity compared with
heaven. And all are running, wrestling, and striving to obtain
a prize. And the prize sought is either such enjoyments as this
world affords, or the enjoyments of heaven. And heaven, in
durable riches, in unfading honors and glories, and in refined
pleasures, as far exceeds all the riches, honors, and pleasure
of this world, as light exceeds darkness, or happiness misery.

To spend our days here in pursuit of worldly good, to the
neglect of running for the prize in heaven, is the greatest wick-

edness and folly. And when the uncertainty of life is considered,to delay preparation for heaven, is the height of folly. And
that depravity of heart must be great, which causes men to
pursue a course to their own ruin, when they might win a
prize so glorious as heavenly and endless felicity.

From this day, let all turn into the narrow way, run the
christian race, and so run as to secure success. Delay not.
If you do, and ruin overtakes you, how must you lament your
conduct, as you make your eternal bed in outer darkness;
when you behold afar off the bliss of heaven, lost to you by
your folly and madness. forever lost by your own perverse-
ness.

NOTES

Referring to different parts of the work.

A Page 31.

THE term *judgm nt* is often used in an indefinite and popular sense, without any regard to metaphysical accuracy. Estimating articles of daily traffic and commerce, or giving an opinion concerning their value, is called judging. Yet here two objects are perceived, and when compared with some standard, it is distinctly seen that one is of more value than the other. Perceiving this difference in their worth, when compared with the standard, is the judgment formed, or conclusion of the person concerning their value. Again. Judicial officers and referees give judgment in cases submitted to their decision. Here the understanding is employed, in investigating the real truth in the cases before them. And when every witness is heard, and every fact or truth is perceived, in relation to the cause pending, the judge comes to a conclusion ; and perceiving what is true or false, right or wrong in the case, he pronounces a decision upon it to the parties concerned. In this process, the final perception of the real truth in the cause before him, and declaring this in words, is called his judgment. Hence in every sense in which the word judgment may be used, it is the understanding which is exercised, in perceiving or taking a view of all the objects necessary to come to a final conclusion and result, which is his judgment. And this is nothing more than a clear perception of the value of an article compared with its standard, or the truth of a cause referred to him. And no *generic*, and no more than a *specific* difference is discernible, between the numerous operations of the understanding. All its operations are no more or less, than perceptions of objects, whether the objects are things, or properties, or qualities, or relations, or connexions between antecedents and consequents.

B Page 46.

The word of God informs us, it is the office of conscience to accuse and condemn, or to excuse, approve, and justify, according as our hearts, actions and lives, agree or disagree with the moral law, our rule of conduct. And it must be obvious to candid minds, that no other than *specific* operations of the understanding are employed, in accusing and condemning, or in approving and justifying. And it will be granted, that the various operations of the mind, when brought into view in the scriptures, are not presented in an accurate and systematic manner, as metaphysicians in examining the operations of the mind arrange them methodically.

Hence it is sometimes the case, that in the word of God we find one faculty of the mind used for another, as the understanding for the heart, and heart for the understanding. And sometimes what is in the word predicated of one faculty, in strict truth belongs to another. By observing these things, we may readily see that every thing, which is affirmed of conscience in the word, will agree with the view given of it in this essay. We read of a pure, a good, a peaceable, an inoffensive conscience ; and of an evil, defiled, and seared conscience. When conscience does not condemn, but justify us, it is called good, and without offence. This is what Paul means, when he said he had lived in all good conscience ; had maintained a conscience, not only good, but without offence. Whatever the reason was, his conscience in different periods of his life did not condemn but justify him. A conscience is *pure*, when free from error in its decisions. When conscience is said to be purged from dead works, to be alive, and washed, it is then awake to perform its office faithfully ; to condemn or justify, according to a person's real conduct or deserts. And when persons have for a long time stifled and silenced the voice of conscience, and refused to regard its decisions and remonstrances ; when it is silent, and ceases to perform its office in accusing and condemning, it is then styled a *seared conscience*. As when the warnings, admonitions, and counsels, we give to persons for evil conduct, have been long disregarded, we become silent, cease to warn them any longer, but give them up to ruin. So conscience ceases to warn, and the person is left to the dominion of an evil heart, to effect his own destruction. Here the fact is, the *heart* is become so hardened in a course of sin and rebellion, that the voice of conscience produces no effect, and makes no impression upon it. Then this hardness of heart is predicated of conscience, which is expressed by the term *seared*. When the true meaning is, conscience is silent, no longer performs its office towards a person so hardened in sin. This is the awful case, it is feared, with many persons.

It is certain that conscience may err and misjudge, through the blinding influence of the heart. Paul, while a pharisee, lived in all good conscience ; during this time it did not condemn, but justify him, in persecuting the church. All this time his conscience erred, or pronounced a false sentence. But when he was converted, it condemned him for the very deeds for which it had before justified him. When it thus errs it is blinded, evil, and polluted, precisely as a judge is, when he is led to wrong decisions, through the influence of bribes, or prejudices of heart. Here the fault is not in the conscience, but the heart, which binds it to give erroneous decisions. In all instances where moral good and evil seem to be predicated of conscience, these and similar terms are used figuratively for the heart. And if the term heart, in such instances, had been used instead of conscience, the sense would have been clear and obvious. If conscience always enjoyed *sufficient light*, and judged entirely free from the influence of a wicked heart, it would always judge correctly. If it errs, and its decisions are wrong, it is owing to the deficiency of light, or the influence of an evil heart. A judge on the bench, if he has sufficient light on every cause, and is wholly free from the influence of bribes, and of an evil heart, will render a just sentence. When the judgment he renders is unjust, it is imputed to the want of sufficient light, and then he is not censured ; or to an evil heart, which has prejudiced and blinded him, in which case he is always blamed and condemned by public opinion. Yet the fault for which he is condemned, is not the erroneous judgment pronounced ; but the wickedness of his heart, which led him to it. If we say his sentence is unjust, we yet consider the real crime for which we blame him to be an evil heart, which led to this decision. Error of judgment is not considered a crime. For criminality in the case, we search for the exciting cause of this error ; and for this a judge is blamed. This applies to conscience, when it judges of moral conduct. Hence nothing said in this essay on conscience, will be found inconsistent with the word of God, if we keep all the illustrations here given clearly in view.

C. Page 70.

Some may find it difficult to perceive a difference between an *appetite*, and the faculty called *taste*. The real difference is the same, as between a *species* and *genus*.

A *genus* includes all the *species* under it. The faculty or taste is a genus, which includes all the appetites. Hence an appetite differs from the taste, as a species does from its genus. If all objects of perception were separated into distinct classes, then one appetite is suited to one class of objects, and another appetite to another class, and all the appetites prepare the mind to be affected with pleasure or pain by all objects, which are objects of perception. Hence the taste is a fitness to feel pleasure or pain in view of *all* objects ; and a single appetite is suited to be affected with only one *class* of objects.

This distinction is verified by experience and facts. All men by experience know their feelings vary, alter, and change, very frequently. Such changes are produced by the ascendancy, which one appetite gains over another. And it is a fact, that mankind are very changeable in their pursuits. One hour a love for their offspring governs ; then they are frugal. The next hour their love or appetite for pleasure in excessive indulgence governs ; then they waste their property, though it reduce their children to poverty. This also agrees with the word of God. When the guests were invited by Christ to the gospel supper, why did they not all make the same excuse ? Because different appetites predominated in them, and each went away in pursuit of that object, which was then most valued. Another day their excuses might have been reversed. If the taste, or what some call a capacity for pleasure and pain, were a *simple faculty*, why are not all mankind pleased or disgusted with the same objects ; why are not their pursuits the same without any change ? It has always been a mystery, why men are so differently affected in view of the same objects. But admitting the existence of different appetites, it is very easy to account for the various feelings excited by the same objects, and the changes in the conduct of the same person from time to time ; and especially, when we consider that the appetites are capable of different cultivation and improvement, for the better or the worse ; and more especially when we consider the *secondary* affections, which arise from those *primary* in the heart. The attachment of the heathen to the same idol is a secondary feeling, which arises from their *primary* love to created objects, and the direction given to this primary appetite by education.

Again. Admit that distinct appetites are implanted in us by our Creator for wise ends, we may then see, that the appetites constitute the faculty of taste or heart, as several *species* constitute a *genus*. Also the loss of an appetite, and the restoration of it, no more affect the taste as a faculty, than the destruction of one species of animals or vegetables affects the genus under which they are included ; or than the loss of an appetite for one article of food, destroys the palate. The *genus* remains the same, though one species belonging to it is annihilated ; and the bodily taste would remain, though one appetite, for instance an appetite for honey, should be lost. And if an appetite to be pleased with the character of God is lost, the taste as a faculty remains, and governs the man according to the ascendancy of the remaining appetites, which were implanted in him at his creation. The more candidly and attentively any person considers this subject in all its relations, the more he will be convinced of its truth, and its agreement with experience, facts, and the word of God. If a person is deprived of any particular appetite, the others which remain will govern ; and as the person is endued with all the faculties and powers, which are necessary to render him a fit object of praise or blame, he will be worthy of one or the other according to the *nature* and *operation* of those appetites, still remaining in his heart. This will remain true as long as he is possessed of appetites, which as active principles govern, whether their number is greater or less ; whether any one is lost or restored, he is still a moral agent.

D. Page 106.

Some readers may think it is a new idea, and very erroneous, to assert that the faculty of taste is of a *moral nature*, the seat of all vice and virtue.

But if they had that intuitive view of the heart of an infant, which God hath, and clearly saw it had a heart or taste of such a nature as would prompt it, if unrestrained, as it advanced in life, to deceive men, oppress, steal, rob, and murder; would they not consider the heart of this infant *morally* depraved, and very wicked ?

Now, facts prove that mankind are born with such hearts, and do commit such crimes, if not restrained. Their lives daily manifest this depravity. And such characters are deemed very vile, whether knowing or ignorant, whether the powers of their minds are very strong or weak. This proves that we estimate their moral character according to the nature of their hearts, and not according to their knowledge or ignorance, their power or weakness ; though it is granted, that light and power may aggravate their guilt. And the reason why all men do not, until renewed, daily perpetrate such crimes, is not any difference in the malignity of their hearts ; but the numerous restraints laid on some, which are not on others.   This is true according to scripture declarations ; and if we had a clear view of sinners in hell, where all restraints on the wicked heart are taken off, we should see no difference in their moral characters.   And did we see the heart as God does, we should be convinced, that all vice and virtue do belong to this *feeling* faculty, which is the primary principle of action in all moral agents.

E. Page 146.

It may be readily perceived, from what has been said, on supposition man is endued with only two faculties, the understanding and the will, that no one can act with *design*, or under the influence of motives.   For aim and design imply, that an agent has an *end* in view, and *means* to attain it.   If the end is pleasing to his heart, by this he is influenced and excited to use the means necessary to reach the end, and while acting, his aim and design is the end he seeks.   He keeps the end steadily in view.   And the end, by its *agreeableness* to his heart, is the motive by which he is governed.

Hence, if he has only the faculties of the understanding and will, there is nothing existing in him on which motives can have any influence.   Motives cannot *affect past volitions*, for they are past and gone, like fleeting moments ; and have no *continued existence*.   They cannot have influence on the volition to be exercised, for that is future, and has no existence, until it is exercised ; and surely motives cannot affect that, which has no being ; and when it exists, then it is too late for the influence of motives.

Proceeding on the supposition we have only the two faculties named, it is impossible for us to be governed by motives. And if we are not influenced by them, we must act without design.   And a being, who is not governed by motives, and does not act by *design*, is not an agent, and surely he is not a *moral agent* ; for a moral agent acts with aim and design, and is influenced by motives in all his voluntary actions, as all will grant. Hence, whatever theory of the mind is admitted, if a third faculty, the taste, is rejected, the theory followed in its consequences destroys moral agency, and contradicts experience. For our experience testifies, that we do act by design, and under the influence of motives. The ideas of acting by *design*, and being *governed* by *motives*, are inseparably connected. If one is denied, the other must be rejected. And as it is now evident that mankind cannot be influenced by motives, unless they are endued with *something* capable of pleasure and pain, whether it is called taste, or by any other particular name ; excluding from the theory of the mind this *something*, or *feeling* faculty, it will follow that we are not moral agents. Such a feeling, governing faculty is the most essential property, in constituting man a moral agent. Without this he is not a moral agent.

F. Page 178.

While in this world, we have bodies, which we have to support. And the appetites, which have been enumerated and described, are active principles, prompting us to seek the things and pursue the ends, requisite to the life and comfort of our bodies, and of our posterity.

We have also souls, for which we ought to make everlasting provision, that we may be happy after death. A benevolent appetite is necessary, to excite us to use the means appointed for the good of the soul, here and forever. As Adam at his creation was endued with all the appetites, needful to seek the good of the body and soul here and hereafter, he was perfect ; no other active principles were necessary, in order to his subsistence in time, and his endless bliss beyond the grave.

When he ate the forbidden fruit, he was deprived of his benevolent appetite, which constituted the moral image of God ; but his other appetites remained entire, and unaltered, as facts prove. While he remained holy, his love to God was the governing principle of his heart ; and all his other appetites operated in subordination to the ends and designs of his supreme regard for God ; and all the distinct faculties of his mind harmoniously aimed at the glory of his Maker. But when deprived of the moral image of God, his remaining appetites had the entire government. As these were given him, to move him to make provision for the body while in this world, it is evident, as *facts prove*, that he would forsake God, and seek happiness in broken cisterns, or created worldly objects.

But philosophers, through mistaken views of the nature of sin, and not distinguishing as they ought between *absolute* and *relative good* and *evil*, have made themselves believe that our natural appetites and propensities are not, neither can be considered as evil; so are ready to exclaim, what, is *hunger* a *sinful* appetite? Here let every one candidly consider what sin is. Now all will grant, that a propensity to *evil* is an *evil* propensity; and if this is an *active* principle, inherent in a being who is a proper *moral agent*, it is a *moral evil*; and moral evil is sin. It is generally granted, that our appetites may be gratified either lawfully or unlawfully.

When a person eats no more than is necessary to the life and support of the body, he gratifies his hunger no more than God allows. But if he eats to *excess*, is *intemperate*, all say he is wrong, and has done what the law forbids. And it is as wrong to gratify any other appetite to *excess*.

Again. Every agent, in all he does, aims at some *ultimate end*; otherwise he aims at no end in any thing done. He must aim at some end ultimately, or do one thing for the sake of another, *ad infinitum;* which is aiming at nothing; and is a thing impossible in a moral agent. And if an agent's ultimate end is evil, it must be granted all he does with such an aim is wrong. What then is the *ultimate end* of all men, while unrenewed? Let any person give a full attention to this subject, and he will say, no unrenewed man aims at any thing higher, than the *gratification* of his own *personal desires ;* self gratification is his end as far as he is able, without any regard for the glory of God, or the happiness of his kingdom.

Now then, what is the ultimate end of unrenewed persons in eating? On examination, every one must come to this conclusion; that he eats for the sake of the pleasure food affords, or to gain strength and preserve life with a view to further ends; and his last end is to gratify some personal desire, without any regard to God or the happiness of man. Is not his aim then in eating sinful? Do not the desires of this appetite lead him to pursue a course, which is hostile to God, and the general good? And as this appetite will operate in all unrenewed men; in the same manner all his *other* appetites will operate; and whether he gratifies them to *excess* or not, his ultimate aim is the gratification of some personal desire, without any regard to the authority or honor of God ; and hence in all he does, while such is his end, he is committing sin.

But to represent our appetites, such as hunger, thirst, and what are termed natural affections, as sinful or evil in their tendency and operation, appears so shocking to many, that they discard the sentiment at once ; and scarcely any will give the subject a candid examination. Yet, as the word of God and facts prove, that mankind are governed by corrupt principles, they adopt some other theory to account for the prevalence of sin. Hence some have believed, that when Adam ate the forbidden fruit, he not only lost the moral image of his Maker, but had produced in him a *principle of selfishness*, which is the root or fountain from which all sinful acts proceed in moral agents.

This selfishness has been defined and described in different ways. Some say it is *self-love*, or a *love* for *self ;* or setting up a *private interest* in opposition to *public good*. However it may be defined, we ought to inquire what ideas the terms communicate. Is this selfishness an active principle distinct, and different in its nature, from the appetites we have considered ?

All must grant selfishness has some ultimate end ; this end must be agreeable to the feelings of this principle ; *desires* must arise from it to obtain its end ; and those will govern the person in all his pursuits and actions. What then is its ultimate end ? Is it the glory of God, or happiness of mankind, or good of God's kingdom? No. What then ? It may be answered, it is the person's own individual good or interest. And what is this, only the gratification of his own desires ? Suppose riches be his end. What good occurs to him from them ; except the gratification of his numerous desires ? In this all the happiness he enjoys consists. And as far as his desires are gratified, he has obtained all he does, or in fact, can desire. So far he has arrived to his ultimate end. Here this selfishness aims at the gratification of its desires as its final end. The same is true of the appetites, as they have been described. Selfishness may be gratified, as is necessary for the support and comfort of the body, and no further ; and as its ultimate end is sinful in all its operations, it is itself sinful. What then is the difference between this selfishness, in its nature and operations, and the nature and operations of the appetites, as they have been represented ? According to each theory, it is wrong to gratify these active principles to an *excess;* and to aim, in all that is done, at a wrong or bad end ultimately. Of course, there is no difference in their nature and operation. And no one can conceive of any selfishness more ruinous to the general good, than those appetites are, when they operate without any regard to the authority, and glory, or happiness of God's kingdom, as they always do, when there is no benevolent principle to govern and regulate them. And if we consult *experience,* we shall find it testifies in favor of the sentiments advanced.

Are mankind conscious of any active principle in them, entirely distinct in its nature and operations, from the appetites which have been described? When they eat, is it hunger which prompts them, or some selfish principle distinct from it? When parental affection moves parents to promote the good of their children, are they conscious of some other principle as governing them, distinct from the affection they have for their offspring? And the same question may be asked in relation to all their other appetites. Experience does not teach men, that they are governed by any other active principles, than these appetites. We know it is hunger, which prompts us to eat ; it is a feeling of love parents have for their children, which leads them to seek what they view as necessary to their good. We know it is a natural propensity, which inclines the different sexes to unite in matrimony. And neither *experience* nor *observation* teaches, that mankind are governed by any other principles, than these several appetites. These are selfish in all their operations ; and aim ultimately at nothing higher or better, than the gratification of the desires arising from them, as far as men are able. And no principle can be conceived, more ruinous to happiness finally, than the effects these appetites have produced, and will continue to produce.

Hence as soon as Adam lost the moral image of God, the appetites, created in him with a view to his good in this world, were the only active, governing principles remaining in him. From that day he loved the objects of this world supremely. He at once experienced a desire to accumulate property, to be esteemed by men ; and he pursued the means necessary in his view to these ends ; and as he had no love for God, his heart was in fact placed supremely on this world. He served the creature, and not the Creator ; he forsook God, the living fountain, and sought broken cisterns to satisfy his thirst. In like manner his posterity have lived. These appetites were now, in their operation, positively wrong or sinful. But this did not constitute his primary depravity. A total want of love to God was that, in which his imperfection, or moral depravity, *primarily* consisted. As long as love to his Maker governed, all he did was in harmony with the law, authority, and honor of his God. And as soon as this love ceased, all he did terminated in self gratification ultimately, and was sinful.

I know many ridicule the idea of placing any part of our depravity in a mere privation. But is the body perfect, if eyes are wanting? Does not the privation of this sense constitute a great imperfection? If a man as long as he has eyes, would walk in the right way, and would certainly deviate from it, as deprived of this sense, would not all consider eyes to see a great blessing, and the want of them a great evil? So the want of a benevolent appetite is a great moral imperfection and evil; in consequence of which, all the other senses or appetites lead us astray from God, as both facts and experience have abundantly proved, from the day in which man revolted from God.

G. Page 184.

The kind and degree of *power*, necessary to constitute a moral agent, or fit object of praise and blame, has long been a subject of dispute; and there is not much hope of bringing it soon to a satisfactory conclusion. With a view, however, to this end, this note is added. Two ideas are implied in all the actions of a moral agent. One is, that he is governed by *motives*; and the other, that in all his actions he has some *aim* and *design*. That he is a designing agent, and is influenced by motives, all will grant. This implies, that in all his actions he *aims* at the attainment of some object or *end*, by such means as, in his view, are adapted to it. The end operates as a motive. If the end is pleasing to his feelings, he is influenced to use every exertion to attain it. If an object is disagreeable or painful, he will be influenced to avoid it. This necessarily implies, that his mind is endued with some property, which is pleased or disgusted by all objects within his view; a property, which is affected antecedent to action, and which gives rise to every exertion. This is requisite, in order for him to be influenced by motives, and to act with design.

Some contend for a self-determining power; and some, for an *efficiency* in men to produce all their voluntary exercises, as essential to praise and blame. According to these theories, man is endued with a *power* antecedent to volition, a power which is to produce volitions. In order for this power to operate, or exert itself to produce volitions, some object must please or disgust it, and in this way influence it to act. If this be not the fact, the agent, in exerting his power, is not governed by any motive. And if objects are neither pleasant nor painful to this power, it is in a state of indifference; and if a man can exercise his power in this state, he must act without design. For his supposed power is not inclined towards any object, and of course he cannot aim at one object more than another; or, in such a state, he aims at no object, or acts without any design. I see no way to avoid this conclusion. Hence, if moral agents are influenced by motives, and act with design, then this supposed power is of such a nature, that in view of objects it is pleased or disgusted, and in this way influenced to obtain the object, if agreeable, and to avoid it, if painful. Then what is the difference between this power, whether self-determining, or efficient, and what is called by me the faculty of taste, or the heart? The taste, and this supposed power, are each of them pleased or the contrary with all objects in view; and by this means are influenced to act, to seek, or avoid the object, and in the pursuit aim at the possession, or avoidance of it, according to the pleasure or pain the object or end affords.

If this self-determining and efficient power is totally destitute of any *feeling*, than how is it to be put in motion, or excited to exertions? It certainly cannot be influenced by motives, nor act with design. Power, which has no *feeling*, does not differ in its nature from those powers we call a *lever*, or a *screw*. And if it ever exerts itself, it must be put in motion by some antecedent power. The agent must have in view some pleasing object, and have a desire to obtain it. Then the agreeable object operates as a motive, and influences him to exert this supposed power to reach it, just as we use a screw to raise a weight. And for this antecedent to act, its nature must be the same with the nature of the faculty termed taste. Hence, whatever *power* may be considered as essential to praise and blame, on examination it will appear insufficient to answer the end for which it is invented ; or else it will be found not to differ in its nature from the faculty of taste, or the heart, as described in these essays.—We must then come to this conclusion, that wherever we behold a created being, who is endued with the faculties of the understanding, taste, and will, and also with liberty, he has all the powers necessary to render him a moral agent, or proper object of praise and blame, and future rewards. Then, to determine whether he is praise or blameworthy, we only have to ascertain his moral character, or the nature of his heart, whether it be holy or sinful. Here we must rest satisfied. For, by the most careful examination we shall find, there is no rational being in the universe, created or uncreated, who is possessed of any other powers, than the faculties which have been described. We know of no others. And we are not conscious of any more, than three distinct classes of opeiations ; *perceptions, affections.* and *volitions.* And as the operations of these differ from each other, they necessarily imply three distinct faculties, to one of which they are to be referred.

INDEX.

ERRATA.

Page 44, line 18 from top, insert *and* between *subject* and *predicate.*
Page 127, line 11 from bottom, for *it*, read *if.*
Page 168, line 6 from top, for *take*, read *like.*
Page 190, title of the essay, for *Arminians*, read *Arminian.*
Page 213, line 20 from top, for *Josiah*, read *Isaiah.*
Page 224, line 13 from top, for *different*, read *distinct.*
Page 225, line 13 from bottom, for *in*, read *on.*
Page 232, line 6 from beginning of the essay, for *they*, read *the.*
Page 287, line 2 from top, for *every*, read *any.*
Pare 288, bottom line, dele *his.*
Page 316, line 5 from bottom, before *for*, add *except.*
Page 321, top line, for *others*, read *then ;* line 15 from top, for *in*, read *into.*
Page 335, line 15 from top, for *or*, read *as.*
Page 341, line 6 from bottom, for *is*, read *was.*
Page 358, line 2 from bottom, dele the letter *y.*
Page 366, line 11 from top, for *scorn*, read *seem.*
Page 367, line 9 from top, after *man*, insert *is*, and dele the comma.
Page 386, line 12 from top, dele *of course.*
Page 392, line 13 from bottom, for *terms note*, read *terminate.*